STUDIES IN IMPERIALISM

General editor: Andrew S. Thompson
Founding editor: John M. MacKenzie

When the 'Studies in Imperialism' series was founded more
than twenty-five years ago, emphasis was laid upon the
conviction that 'imperialism as a cultural phenomenon
had as significant an effect on the dominant as on the
subordinate societies'. With well over a hundred titles now
published, this remains the prime concern of the series.
Cross-disciplinary work has indeed appeared covering the
full spectrum of cultural phenomena, as well as examining
aspects of gender and sex, frontiers and law, science and
the environment, language and literature, migration and
patriotic societies, and much else. Moreover, the series has
always wished to present comparative work on European
and American imperialism, and particularly welcomes the
submission of books in these areas. The fascination with
imperialism, in all its aspects, shows no sign of abating,
and this series will continue to lead the way in encouraging
the widest possible range of studies in the field. 'Studies
in Imperialism' is fully organic in its development, always
seeking to be at the cutting edge, responding to the latest
interests of scholars and the needs of this ever-expanding
area of scholarship.

New Zealand's empire

Manchester University Press

SELECTED TITLES AVAILABLE IN THE SERIES

WRITING IMPERIAL HISTORIES
ed. Andrew S. Thompson

MUSEUMS AND EMPIRE
Natural history, human cultures and colonial identities
John M. MacKenzie

MISSIONARY FAMILIES
Race, gender and generation on the spiritual frontier
Emily J. Manktelow

THE COLONISATION OF TIME
Ritual, routine and resistance in the British Empire
Giordano Nanni

BRITISH CULTURE AND THE END OF EMPIRE
ed. Stuart Ward

SCIENCE, RACE RELATIONS AND RESISTANCE
Britain, 1870–1914
Douglas A. Lorimer

GENTEEL WOMEN
Empire and domestic material culture, 1840–1910
Dianne Lawrence

EUROPEAN EMPIRES AND THE PEOPLE
Popular responses to imperialism in France, Britain, the Netherlands, Belgium, Germany and Italy
ed. John M. MacKenzie

SCIENCE AND SOCIETY IN SOUTHERN AFRICA
ed. Saul Dubow

New Zealand's empire

EDITED BY KATIE PICKLES AND
CATHARINE COLEBORNE

MANCHESTER
UNIVERSITY PRESS

Published by MANCHESTER UNIVERSITY PRESS
OXFORD ROAD, MANCHESTER M13 9PL

www.manchesteruniversitypress.co.uk

British Library Cataloguing-in-Publication Data
A catalogue record for this book is available from the British Library

Library of Congress Cataloging-in-Publication Data applied for

ISBN   978 0 7190 9153 7   hardback
ISBN   978 1 5261 7172 6   paperback

First published 2016
Paperback published 2023

Typeset by
Servis Filmsetting Ltd, Stockport, Cheshire

CONTENTS

List of figures—vii
List of contributors—ix
Acknowledgements—xiv
Abbreviations—xv

Introduction: New Zealand's empire   1
Katie Pickles and Catharine Coleborne

PART I 'Empire at home'

1 *Te Karere Maori* and the defence of empire, 1855–60   13
   Kenton Storey
2 An imperial icon Indigenised: the Queen Victoria Memorial
   at Ohinemutu   28
   Mark Stocker
3 'Two branches of the brown Polynesians': ethnographic
   fieldwork, colonial governmentality, and the 'dance of
   agency'   51
   Conal McCarthy

PART II Imperial mobility

4 Travelling the Tasman world: travel writing and narratives
   of transit   71
   Anna Johnston
5 Law's mobility: vagrancy and imperial legality in the trans-
   Tasman colonial world, 1860s–1914   89
   Catharine Coleborne
6 'The world's fernery': New Zealand, fern albums, and
   nineteenth-century fern fever   102
   Molly Duggins

PART III New Zealand's Pacific empire

7 From Sudan to Sāmoa: imperial legacies and cultures in New
   Zealand's rule over the Mandated Territory of Western
   Samoa   127
   Patricia O'Brien

8 'Fiji is really the Honolulu of the Dominion': tourism, empire, and New Zealand's Pacific, ca. 1900–35   147
Frances Steel

9 Empire in the eyes of the beholder: New Zealand in the Pacific through French eyes   163
Adrian Muckle

10 War surplus? New Zealand and American children of Indigenous women in Sāmoa, the Cook Islands, and Tokelau   179
Judith A. Bennett

PART IV Inside and outside empire

11 Official occasions and vernacular voices: New Zealand's British Empire and Commonwealth Games, 1950–90   197
Michael Dawson

12 Australia as New Zealand's western frontier, 1965–95   213
Rosemary Baird and Philippa Mein Smith

13 Southern outreach: New Zealand claims Antarctica from the 'heroic era' to the twenty-first century   229
Katie Pickles

14 A radical reinterpretation of New Zealand history: apology, remorse, and reconciliation   245
Giselle Byrnes

Index—262

LIST OF FIGURES

2.1 Queen Victoria, Ohinemutu. Sculpture by anonymous
Italian carver, 1874; pedestal by Patu Whitiki, 1900;
canopy by Tene Waitere, 1901. Postcard: Tanner Brothers,
Wellington, after 1920.   29

2.2 Queen Victoria, Ohinemutu, ca. 1970, Photograph D. I.
Therkleson, 'Rotorua Scenic Gems' (Peter Cadogan,
University of Otago).   30

2.3 *Te Arawa* (Queen Victoria, Ohinemutu), 1986.
Photograph taken from Nicholas Thomas, Mark Adams,
James Schuster and Lyonel Grant, *Rauru: Tene
Waitere, Maori Carving, Colonial History* (Dunedin:
University of Otago Press, 2009), p. 59
(courtesy of Mark Adams).   32

2.4 *Queen Victoria*, Windsor Castle, 1869–72. Joseph Edgar
Boehm. Postcard: F. Frith & Co., Reigate, 75189.   34

2.5 Queen Victoria, Ohinemutu, 1985. Photograph by John
Dixon (courtesy of Rotorua Museum Te Whare Taonga o
Te Arawa (OP-5403)).   40

2.6 Queen Victoria Bust – Houtaiki flag pole, Ohinemutu, ca.
1900. Photograph by Edward W. Payton (1859–1944)
(courtesy of Rotorua Museum Te Whare Taonga o Te
Arawa (OP-1475)).   44

2.7 Queen Victoria, Ohinemutu, 2011, Mark Stocker
(courtesy of photographer).   45

6.1 *Cyathea dealbata*, fern specimen on paper, 'Ferns of
Australasia', ca. 1900, Mary Ann Armstrong (State Library
of Victoria, H94.11/7).   103

6.2 Mary Ann Armstrong (1838–1910), ca. 1890 (courtesy of
Richard Daffey).   109

6.3 'White Terrace Rotomahana N. Z.', albumen print and
fern specimens on paper, 'New Zealand Ferns', 1886–87,
Frank Arnold Coxhead and Mary Ann Armstrong
(courtesy of Hans P. Kraus, Jr., New York).   111

6.4 'Giant Tree Fern (*Dicksonia billardierii*)', engraving,
South Pacific Fern Album, ca. 1889, George Treeby (State
Library of Victoria, 587.3 T93).   117

7.1 'Action near Rosaires', map from Winston Churchill, *The
River War: An Historical Account of the Reconquest of*

the Soudan (London: Longman Green and Co., 1899)
Volume 2, opp. p. 344.   128

7.2   Sir Charles Fergusson. Crown Studios Ltd., negatives and
prints, ref: 10x8-2185-F (Alexander Turnbull Library,
Wellington, New Zealand).   129

7.3   Portrait of General George Spafford Richardson with
Samoan children. Rutherford, Alexander Mathieson,
1915–. Photographs of Samoa. Ref: PA1-o-446-61-2
(Alexander Turnbull Library, Wellington, New Zealand).   130

7.4   Portrait of Ta'isi O. F. Nelson reproduced in N. A. Rowe,
Samoa Under Sailing Gods (London: Putnam, 1930).   134

7.5   'Reinforcement for the administration police at Samoa;
the departure from Auckland last Saturday morning', staff
photographer, *Auckland Weekly News*, 26 April 1928
(Auckland Libraries, Sir George Grey Special Collections,
AWNS-19280426-38-3).   138

7.6   'Keeping the peace in New Zealand's mandated territory
at Samoa', photograph by A. J. Tattersall, *Auckland
Weekly News*, 13 September 1928 (Auckland Libraries, Sir
George Grey Special Collections, AWNS-19280913-40-3).   138

12.1 Trans-Tasman Permanent and Long-Term Migration
Flows, Year Ended 31 March 1948–2013 (Source: www.
stats.govt.nz, International Travel and Migration).   216

13.1 Robert Falcon Scott and his wife Kathleen, on Quail
Island (Alexander Turnbull Library, Wellington, New
Zealand).   232

13.2 Hillary, Wright and Ellis on tractors, Commonwealth
Trans-Antarctic Expedition, Stan McKay photograph
(Canterbury Museum, reproduced with permission of the
Christchurch *Star*).   235

13.3 Unveiling of the Pou Whenua carving at Scott Base
(Fairfax Media New Zealand).   240

LIST OF CONTRIBUTORS

Rosemary Baird completed her history PhD thesis, 'Across the Tasman: Narratives of Kiwi Migration to and from Australia, 1965–1995' at the University of Canterbury in 2012. As an oral historian, she has done many interviews focused on the Christchurch earthquakes, contributing to the National Council of Women's online interview archive 'Women's Voices', the Ministry for Culture and Heritage's 'Remembering Christchurch' oral history project, and the University of Canterbury's Department of Management MBIE-funded project on resilient infrastructure organisations. She currently works at Heritage New Zealand in an outreach role, as well as contributing to CERA's Learning Legacy and Lessons programme. In her spare time she works on her personal research interest: oral histories with men and women involved in the construction of the Manapouri hydro scheme.

Judith A. Bennett teaches Pacific and environment history at the University of Otago. Her publications include *Wealth of the Solomons: A History of a Pacific Archipelago, c.1800–1978* (1987); *Pacific Forest: A History of Resource Control and Contest in Solomon Islands, c. 1800–1997* (2000); and *Natives and Exotics: World War Two and Environment in the Southern Pacific* (2009). With Angela Wanhalla, she has just completed an edited manuscript, 'Mothers' Darlings: The Children of Indigenous Women and US Servicemen in the South Pacific, World War Two' and is co-producer of a documentary on the same, shown on New Zealand Maori TV on Anzac Day, 2014.

Giselle Byrnes is Professor and Pro Vice-Chancellor of the Faculty of Law, Education, Business and Arts at Charles Darwin University, in Darwin, Australia. Prior to her current role, she was Professor of History and Pro Vice-Chancellor (Postgraduate) at the University of Waikato. Giselle has published extensively on aspects of cross-cultural histories and is the author of *Boundary Markers: Land Surveying and the Colonisation of New Zealand* (2001), *The Waitangi Tribunal and New Zealand History* (2004) and is editor of *The New Oxford History of New Zealand* (2009). In 2006, Giselle was Fulbright Visiting Professor in New Zealand Studies at Georgetown University, Washington DC. She has served on a number of boards and is a past President of the New Zealand Historical Association. She is currently examining how contemporary political and quasi-judicial processes use historical evidence to address longstanding historical injustices, focusing on the issues of apology and reconciliation.

Catharine Coleborne is Professor of History at the University of Waikato in New Zealand. Her research focuses on the histories of insanity, institutions, medicine, law, and health in colonial Australia and New Zealand. Her book *Insanity, Identity and Empire* is forthcoming with Manchester University Press. She is the author of *Madness in the Family: Insanity and Institutions in the Australasian Colonial World, 1860–1914* (2010), and the co-editor of six books including, with Angela McCarthy, *Migration, Ethnicity, and Mental Health: International Perspectives, 1840–2010* (2012), and with Diane Kirkby, *Law, History, Colonialism: The Reach of Empire* (2001, 2009). Her current project focuses on the regulation of colonial mobility in Australia and New Zealand through an examination of vagrancy laws.

Michael Dawson is Professor of History at St Thomas University in New Brunswick, Canada. He is the author of *The Mountie from Dime Novel to Disney* and *Selling British Columbia: Tourism and Consumer Culture, 1890–1970* and co-editor, with Christopher Dummitt, of *Contesting Clio's Craft: New Directions and Debates in Canadian History*. His contribution to this volume forms part of a larger project examining the Commonwealth Games and national identity in Canada, Australia, and New Zealand.

Molly Duggins is a lecturer in the Department of Art History and Theory at the National Art School, Sydney, and in the Department of Art History and Film Studies at the University of Sydney. In 2012 she completed her PhD at the University of Sydney with a dissertation on nature and the colonial album. She has been awarded fellowships at the State Library of New South Wales (2012) and the Yale Center for British Art (2012). Select publications include, 'Montage and Modernity: Late Nineteenth-Century Colonial Graphic Culture', in *Surface and Deep Histories: Critiques and Practices in Art, Architecture and Design* (2014), and 'Arranging the Antipodes: The Archer Family Album as Metaphorical Cabinet', *Australasian Journal of Victorian Studies* (2009). She is currently co-editing a volume on art, science, and the commodification of the ocean world in the long nineteenth century.

Anna Johnston is an Australian Research Council Future Fellow and Associate Professor in English at the University of Tasmania. Her areas of research include missionary writing and empire, colonial and postcolonial literatures, and travel writing. She is the author of *The Paper War: Morality, Print Culture, and Power in Colonial New South Wales* (University of Western Australia Publishing, 2011) and *Missionary Writing and Empire, 1800–1860* (Cambridge, 2003). She is also co-editor of a number of books: *The Complete Indian Housekeeper and Cook* (with Ralph Crane, Oxford, 2010), *Reading Robinson: Companion Essays to* Friendly Mission (with Mitchell Rolls, Quintus, 2008; Monash University Publishing, 2012), and *In Transit: Travel, Text, Empire* (with Helen Gilbert, Peter Lang, 2002).

Conal McCarthy is an Associate Professor and Director of the Museum & Heritage Studies programme at Victoria University of Wellington, New Zealand. Conal has degrees in English, Art History, Māori language, and Museum Studies and has worked in galleries and museums in a variety of professional roles. He has published on museum history, theory, and practice, and in particular the Indigenous engagement with collecting and display, including the book *Museums and Māori: Heritage Professionals, Indigenous Collections, Current Practice* (2011). His next book is *Museum Practice: The Contemporary Museum at Work* (2015).

Philippa Mein Smith is Professor of History and Head of History and Classics at the University of Tasmania, Hobart. Previously she was Professor of History and Director of the New Zealand Australia Research Centre at the University of Canterbury, Christchurch. She is the author of six books, including *A Concise History of New Zealand*, Cambridge Concise Histories Series (Cambridge and Melbourne: Cambridge University Press, 1st edition 2005, 2nd edition 2012); *Remaking the Tasman World* (Christchurch: Canterbury University Press, 2008), co-authored with Peter Hempenstall and Shaun Goldfinch; and *A History of Australia, New Zealand and the Pacific*, Blackwell History of the World Series (Oxford and Malden MA: Blackwell, 2000), co-authored with Donald Denoon and Marivic Wyndham.

Adrian Muckle is a Senior Lecturer in the History Programme at Victoria University of Wellington, New Zealand. His main research areas are nineteenth- and twentieth-century Pacific history, colonialism and colonial societies, decolonisation, violence and race relations. Much of his research focuses on New Caledonia including the dynamics of colonial rule and power relations, Indigenous (Kanak) experiences of the Great War, New Caledonia's links with the wider Oceanian region, including New Zealand, and recent political developments. He is the author of *Specters of Violence in a Colonial Context: New Caledonia, 1917* (University of Hawai'i Press, 2012) and is now working on a collaborative study of the *indigénat* regime and its Oceanian legacy. He is a member of the Research Group on New Caledonia and currently the Book Review Editor for the *Journal of Pacific History*.

Patricia O'Brien specialises in the colonial and gendered histories of Australia and the Pacific, race relations, and Indigenous histories within a broad arc of British imperialism. She was visiting Associate Professor in the Center for Australian and New Zealand Studies and the Department of History in the Edmund A. Walsh School of Foreign Service at Georgetown University, Washington DC, before she was awarded an Australian Research Council Future Fellowship in 2013. In 2014 she commenced this fellowship in the School of History in Research School of Arts and Social Sciences at the Australian National University. In 2012 she was JD Stout Fellow in New Zealand Studies at Victoria University Wellington, where she researched New Zealand's Mandate over Western Samoa, focusing particularly upon the nationalist leader Ta'isi O. F. Nelson. In 2011 she was the John I. Kislak Fellow in American Studies at the John W. Kluge Center at the Library of Congress, Washington DC. She is the author of *The Pacific Muse: Exotic Femininity and the Colonial Pacific* (Seattle, 2006), as well as numerous chapters and articles on colonialism and culture.

Katie Pickles is Professor of History at the University of Canterbury. Her work explores empire and the colonial past in New Zealand, Canada, Australia, and Britain. She is the author of many journal articles and book chapters on the topic, and the monographs *Transnational Outrage: The Death and Commemoration of Edith Cavell* (2007/2015) and *Female Imperialism and National Identity: Imperial Order Daughters of the Empire* (2002, 2009). She is the co-editor, with David Monger and Sarah Murray, of *Endurance and the First World War: Legacies and Experiences in New Zealand and Australia* (2014); with Myra Rutherdale, *Contact Zones: Aboriginal and Settler Women in Canada's Colonial Past* (2005); with Lyndon Fraser, *Shifting Centres: Women and Migration in New Zealand History* (2002); and she is the editor of *Hall of Fame: Life Stories of New Zealand Women* (1998). A new book, *Christchurch Ruptures*, is due for publication in 2015.

Frances Steel is Senior Lecturer in History at the University of Wollongong. Her research focuses on the intersections of empire, shipping, and mobility in the Pacific world. She is currently researching the history of the trans-Pacific passenger liner trades between Australasia and North America (ca.1870s–1950s), and is also engaged in a collaborative project on the transcolonial cultures of male domestic service in the Asia-Pacific. She is the author of *Oceania Under Steam: Sea Transport and the Cultures of Colonialism, c.1870–1914* (2011), as well as a number of articles and chapters, including those in *Journal of Colonialism and Colonial History* and *Australian Historical Studies*.

Mark Stocker was recently appointed as the Curator (Historical and International Art) at the Museum of New Zealand Te Papa Tongarewa. Prior to that he taught for over ten years at the Department of History and Art History at the University of Otago. He has published extensively in the area of public monuments and sculpture, as well as in numismatics, in such journals as *Apollo*, *The British Numismatic Journal*, *The Burlington Magazine*, and the *Sculpture Journal*. A long-time royal watcher, Mark's PhD was on Queen Victoria's favourite sculptor, Sir Joseph Edgar Boehm; he was surprised and delighted to see that the Ohinemutu carving of the Queen was clearly based on Boehm's original in Windsor Castle, and to learn of and retell here its fascinating story.

Kenton Storey completed his first degrees at the University of Manitoba, Canada, and is currently a postdoctoral fellow in Western Canadian Social History at the University of Manitoba. His doctorate, awarded by the University of Otago in 2011, explores the way in which the nineteenth-century press connected Vancouver Island and New Zealand with the Anglophone world, and argues that concerns about surveillance in Great Britain shaped media portrayals of Indigenous peoples and contributed to the persistence of humanitarian racial discourses in both colonies. This thesis, in book form, is forthcoming from UBC Press.

ACKNOWLEDGEMENTS

The staff at Manchester University Press have been a pleasure to work with.

University of Waikato Research Trust Contestable Funding, and an External Research Award from the Vice Chancellor's Office at the University of Waikato, have supported the tireless editorial work of Dr Fiona Martin: we are indebted to her assistance in preparing our manuscript for submission to the press. These funds also supported some travel costs, allowing conversations and meetings between us as editors of this book. We are also grateful to the School of Humanities and Creative Arts at the University of Canterbury for awarding funds to assist with the editing process.

We thank all our contributors for their work in realising our aims in their chapters, and for entering into the spirit of the concept of 'New Zealand's empire'. We are enormously grateful for the anonymous reader's report on this volume which was positive, thorough and insightful.

Every reasonable attempt has been made to obtain permission to reproduce the copyright images. Images have been included but if any proper acknowledgement has not been made, copyright holders are invited to contact the editors via the publisher.

Our colleagues at the University of Canterbury and at the University of Waikato have supported our work amid busy administrative and teaching loads. We especially acknowledge here our families for their time, love and support: Mike, Eve, Clara, and James; and Craig and Cassidy.

ABBREVIATIONS

NZPD	*New Zealand Parliamentary Debates*
USSCo.	Union Steam Ship Company of New Zealand

Archives

ACA	Auckland Council Archives, Auckland
ANZ	Archives New Zealand, Wellington branch
ATL	Alexander Turnbull Library, Wellington
CADN	Centre des archives diplomatiques de Nantes, Nantes
CAOM	Centre des archives d'outre-mer, Aix-en-Provence
HC	Hocken Collections, University of Otago, Dunedin
MAE	Archives du Ministère des affaires étrangères, Courneuve, Paris
NA	National Archives, London
NAF	National Archives of Fiji, Suva
NASB	National Archives of the USA, San Bruno, California
NAUSA	National Archives of the USA, College Park, Maryland
PMB	Pacific Manuscripts Bureau, Canberra
RDL	Rotorua District Library, Rotorua
SL	State Library of New South Wales, Sydney
WCA	Wellington City Archives, Wellington

INTRODUCTION

New Zealand's empire

Katie Pickles and Catharine Coleborne

New Zealand's empire revises, expands, and complicates received histories of empire and imperialism: specifically their significance to, in, and from New Zealand. In the study of the imperial past, both colonial and postcolonial approaches have often asserted the dualism of core and periphery, with New Zealand firmly positioned on the 'edge', or as an outlier of empire. Meanwhile, nation-centred approaches have tended to under-emphasise the connections between New Zealand and the rest of the world.[1] Turning the theme of 'empire' on its head, contributors show how a focus on New Zealand as being at the centre of a local world of imperialism throws older debates about New Zealand as a 'periphery' into sharp relief. With historians building upon and revising existing approaches to New Zealand history, there is now a literature that traverses nation and empire, variously placing New Zealand as a part of a 'British world', a 'Tasman world', an 'Anglo world', and networked 'webs of empire'.[2] Yet what of New Zealand's own 'imperial' ambitions, and its awkward interactions with 'empire' over time? This volume argues that New Zealand could assert its own forms of 'imperialism', both 'at home', and also in the Pacific, Australia, and Antarctica, and that New Zealanders have constantly grappled with ideas of and about imperialism, from a range of vantage points.

By conceiving of New Zealand as an imperial power in its own right, as well as viewing New Zealand as being in a complex and evolving relationship with and within the British Empire, this volume addresses issues at the frontline of the study of imperialism in a fresh and interesting way. New Zealand as a European 'place' had its own imperial aspirations, witnessed in its ongoing interactions with Māori and Pacific peoples, and often in relation to progressive state welfare policies.[3] As the next step into the study of imperialism, taking new directions in both historiographical and empirical research, the essays

[1]

in this volume span social, cultural, political, and economic history to raise questions and test the concept of 'New Zealand's empire'.

The relevant historiographies of empire and nation, and where they intersect, inform readers about how the present volume produces new ideas about New Zealand's history. An Oxford History of the British Empire Companion Series includes titles such as *Australia's Empire*, edited by Deryck M. Schreuder and Stuart Ward, *Canada and the British Empire*, edited by Phillip Buckner, David McIntyre's *Winding up the British Empire in the Pacific Islands*, and *Ireland and the British Empire*, edited by Kevin Kenny.[4] Schreuder and Ward comment that the scholars lamenting the 'end of Empire' have had less resonance in the Australian context, where hints and fragments of imperial histories had seemed less important to historians over a longer period of time than the relevance of the task of depicting Australia's national past: the history of a nation being forged as a separate and important entity. As they write of Australia in the twenty-first century, 'the trappings of Empire have been quietly relegated to the museum'.[5] Finding how to 'moor' Australia once again inside an imperial history is not, as Schreuder and Ward suggest, a retrograde step or one coloured by a sense of loss of 'empire', but rather, an opportunity to critically interpret the many complex forms taken by 'empire' in Australia's past, and we take a similar view in relation to New Zealand.[6] Kenny's volume on Ireland explores the island as a 'laboratory for Empire', a concept also useful when applied to New Zealand. Kenny's volume is also concerned with culture and imperialism, which is an important strand running through the chapters in *New Zealand's empire*.[7]

From a popular point of view, New Zealand's attachment to the British Empire has been more pronounced than Australia's. Where Schreuder and Ward point out that Australia's sense of itself and its achievements was determined over time as being about 'independence' from Britain, in New Zealand, comparable developments – including a movement towards republicanism – are relatively muted. As chapters in this volume suggest, New Zealand's relationship with the British Crown is an ongoing vital concern for issues of Māori sovereignty and unfinished business. In addition, there is much nostalgia for the place of the monarchy and for being a loyal nation that perpetuates many of the values that have been present, albeit in an evolving form, since British colonisation. The British colony of New Zealand was 'settled' in formal terms during the 'age of empire'. In 1840 the Treaty of Waitangi was signed between the British Crown and Māori iwi. As a 'living document' with multiple interpretations and meanings, the Treaty occupies a complex place in both the past and the present.[8] The colony's formative years were dominated by the mobility of imperial peoples and ideas, including contestation over land ownership, cultural beliefs, and the dominance of European world views. New Zealand came to be understood as a largely 'English' society, though with immigrants from all parts of the British Isles, a strong Scottish character, and Europeans and Pacific peoples traversing its spaces.[9] Moreover, New Zealand and its peoples came to understand itself – and themselves – over time as part of the empire, the dimensions and style of which took many different forms.

Where *Australia's Empire* and *Canada and Empire* rightly place Australia or Canada as centre-stage in the range of histories of contact, cultures, and politics of the empire, we consider New Zealand as being a rather different national and imperial stage for complex notions of 'nation' and 'empire' to develop and take social and cultural forms. First, as chapters in this volume attest, New Zealand's history intersects in both spatial and cultural ways with Australia. New Zealand was part of a wider Tasman world. Second, New Zealand's role in the Pacific, and the place and meanings of 'the Pacific' in New Zealand, are a vital part of 'New Zealand's empire', and hence are central to this volume. Unlike *Winding up the British Empire in the Pacific Islands*, this volume considers New Zealand as part of the Pacific Islands, and goes beyond the British influence, including a chapter about New Zealand in the Pacific region from the point of view of the French imperialists, who looked upon the British Empire in distinctly different ways. New Zealand's experience of relationships with Sāmoa and Fiji, and the Cook Islands, is examined in separate chapters which articulate the finely tuned ways and means of Pacific 'belonging' for New Zealand's history, themes which also speak to the contemporary significance of the Pacific and its peoples in New Zealand's histories. Importantly, contributors to this book locate New Zealand spatially, historically, and intellectually within new understandings of these shared histories across and within the Australasian and Pacific regions.[10]

There is already a strong body of work about New Zealand, Britishness, and hegemony that, with gender and empire to the fore, has interrogated aspects of the construction of colonial identity in New Zealand. Influenced by the work of John M. MacKenzie, and many of the volumes in the Studies in Imperialism series, written during the past two decades, this work has followed on from MacKenzie's importance of the 'informal empire' of patriotic clubs and societies, allowing for the importance of women imperialists to be uncovered and recognised as a vital part of the colonial past.[11] While male politicians worked in the public sphere that overall implicitly advanced New Zealand's place within the British Empire; from a maternal sphere, female imperialists took on the mantle of empire, believing that they had a central part to play in imperial concerns. Indeed, their efforts in promoting Anglo-Celtic hegemony and versions of 'Britishness', especially through work with children, are a vital part of New Zealand's imperial past.[12] A theme in this work was New Zealand's claiming of the British Empire, and forming a national identity out of a strong attachment to, and mimicking of, Britain. Along similar lines, New Zealand has claimed the imperial centre of Britain, and in particular London, as work by Hannah-Lee Benbow and Felicity Barnes argues.[13] 'New Zealand's London' demonstrates the imperial relationship between imperial centre and colony, and the imagined ownership that came from being a white settler society, emulating the 'mother country'.

To explore and test the concept of New Zealand's empire, this volume is arranged in four thematic sections. Within and across the sections continuity and change over time are highlighted. 'empire at Home' includes essays about attempts to colonise Māori peoples, and their own resistance and responses in the form of cultures of Indigeneity. An important theme throughout *New Zealand's empire* concerns how Māori were subjects of the empire in different ways to their Pākehā invaders. The dynamic and ever-changing meaning of the Crown in New Zealand is in the spotlight through this first section, and re-emerges through the rest of the volume. Discourses of imperialism as conceived by and with Māori are the concern of Kenton Storey's chapter on the early press. His examination of *Te Karere*, the colonial government's bilingual newspaper, during the years 1855–60, addresses internal colonisation of New Zealand by both the Crown and subsequent settler governments. Storey reads *Te Karere* for evidence of racial attitudes, and along with other chapters in the volume concerned with literary sources, he renders explicit the formation of communications networks for what they reveal about racial amalgamation and assimilation.

Mark Stocker's chapter examines Māori's relationship with Queen Victoria through memorials. This is a hybrid history that reveals the significant local aspects of New Zealand's Indigenous history that can emerge through a focus on the wider imperial context. Stocker's chapter on the 1874 Queen Victoria Memorial at Ohinemutu taps into the ways in which Te Arawa forged a unique relationship with Queen Victoria. Significantly, through the chapters in Part I, and throughout the volume, it emerges that imperial mentalities were not restricted to Pākehā, with Māori asserting agency from their position as colonised peoples. Conal McCarthy's chapter explores what he terms the 'dance of agency' regarding the fieldwork and governance of educated and successful Māori leaders in the first half of the twentieth century, a process which in some ways echoes Te Arawa's relationship with the Crown. McCarthy takes the familiar narrative of the Young Maori Party's successful politicians – Sir Maui Pomare, Peter Buck, and Āpirana Ngata – disentangling them from previous nationalist narratives and instead placing them in new networks that stretched out across the Pacific and into North America, forging (or dancing) new pathways as the men collaborated in the Pacific within the context of their times. Tony Ballantyne reminds us that New Zealand also exercised considerable 'intellectual authority' from its capital city, Wellington, over the Pacific, through the work of ethnologists, anthropologists, and museological practices, a theme examined in some depth by McCarthy in this volume.[14]

Part II, entitled 'Imperial Mobility', examines the intersection of New Zealand histories with those of imperial and trans-Tasman movement and mobility, including laws, travellers, and representations. Importantly, this addresses recent 'turns' in historical writing, including cultural histories and histories of the trans-Tasman world, that position New Zealand as part of a wider set of colonial world preoccupations.[15] Featured in this section are the 'narratives of transit' that criss-crossed the imperial and colonial worlds in the form of travel writings, the mobility of peoples, and of laws and legal practices of empire in colonial settings, and the way New Zealand's physical attributes and landscape became part of a much larger emphasis on the physical and representational cultural worlds of 'places' in the nineteenth century. Employing such a framework, Anna Johnston discusses the trans-Tasman colonial world and imperial travellers. She is interested in how nineteenth-century travel writing texts globalised settler colonial models. Her analysis builds upon work by other scholars interested in travellers, their narratives, and the communication of ideas about place and subjectivity.[16]

The trans-Tasman locale also underpins Catharine Coleborne's examination of mobility and vagrancy, and the laws introduced to contain it in New Zealand and other colonies in the second half of the nineteenth century. Coleborne argues that law 'moved across the spaces of empire and into the colonial world as a form of imperial knowledge and practice and brought with it the possibility of a new imagining of spaces'. Making complex the conception that New Zealand laws largely mimicked British ones, Coleborne argues that New Zealand had a legal culture of its own, albeit framed inside an existing imperial world of law and legality. Gender is invoked as a category of analysis to show how the regulation of mobility was shaped through ideas about colonial identities, and how gender intersected with class and ethnicity as unauthorised mobility was interrogated.

Combining commerce, aesthetics, and ecological imperialism, Molly Duggins' chapter suggests that the circulation and export of

New Zealand culture itself happened in all kinds of ways: the sharing of botanical culture, depictions of physical landscapes, and botanical art on the world stage combined to produce a place for New Zealand *inside* empire. Duggins explores New Zealand as 'the World's fernery', drawing upon fern albums, specimens, decorations, and souvenirs. Her chapter addresses a strong current throughout *New Zealand's empire*: several authors, like her, seek to question and explicate the formation of symbols and events for New Zealand's national identity.

If Britain itself, New Zealand internal colonisation and the Trans-Tasman domain are three important spheres of influence and activity for New Zealand's imperial past, then a fourth vital sphere is that termed by Damon Salesa as 'New Zealand's Pacific'.[17] This volume addresses the lack of attention in the context of the British Empire given to 'New Zealand as an empire as well as a colony', involving what Salesa has termed 'The overseas tropical empire of New Zealand – which not only hinged on Pākehā, but also on New Zealand Māori and local Polynesian interlocutions'.[18]

Chapters in Part III examine 'New Zealand's Pacific empire', and include a focus on the French in the Pacific, imperial legacies and cultures of imperialism in Western Samoa, travellers to and from Fiji, and the impact of the Second World War in the Pacific countries of Sāmoa, the Cook Islands, and Tokelau, through the intimate histories of sexual engagements between American troops and local women. Judith A. Bennett asserts in her chapter that '[a]s early as the 1850s New Zealand had dreamt of being a South Pacific power'. Historian of the Pacific, Kerry Howe, insists on the Pacific being forged as an 'imperial' history from its beginnings, by virtue of scholarship's early focus on the presence of imperial powers in Pacific oceans.[19] Adrian Muckle and Frances Steele test the concept of New Zealand's Pacific empire in original ways. Muckle does so by finding evidence of how those who attempted to shape it were viewed through French eyes. He offers French descriptions of New Zealand as an aspiring colonial and imperial power, albeit small enough to be considered 'Lilliputian'. Beliefs about empire circulated via oceanic routes of travel and trade. Frances Steele turns to the sea and tourism in New Zealand's Pacific between 1900 and 1935. A part of 'informal imperialism', tourism was also implicated in empires of trade and settlement. Cultural and commercial influences were often entwined, and Steele's chapter illustrates new ways of examining the history of imperialism beyond formal political influences.

A focus on New Zealand's Pacific empire involves histories of complicity, conflict, and tragedy. Patricia O'Brien looks into the background and influences of Governor-General Charles Fergusson, bringing together his time at the Battle of Rosaires in the Sudan in 1898 with the Black Saturday Massacre in Western Samoa in 1929, to offer a nuanced reading of colonial governance. O'Brien includes the opinions of New Zealand's parliamentarians, who drew comparisons between Sāmoa and New Zealand's 'Native Wars'. As chapters in this book attest, war was a time when articulations of empire were to the fore: imperial international conflict led to New Zealand occupying Western Samoa in 1914 at Britain's request. New Zealand remained in power for almost fifty years. The tragic introduction of the influenza epidemic occurred under New Zealand rule, and played a strong part in Sāmoan Mau opposition against New Zealand.

Judith A. Bennett's chapter combines the American occupation of the South Pacific during the Second World War with the intimate history of 1,000 part-American children across the Islands: Sāmoa, the Cook Islands, Tokelau, and New Zealand. Women were treated as sex objects, to be abandoned when units left the islands. Examining New Zealand's stance on these 'outcomes of intimacy', Bennett argues that in New Zealand territories 'imperial obligations toward the results of the intimacies of the colonised had their limits'. Her research leads her to see the stark application of class and racial hierarchies through the ways in which Island women's bodies were literally 'treated' for sexual favours and sexual diseases.

Part IV of *New Zealand's empire* considers New Zealand 'Inside and outside empire', evoking notions of how New Zealand has looked at itself, increasingly devolved from Britain, and also how it is viewed and perceived from the outside. The emphasis is on New Zealand in the twentieth century and on to the present, allowing the opportunity for themes introduced earlier in on in the volume to resurface. In his examination of the British Empire and Commonwealth Games held in New Zealand in 1950, 1974, and 1990, Michael Dawson traces the evolution of New Zealand's status within the empire through important years of devolution from empire to Commonwealth. Dawson reveals the rise of 'kiwi worship' and partisan coverage of the games, as well as rapidly changing, yet tense, racial attitudes. Redolent of the Māori agency evidenced in Stocker and McCarthy's chapters, Dawson argues that during the British Empire Games in 1950, after being omitted from the official opening and closing ceremonies, Māori created their own place as hosts on their own terms.

In a chapter about late twentieth-century New Zealand outreach to Australia's western frontier, in which they challenge assumptions about the nature of the relationship between the two countries, Rosemary Baird and Philippa Mein Smith pick up themes introduced earlier on in the volume. They rightly point out that between 1788 and 1840, New Zealand was a part of 'Australia's empire', because it was officially governed by New South Wales, and argue that Trans-Tasman connections have been vital from that time onwards. As a part of that world, increasingly, New Zealand has looked to and claimed Australia. Also concerned with mobility, Baird and Mein Smith explore the concept of culture contact, maritime traffic, trade and exchange across the Tasman Sea into the jet age, when New Zealanders have migrated to 'colonise' Australia in large numbers. Using oral history as their evidence, they reveal narratives of migrants seeking a better life for their families in a 'West Island' of opportunity.

New Zealand has cast its imperial eyes in all directions, including to the South. As Katie Pickles argues, taking over when Britain left off, New Zealand has claimed Antarctica through the twentieth century and continues to do so in the twenty-first century. Antarctic endeavours reflect New Zealand's movement away from Britain towards the United States of America, and also highlight the formation of national identity, albeit one that remains imaginatively trapped in the heroic era of a century ago. New Zealand often appears to be stuck in a nostalgic age of high imperialism, as evidenced through claiming a place for Antarctica in the hearts and minds of New Zealanders through evoking heroes at the service of empire. The 2013 placing of the pou whenua at New Zealand's Scott Base in Antarctica displays continuity with past Māori imperialism, present in Stocker's and McCarthy's chapters.

In her chapter about apology, remorse, and reconciliation, Giselle Byrnes continues the theme of internal imperialism raised earlier in the volume, considering the Crown's imperial ambitions and its role as a coloniser, specifically through the case study of the Battle of Gate Pā. In some ways, it is a long way from Gate Pā, via Sir Charles Fergusson, to the appointment of two Māori Governors-General, Sir Paul Reeves (22 November 1985–20 November 1990) and Sir Jerry Mateparae (in office 31 August 2011–present). Such history, captured in this volume, speaks to the unique and evolving relationship between Māori and the Crown and, indeed, the broader formation of New Zealand's imperialism. Employing a diversity of socio-cultural and political approaches to the past, the chapters in this book explore the common theme and heuristic device of 'New Zealand's empire', seeking to frame the history of New Zealand in relation to empire and imperialism. Rather than simplify our collective understanding of that past, they seek to open up new conversations, and to stimulate interest in an area of history that reverberates strongly in the present. Where and when New Zealand was historically responsible for its own power and control over spaces, peoples, and situations, how did it perform? How New Zealand exercised imperial power at home and over its neighbours is under examination in the following pages. Overall, the book entertains a range and variety of concepts of 'empire' in relation to 'New Zealand' and its histories: we aim to open up discussion about just how to conceive of 'New Zealand's empire'.

Notes

1 For a summary of New Zealand historiography in the context of the British Empire, see James Belich, 'Colonization and History in New Zealand', in Robin W. Winks (ed.), *The Oxford History of the British Empire, Vol. 5: Historiography* (Oxford: Oxford University Press, 1999), pp. 182–93.

2 Katie Pickles, 'The obvious and the awkward: Postcolonialism and the British world', *New Zealand Journal of History*, 45:1 (2011), 85–101; Philippa Mein Smith, Peter J. Hempenstall, and Shaun Goldfinch, *Remaking the Tasman World* (Christchurch: Canterbury University Press, 2008); James Belich, *Replenishing the Earth: The Settler Revolution and the Rise of the Anglo-World, 1783–1939* (Oxford: Oxford University Press, 2009); Tony Ballantyne, *Webs of Empire: Locating New Zealand's Colonial Past* (Wellington: Bridget Williams Books, 2012).

3 Tony Ballantyne and Antoinette Burton, *Empires and the Reach of the Global 1870–1945* (Cambridge MA: Belknap Press of Harvard University Press, 2012), p. 96.

4 Deryck M. Schreuder and Stuart Ward (eds), *Australia's Empire*, Oxford History of the British Empire Companion Series No. 6 (Oxford: Oxford University Press, 2008); Phillip Buckner (ed.), *Canada and the British Empire*, Oxford History of the British Empire Companion Series (Oxford and New York, 2010); W. David McIntyre, *Winding up the British Empire in the Pacific Islands*, Oxford History of the British Empire Companion Series (Oxford and New York: Oxford University Press, 2014), and Kevin Kenny (ed.), *Ireland and the British Empire*, Oxford History of the British Empire Companion Series (Oxford and New York: Oxford University Press, 2004).

5 Deryck M. Schreuder and Stuart Ward, 'Introduction: What became of Australia's Empire?', in Schreuder and Ward (eds), *Australia's Empire*, p. 4.

6 Schreuder and Ward, 'Introduction', in *Australia's Empire*, p. 11.

7 Kenny, *Ireland and the British Empire*.

8 On the changing commemoration of Waitangi Day, see Helen Robinson, 'Making a New Zealand Day: The creation and context of a national holiday', *New Zealand Journal of History*, April 46:1 (2012), 37–51.

9 See Lyndon Fraser (ed.), *A Distant Shore: Irish Migration and New Zealand Settlement* (Dunedin: Otago University Press, 2000); Jock Phillips and Terry J. Hearn, *Settlers: New Zealand Immigrants From England, Ireland and Scotland, 1800–1945* (Auckland: Auckland University Press, 2008); Lyndon Fraser and Katie Pickles (eds), *Shifting Centres: Women and Migration in New Zealand History* (Dunedin: Otago University Press, 2002); Lyndon Fraser and Angela McCarthy (eds), *Far from 'Home': The English in New Zealand* (Dunedin: Otago University Press, 2012); Tom Brooking and Jenny Coleman (eds), *The Heather and the Fern: Scottish Migration and New Zealand Settlement* (Dunedin: Otago University Press, 2003); Brad Patterson (ed.), *The Irish in New Zealand: Historical Contexts and Perspectives* (Wellington: Stout Research Centre for New Zealand Studies, 2002); Sean Mallon, Kolokesa Mahina-Tuai, and Damon Salesa (eds), *Tangata o le moana: New Zealand and the People of the Pacific* (Wellington: Te Papa Press, 2012); Tony Simpson, *The Great Migration from Britain to New Zealand, 1830–1890* (Auckland: Godwit, 1997).

10 See Smith, Hempenstall, and Goldfinch, *Remaking the Tasman World*.

11 John M. MacKenzie, *Propaganda and Empire: The Manipulation of British Public Opinion, 1880–1960*, Studies in Imperialism (Manchester: Manchester University Press, 1984); Katie Pickles, 'Colonisation, empire and gender', in Giselle Byrnes (ed.), *The New Oxford History of New Zealand* (Melbourne: Oxford University Press, 1999), pp. 219–41, Sarah Dowling, 'Female Imperialism: The Victoria League in

Canterbury, New Zealand, 1910–2003', MA thesis, University of Canterbury, 2004; Karen Fox, 'Dames in New Zealand: Gender, Representation and the Royal Honours System, 1917–2000', MA thesis, University of Canterbury, 2005; Nadia Gush, 'Beauty of Health: Cora Wilding and the Sunshine League', MA thesis, University of Canterbury, 2003; Diana McCurdy, 'Feminine Identity in New Zealand: The Girl Peace Scout Movement, 1908–1925', MA thesis, University of Canterbury, 2000; Angela Wanhalla, 'Gender, Race and Colonial Identity: Women and Eugenics in New Zealand, 1918–1939', MA thesis, University of Canterbury, 2001; Megan Woods, 'Re/producing the Nation: Women Making Identity in New Zealand, 1906–1925', MA thesis, University of Canterbury, 1997. See also John Griffiths, 'The branch life of Empire: Imperial loyalty leagues in antipodean cities – comparisons and contrasts with the British model', *Britain and the World*, 7:1 (2014): 56–84.

12 See Katie Pickles, 'A link in "the great chain of Empire friendship": The Victoria League in New Zealand', *The Journal of Imperial and Commonwealth History*, 33:1 (2005): 29–50.

13 Felicity Barnes, *New Zealand's London: A Colony and its Metropolis* (Auckland: Auckland University Press, 2012); Hannah-Lee Benbow, 'I Like London Best': London Correspondents for New Zealand Newspapers, 1884–1942', MA thesis, University of Canterbury, 2009.

14 Ballantyne, *Webs of Empire*, pp. 44–5.

15 In this area see foundational work by Catharine Coleborne, *Madness in the Family: Insanity and Institutions in the Australasian Colonial World, 1860–1914* (Houndmills and New York: Palgrave Macmillan, 2009) and Diane Kirkby and Catharine Coleborne (eds), *Law, History, Colonialism: The Reach of Empire*, Studies in Imperialism (Manchester: Manchester University Press, 2001).

16 See Lydia Wevers, *Reading on the Farm: Victorian Fiction and the Colonial World* (Wellington, Victoria University Press, 2010).

17 Damon Salesa, 'New Zealand's Pacific', in Giselle Byrnes (ed.), *The New Oxford History of New Zealand* (Melbourne: Oxford University Press, 2009), pp. 149–72.

18 Salesa, 'New Zealand's Pacific', p. 149. See also Damon Salesa, 'A Pacific destiny: New Zealand's overseas empire, 1840–1945', in Mallon, Mahina-Tuai, and Salesa (eds), *Tangata o le Moana*, pp. 97–122.

19 K. R. Howe, *Nature, Culture, and History: The "Knowing" of Oceania* (Honolulu: University of Hawai'i Press, 2000), p. 59. See also Kerry Howe, 'New Zealand's twentieth-century Pacifics: Memories and reflections', *New Zealand Journal of History*, 34:1 (2000), 4–19.

PART I

'Empire at home'

CHAPTER ONE

Te Karere Maori and the defence of empire, 1855–60

Kenton Storey

When the Taranaki War began in early 1860, the colonial government's bilingual newspaper, *Te Karere Maori* or *The Maori Messenger*, identified the origins of the conflict in an editorial entitled 'The Maori of the Past and the Maori of the Present'. Rather than being a conflict over land between the Crown and Māori, the paper identified the war as a struggle between Māori over the merits of British colonialism. In this case, the Te Ati Awa insurgents led by Wiremu Kīngi Te Rangitāke were accused of seeking to return to the values of the pre-colonial era:

> In former times gross darkness pervaded the land. The Maori was a savage – superstitious, cruel, bloodthirsty. 'Blood for blood' was his only law. Every man's hand was against his neighbour, and his neighbour's hand against him. Wars and rumours of war convulsed the people. No tribe was exempt. The aggressor of to-day was besieged of to-morrow – the tyrant of one time was the oppressed of another. The thick veil of heathenism clung around the minds of men, and the service of the Evil One prevailed. The Maori of the past was little better than the beast of the field.[1]

Here the writer described the society of pre-colonial Māori as a primordial chaos. Thus Māori faced a choice: Christianity and civilisation, or timeless barbarism and an existence outside of history.

This allusion to the power of history in this moment of crisis would not have been surprising to long-time readers of *Te Karere Maori*. Central to the paper's manifesto was the argument that England's own history offered a template for Māori development; just as the Anglo-Saxon progenitors of the British Empire were products of racial amalgamation, so too, it was believed, a similar process as desirable was occurring in New Zealand. Historical narratives, then, functioned as both guides for cultural development and as a means to illustrate the divine attributes of the British Empire and, by extension, the colonial project in New Zealand. *Te Karere Maori* took for granted that Māori Christians were open to further cultural innovation and attempted to appeal to its readers through the language of Christian brotherhood. In this way, *Te Karere Maori* sought to convince its readers to refashion themselves by putting aside all aspects of their customary culture.[2]

Building on work by Alan Lester and Tony Ballantyne regarding the significance of communications networks for colonial societies, this chapter explores how *Te Karere Maori* framed its advocacy for civilising reform and racial amalgamation between 1855 and 1860, the formative years before the Taranaki War.[3] In this period, many Māori were increasingly reassessing the benefits of British colonialism and paying close attention to the intentions of settlers as revealed within networks of colonial knowledge. *Te Karere Maori* attempted to mediate understandings of news that might inspire dissent by crafting ideal-ised portraits of English history and coverage of international news to identify the providential role of the British Empire. But as the chapter suggests, *Te Karere Maori*'s confidence in the British colonial project often veiled anxiety.

Te Karere Maori

Governor George Grey initiated *Te Karere Maori* in 1849 following his arrival at the colony in order to communicate more effectively with Māori. The paper ceased publication in 1854 as a result of his depar-ture and was then revived with the arrival of Governor Thomas Gore Browne in 1855.[4] Its express goal was '[t]o increase the wealth and encourage the industry of the native people of New Zealand'.[5] Its eclec-tic content included local and international news, government legisla-tion, editorials, announcements of land sales, letters to the editor, and market prices for commodities. It focused particularly on increasing Māori participation in the colonial free market economy through modern farming, wage labour, and the individualisation of collectively owned property. Published first as a monthly newspaper, *Te Karere Maori* became a bi-monthly publication in May 1857. Its circulation in 1855 was 1,000 copies per monthly edition, but this was later reduced to 500 copies per edition.[6] Given the Crown's estimate of 30,132 Māori over the age of 14 in 1858, a circulation of 500 newspapers would have equalled one copy per sixty Māori persons.[7]

This level of circulation was much lower than other leading New Zealand papers, and colonists recognised this as an impediment to the paper's effectiveness.[8] In 1859, the editor of Auckland's leading newspa-per, the *New Zealander*, observed that the Māori press was 'by far the most efficient means' for the Crown to educate Māori, but published only a single copy for every 300 Māori readers.[9] This limited circulation reflected the fact that the Native Department operated on a small budget. However, a combination of factors facilitated this newspaper's broad reach, including high rates of Māori literacy in the mid-1850s, the oral transmission of newspaper content, and Māori receptivity to publications in their own language.[10] Indeed, Arthur S. Thomson reported in 1859 in *The Story of New Zealand* that one half of adult Māori could read Māori and one third could both read and write.[11] The Native Department distributed copies of *Te Karere Maori* to prominent Māori rangatira, government officials, and missionaries, who then shared the newspaper within their communities. *Te Karere Maori*, then, represented an affordable and relatively efficient means for both Grey and Browne to disseminate information to Māori.

The importance of this paper only increased following the outbreak of the Taranaki War in 1860. This conflict originated in the province of Taranaki over a contested land sale that pitted members of the Te Ati Awa iwi against each other and the Crown. Memoranda detail that the Native Department increased *Te Karere Maori*'s circulation to 1,000 copies per edition in 1860.[12] This increased circulation appears to have continued throughout the war.[13] Also during the conflict, the Native Department published the extensive proceedings of the Kohimarama conference, which featured detailed reportage of many Māori leaders' speeches of support for Governor Browne.[14] This was a significant expenditure and illustrates the importance that Native Secretary Donald McLean placed on the paper to rally support for the Crown.[15]

Te Karere Maori was also closely integrated within New Zealand's settler press. Not only did editors pay attention to the paper's content as an indicator of the Crown's policy towards Māori, it was also edited from 1849–60 by David Burn, a member of the Auckland press.[16] He worked alongside C. O. Davis, *Te Karere Maori*'s Māori language editor, until his departure in 1857.[17] During his editorship, Burn came into conflict with *Te Karere Maori*'s translators and constantly challenged attempts to reduce his salary.[18] Burn's correspondence to the Native Secretary reveals how the Native Department attempted to publish *Te Karere Maori* with the utmost economy, leaving the paper's organisation under his control as 'almost the exclusive writer of the Maori Messenger'.[19]

Te Karere Maori, like other colonial papers across the British Empire, provided its readers with both commercial and editorial content. Burn's diaries detail the key role he played in shaping both *Te Karere Maori*'s commercial stories and many leading articles.[20] At the same time, though, Burn worked as a journalist and editor at several Auckland newspapers, including the *Southern Cross*, the *New Zealander*, and the *Auckland Weekly Register*. These close ties were no doubt strengthened by the fact that W. C. Wilson, Burn's employer and the controller of both the *New Zealander* and the *Auckland Weekly Register*, often printed *Te Karere Maori*. Burn's significant involvement in the Auckland press made him keenly aware of local coverage of international news and likely influenced *Te Karere Maori's* commentary on events within the British Empire. At the same time, Burn brought to *Te Karere Maori* the same range of skills that he employed within other Auckland newspapers. A constant feature within *Te Karere Maori* was the provision of commercial information, including market prices and shipping news, and according to Burn, this was its most popular content.[21]

The analysis in this chapter is based solely on *Te Karere Maori's* English text. As Lachy Paterson argues, *Te Karere Maori's* parallel Māori and English texts did not always share the same meanings.[22] Indeed, Paterson suggests that Māori readers most likely ignored the English text, which was itself probably crafted primarily for colonists, Crown administrators, and members of the Colonial Office.[23] On the surface, though, both English and Māori texts were expected to feature similar meanings. While it is difficult to measure the impact of this paper among its Māori readers, an interpretation of *Te Karere Maori's* English text offers valuable insights into the Native Department's vision for Māori.

Te Karere Maori *and the history of England*

History was not the equivalent of Māori tradition, according to *Te Karere Maori*. Māori myth might 'amuse the fancy', but it could not 'inform the understanding'.[24] The value of history lay in its reliability, its recitation of 'the actions of men who have really existed ... [which] affords us an opportunity of acquainting ourselves with the manners and customs of former times'.[25] This interpretive framework privileged print culture and associated Māori orality with barbarism and a timeless pre-historical chaos. Not only had the British brought the *Word* but they had brought *time* as well. *Te Karere Maori* employed historical narratives to illustrate 'how other nations that have been in a state of barbarism have progressed in civilization and improvement'.[26] By introducing its readers to models of Western temporality and cultural development, *Te Karere Maori* purported to introduce Māori into history itself.

Te Karere Maori's articles on English history drew upon a theory of human development which had its antecedents in the Scottish Enlightenment, particularly with the moral philosophers Adam Smith, John Millar and Adam Ferguson.[27] These early historians had popularised a stadial theory of history that identified human development over time within four recognisable stages, predicated upon distinctive modes of subsistence with agriculture, commerce, and property as signifiers of civilisation. The accounts of English history in *Te Karere Maori* utilised this same theory of history to emphasise how change over time had progressively led to the creation of the British Empire. These narratives were intended to naturalise the cultural disjunctions which Māori were experiencing as a consequence of British colonisation, especially the replacement of some aspects of their culture. The importance of these editorials is evidenced by the fact that Governor Browne himself authored several chapters on the history of England.[28]

Te Karere Maori's historical articles also explicitly drew upon a Judeo-Christian worldview. In series such as 'Geography, or the world we live in', 'Letters on history', and 'History of the world', *Te Karere Maori* described the world's Biblical origins, its ancient civilisations, European exploration and colonisation, and the cultural differences of foreign nations. These narratives stressed the veracity and continuity of Biblical narratives and highlighted cultural differences within descriptions of pagan religiosity. This interpretive framework characterised the Bible itself as a history text; its claims to reliability could increasingly be corroborated with new archaeological and historical research from the Middle East. Explicitly, these narratives increased Māori readers' general knowledge of the world. At the same time, too, *Te Karere Maori* established a seamless timeline from the Biblical Age of the Patriarchs through to the rise of the British Empire. This was an Anglocentric vision of world history in which divine agency could be clearly discerned.

England's history received particular attention as an archetype of civilising reform and as an example of God's continued work in the world. *Te Karere Maori* explained the process by which the modern English nation had formed, focusing particularly on its legacy of racial amalgamation. Series of articles such as 'The early history of England', 'The ancestors of the Pakeha', and 'The people of England' described the transformation of England by successive invasions. Pagan Celts were conquered first by the Roman Empire, then Christianised Celts were invaded by Saxons, then Danes, and finally by the Normans. Moreover, each successive invading force melded with the other to create a people greater than the sum of its parts:

> But even out of all this tyranny and misery the God who orders all made good come forth. The conquerors learnt from the men they had subdued many good laws and customs which before had been unknown to them, and the English never would have been the men they are had they not the Nooman [sic] courage and the Norman higher power of mind been added to the Saxon temper which did not rise enough above the pains and pleasures enjoyed by beasts as well as men.[29]

[17]

As this passage makes clear, the editor emphasised that these conquests and the related work of racial amalgamation were part of God's plan.

Christianity and Te Karere Maori

Christianity functioned as a bridge for the writers of *Te Karere Maori*, as they sought to normalise British colonialism, exploit Māori openness to innovation, and correct what they perceived to be deviations from orthodoxy. This strategy built upon Māori readers' familiarity with the Bible and the development of the nation of Israel as God's chosen people. Drawing on this interpretive framework, readers were invited to recognise the British Empire as God's agent in the world and, by extension, the divine inspiration for the British colonial project in New Zealand. Here we see the centrality and significance of Christianity to *Te Karere Maori* and its attempts to engage Māori readers.

While the majority of Māori prior to the Taranaki War had relatively little direct contact with the colonial government's administrative apparatus, large numbers of Māori were members of both Protestant and Catholic denominations. Indeed, much had changed within Māori communities since the arrival of European newcomers. According to Lyndsay Head, 'the arrival of Europeans in the early nineteenth century destroyed the intellectual and moral coherence of existing Maori political culture, which was based on the spiritual and temporal authority of chiefs'.[30] Māori Christian conversion, then, had entailed a shifting belief in the primacy of customary tapu to the authority of a Christian deity. It is important to recognise that both Māori spirituality and European forms of Christianity were unstable formations, encountered by Māori through a syncretic interface of both knowledge systems.[31] It is also important to remember Gauri Viswanathan's insight that 'conversion is not necessarily a mode of assimilation to a predetermined reality, identity, or system of thought'.[32] Conversion in New Zealand was instead a dynamic and dialogical process shaped by both the 'ideal system to which the convert aspires' and the convert's pre-existent worldview.[33]

Māori cultural perspectives informed their Christian practice; Māori did not simply put aside certain cultural practices such as cannibalism, polygamy, and moko upon conversion. Rather, conversion entailed dynamic discontinuities between the social organisation of pre-Christian Māori culture and its subsequent Christian incarnation.[34] Recognising agency entails an acknowledgment that Māori utilised Christian practice to reject some aspects of their cultural worldview

[18]

in their pursuit of modernity. What troubled colonists, though, is that Māori engagement with Christianity also resulted in novel interpretations and practice, which, like the Kīngitanga, drew upon scriptural authority to resist the Crown. The Kīngitanga was a political movement whereby a Māori king was elected in 1858 as a symbol of Māori commitment to end land sales with the Crown and implement an alternative code of laws. Kīngitanga leaders such as Wiremu Tamihana likened the experience of Māori to the people of Israel, illustrating how Biblical narratives could inspire unexpected interpretive meanings far beyond that which British missionaries had intended in their translation and publication of the Bible into Māori.

It is clear that the writers of *Te Karere Maori* took for granted that Māori were receptive to cultural innovation. They based this belief on the fact that many Māori were sincere Christians, and that they had willingly rejected aspects of their customary culture. Letters to the editor from Māori writers in *Te Karere Maori* touch on this enthusiasm for aspects of modernity. While the interpretation of Māori correspondence is fraught, as questions pertaining to translation, motivation, and representational quality must be considered, it is fascinating how Māori correspondents often readily accepted that their Christian conversion had entailed the rejection of some aspects of their former culture.[35] Māori society in the mid-nineteenth century was in flux, and Indigenous forms of Christianity played a significant role in this transformation.

Worth noting, however, is how the explicit religiosity of *Te Karere Maori* led Alan Ward to dismiss the paper as 'tawdry' and Keith Sinclair to consider it as 'a hotchpotch of sloppy piety, dull moralizing, and condescending didacticism'.[36] These relatively contemporary assessments endorsed the view that *Te Karere Maori*'s fervent Christian themes were unattractive to Māori readers. Here both Ward and Sinclair reiterated the more extreme denunciations of the paper that appeared within the colonial New Zealand press in the mid-nineteenth century.[37] Then public critics of *Te Karere Maori* had asserted that the paper's religious themes were misdirected because Māori were not really Christians. Indeed, Māori Christianity was itself a subject of controversy. From New Zealand's foundation in 1840, both British settlers and missionaries had fought over the shape of local colonialism. In these debates, the conversion and Christian faith experience of Māori believers had been deployed as a rationale for their protection by the Crown. The use of the language of Christian brotherhood by *Te Karere Maori* signified a particular, and hotly contested, humanitarian worldview with roots in both the Abolitionist Movement and the work of the Aborigines Protection Society.

Racial amalgamation diluted

Te Karere Maori's historical narratives asserted that British settlement in New Zealand had initiated a process of racial amalgamation. But as this chapter will uncover and discuss, this promised vision of a Māori future tense had complex meanings. For example, narratives of English history revealed how racial amalgamation was a messy and lengthy process involving coercion, violence, invasion, and the coupling of many peoples. But *Te Karere Maori* made no mention of racial amalgamation as a process of racial fusion tying Māori to colonists through intermarriage. As both Damon Salesa and Angela Wanhalla have shown, New Zealand did feature a significant half-caste population by the mid-nineteenth century, itself a legacy of intermarriage and partnership between European newcomers and Māori.[38] However, encouraging further racial mixing was not respectable and did not garner attention or encouragement.

Instead, *Te Karere Maori* described racial amalgamation as the transformation of customary Māori cultural practices, with emphasis on the reformation of the Māori body – corporeal and politic – through personal hygiene, individual land tenure, English law, and education. As Salesa has recently illustrated, the origins of the Crown's policy of racial amalgamation lay in the pre-settlement prospectus of the New Zealand Company (NZC), which had outlined plans to avoid the separation of the races in New Zealand by intermixing Māori reserves alongside colonists and maintaining the social order of Māori through special land grants to Māori rangatira.[39] According to Salesa, the NZC's humanitarian mandate has not been taken seriously because it failed spectacularly; the reality of Māori–settler relations never matched the naïveté of NZC propaganda.[40] At the same time, however, the humanitarian policy of racial amalgamation as imagined by the NZC became enshrined as a policy objective of both the Colonial Office and colonial executives in New Zealand during the 1840s and 1850s. Articulated most clearly within *Te Karere Maori*, the policy of racial amalgamation became diluted into a merger of two cultural systems, the weaker Māori with the stronger Anglo-Saxon. This bias against Māori culture reflected a particular humanitarian worldview – that Māori were capable of civilising reform but would only be civilised when they were no longer Māori.

But while the policy of racial amalgamation was rather vague, *Te Karere Maori*'s writer was quick to note the differences between England's historical experiences versus those of New Zealand:

> The difference is very great between the robbers of those days who seized what pleased them, and the settlers of the time we live in, who pay for

the land they live on, and are willing to share with those amongst whom they dwell the advantages of their laws and civilization.⁴¹

In other words, British colonists were not invaders. As Chief Justice William Martin argued in 'The Laws and Customs of the Pakeha', England's prosperity and its divine mission drew upon the Christian faith. Formerly England had been like New Zealand, 'in a state of ignorance', but '[a]fter the introduction and establishment of Christianity it began to rise; for God is mindful of the people who are mindful of Him'.⁴² In this way, *Te Karere Maori* utilised England's history of invasion to stress the beneficial conditions in which Māori had encountered the British. As Martin emphasised, the historic relationship between Māori and the British Empire was founded on integrity. Great Britain had been invited by Māori to colonise New Zealand and in doing so was an agent of God's blessing. By embracing Christianity, too, Māori had embarked upon the same path as the ancient English. Great Britain could easily have invaded New Zealand.⁴³ In its historical narratives and appeals to Māori to embrace racial amalgamation, *Te Karere Maori* offered an idealised view of the past and an undefined vision of the future; these narratives broke down amid the uncertainties of mid-nineteenth-century news.

News, anxiety, and Māori rebellion

From time to time we hear of reports being in circulation amongst them the tendency of which is to disturb the friendly relations subsisting between the two races and to impair the confidence which the Maori people have hitherto placed in the Government. A vague and indistinct suspicion of some imaginary harm intended them by their Pakeha neighbours is entertained by some of the less intelligent and well-informed, suggested probably in the first instance by the mischievous and disaffected.⁴⁴

Written in 1859 in a period of growing interracial tension, here the writer explicitly sought to allay Māori anxiety. This passage reminds us that the historical narratives and interpretive news stories of *Te Karere Maori* were articulated against public discourses which suggested that the British intended harm to Māori. The 1850s featured the beginning of what James Belich refers to as 'swamping', whereby the population of immigrant colonists grew rapidly alongside a demographic decline of Māori.⁴⁵ The population growth of colonists versus the diminishing Māori population was widely recognised.⁴⁶ At the same time, while the early 1850s had featured strong Māori participation in an export-oriented agricultural economy which had supplied the Australian gold fields with foodstuffs, this market collapsed in the mid-1850s, causing considerable harm to Māori agriculturalists.[47] During the Taranaki War, too, rumours abounded that the Crown intended to enslave all Māori and steal their territories.[48]

It appears that *Te Karere Maori*'s narratives of English history may have also played a role in fomenting anxiety. For example, Hugh Carleton, editor of the Auckland newspaper the *Southern Cross*, noted on 17 May 1859 what he considered to be the ingenious way in which Māori had adapted British knowledge.[49] Carleton referred to how local Māori objected to the construction of a road from Auckland to Ahuriri based upon the logic that the Roman Empire's successful invasion of Britain had occurred through road building. Paterson provides a similar anecdote from F. D. Fenton, the Resident Magistrate for Waikato, collected on 29 July 1859, which details Māori opposition to road construction based upon a Roman precedent.[50] Neither Carleton's nor Fenton's accounts linked this usage of English history to the content of *Te Karere Maori*, despite the fact that several editorials detailing the Roman invasion of England were published in this paper in 1857.[51] This usage of English history evidences a dynamic engagement with *Te Karere Maori*. Waikato Māori accepted the premise that the experience of the ancient Celts paralleled their own, but they were not reassured. Instead, these leading articles inspired strategic resistance.

The links between rumour and editorial content suggest that *Te Karere Maori*'s expositions on world history may have been more intentional in their purpose than is explicitly apparent. Not surprisingly, *Te Karere Maori* interpreted international events within celebratory Anglocentric narratives. For example, in June 1855–56 *Te Karere Maori* published three leading articles concerning the Crimean War.[52] These pieces detailed the moral justification of Great Britain's partnership with Turkey and France against a Russian oppressor, characterising the war as a defence of mankind's liberty, and also stressed how the numerically inferior British and French military forces had defeated their Russian foes. These leading articles are unremarkable propaganda at first glance. However, comments by Henry Sewell shed light on their actual purpose. Sewell was a prominent Canterbury colonist and member of the House of Representatives. In 1855 he recorded in his diary that relations between colonists and Māori were dire, exacerbated not only by intertribal violence in the province of Taranaki but also by visiting American whalers.[53] According to Sewell, these American whalers were:

> preaching sedition all through the Colony, persuading the Natives that Russia has destroyed all our fleets and armies, and that the Troops are

about to be recalled. Then they say – Hand over New Zealand to America, she will protect your Land Rights.[54]

Governor Browne echoed Sewell's concern, complaining to the Colonial Office that '[t]he American whalers who are very numerous in our ports take every opportunity to aggravate this [Māori] discontent'.[55] These comments cast *Te Karere Maori*'s exposition of British military successes in the Crimea in a different light. Their celebratory tone can be interpreted as an attempt to counteract rumours of British imperial weakness. This example has several connotations worth discussing. First, Sewell's and Browne's concerns illustrate a significant degree of anxiety that misinformation about the British Empire might adversely affect local relations with Māori. Second, these fears reveal how Māori were integrated within unregulated networks of information transmission to sites where anti-British rhetoric flourished. Not only could Māori misinterpret the news but they might also be deceived by enemy propaganda.

In the same way, *Te Karere Maori*'s response to the Indian Rebellion was inspired by misinformation, and sought to influence Māori understandings of the conflict. In early 1858, Browne wrote to Henry Labouchere at the Colonial Office complaining that *Te Karere Maori*'s former editor, C. O. Davis, had printed accounts of the Indian Rebellion within a Māori language paper (*Te Waka o Te Iwi*), which might incite insurrection.[56] *Te Karere Maori* subsequently published a series of articles on the Indian Rebellion in 1858 and 1859.[57] As Ballantyne notes, these articles detailed the Rebellion's origins and emphasised 'the swift reassertion of British authority'.[58] These narratives also stressed that the Indian Rebellion had been initiated by 'traitorous' Indian Sepoys who had betrayed the British by perpetrating 'diabolical cruelties … upon the helpless and unoffending women and children who fell into the hands of the rebels'.[59] Explicitly, *Te Karere Maori* observed that while Māori readers were probably aware of the Indian Rebellion, their 'imperfect information' probably would not allow them to 'form very distinct or correct notions on the subject'. These leading articles sought to remedy this deficit by elaborating how Great Britain's war in India was just, fought only in self-defence, and warranted by the Indian rebels' atrocities.

Te Karere Maori's description of the Indian Rebellion, though, was paired with an historical article detailing the development of Great Britain's presence in India. According to the writer, English troops had not conquered India through numerical superiority. Rather, British hegemony had occurred over an extended period, facilitated by Indian leaders' partnership with the English, who 'soon found that the

[23]

religion of the Christians made them act very differently from any of the Idolatrous Sovereigns who had hitherto ruled over their country'. England's presence in India had been facilitated by its integrity and non-interference in Indian culture. But a purported hundred years of excellent treatment of Indian soldiers had been rewarded with betrayal. Here too, an historical narrative contextualised a contemporary event within an Anglocentric frame, emphasising the British Empire's providential role.

Te Karere Maori devoted considerable attention to the Indian Rebellion for several reasons. First, the Indian Rebellion was the most significant news story in 1857 and 1858, and garnered a vast amount of coverage within New Zealand papers, information which was accessible to Māori. Second, the antagonistic racial language employed within metropolitan descriptions of the Indian Rebellion as a war of the races undermined the Native Department's own characterisations of the British Empire's providential role in the world. Local papers in New Zealand reproduced in detail news of the summary executions of rebel Sepoys and arguments that Delhi should be annihilated in the same manner that God had destroyed Sodom and Gomorrah in the Old Testament. The custom of publishing extended metropolitan coverage of the Rebellion reproduced the language of racial warfare and a vengeful and antagonistic portrait of British and Indian relations.[60] In effect, the mechanics of cut-and-paste journalism prevalent in this period allowed narratives of the Indian Rebellion – which had been crafted for Anglo-Indians and metropolitan Britons – to resonate in New Zealand in an unfiltered way. Interestingly, leading members of New Zealand's colonial press did not draw parallels between the situation in India and local race relations. The discourses surrounding the Indian Rebellion were too fraught with racial antagonism to be employed in New Zealand with its own deepening racial crises.

Conclusions

Te Karere Maori had an ambitious goal: to convince its Māori readers to transform themselves into the very image of the British settlers who were increasingly encroaching on their territory. Through historical narratives, *Te Karere Maori* provided the requisite roadmap – English people and, by connection, the British Empire, had been propelled to pre-eminence by a divinely inspired process of racial amalgamation. These narratives of Roman conquest and road-building were intended to be comforting; instead, they sometimes inspired strategic resistance. As this example illustrates, too, Māori responses to the content of *Te Karere Maori* were not fixed, just as their Indigenous forms of

Christianity were not simply replications of British practice. Perhaps most significantly, this contextualised analysis of *Te Karere Maori* allows us to read through the rhetoric of imperial propaganda. *Te Karere Maori* responded reactively to correct its readers' understandings of the Crimean War and the Indian Rebellion precisely because both agent provocateurs and the public discourses of New Zealand's colonial press contradicted the paper's own idealised narratives. Inspired by the anxiety of the colonial administration, *Te Karere Maori* sought to alleviate the fears of its Māori readers yet sometimes did the very opposite.

Notes

1   *Te Karere Maori* (31 May 1860), p. 1.
2   Lachy Paterson, *Colonial Discourses: Niupepa Māori 1855–1863* (Dunedin: Otago University, 2006), p. 12. Paterson's book offers the most in-depth study of *Te Karere Maori*.
3   Alan Lester, 'British settler discourse and the circuits of empire', *History Workshop Journal*, 1:54 (2002), pp. 24–48; Tony Ballantyne, 'Teaching Māori about Asia: Print culture and community identity in nineteenth-century New Zealand', in Henry Johnson and Brian Moloughney (eds), *Asia in the Making of New Zealand* (Auckland: Auckland University Press, 2006).
4   Phil G. Parkinson and Penny Griffith, 'The Maori Messenger = Te Karere Maori (1855–1861)', in Phil G. Parkinson and Penny Griffith (compilers), *Books in Māori, 1815–1900: An Annotated Bibliography / Ngā Tānga reo Māori, 1815–1900: Ngā Kohikohinga me ōna Whakamārama* (Auckland: Reed, 2004), pp. 749–51.
5   *Te Karere Maori* (July 1855), p. 1.
6   Ross Harvey, 'Economic aspects of nineteenth-century New Zealand newspapers', *Bibliographical Society of Australia and New Zealand Bulletin*, 17:2 (1993), 59.
7   Registrar General, *Statistics of New Zealand for 1858* (Auckland: W. C. Wilson), No. 10.
8   In 1857 New Zealand's leading newspaper, the *New Zealander*, published one edition for every ten adult colonists in Auckland.
9   *New Zealander* (25 May 1859), p. 3.
10 Paterson, *Colonial Discourses*, pp. 37–48; Ballantyne, 'Teaching Māori about Asia', pp. 21–3; Walter Brodie, *Remarks on the Past and Present State of New Zealand, Its Government, Capabilities, and Prospects* (London: Whittaker & Co., 1845), pp. 109–10.
11 Ballantyne, 'Teaching Māori about Asia', p. 19; Arthur S. Thomson, *The Story of New Zealand: Past and Present – Savage and Civilized*, Vol. 2 (London: John Murray, 1859), p. 297.
12 Archives New Zealand, Wellington (hereafter ANZ), MA-1-831-1860/23, Thomas Henry Smith and Frederick Whitaker to Thomas Gore Browne, 'Memoranda – Native Department', 22 March 1860; ANZ, MA-1-831-1860/42, Donald McLean to the Native Secretary, 'Memoranda – Native Department', 20 April 1860.
13 ANZ, MA-24-8/16, Native Secretary, 'Memoranda – Native Department'.
14 *Te Karere Maori* (14 July 1860), pp. 1–48; *Te Karere Maori* (31 July 1860), pp. 1–62; and *Te Karere Maori* (1 September 1860), pp. 1–79.
15 Native Secretary, Memoranda, ANZ, MA-1-831-1860/156. For a more in-depth discussion see Lachy Paterson, 'The Kohimarama Conference of 1860: A contextual reading', *Journal of New Zealand Studies*, 12 (2012): 29–46.
16 *Auckland Examiner* (30 March 1859), p. 2; *New Zealander* (25 May 1859), p. 3; *New Zealander* (31 August 1859), p. 3; *Auckland Examiner* (4 April 1860), p. 2; *Auckland*

Examiner (11 April 1860), p. 2; *Taranaki Herald* (15 December 1860), p. 2; *Southern Cross* (19 February 1861), pp. 2–3.

17   State Library of New South Wales, Sydney (hereafter SL), Microfilm-CY 1094, David Burn, Diary, 11 January 1856.

18   SL, Microfilm-CY 1094, David Burn, Diary, 11 January 1856; ANZ, IA-1-222-1861/2131, Burn to the Native Secretary, 'General Inwards Correspondence to the Colonial Secretary'.

19   ANZ, Burn to the Native Secretary, 'General Inwards Correspondence', 7 October 1861.

20   SL, Microfilm-CY 1094, David Burn, Diary. Burn's diary gives significant details of activities. He wrote articles relating to New Zealand events (1 March 1856; 4 February 1858); agricultural topics (7 May 1856; 30 November 1856; 9 February 1857); the Crimean War (21 May 1856); leading editorials – the dates correspond with articles describing Browne's trips to the Bay of Islands and Taranaki, and an editorial on Māori land ownership (6 January 1858; 27 January 1858; 31 March 1858), and on the topic of Māori debt (2 July 1858).

21   ANZ, Burn to the Colonial Secretary, 'General Inwards Correspondence to the Colonial Secretary', 7 October 1861.

22   Paterson, *Colonial Discourses*, pp. 49–67.

23   Paterson, *Colonial Discourses*, pp. 49–50.

24   *Te Karere Maori* (1 September 1855), p. 13.

25   *Te Karere Maori* (1 September 1855), p. 13.

26   *Te Karere Maori* (30 August 1856), p. 1.

27   Adam Ferguson, *An Essay on the History of Civil Society* (London: A. Millar & T. Cadell, 1768); Adam Smith, *An Inquiry into the Nature and Causes of the Wealth of Nations* (London: T. Cadell, 1776); John Millar, *An Historical View of the English Government* (London: J. Mawman, 1803).

28   David Burn, Diary, 1 July 1856 and 4 September 1856.

29   David Burn, Diary, 30 June 1859.

30   Lyndsay Head, 'Land, Authority and the Forgetting of Being in Early Colonial Maori History' (PhD thesis, University of Canterbury, 2006), p. 2.

31   Michael J. Stevens, 'Muttonbirds and Modernity in Murihiku: Continuity and Change in Kāi Tahu Knowledge' (PhD thesis, University of Otago, 2009), pp. 15–16.

32   Gauri Viswanathan, *Outside the Fold: Conversion, Modernity, and Belief* (Princeton: Princeton University Press, 1998), p. 122.

33   Viswanathan, *Outside the Fold*, p. 122.

34   Bronwyn Elsmore, *Mana from Heaven* (Tauranga: Moana Press, 1989).

35   *Te Karere Maori* (28 February 1857), pp. 11–12; *Te Karere Maori* (31 March 1857), pp. 9–13; *Te Karere Maori* (30 June 1857), p. 3; *Te Karere Maori* (15 September 1857), pp. 8–12; *Te Karere Maori* (15 December 1857), pp. 4–5; *Te Karere Maori* (31 May 1858), pp. 3–6; *Te Karere Maori* (16 August 1858), pp. 8–9; *Te Karere Maori* ([?] January 1860), pp. 11–13.

36   Keith Sinclair, *The Origins of the Maori Wars* (Wellington: New Zealand University Press, 1961), p. 41; Alan Ward, *A Show of Justice: Racial 'Amalgamation' in Nineteenth Century New Zealand* (Toronto: University of Toronto Press, 1974), p. 92.

37   *Auckland Examiner* (30 March 1859), p. 2; *Auckland Examiner* (4 April 1860), p. 2; *Auckland Examiner* (11 April 1860), p. 2; *Taranaki Herald* (15 December 1860), p. 2; *Southern Cross* (19 February 1861), pp. 2–3; John Eldon Gorst, *The Maori King* (London: Macmillan and Co., 1864), pp. 52–3.

38   Damon Ieremia Salesa, *Racial Crossings: Race, Intermarriage, and the Victorian British Empire* (Auckland: Oxford University Press, 2011); Angela Wanhalla, *Matters of the Heart: A History of Interracial Marriage in New Zealand* (Auckland: Auckland University Press, 2013).

39   John Ward and Edward Jerningham Wakefield, *The British Colonization of New Zealand* (London: John W. Parker, 1837). Of anonymous authorship, this book was

published 'For the New Zealand Association', and later attributed to Ward and Wakefield.
40 Salesa, *Racial Crossings*, p. 43.
41 *Te Karere Maori* (30 June 1859), p. 3.
42 *Te Karere Maori* (31 March 1856), p. 5.
43 *Te Karere Maori* (31 August 1859), p. 2.
44 *Te Karere Maori* (31 August 1859), p. 1.
45 James Belich, *Making Peoples: A History of New Zealanders, from Polynesian Settlement to the End of the Nineteenth Century* (Honolulu: University of Hawai'i Press, 2001), pp. 247–72.
46 *New Zealander* (31 August 1859), p. 3; *Southern Cross* (6 September 1859), p. 3; *Southern* Cross (13 September 1859), p. 3; *Te Karere Maori* (30 September 1859), p. 5.
47 Hazel Petrie, *Chiefs of Industry: Māori Tribal Enterprise in Early Colonial New Zealand* (Auckland: Auckland University Press, 2006), pp. 253–60; Paul Monin, 'Maori economies and colonial capitalism', in Giselle Byrnes (ed.), *The New Oxford History of New Zealand* (Auckland: Oxford University Press, 2009), p. 133.
48 McLean to Browne, 6 March 1861, No. 12, Enclosure No. 1, *Correspondence and Other Papers Relating to New Zealand, 1862–64*, Vol. 13, British Parliamentary Papers (Shannon: Irish University Press, 1970), p. 39; Browne to Newcastle, 26 September 1861, No. 41 (No. 125), pp. 99–101.
49 *Southern Cross* (17 May 1859), p. 2.
50 Paterson, *Colonial Discourses*, pp. 111–12; *Appendices to the Journal of the House of Representatives*, E-1C, 1860, p. 17. F. D. Fenton, Resident Magistrate of Waikato, recorded in his journal to 29 July 1859: 'I have heard mention made of the Romans and their bridges, and of the consequent subjugation of England.'
51 *Te Karere Maori* (15 March 1859; 31 July 1857; 30 November 1857).
52 *Te Karere Maori* (1 June 1855), pp. 1–2; *Te Karere Maori* (30 June 1856), pp. 4–15; *Te Karere Maori* (31 July 1856), pp. 1–3.
53 David W. McIntyre, *The Journal of Henry Sewell, 1853–7*, Vols 1–2 (Christchurch: Whitcoulls Publishers, 1980), pp. 242–3, p. 251.
54 McIntyre, *The Journal of Henry Sewell*, pp. 242–3.
55 McIntyre, *The Journal of Henry Sewell*, pp. 242–3; Alexander Turnbull Library, Wellington, New Zealand (hereafter ATL), QMS-0284, Thomas Gore Browne to Herman Merivale, 'Sir Thomas Gore Browne Letterbook', 2 July 1856.
56 ATL, CO 209/145, Browne to Labouchere, 18 February 1858.
57 *Te Karere Maori* (30 June 1858), pp. 1–5; *Te Karere Maori* (15 July 1858), pp. 1–6; *Te Karere Maori* (31 December, 1858), pp. 4–5; *Te Karere Maori* (15 June 1859), p. 6.
58 Ballantyne, 'Teaching Māori about Asia', 22–3.
59 *Te Karere Maori* (30 June 1858), p. 2.
60 *Southern Cross* (15 December 1857), p. 3.

CHAPTER TWO

An imperial icon Indigenised: the Queen Victoria Memorial at Ohinemutu

Mark Stocker

The vast majority of sculptural memorials to Queen Victoria in the British Empire were erected in the period that spanned her Golden Jubilee (1887) and the opening decade of the twentieth century. The most familiar examples in New Zealand, located in the metropolitan centres of Auckland, Wellington, Christchurch, and Dunedin, are no exception; they date from 1899 to 1905.[1] Stylistically and iconographically, their conventionally realist portraiture and accompanying reliefs rendered them highly acceptable as public art, proud products from the 'core' of the Empire (made in London and Esher, UK), and commissioned by the loyally imperial colonial 'periphery'. Only in two instances do they contain obviously local references. In a pedestal relief on F. J. Williamson's memorial in Christchurch (1901–05), a Māori man beholds the arrival of the first four migrant ships in Lyttelton Harbour, while in another an Athena-like 'Canterbury' farewells her province's Second Boer War volunteers. The Wellington Victoria (1901–04) boasts Alfred Drury's much-admired depiction of the signing of the Treaty of Waitangi, subsequently reproduced on banknotes and postage stamps.[2]

Altogether less familiar, but arguably of greater interest in testing the concept of 'New Zealand's empire' central to this book, is the over-life-sized, half-length wooden carving of Queen Victoria in Ohinemutu, as represented in Figures 2.1 and 2.2 (1874). Ohinemutu, a lakeside settlement steeped in history and adjacent to the tourist city of Rotorua, was described in 1870 by the Governor, Sir George Bowen, as lying 'in the very heart ... of the native districts of New Zealand, and of the country most renowned in Maori song and legend'.[3]

The Ohinemutu Queen Victoria, like the monarch herself, is sui generis. Portraying the Queen in her early 50s, it is by far the earliest such memorial in New Zealand, preceding that of Auckland by almost twenty-five years. It is distinctive in that it was made of wood at a time

Maori Children, Ohinemutu, Rotorua. N.Z. 5035.

2.1 Queen Victoria, Ohinemutu. Sculpture by anonymous Italian carver, 1874; pedestal by Patu Whitiki, 1900; canopy by Tene Waitere, 1901. Postcard: Tanner Brothers, Wellington, after 1920.

when bronze and marble were de rigueur for such commissions, and it is unconventional in being taller than a bust but shorter than a statue. Yet the memorial was one of special resonance for its Māori recipients. Its later pedestal and canopy (1900–01), made by Ngāti Tarawhai carvers Patu Whitiki and Tene Waitere respectively, make it a marvellous – and literal – instantiation of the 'framing' that Western culture receives when translated into different contexts.[4] And while the memorial may be read as a potent signifier of integrated acculturation and hybridity, it goes intriguingly against the standard postcolonial grain. Far from embodying resistance to imperialism, its more obvious political connotations, of monarchical maternalism and concomitant imperial compliance of a subaltern people, make the carving a 'popular, indigenous expression of loyalty', as identified by Maya Jasanoff.[5] Perhaps it subsequently paid a price for this, as currently the carved portrait – wrenched from its architectural context – languishes ignominiously in a damaged state in the basement of the local Whakaturia wharekai. Yet given its chequered history, the fate of the Ohinemutu Queen Victoria may well change once more. This chapter examines the circumstances behind the original commission, its delayed delivery, and its initial, controversial, location at Ohinemutu. It then considers its relocation and remarkable beautification at the hands of local Indigenous carvers immediately prior to the Queen's death, and the attendant

2.2 Queen Victoria, Ohinemutu, ca. 1970, Photograph D. I. Therkleson, 'Rotorua Scenic Gems'.

anthropomorphic identity that the carving and memorial thereupon assumed. Almost a century of relatively quiescent and 'picturesque' history ensued, only to be disrupted by its contested relocation during the 1980s and an abrupt, unauthorised removal and return in the course of a few weeks in 1995. The aim here is to construct something more than a chronological narrative; rather, it is to reveal how a relatively naïve carving can become the contested site of imperial and Indigenous, core and periphery, 'loyalist' and 'activist' political discourse.

'... admirably carved, and the likeness is unmistakable'

The presentation of the carving probably followed an informal promise made on behalf of Queen Victoria's second son, Prince Alfred, Duke of Edinburgh (1844–1900), who visited New Zealand on three occasions during a naval tour of duty between 1869 and 1870.[6] The Arawa confederation, and the Ngāti Whakaue iwi in particular, were accorded particular favour for their role as kūpapa who, as the New Zealand Times put it, had 'in the Native wars lent valuable aid, in the field and otherwise, to bring about submission to Her Majesty and the tranquillity of the country. Apparently they desired to have among them some visible evidences of the powerful but faraway Queen under whose banner they had fought.'[7] Although both Victoria and Alfred would have applauded the sentiments behind the carving, archival documentation in the Don Stafford Collection of the Rotorua District Library reveals that the Native Affairs Department in Wellington formally commissioned and funded it in February 1874.[8] From the outset, it was intended for the Ngāti Whakaue, whose epicentre was – and remains – the Papa-i-Ouru marae at Ohinemutu.

Ngāti Whakaue had hoped that the carving would be completed for the opening of Tamatekapua, their wharenui on Papa-i-Ouru, in 1872, but both the commission and the presentation of the carving were considerably delayed. The earliest known record appears in a letter from Ngāti Whakaue elder Paora Te Amohau to the Native Affairs minister Donald McLean, dated December 1873 and requesting that delivery be hastened.[9] Henry Tacy Clarke, resident magistrate at Tauranga, told McLean that the bust had been approved over twelve months previously. The minister promptly arranged via the Agent-General in London, Isaac Featherston, for the work to be put out to tender. It was specified that it must be a wooden portrait, life-sized and bearing a gilt crown.[10] While the first and the last conditions would be satisfied, the eventual carving, 92 cm high excluding the crown, is noticeably larger than life. The sculptor was accordingly described as having 'taken the usual liberty of improving ... on the idea'.[11]

2.3 *Te Arawa* (Queen Victoria, Ohinemutu), 1986. Photograph taken from
Nicholas Thomas, Mark Adams, James Schuster and Lyonel Grant, *Rauru:
Tene Waitere, Maori Carving, Colonial History* (Dunedin: University of
Otago Press, 2009), p. 59.

No one has previously commented on the consonance between
the wooden material and Māori woodcarving traditions, of which the
Arawa/Ngāti Tarawhai genus (and genius) proved to be by far the most
enduring (see Figure 2.3).[12] Probably the underlying explanation owes
more to economy than to cultural sensitivity; wood was cheaper than
marble or bronze, and was more durable than terracotta or plaster. In
September 1874 Featherston chose 'a design by a clever Italian artist,
whose tender for seventy guineas' had been accepted; estimates had
been 'varying in amount up to £350'.[13]

Unfortunately, the artist's identity remains anonymous. One factor
influencing its anonymity is its lack of originality; it derives closely
from the full-length marble statue of Victoria in the Grand Vestibule of
Windsor Castle (1869–72), the first major royal commission of the later
Sculptor-in-Ordinary to the Queen, Joseph Edgar Boehm (see Figure
2.4). The sculptural showpiece of the 1872 International Exhibition,
held at the recently opened Albert Hall in London, the *Art Journal*

described it as 'the most careful statue of the Queen that has yet been executed'. The royal collar and the stars of the orders of the Garter and the Thistle were punctiliously rendered, as was Boehm's consistently intelligent eye for a likeness. Although the sagging chin makes a concession to the Queen's advancing middle age, the *Art Journal* still felt that she was portrayed 'somewhat younger than she is', a point echoed in the response to her Ohinemutu likeness. In Boehm's version, the Queen's left arm is directed towards her pet collie, 'Sharp'. This imparts a domesticity that pleased contemporaries, a sense 'more of social ease than of stately form'.[14] Emphasis on regality and mana were, however, the prime requirements for Ohinemutu, while the half-length format necessitated alterations to the arms and hands.

The carving was finished by late 1874, and on its arrival in May 1875 Thomas Lewis, Under-Secretary to the Native Affairs Department, arranged for it to be photographed and 'a dozen or two copies struck off. It would make a nice picture which many of the natives would like to receive as a present.' The cost 'would be very slight', but the aura of the reproductions considerable. Lewis's memorandum adds that the 'bust [was] painted by order cost of three pounds'.[15] Although these early photographs are untraced, a newspaper account of June 1897 indicates that 'Her Majesty was originally white', apparently in imitation of Boehm's marble.[16] As well as the crown, the sceptre was very likely gilt. The sash – evident in outdoor photographs of the carving dating from 1900 – was probably first painted at that time, but the blue eyes and red lips seen in mid-twentieth-century colour photographs were later additions (see Figure 2.5).

The *New Zealand Times*, in a widely syndicated article, wrote: 'The features are admirably carved, and the likeness is unmistakable. Anyone who has seen her Majesty cannot but at once perceive the admirable portrait the artist has achieved.' Her small crown, sceptre, collar, and insignias were 'all well carved. It is possible, however, that the artist found some difficulty with his wood, and having succeeded so admirably with the face, both full and in profile, did not care to run the risk of spoiling his work by cutting the hands smaller.' The account nonetheless concluded that 'there is a happy air of dignity in the countenance, together with that peculiar look of matronly love which distinguishes Her Majesty'.[17] It is difficult for viewers today to share the original critic's obvious enthusiasm. Subsequent accretions of paint, particularly the latest application of household white, do not flatter the carving; future restoration may better confirm this description (see Figure 2.7).

A full eight years elapsed before the carving was delivered to Ohinemutu. For most of this period (1875–83), Victoria inhabited the General Assembly Library in Wellington, which functioned as a

2.4 *Queen Victoria*, Windsor Castle, 1869–72. Joseph Edgar Boehm. Postcard: F. Frith & Co., Reigate, 75189.

museum-like repository for such (future) curios as a scarf knitted by the elderly Queen for a New Zealand trooper in the Second Boer War, a collection of captured war flags, and the Bishop Monrad Collection of Old Master prints.[18] The loan of the carving, still the property of Native Affairs, to the 1881 Wellington Industrial Exhibition probably prompted Ngāti Whakaue to renew their request. A letter to John Bryce, Minister of Native Affairs, from Petera Te Pukutua and Whitiera Te Waiatua, reminded him in January 1883 of 'the promise respecting which was conveyed to us by the Government in Sir Donald MacLean's time'.[19] Bryce immediately assented; 'the present to the Arawa tribe' would be placed 'in their carved house at Ohinemutu'.[20] A 'very fine' pedestal was commissioned, and despatch arranged. However, when the carving was being placed into position within Tamatekapua in April 1883, 'a cart arrived with an escort of police, who took possession of the illustrious figure and carried it off to the lock up'. The seizure was probably intended to forestall exposure prior to an appropriate ceremonial unveiling, though it caused 'considerable amusement and consternation' in the process.[21]

'Monsters in the district'

The sculpture endured almost a year in solitary confinement before its unveiling in March 1884. The reasons for this delay remain conjectural, but possible explanations include bureaucratic inertia, and a lack of further reminders from Ngāti Whakaue. There may also have been an unspoken apprehension that Ohinemutu was still too 'primitive' a locale for such a carving, with its 'old fighting pa stockades' still standing in the early 1870s, a single store opening in 1873, and no regular village school until 1878.[22] In the same issue of the *Bay of Plenty Times* (April 1883) that reported the projected unveiling, a correspondent held forth on the 'heaps of stable manure' on the side of the settlement's main road, which filled up the water tables and choked the culverts.[23] With Tamatekapua and the remarkable Houtaiki flagstaff (1878) – for several years the Queen's immediate neighbour[24] – and its ubiquitous steaming geothermal vents, Ohinemutu must have afforded a memorable juxtaposition of splendour and squalor.

Newspaper accounts of the unveiling in March 1884 by the Governor, Sir William Jervois, provide a corrective to the supposed harmonious relationship between European settlers and Te Arawa. It is extremely rare to encounter political dissent in the often platitudinous speeches that formed part of such ceremonies, but this occasion was exceptional. The 'leading chiefs' proclaimed their people to be 'the most loyal natives in the Colony', and in turn they 'expected to be protected by the Government'.[25] At the ceremony Wiremu Maihi Te Rangikaheke, of the Ngāti Rangiwewihi iwi of Te Arawa, who had been a friend of and scholarly collaborator with the Governor and more recently Premier Sir George Grey, held forth. He told the assembled throng of some three or four hundred people that 'there are two monsters in the district which are devouring them, and asked the Governor to have them driven away. These monsters are the private land companies and the Native Land Purchase Department.'[26] Henare Pukuatua offered a similar message: 'We have no fault to find with the Governors of the colony, but with your Minister we have many complaints regarding our lands.'[27] Here they were to be repeatedly disappointed; indeed, historian Richard Hill asserts that Te Arawa 'suffered at the hands of the Crown', not-withstanding 'its "loyalist" reputation'.[28] This is the central thesis of Vincent O'Malley and David Armstrong's exhaustive *The Beating Heart: A Political and Socio-Economic History of Te Arawa*.

The complex question of the Native Land Court cannot be addressed in detail here. It has long been regarded as a cause of 'serious damage to Maori economic and social well-being' in the late nineteenth century. Recently, however, Paul Monin has suggested a subtler, revisionist picture whereby the changing economy and individualistic attitudes to property 'contributed to the Maori wish to engage with the new land system'. He argues that there was an element of 'agency' involved: 'Maori chose to accommodate and negotiate with colonisation as well as to resist it.'[29] This was precisely the approach of Te Rangikaheke as a Native Land Court assessor, witness, and claimant between 1867 and 1889. Yet his outspoken disaffection at the unveiling testifies to a depth of feeling and the sense of a sorely tried loyalism. In his diplomatic reply, Jervois felt cheered by 'the expressions of goodwill towards himself and the Queen'. He had come to Ohinemutu 'for the purpose of performing a very gratifying duty – namely to unveil the bust of the Queen and present it to the Ngātiwhakaue tribe … New Zealand is the brightest gem which the British Empire possesses'. Jervois envisaged a railway being constructed to serve the area and felt confident that when this was done, 'and the leases of the township satisfactorily settled, the natives would reap incalculable benefits from them'.[30] Such aspirations reflected a widespread colonial belief that 'Maori would be able to engage more successfully in the commercial economy … playing an active part in the development of the colony to their benefit'.[31]

That was a rosy vision of the future. Although in earlier times they had been reluctant signatories to the Treaty of Waitangi, by the late 1850s Te Arawa leaders ardently believed in its ideals. In 1857, not long before the recurrence of war, Temuera Te Amohau withheld his people's support from the pan-tribal (and, to most European colonists, disloyal) King Movement, declaring: 'One of our chiefs, Timoti, was the only man of the Arawa people who signed the Treaty of Waitangi, but we shall not depart from the pledge he then gave. We will not join the king tribes. My king is Queen Victoria.' ('Taku kingi ko Kuini Wikitoria.')[32] In the face of war and post-war adversity, Te Arawa had staunchly maintained their loyalty. At the same time, they revealed sophistication in distinguishing between Queen Victoria as the benign personification of the Crown (evident in her spotless white carving) and the perceived shortcomings of Crown agency in the form of successive colonial governments. Further Arawa disaffection that formed the background to the unveiling came from the introduction of trout to local lakes, which decimated customary food supplies. The advent of European tourism had moreover been a mixed blessing, bringing 'drunkenness and excesses of all kinds' to the neighbourhood.[33] Although a famous early tourist, Anthony Trollope, was probably blameless in these respects on his visit in 1872, he relished bathing in the nude back-to-back with Te Arawa belles in an Ohinemutu hot pool, safely outside his wife's purview and not yet within Queen Victoria's.[34]

The installation of the carving inside Tamatekapua caused immediate concern amongst puritanical Europeans, with the *Bay of Plenty Times* referring to 'the bust of Her Most Gracious Majesty ... which is to adorn Tamati Kapua [*sic*] being placed among the obscene Maori carvings'.[35] The perceived obscenity or hideousness of traditional Māori woodcarving as creations of the heathen and 'ignoble savage' has a long literature.[36] P. W. Hutton, a bookseller and photographer visiting from Timaru, noted how 'The Maoris treat this bust with great respect, but ... [he] was sorry to see that it was surrounded by carved figures which much disgusted him.'[37] Somewhat subtler was the response of W. H. Lyon in his 1873 'Holiday Notes' on Tamatekapua: 'the carvings of the present day are a little less offensive than those of past years, but are quite as ugly and grotesque'.[38] The visiting historian and biographer J. A. Froude in turn observed the 'hideous carved monsters' in the wharenui, while noting 'the veiled statuette [*sic*] of the Queen, which was uncovered on serious occasions'. Deference to puritanical sensibilities seems likely here, and Froude – like Hutton – recognised that 'the poor Maori had meant well'.[39] Shortly after Froude's visit, the 1885 Christmas dinner hosted by the Ngāti Whakaue Native Committee found Victoria 'beautifully adorned with bouquets of flowers, and Maori-like a "Tiki" pendant was suspended around Her Majesty's neck'. The hosts expressed 'their loyalty to our beloved Queen Victoria' and fondly hoped that 'Her Majesty would know of their proceedings that day'.[40]

In the final analysis, any concerns over the offence created by the Queen's proximity to the traditional carvings were probably less a source of concern for Ngāti Whakaue than questions of protocol. Her presence as a female within Tamatekapua had evidently offended Te Kooti, Te Arawa's erstwhile foe and quarry in the final years of the New Zealand Wars, who visited Ohinemutu on several occasions in his later years. Highly relevant in this context was Te Kooti's leadership of the Ringatu Church, whose services were commonly held at different wharenui, Tamatekapua included. Ngāti Tarawhai master carver Tene Waitere, maker of the canopy for the Queen's carving, was himself an adherent of that faith.[41]

Hybridising Victoria: a pedestal and a canopy

The relocation of the sculpture to an outdoor setting on Papa-i-Ouru, where it would remain between 1900 and 1995, was prompted by several considerations, most obviously the renovation and enlargement of Tamatekapua, which was completed in 1905. Another important factor was the celebration of the Queen's Diamond Jubilee in 1897, and the attendant epidemic of world-wide 'statuemania' exerting a roll-on effect.[42] In a letter to James Carroll, Native Affairs minister, Kokiri Te Wharepurangi alluded to 'the carved pedestal for the Queen's Statue for the Diamond Jubilee'.[43] The four metropolitan memorials, mentioned above, all dated from the years immediately following the Jubilee. Civic beautification as well as imperial celebration was equally the order of the day for Ohinemutu. The carving's easy portability when located in Tamatekapua had provoked angry exchanges over its proposed loan to the Rotorua Town Board for Jubilee celebrations. This culminated in physical conflict between two locals: Te Arawa tourist guide Alfred Warbrick and Te Miri o Raukawa. The *Hot Lakes Chronicle* memorably headlined the episode 'A Diamond Jubilee Bust Up' and reported how an angry Warbrick insisted that 'he would not allow the bust to be taken out of the house'.[44]

At the same time, members of the Town Board expressed concerns about 'the disreputable condition in which the bust ... had fallen'. Roger Dansey, the Postmaster, believed that 'next to the erection of a brand new statue the restoration of the present one, which presents the lineaments of our revered Queen in all her girlhood's [sic] beauty would be an appropriate recognition of her long and beneficent reign ... the Queen's countenance was getting very black indeed'. This caused Stephen Brent, Rotorua's principal hotelier, to quip 'as to her getting black – why, the natives probably preferred a queen of their own colour'. The medical officer Alfred Ginders was highly amused but the comment evidently shocked the acting clerk and local architect, Benjamin Corlett, not because of what a later age would consider racist but because Corlett was reportedly 'loyal right from skull to boots'.[45]

The new location stood some 200 metres north of Tamatekapua, close to the Houtaiki flagstaff and the original St Faith's Church. Like the wharenui, Queen Victoria was given a new lease of life. In March 1900, the *Bay of Plenty Times* reported that a solid tōtara pedestal for the carving, measuring 20 inches square and 12 feet high, was in the process of erection, as depicted in Figure 2.5.[46] Its unveiling in early May received little press attention, although the pedestal was described as 'cleverly carved in approved Native style by a Maori wood worker'.[47] Hemi Te Tupara and Petera Pukuata promptly petitioned Carroll, requesting £100 for red, white, and blue paint 'about a hundred pounds weight, wherewith to paint her Majesty the Queen's statue, also the fence surrounding it'.[48] Their request was given a more practical footing by Captain A. C. Turner, District Road Surveyor, who explained: 'What it really requires is an ornate fence around it, concreted footing at base of pedestal, and a nice Canopy to protect it from the rain and sun. All will require painting as well as the bust ... The bust is already getting disfigured by exposure'[49] (see Figure 2.6). Tene Waitere was indeed about to provide 'a nice Canopy', while an 'ornate fence' is evident in photographs dating from the Duke and Duchess of York and Cornwall's visit in June 1901. The addition of the canopy involved a regrettable truncation of the recently erected pedestal.

The seemingly parochial matter of paint colour is of considerable interest here. The colour of the pedestal is difficult to determine from early monochrome photographs, but it had originally been painted black. Ngāti Whakaue met Nina, Dowager Countess of Seafield, when she visited Rotorua and Tauranga in 1900. She recounted to them 'many little incidents about Queen Victoria, in order to foster their loyalty'. In turn, they entrusted Lady Seafield 'with loving and loyal messages, which she, in virtue of rank, was able to send direct to the Queen herself'. This included news of the portrait and pedestal, with Ngāti Whakaue saying of the latter: 'We paint it black, for the great Queen, our white mother, constantly mourns and weeps for her braves who have fallen in South Africa, and we, too, mourn for our brothers now lying under the sod for the cause of freedom and for our great nation.' In the Queen's eventual reply, penned by a lady-in-waiting, the near blind and infirm monarch expressed her 'gracious thanks for the devoted loyalty shown by the Maoris. The Queen is much touched by their feeling for her in the very many sorrows and anxieties which this sad year has brought ... Her Majesty says: "Tell my dear Maori subjects how I love them. I am proud of their sympathy and devotion."'[50]

[39]

2.5 Queen Victoria, Ohinemutu, 1985. Photograph by John Dixon.

The Queen's message, dated 1 December 1900, reached Lady Seafield on 18 January 1901; four days later the Queen was dead. The episode substantiates scholarly assertions that 'Victoria seemed to validate imperialism and render it harmless, even comforting',[51] and that 'the insinuating nature of Victoria's presence ... helped to symbolize her as the Mother of her People and the Great White Empress'.[52] Yet a more generous 'post-postcolonial' interpretation of Victoria would recognise, as does the *Oxford Dictionary of National Biography* entry about her, that to the bitter end she was 'honest and humble in the face of virtue in others'.[53] Whatever the interpretation, she was indubitably 'central to the ideological and cultural signifying systems of her age',[54] which in this case the agency of Ngāti Whakaue crucially redefined through the recontextualisation and beautification of her carving.

The new pedestal and canopy studiously avoided anything that might be considered obscene or even disrespectful to the Queen, but atop each side of the pedestal in red ochre and white featured four bold koruru (see Figure 2.3). Although they are briefly mentioned in Roger Neich's magisterial monograph *Carved Histories: Rotorua Ngāti Tarawhai Woodcarving*, they have been little studied and there is a comparable dearth of published information on their creator, Patu Whitiki of Horohoro.[55] Their teeth, conveying fearsomeness, are considerably more prominent than in equivalent poupou figures by such carvers as Wero Taroi and Tene Waitere. Tene Waitere's low relief carvings of the maihi are deliberately discreet and dignified, yet they function as more than architectural embellishment. They comprise a repeated series of profiled manaia, mythological creatures who probably serve here as figures of protection and guardians against evil, subtler reinforcements of the koruru. The ubiquitous motif of three fingers has multiple meanings, including the trinity of birth, life, and death. The maihi are pitched at a more acute angle than is normally found in equivalent wharenui or pātaka.

As Nicholas Thomas has observed, Māori – and Te Arawa not least – from the outset of contact 'embraced signs of European power and sovereignty, and made them serve their own ends'.[56] Even if they appeared at a low ebb in terms of population, prosperity, and political power in 1900, Māori constituted a dynamic society and had demonstrated themselves readily and selectively capable of borrowing material culture and ideas that had a compatibility and adaptability to their own, ever-changing world. Within this process, identity and mana were preserved and proudly expressed, not least in the Ohinemutu Victoria. In her turn-of-the-century incarnation, she represented a singular, Indigenous appropriation and redefinition of that supposedly most imperialist of cultural forms – the public sculpture of a queen and empress. The sculpture – and with it Queen Victoria herself – underwent an animistic transformation into 'Kuini Wikitoria', Ngāti Whakaue's beloved and revered 'white mother', protected and supported by her kokowai infrastructure. Hence this author's statement in a public lecture delivered at Ohinemutu that 'while I may sometimes refer to the sculpture as "it", really it is almost disrespectful not to say "she"', a point warmly endorsed by the Ngāti Whakaue present.[57]

Royalty and waiata

The Duke and Duchess of York and Cornwall, later King George V and Queen Mary, visited the Ohinemutu Queen Victoria sculpture in June 1901 as a part of their official visit to New Zealand. The visit provided an occasion both to deliver mournful waiata dedicated to the recently deceased Queen, the Duke's grandmother, and to joyfully welcome the royal party. One such waiata rhetorically asked:

> O Prince, where is the Great Mother?
> She is fallen, she is dead
> There by the far-off slopes of London.
> Fling Death heading to the lowest regions.
> And there let it lie!
> Welcome, O Prince
> Welcome![58]

At Rotorua, Carroll – who was of Ngāti Kahugnunu kūpapa background and an eloquent orator – pronounced in his address:

> This is a great day – a day that will live in our memory of our race while God permits them existence. Yet it is a day of mourning. We mourn the Great Queen to whom our fathers ceded by treaty the sovereignty over these Isles; who was the guardian of our rights and liberties from that time until she slept with her fathers. We, the humblest of her children, alien in blood, yet kin by law and allegiance, mourn the loss of a mother who sought the good of high and low alike ... Pass, O Mother, to rest with the mighty dead who went before thee.[59]

At the foot of the memorial were laid out gifts for the visitors, 'several very fine flax mantles and mats, together with a greenstone mere'. Pirimi Mataiawhea explained how this was 'in accordance with the custom of laying down presents in memory of those who are departed. They are tokens of our love, therefore we beg Your Royal Highnesses not to disregard these small presents, unworthy though they may be, but to take them with you. This is all. We here are the Arawa.'[60]

Subsequent royal visits to Rotorua and Ohinemutu affirmed such relationships, even if accounts of them dwell less specifically on the Queen Victoria memorial and more on the Treaty of Waitangi. In April

1920 the Prince of Wales (later King Edward VIII), like his parents, processed from Tamatekapua to the memorial, where he 'stood for a few moments contemplating it, the assemblage maintaining a reverent silence'.[61] In January 1954, Te Arawa reminded Queen Elizabeth II of the historical links between the confederation and her forebears: 'O Royal daughter of an illustrious line, we are proud that you should perpetuate the traditions of your race and house ... walk therefore among the Maori people, sure of their hearts, fostering therein the love they bore the great Queen Victoria and those who have followed her.'[62] The same visit prompted an illustrated article 'Papa I Ouru Marae Ohinemutu', by W. J. Phillipps in *Te Ao Hou: The New World*, a magazine published by the Department of Māori Affairs. While Phillipps's didactic intentions were laudable, he compounded previous historical inaccuracies by claiming that the Duke of Edinburgh 'brought with him, as gifts, a marble bust of the Queen'.[63] The memorial received sporadic mention in Rotorua newspapers through the century, the most interesting of which was Tene Waitere's obituary in 1931, which noted 'The striking shelter for the statue of Queen Victoria at Ohinemutu [as] one well-known carving carried out by the old Arawa craftsman'.[64] In his book *The Founding Year in Rotorua: A History of Events to 1900*, D. M. Stafford belatedly corrected assumptions that the sculpture of Victoria was a present from the Duke of Edinburgh in return for his hospitality from Te Arawa, and provided a succinct and sensible summary of the place of the sculpture, and indeed Queen Victoria, in local history.[65]

Trampling on sanctity?

The same year as Stafford's landmark publication, the memorial received renewed attention when, after heated discussions among the Papa-i-Ouru trustees and other Ngāti Whakaue, it was moved 15 metres south west across the marae to make way for the Whakaturia wharekai.[66] An evocative photograph by Mark Adams, taken just weeks after the relocation and subsequently published in his co-authored *Rauru: Tene Waitere, Maori Carving, Colonial History*, shows the tired but essentially intact memorial with a trailer, camper van, and pile of rubble beside it, as shown in Figure 2.3.[67] The original moko patterns of the koruru had been effaced, while the pāua inlay punctuating Patu Whitiki's column had also long since gone. The eyes and teeth remained white. However, within a few years the pedestal was coated entirely in monochromatic red ochre; and the colour of Queen Victoria, a defining feature given that her crown had been gilt almost immediately after her arrival in New Zealand, was effaced by an application of uniform white. This remains its current appearance. The coincidence of this

'once-over' with the cultural awakening of traditional Māori art, signalled at the exhibition 'Te Maori' at the Metropolitan Museum of Art
New York (1984) and its triumphant homecoming, seems deeply ironic.
That more protest did not arise is probably attributable to two factors:
a universal one – Robert Musil's famous dictum that a monument is
paradoxically immune from public attention and thus 'invisible' – and
a more local one, that of the 'Maori Renaissance' which 'sat within
the international context of decolonisation and radical action movements'.[68] Carroll's reverence for the 'Great Queen to whom our fathers
ceded by treaty the sovereignty over these Isles' did not sit comfortably
with late twentieth-century Māori autonomist aspirations. The very
term kūpapa, applied in 1892 to 'the friendly Maoris in the wars of the
sixties', who were also known as 'loyalist' and 'Queenite', was redefined by the publication *Te Iwi o Aotearoa* (1990) as denoting 'Maori
traitors or collaborators'.[69]

The 'kidnapping' of Queen Victoria in September 1995 and the
damage that she sustained in the process with the physical (and surely
symbolic) loss of her crown, should be understood in this context. The
episode was comparable to the respective Māori 'activist' decapitation

2.6 Queen Victoria Bust – Houtaiki flag pole, Ohinemutu, ca. 1900.
Photograph by Edward W. Payton (1859–1944).

of Sir George Grey's statue in Albert Park, Auckland (1987), and that of his fellow premier, John Ballance, in Moutoa Gardens, Whanganui (1995), and was based on similar interpretations of New Zealand colonial history. Both figures were constituted as colonial oppressors of Māori, and in Grey's case, as a racist.[70] While James Belich quoted Grey's exasperated comment on Māori as 'a semi-barbarous people puffed up with the pride of imagined equality' and unwittingly influenced the attack on his statue,[71] Ballance's role as Native Affairs Minister (1884–87, 1891) has been claimed as a remarkably benign and non-confrontational one for the period.[72] However, historical rationalism carried little sway in such a politically impassioned climate. The response of Don Stafford to Victoria's removal was scathing: 'I assume it was taken by someone who dislikes any symbol of the European but they are obviously ignorant of the background of the bust ... It was not a symbol put up by the pakeha. It is an historic item in its own right. It represents the long association of the people of Te Arawa with the Crown.'[73] Figure 2.7 illustrates the somewhat faded glory of the bust itself.

2.7 Queen Victoria, Ohinemutu, 2011, Mark Stocker.

The carving disappeared on 7 September 1995; local police initially suspected that a bomb scare made to the Rotorua *Daily Post* and Radio 97FM was 'a blind to tie up officers' at the time of its removal. One of the first to deplore the action was the chair of the Papa-i-Ouru trustees, Wihapi Te Amohau Winiata, whose language was relatively temperate: 'grim – not in accord with protocol'. Bishop Kingi, a Ngāti Whakaue elder, summarised widespread local feelings: 'because the bust's shelter and plinth remained, he believed the monument was still at the village [Ohinemutu] in spirit. "But I still wish them [those responsible] to hell."'[74] Particular distress was caused by what another elder, Don Bennett, regarded as an act that trod on 'the mana of the Ngāti Whakaue people. That marae is the paramount marae of Te Arawa. It is looked on as sacrosanct and they have trampled on that sanctity.'[75] A local kuia, Witarina Harris, was memorably pictured keeping vigil beside the empty memorial, describing her presence as a 'gesture of mourning'.[76] The return of the carving, deposited on the doorstep of the Te Ao Marama hall on Papa-i-Ouru, came in May 1996, 'as mysteriously as it disappeared eight months ago'.[77] This rapidly followed an eloquent appeal from Winiata, who invoked his mana as a priest, woodcarver, and rangatira. Winiata stopped short of pronouncing a traditional mākutu, or curse, which would have been incompatible with his devout Anglicanism, but warned those responsible of the 'karmic' consequences with clearly decisive effect.[78]

Restoration and closure?

Although professional restoration and reinstatement was initially proposed and repairs were undertaken to Victoria's damaged arm, the carving has subsequently remained in safekeeping in the Whakaturia wharekai due to security concerns. Periodically, however, as on the occasion of the visit by Prince Andrew, Duke of York in March 2007, it has been removed and temporarily reaffixed to the pedestal.[79] While this is fully consistent with the Ngāti Whakaue and Te Arawa love of ceremony eloquently manifested on previous royal visits – particularly between 1901 and 1954 – rather more profound is the visible reaffirmation of the marae-framed relationship under which the Treaty of Waitangi is sealed by this, the historic taonga of Queen Victoria's effigy.

What then of the sculpture's future? The Whakaue kairaupi have expressed a not altogether unsurprising aesthetic and political dissatisfaction with the 'empty plinth'.[80] In this regard, Shaloh Mitchell has recently suggested that 'ideally he wanted to get a bronze cast made of the bust', with the original being loaned to the Rotorua Museum of Art and History.[81] Agency in any new chapter necessarily lies with its original recipients, Ngāti Whakaue of Ohinemutu, acting on behalf of Te Arawa, as the past and future makers of that particular corner of 'New Zealand's empire'. Whatever the outcome, the taonga that Ngāti Whakaue possess in the Queen Victoria, what they have in the past made of the sculpture and for the sculpture, both materially and spiritually, and what they may make of it in the future, constitutes a unique testament to Indigenous pride and particularity, and one that powerfully resonates in the context of the imperial revisionism central to this volume.

Acknowledgements

I am very grateful to Phil Andrews, Tony Ballantyne, Roger Fyfe, Maya Jasanoff, Shaloh Mitchell, Heather Morrison, Su Potter, Ike Reti, Jane Strachan, and Paul Tapsell for their invaluable assistance with my research for this essay. Tena rawa atu koutou!

Notes

1 Jennifer Powell, 'The dissemination of commemorative statues of Queen Victoria', in Penelope Curtis and Keith Wilson (eds), *Modern British Sculpture* (London: Royal Academy of Arts, 2011), pp. 282–8.

2 Mark Stocker, 'Queen Victoria memorials in New Zealand: A centenary appraisal', *Journal of New Zealand Art History*, 22 (2001), 7–28.

3 'The Hot Lakes in the North Island', *Nelson Examiner* (11 November 1871), p. 6.

4 Robert J. C. Young, *Colonial Desire: Hybridity in Theory, Culture and Race* (London and New York: Routledge, 1995), p. 162.

5 Maya Jasanoff added that these 'deserve considerably more research' in her unpublished plenary address, 'The British Monarch as Global Emperor', Historic Royal Palaces, 'The Making of a Monarchy for the Modern World', Kensington Palace, London, 7 June 2012.

6 R. A. Loughnan, *Royalty in New Zealand: The Visit of Their Royal Highnesses the Duke and Duchess of Cornwall and York to New Zealand* (Wellington: Government Printer, 1902), pp. 368–71.

7 'Present of a wooden bust of Her Majesty to the Natives', *Taranaki Herald* (7 July 1875), p. 2. The last shot of the New Zealand Wars would only be fired in February 1872. See James Belich, *The New Zealand Wars and the Victorian Interpretation of Racial Conflict*, 2nd edn. (Auckland: Penguin, 1998), p. 286.

8 Rotorua District Library/Te Whare o te Maatauranga (hereafter RDL), the Don Stafford Collection, Donald McLean to Daniel Pollen, Colonial Secretary, 'Carved Houses', 2 February 1874.

9 RDL, Paul Amohau Tamati to Donald McLean, 4 December 1873. Tamati wrote on behalf of 'all Whakaue'. See also D. M. Stafford, *The Founding Years in Rotorua: A History of Events to 1900* (Rotorua: Ray Richards and Rotorua District Council, 1986), pp. 200–2.

10 RDL, Donald McLean to Daniel Pollen, 6 February 1874.

11 'Present of a wooden bust of Her Majesty to the Natives', *Taranaki Herald* (7 July 1875), p. 2.

12 See especially Roger Neich, *Carved Histories: Rotorua Ngāti Tarawhai Woodcarving* (Auckland: Auckland University Press, 2001).

13 RDL, Featherston to McLean, 18 September 1874.

14   'The International Exhibition', *Art Journal*, New Series 11 (1874), 249. For Boehm, see Mark Stocker, *Royalist and Realist: The Life and Work of Sir Joseph Edgar Boehm* (New York: Garland, 1988).
15   RDL, Thomas Lewis to Henry Clarke, 6 May 1875.
16   RDL, Unidentified newspaper clipping, 'Events 1897' (5 June 1897), unpaginated.
17   'Present of a wooden bust of Her Majesty to the Natives', *Taranaki Herald* (7 July 1875), p. 2.
18   John E. Martin, *Parliament's Library: 150 Years* (Wellington: Steele Roberts, 2008), p. 92.
19   RDL, Petera Te Pukuatua and R. Whitera Te Taiatua to the Minister of Native Affairs, 'Carved Houses', 8 January 1883.
20   RDL, Thomas Lewis, memorandum, 18 January 1883; John Bryce, memorandum, 19 January 1883.
21   'Resurrexi', *Thames Star* (24 April 1883), p. 2.
22   Stafford, *Founding Years*, pp. 98–100.
23   'The Bay of Plenty Times and Thames Valley Warden', *Bay of Plenty Times* (26 April 1883), p. 2.
24   Stafford, *Founding Years*, pp. 115, 142–3.
25   'Arrival of the Governor at Ohinemutu', *Bay of Plenty Times* (27 March 1884), p. 2.
26   'Arrival of the Governor at Ohinemutu', *Bay of Plenty Times* (27 March 1884), p. 2. For Te Rangikaheke, see Jennifer Curnow, 'Te Rangikaheke, Wiremu Maihi', in *Dictionary of New Zealand Biography*, Te Ara Encyclopedia of New Zealand, www.teara.govt.nz/en/biographies/1t66/te-rangikaheke-wiremu-maihi, accessed 30 January 2013.
27   'The Governor at Ohinemutu', *Auckland Star* (25 March 1884), p. 3.
28   Richard Hill, in Vincent O'Malley and David Armstrong, *The Beating Heart: A Political and Socio-Economic History of Te Arawa* (Wellington: Huia, 2008), unpaginated.
29   Paul Monin, 'Maori economies and colonial capitalism', in Giselle Byrnes (ed.), *The New Oxford History of New Zealand* (Melbourne: Oxford University Press, 2009), p. 139.
30   'Arrival of the Governor at Ohinemutu', *Bay of Plenty Times* (27 March 1884), p. 2.
31   Monin, 'Maori economies', p. 138.
32   James Cowan, *The New Zealand Wars: A History of the Maori Campaigns and the Pioneering Period: Volume I (1845–64)* (Wellington: R. E. Owen, 1955), p. 150.
33   Stafford, *Founding Years*, p. 243. For fishing, see O'Malley and Armstrong, *The Beating Heart*, pp. 266–9.
34   A. H. Reed (ed.), *With Anthony Trollope in New Zealand* (Wellington: A. H. & A. W. Reed, 1969), pp. 119–20.
35   *Bay of Plenty Times* (26 April 1883), p. 2.
36   Neich, *Carved Histories*, pp. 137–9.
37   'Town and country', *Timaru Herald* (12 March 1895), p. 2.
38   Neich, *Carved Histories*, p. 158.
39   J. A. Froude, *Oceana, or, England and her Colonies* (London: Longmans, Green, 1886), p. 234.
40   'Rotorua', *Bay of Plenty Times* (29 December 1885), p. 3.
41   Judith Binney, *Redemption Songs: A Life of Te Kooti Arikarangi Te Turuki* (Auckland: Auckland University Press with Bridget Williams Books, 1995), p. 325. For Te Kooti's visits to Ohinemutu, see Stafford, *Founding Years*, pp. 198–9, 415–16.
42   See for example Erika Doss, *Memorial Mania: Public Feeling in America* (Chicago: University of Chicago Press, 2010).
43   RDL, Kokiri Te Wharepurangi to James Carroll, 12 May 1900 (translation).
44   *Hot Lakes Chronicle* (24 July 1897), p. 2. For Warbrick, who was of Ngāti Rangitihi ancestry, see 'Warbrick, Alfred Patchett', in *Dictionary of New Zealand Biography*, Te Ara Encyclopedia of New Zealand, www.teara.govt.nz/en/biographies /2w7/ warbrick-alfred-patchett, accessed 29 June 2013.

45 RDL, Unidentified newspaper clipping, 'Events 1897' (5 June 1897), unpaginated. Although there is no documentation of a restoration of the carving, cleaning and painting prior to its relocation seems highly probable.
46 Untitled, *Bay of Plenty Times* (30 March 1900), p. 2.
47 'Omnium gatherum', *Otago Daily Times* (8 May 1900), p. 18.
48 RDL, Petera Pukuatua to James Carroll, 23 May 1900 (translation).
49 RDL, A. C. Turner to the Assistant Surveyor-General, 6 July 1900.
50 'A gracious message to the Maori people', *Otago Witness* (20 February 1901), p. 54.
51 John Plunkett, *Queen Victoria: First Media Monarch* (Oxford: Oxford University Press, 2003), p. 247.
52 Margaret Homans and Adrienne Munich (eds), *Remaking Queen Victoria* (Cambridge: Cambridge University Press, 1997), p. 2.
53 Colin Matthew and Kim Reynolds, 'Victoria (1819–1901), Queen of the United Kingdom and Ireland, and Empress of India', *Oxford Dictionary of National Biography* (Oxford: Oxford University Press, 2004–11), www.oxforddnb.com/view/printable/36642, accessed 20 May 2011.
54 Homans and Munich (eds), *Remaking Queen Victoria*, p. 2.
55 Neich, *Carved Histories*, pp. 69, 373.
56 Nicholas Thomas, Mark Adams, James Schuster, and Lyonel Grant, *Rauru: Tene Waitere, Maori Carving, Colonial History* (Dunedin: University of Otago Press, 2009), p. 25.
57 Mark Stocker, 'Kuini Wikitoria: The Adventures of the Queen Victoria Carving in Rotorua', lecture, Whakaturia wharekai, Ohinemutu, 16 November 2013.
58 Loughnan, *Royalty in New Zealand*, p. 375 (translation).
59 Loughnan, *Royalty in New Zealand*, p. 80.
60 Loughnan, *Royalty in New Zealand*, p. 87.
61 'At Rotorua: Enthusiasm of Maoris. Mat and Huia Feathers Worn by Royal Visitor', *Colonist* (29 April 1920), p. 5. Unfortunately the Prince of Wales did not mention the carving to his then lover, Freda Dudley Ward, although he complained to her of 'long and tedious Maori ceremonies at the native villages and had to submit to being made to look the most hopeless B F dolled up in mats and other things while inane Maoris danced & made weird noises at me!' See O'Malley and Armstrong, *Beating Heart*, pp. 250–2.
62 O'Malley and Armstrong, *Beating Heart*, p. 314. See also D. M. Stafford, *The New Century in Rotorua: A History of Events from 1900* (Rotorua: Ray Richards and Rotorua District Council, 1988), pp. 276–7.
63 W. J. Phillipps, 'Papa i Ouru Marae Ohinemutu', *Te Ao Hou: The New World*, 7 (1954), 39.
64 'Famous carver goes to rest', *Rotorua Morning Post* (29 August 1931), p. 7.
65 Stafford, *The Founding Years*, pp. 200–2. See also Stafford, *New Century*, p. 20.
66 'He Panui', *Daily Post* (27 November 1985); Ike Reti, interview with Mark Stocker, Ohinemutu, 5 May 2012.
67 Mark Adams, 'Te Arawa', in Thomas, Adams et al., *Rauru*, p. 59.
68 Richard S. Hill, 'Maori and state policy', in Byrnes (ed.), *New Oxford History of New Zealand*, p. 533.
69 Monty Soutar, 'Kupapa: A shift in meaning', *He Pukenga Korero*, 6:2 (2001), 36.
70 See especially Mark Stocker, 'Te kai-hautu o te waka'/ Director of the canoe: The statue of Sir George Grey in Auckland', in Julie F. Codell (ed.), *Transculturation in British Art, 1770–1930* (Farnham: Ashgate, 2012), pp. 125–42.
71 James Belich, *New Zealand Wars*, p. 120. In the same paragraph, however, Belich notes that Grey 'deplored vulgar prejudice directed against' Māori.
72 Tim McIvor, 'Ballance, John', in *Dictionary of New Zealand Biography*, *Te Ara Encyclopedia of New Zealand*, www.teara.govt.nz/en/biographies/2b5/ballance-john, accessed 29 June 2013.
73 'Missing bust has colourful history', *Daily Post* (9 September 1995), p. 3.
74 'Police suspect hoax-theft link', *Daily Post* (8 September 1995), p. 1.
75 'Missing bust has colourful history', *Daily Post* (9 September 1995), p. 3.

76 'Police suspect hoax-theft link', *Daily Post* (8 September 1995), p. 1.
77 'Historic bust returned', *Daily Post* (24 May 1996), p. 1.
78 Reti, interview, 5 May 2012. For Winiata, see Damian Skinner, *The Carver and the Artist: Maori Art in the Twentieth Century* (Auckland: Auckland University Press, 2008), pp. 180–1.
79 I owe this information to Ike Reti and Shaloh Mitchell. For Prince Andrew's visit, which commemorated Second World War hero Lance-Sergeant Haane Manahi, see O'Malley and Armstrong, *Beating Heart*, pp. 330–1.
80 Ike Reti and Shaloh Mitchell, interview with Mark Stocker, Ohinemutu, 5 May 2012.
81 Matthew Martin, 'Shedding light on carved bust', *Rotorua Daily Post* (15 November 2013), p. 6. This newspaper was known as the *Daily Post* until March 2013.

CHAPTER THREE

'Two branches of the brown Polynesians': ethnographic fieldwork, colonial governmentality, and the 'dance of agency'

Conal McCarthy

In the pre-dawn dark, a ship anchored off the shore of a Pacific island. Passengers could see the craggy outline of the tropical island and heard the surf pounding on the beach. One of them was particularly excited at hearing the sound of boats approaching, crewed by local men, who drew alongside to unload the ship. Their language was familiar, the same speech as his own with a few dialectical differences. He went ashore in a boat, looking closely at the crew, noticing that only straw hats betrayed the 'tropical variety of an ancient race'. For they were, he noted with pride, 'distant kinsmen of my own'. This landfall was an event of huge emotional significance for him. 'We landed in the dark,' he wrote, 'and my foot trod the ancient land that my ancestors had left in 1350 AD.'[1]

The man was Peter Buck, a Māori politician, decorated soldier and doctor who later became a famous anthropologist of the Pacific. After this trip to Rarotonga in the Cook Islands in 1910, Buck (Te Rangihīroa) wrote about the historical and political links between the Māori of Aotearoa and the islands that were now part of New Zealand's Pacific empire. When Premier Richard Seddon abandoned the Munroe doctrine and annexed the Cooks and other Islands in 1900, Buck noted, the scheme had the effect of forming a link 'between two branches of the brown Polynesians'. The Cook Islands were 'more nearly allied by dialect, history and pedigree' to the Māori of New Zealand. 'Imagine therefore the feelings of the latter branch on visiting the Cook Group with all its historic associations,' he wrote, 'It was a pilgrimage to a holy land.'[2]

After this first 'homecoming' to Rarotonga, Buck returned to live and work in the Pacific, his research providing a template for colonial administration. In this chapter, I use analytical tools derived from historical sociology and STS (Science and Technology Studies) to trace the links between Māori and Pacific Islanders, and scientific activities such as fieldwork anthropology on the one hand, and colonial governmentality on the other. This examination focuses on Native policy within New Zealand and New Zealand policy in the Cook Islands and Sāmoa between 1914 and 1939.[3] Rather than recounting a tale of Pākehā administration of Island populations and Indigenous resistance or, in other words, of coloniser and colonised, self and other, of a kind which has become familiar in the field of postcolonial studies,[4] I want to take a different approach and explore the collaboration and critical engagement of Māori politician Āpirana Ngata with government machinery in Wellington and his Pacific 'subjects' in the Islands.

This ambiguous relationship is revealed in particular through the correspondence between Ngata, directly involved in administration, and Peter Buck, engaged in ethnographic research in the Pacific for the Bishop Museum in Hawai'i. I argue that while the collecting of artefacts, photographs, and other material in the field was directly related to the assembling and governing of New Zealand's empire, it simultaneously produced a platform for Native survival and development within the nation and empire. In making sense of this complex situation – especially the ways in which objects, people and institutions were intertwined in a ceaselessly open-ended emergence – I deploy Andrew Pickering's notion of the 'dance of agency' which is performed through what he calls the 'mangle of practice'.[5] Individuals and things are not simply constituted from above, through structures, but from below, through social practices; they actively create, mediate, and contest the world around them in a constant back-and-forth dialectical negotiation, resistance, and accommodation. Fresh theories allow a more fine-grained analysis of the spaces in between government and the Māori social, the assemblage of ethnology/government/Native policy which I have called 'anthropological governance'.[6] In doing so this chapter revises and expands the history of New Zealand's empire, like others in this volume, by breaking down neat divisions between Māori and Pākehā, Māori and Pacific Islanders, nation and Native, here and there.

Re-theorising colonial relations

Many scholars have examined colonial relations in the Pacific, and the connections with New Zealand and the world,[7] and some have looked at the interconnections between Pacific and Māori people.[8] In the international and local scholarship, the analysis of empire framed by postcolonial theory has been very influential.[9] Anthropology and museums, often seen as tools of empire, have been a key foci of this literature.[10] The phrase 'colonial governmentality' was coined by David Scott to describe the indirect rule of colonial subjects and their assimilation into Western European culture through what Foucault called the 'conduct of conduct', in other words the self-regulation of Natives by themselves.[11] Likewise, historical sociologist George Steinmetz drew on Pierre Bourdieu's work in his concept of 'ethnographic capital', seen for example through German Native policy in Sāmoa, where the re-traditionalisation of fa'a Samoa, produced through ethnographic fieldwork and artefacts collected by anthropologist-administrators like Wilhelm Solf, acted on the social to draw the local people into the colonial state (while at the same time creating some degree of mediation by local people).[12] In New Zealand, the critique of Orientalism has been applied to the European settler government which not only directly ruled the Indigenous population but facilitated their assimilation through the self-regulating field of the social, using institutions and practices that drew on the discourse of the 'old time Māori' produced by ethnology, museums, books, and other public discourses.[13] The very notion of classic pre-European Māori culture, then, was constructed through museum display and anthropology and circulated in public discourses about race, civilisation, and material progress, making possible the authorising, describing, regulating, and ruling of both Indigenous and settler populations.

However, the postcolonial analysis of history has been criticised for back-projecting the concerns of the present on to a flattened and simplified past,[14] with calls for a more rigorously historicised analysis of anthropology, ethnology, museum collecting, and their complex interactions with empire on the one hand and Indigenous peoples on the other.[15] My own work has explored the ways in which, despite the devastating impact of colonisation, Māori people as 'brown Britons'[16] actively participated in the settler state along with its cultures of collecting and display, steering government heritage campaigns to their own ends, for example the scenery preservation movement and the Antiquities legislation in the 1900s, and the revival of arts and crafts in the 1920s.[17]

A greater attention to agency is apparent in ANT (Actor Network Theory) and STS, which have opened up novel perspectives on social and material agency, offering powerful methods for 'reassembling the social' by integrating the study of human and non-human, subjects and objects, culture and economy.[18] This work moves away from the postmodern preoccupation with language and discourse towards non-representational paradigms such as objects, performance, embodiment, and affect. English physicist Andrew Pickering uses a distinctive theoretical framework fusing agency, material culture, and history. His reconceptualisation of research practice as a 'mangle', like the machine used to squeeze the water out of the washing, an open-ended, evolutionary, and performative interplay of human and non-human activity in a 'dance of agency', moves beyond language-based theories of representation. The dance of agency is emergent, post-humanist, and de-centred, and sees science (and other activities) as a *practice* which is a performative rather than a representational idiom.[19] As Pickering puts it, actors engage with the material world in 'a temporally extended back and forth dance of human and non-human agency in which activity and passivity on both sides are reciprocally intertwined'.[20]

Māori politicians and ethnological research

In the interwar years, Māori people staged a rapprochement with main-stream Pākehā society through the work of a remarkable group of intel-lectuals known as The Young Māori Party, which included Sir Māui Pōmare (Minister of Health), Peter Buck (or Te Rangihīroa) (Director of Maori Hygiene), and Āpirana Ngata (Native Minister who, even when in opposition, had a major influence on government policy).[21] All three collaborated in researching and writing about their native culture and traditions, at times through an anthropological framework targeting political goals, namely maintaining a distinct and independent Māori identity within modern New Zealand through the idea of 'cultural adaptation'.[22] Alongside health, housing, education, employment, and land development schemes, their social and economic development programmes were intimately linked to, and in part underpinned by, the collection, preservation, and revival of visual and performing arts, tribal traditions and history.

The key instrument for the control and funding of this Indigenous heritage campaign was the little-known Board of Maori Ethnological Research, which behind the scenes directed scientific activities towards Māori social and cultural goals: namely the Dominion Museum and its ethnological expeditions, and the Polynesian Society and its journal. The Board of Maori Ethnological Research was set up by Ngata in 1923 with the support of the other Māori MPs, his friend the PM Gordon Coates, and sympathetic Pākehā scholars. Ngata believed that the new Board should take control of research and publishing. Its purpose was stated as follows:

> the study and investigation of the ancient arts and crafts, language, customs, history, tradition, and antiquities of the Maori and other cognate races of the South Pacific Ocean, the acquirement and collection of records, manuscripts, drawings and Maori antiquities pertaining to any of the said races and the publication, perpetuation or preservation in any way of any matter or thing in connection therewith that the Maori

Ethnological Research Board, hereinafter referred to, may deem necessary or desirable.[23]

Ngata had in mind specifically Māori objectives for the Board, explaining 'as the fund will be derived almost entirely from Maori sources, that certain conditions may be attached on behalf of the race by its Parliamentary representatives. Maori want access to published material on tradition and history, genealogical tables and song etc'.[24] Indeed, evidence suggests the Māori agenda was paramount, with a few token Pākehā added to the Board who were expected to go along with Ngata's plans. Museum ethnologist Elsdon Best confided in his friend T. W. Downes, expressing his delight at finally having his work published and making it clear who was in charge – the Board 'is Maori out and out', he said. 'The Board does not want us Pakeha to control activities,' he added, 'but highly appreciates the work of the Polynesian Society.'[25]

Over the next decade Ngata's political and cultural programmes were woven together, one supporting the other as he worked inside the system to create space, resources, and support for economic and social development through a framework that retained cultural difference and resisted assimilation. The Board's work, through its research funding, official publications, and its community activities, sparked but also responded to a nation-wide revival of Māori interest in genealogy, tribal traditions, and visual and performing arts, as well as other aspects of customary culture. An example of the confluence of science and community work at the flax roots is described by Felix Keesing. At a hui in January 1928 at Motuiti pā in the Manawatū district, six resolutions were passed including land, finance, education, and agricultural instruction, with one mentioning ethnology in the form of the 'revived interest in the collection and annotation of Maori songs etc'. To assist this work, it recommended that the Maori Ethnological Research Board set up 'departments of ethnology and social science in universities' which would 'train workers over Maoridom and also native races in Island dependencies of the Dominion'. This 'practical laboratory' for both races would serve 'to guide and co-ordinate the constructive movements, external and internal, affecting the Maori people'.[26]

Ngata pursued this vision with great energy for a number of years. In the early 1930s a proposal arrived from Raymond Firth to establish a Chair of Social Anthropology in a new university department, attached to the Board of Maori Ethnological Research, in which the professor would lecture to students and government officials. Ngata picked up the idea, trying to lure Buck back for the role, and describing the advantages of staff and students conducting fieldwork in the Pacific in addition to academic study, for example testing out their ideas and methods among iwi. He went as far as applying to the Rockefeller Foundation for funding, not just for a chair in Māori but also for practical health and farming programmes for Māori communities.[27] Needless to say, this scheme was not realised, but like many of Ngata's ideas, it is important to be aware of the dead ends and paths not taken as they give us a better sense of Māori aspirations at a time when leaders saw anthropology as a tool of cultural development rather than assimilation.

In the 1920s and 1930s Māori politicians, scholars, and artists were actively involved in the assembling of 'classic' Māori culture and its deployment in social governance (but also the mediating of that social governance). Consequently we find ideas of 'traditional' social organisation informing the work of the Native Department in the interwar period, when policy shifted from buying Māori land to incorporation and consolidation of fragmented collective holdings to enable Māori owners to develop farms. That this work took place along tribal lines and under hereditary leadership is testament to the customary notions of rangatiratanga and iwi, hapū and whānau, which were assembled in part through the Māori-funded ethnographies of Elsdon Best – but we should not dismiss this 'invention of tradition' as some inauthentic representation but rather see it as a genuine Indigenous intervention, another step in the dance of agency. This in turn produced ethnographic capital, which, like Felix Keesing's study of *The Changing Maori* (published by the Board in 1928), shaped the work of the Department of Native Affairs in the New Zealand Government 1920–35. An example was Ngata's sheep and dairy farming schemes which can be understood as 'anthropology in action: not an end in themselves but a catalyst for community regeneration'.[28]

It would not be overstating the case to say that, in collusion with their Pākehā allies, these Māori scholars *invented* anthropology in New Zealand, employing it to advance their position in recolonial New Zealand when, as Belich suggests, Māori status was on the rise as 'brown Britons' whose artistic treasures adorned the new nation state. Rather than see Ngata and others as collaborators within a system inured to influence from within and below, this back and forth negotiation can be seen as a 'dance of agency', an immanent practice of resistance and accommodation through which a socio-political-technical assemblage centred around anthropological governance operated within, outside, and between government and tribes. Therefore, the connections between anthropology and colonial governmentality were not a simple case of the clash of cultures, duelling discourses, or the racial politics of Māori versus Pākehā, but a heterogeneous assemblage of objects, texts, people, practices, and institutions, all 'mangled' together in web-like networks of social and material agency.

Applied anthropology in New Zealand's Pacific empire

The network described above extended out into the Pacific, through close links between Native policy in New Zealand and the administration of the colonies in its fledging empire in the Cook Islands, Niue, and Sāmoa. These links have a distinctly ethnographic tinge. As mentioned above, the Board of Maori Ethnological Research was set up with the express desire to conduct fieldwork on 'cognate races of the Pacific' and in fact by 1933 Buck thought it should be renamed the Board of *Polynesian* Research.[29] Its work included several Pacific projects: a Solomon Islands dictionary, a translation of Kramer's work on Sāmoa from the German, and funding several articles in the *Journal of the Polynesian Society*. In addition to this, there was some interest in extending the provisions of the legislation on antiquities and arts and crafts to the Island territories. Importantly, the Board funded Buck's trip to the Cook Islands for ten weeks in 1926, later published as *The Material Culture of the Cook Islands (Aitutaki)*, which in turn led to an offer to join the Bishop Museum's five-year expedition to the South Pacific. Buck, who eventually became Director of the Museum and Professor of Anthropology at Yale, saw his work on material culture in the Pacific as a natural extension of his Māori research on weaving and other topics at home. Aside from the many parallels in culture and society explored in Buck's published work – which dominated the field of Pacific Anthropology[30] – there were clear contemporary affinities and interests between Māori and Pacific Island people in terms of their responses to European technology, particularly this theme of cultural contact, change, and adaptation. Ngata asked Buck to produce a series on 'Nga moutere o te moana nui a Kiwa' (the islands of the great Ocean of Kiwa) for the Board's Māori language magazine *Te Wananga*. He added that his 'observations on the overseas branches of the race' will be of 'extraordinary interest for our people'.[31]

Buck's colleagues attested to his success as a fieldworker because of his language skills, his collaborative methods of gathering data, and the respect in which he was held by local people, to whom Te Rangihīroa was an 'honest kinsman, descended from common ancestors'.[32] His colleagues at the time commented on Buck's relationship with Pacific Islanders. 'By his knowledge of the Polynesians,' wrote H. F. Ayson in 1926, 'Dr Buck is able to gather info which perhaps no other scientist would be able to get. He has been extremely popular with the native people and they have taken great interest in his work.'[33] As J. B. Condliffe recounts, when Buck went to Aitutaki to do fieldwork in 1926, he managed to complete research in five weeks that his American colleagues thought would take six months. Unlike some anthropologists of the time, he knew that the local people were smart, and they wanted to know why he was 'prying around' asking innumerable questions, so he called a meeting of the elders, explained the project to them and appealed to their pride – the result was a community effort to collect and record ethnological data across the island. He wrote home to Ngata explaining the advantage his Māori ancestry gave him, and the similarities to Māori crafts he was familiar with from the museum expeditions. 'The Polynesian corpuscles carry us behind the barrier that takes a pakeha some time to scale and the key of speech cuts out some other months,' he wrote, 'then the plaiting technique of Wanganui, the net strokes of Waiapu, etc etc cuts out one or two more months.'[34]

While Buck was conducting research around the Pacific from the late 1920s, and now and then acting as a government official, back in Wellington Ngata was in the centre of government at the helm of the Department of Native Affairs and also responsible for the Cook Islands (he was also offered Sāmoa, while Pōmare had previously been responsible for the Cook Islands, Sāmoa and Niue). Up to the late 1930s Ngata and Buck's close relationship was maintained through a lengthy correspondence, which shows how mutual interests in anthropology shaped, and were shaped by, problems of cultural adaptation, identity, and race. This research was not seen as a purely European academic exercise but an 'applied' or 'empirical' anthropology which was inflected with a Polynesian perspective and ultimately directed towards the welfare of their people. Rather immodestly Te Rangihīroa told Ngata that, as Māori, they had an insider view of the field of study, which gave them an advantage over their European colleagues. 'In Polynesian research,' Buck wrote, 'it is right and fitting that the highest branch of the Polynesian race should be in the forefront and not leave the bulk of the investigations to workers who have not got the inside angle that we have.' He added: 'They miss things that are significant to us.'[35]

In his letters to Ngata, Buck told him about the famous anthropologists he met at Yale and elsewhere, including Boas, Malinowski, Wissler, and Radcliffe-Brown. Ngata responded positively to Buck's invitation to meet up with him at a 1931 congress in Vancouver so as to view 'the eminent anthropologists from a Polynesian angle'.[36] While he saw himself as an anthropologist, Peter Buck was quite prepared to criticise the theoretical tendencies of the discipline unconnected with material culture, or the style of work which disconnected objects from social life. In a letter to Johannes Anderson (a colleague on the Board of Maori Ethnological Research) from Mangareva in 1934, he complained about the dry formal analysis of artefacts by H. D. Skinner, the Cambridge-trained curator and lecturer at the University of Otago and the Otago Museum in Dunedin. Buck wrote that 'his description of objects remains dead unless it is woven into the living culture of the people'.[37] 'There are times when I feel it is a hard problem to express the Polynesians' feelings in a manner intelligible to the pakeha,' he confessed to Ngata, adding, 'He on his side has no diffidence in the matter and I wonder at times if the errors of the past will not continue to be recorded but in more pretentious language.'[38]

For his part, Ngata was aware of the usefulness of ethnological field-work for 'the government of native races in the Pacific',[39] but was criti-cal of scholars who travelled around picking up a 'smattering' of various native languages compared to Buck's 'fundamental work on Samoa and Cook Islands'.[40] His fieldwork provided the platform, he felt, for good administration:

> Dr. Buck is the first student who has examined the culture and sociol-ogy of the Cook Island peoples having in his possession the key to their psychology, and I am sure, that when his work is published will form the best foundations for government and administration in keeping the mind of the people concerned.[41]

Buck returned to New Zealand rarely, and Ngata only went to Rarotonga once, but they were always working on projects of mutual benefit aimed at connecting peoples across the South Pacific. Ngata for his part sent Cook Island carvers to train with the School of Arts and Crafts (set up through government legislation in 1926), and arranged for a visiting party from Rarotonga to tour New Zealand (including marae) in the early 1930s; this resulted in a lasting connection with the Ngāti Porou people of Tokomaru Bay on the East Coast, through the meeting house Te Hono ki Rarotonga – both attempts to 'bring the Cook Islander closer to his New Zealand relative'.[42] Buck also spoke of 'a wider Polynesian spirit and consciousness among the various branches' which he hoped Ngata's Native Department could foster, though he acknowledged this was difficult because 'the pakeha politicians do not see as we see'.[43] Buck also tried to get Ngata interested in various aca-demic initiatives, and Ngata in turn attempted to find his friend a local university job so he could support his political projects. At one point they considered working on a joint conference paper to expound their theory about 'cultural contacts and adaptations'. Ngata wondered how they should approach the topic, arguing for a 'native viewpoint' rather than looking at it 'through Pakeha spectacles'.[44]

The lessons for colonial administrators from Buck's research in the Pacific were the same as in New Zealand, the gradual adjustment of Native people to European culture through sympathetic knowledge and understanding, while retaining the 'best' of their ancestral culture. On a visit to New Zealand in 1936, Buck told a reporter about his anthropological research in the Pacific, stressing this theme of the persistence of cultural forms that Ngata also preached:

> Speaking about the culture being manifested by the native peoples in the Pacific, Dr Buck said it was really strange that the new culture was really native in spite of European food, clothes, utensils and manners. There was a change in the material and economic life, but the spirit at the back of it all was thoroughly Polynesian.[45]

Peter Buck's enthusiasm for anthropology did not blind him to the negative effects of colonisation. In Hawai'i, where he admitted to being 'mokemoke' at times, he was disappointed to find 'so little' of Indigenous culture left, and 'appalled' at the commercialism of US culture, viewing it with the somewhat superior attitude of a British subject. 'One would like to stand up on a marae and make a speech,' he told Ngata, 'but this is the area of the Pakeha.'[46] In the letters between these two men we can see how they dealt with the changing world around them – at times adopting colonialist, at times British, and at other times staunchly Māori positions – their views shifting as circumstances demanded. We can understand these assertions, compromises, and contests as a dance-like movement in which Indigenous agents were engaging with the state, the nation, and the empire but also working against it, reserving a space for Native people just as they were preserving Native artefacts and traditions.

Māori and the Sāmoan 'problem'

How did New Zealand, praised for an apparently successful record in dealing with the so-called 'Māori problem', fare in the Pacific, especially when the execution of government policy was in the hands of Māori politicians? The record is decidedly mixed. Whereas the Cook Islands were seen at the time to be governed successfully through the Native Department by Pōmare, and later Ngata, along the lines followed by the Native Department in New Zealand, the administration of Sāmoa was seen as a disaster. Taken over in 1914 from Germany, in 1920 the League of Nations handed over Western Samoa to New Zealand as a mandated territory. Under the Samoa Act 1921, an administration governed the islands through a Legislative Council and a Fono made up of high chiefs. In 1918 there was a disastrous influenza outbreak due to New Zealand negligence, and in 1929 the Mau nationalist movement was met with violent suppression and the death of its leader Tamasese.[47] Pōmare in particular, who, as Patricia O'Brien has shown, had a close relationship with one of the leaders of the Mau, the half-caste businessman Ta'isi Nelson, denounced government actions and called for independence or 'Samoa for Samoa' (Samoa mo Samoa).[48] Ngata was also publicly critical of New Zealand's 'imperial' pretensions and 'blustering' tactics. He told the Institute of Pacific Relations:

> Here was the opportunity for our ethnologists to survey the social setting of the Samoan race, to appraise the extent to which contact with European culture had affected the native culture and to adapt our New Zealand and Rarotongan experience to the conditions revealed.[49]

Ngata argued in parliament that 'Maori methods' should be applied cautiously to Sāmoans, but disagreed with the policies of the Department of External Affairs. The problem was, he felt, that Sāmoa was *not* run through the Native Department and the Department of External Affairs lacked an understanding of the people and their culture.[50] Buck said if *he* had been sent to do 'ethnological research' in Sāmoa, he would surely have found out more easily what the local feeling was and possibly averted the disaster.[51] Later he complained that it was 'criminal' that the government never made use of the Native Affairs Department. There was, he added, 'too much of the egotistical pakeha superiority'.[52] Ngata replied, agreeing that Pakeha administrators acted in a 'superior supercilious fashion ... as if they know better what is good for a Polynesian than Polynesians who have found it out for themselves'.[53] They felt that in the Cook Islands, where Ngata's own official and personal involvement was much closer, the administration's record was more successful. Ngata put this down to a closer cultural affinity between Cook Island Māori and New Zealand Māori, a connection made visible through ethnological research. However, Ngata himself felt unsure how to approach Cook Island culture, but told the anthropologist Felix Keesing that he sensed a common Polynesian base underlying the layers of Christian colonial culture. The 'Rarotongan heart' had altered little, however much it conformed to Western civilisation on the outside, like 'our own people' who despite outward appearances had the same 'ngakau Maori'.[54]

New Zealander Felix Keesing, who had written his first book about the 'changing Māori' with Ngata's encouragement, went on to do similar field work on culture contact among Native Americans and Sāmoans.[55] Ngata exchanged letters with him comparing the administration of Māori, Sāmoans, and Native Americans. Buck also met Keesing and told Ngata that Keesing's research confirmed their views about Māori resilience. 'Keesing says that Samoan culture has undergone considerable change,' he wrote, but 'in spite of this the Samoan background is Samoan.' Likewise Māori material life had changed 'and yet you are using the tribal mechanism and psychology with success in your very advanced development schemes' by recognising 'certain survival features in native culture'.[56]

However, Keesing was highly critical of Richardson's administration in Sāmoa, writing:

> Until some sort of intensive anthropological survey is made (to my thinking the most urgent need), until there is some intelligent working out of policy, securing of continuity, and training of staff, until there is an adequate bridging of the language gap by interpreters, the authority of New Zealand will lie as it so largely does today in the hands of a scattering of youthful policemen rather than in the civil administration.[57]

While Ngata and Buck agreed on the utility of ethnology for liberal native policy, and a pan-Polynesian affinity between Māori and Pacific peoples, their correspondence is full of negative and patronising attitudes to 'backward' Sāmoa and Sāmoans. Buck, who had spent a lot of time in Sāmoa in the 1920s, thought the 'debacle' could have been avoided but dismissed the Mau as wrong in 'principle'.[58] Ngata was equally critical: the Sāmoan philosophy was 'narrow, conceited, and self-centred' but 'adequate to limited needs'. In a tropical environment where food was abundant, life was too easy compared to New Zealand, he argued, quoting the proverb, 'Hawaiki kai – te kai i rari noa mai te raweketia e te ringaringa' ('Prolific Hawaiki – where food untouched by human hand is in great abundance').[59] 'If Samoa for Samoa means that,' concluded Ngata, 'then we are wasting time and money in our method of administration.'[60] One interesting point of contrast was their criticism of the Sāmoan prejudice against half-castes, compared to Māori who had embraced hāwhe kāehe like James Carroll in New Zealand.[61] Keesing also remarked on critical Sāmoan attitudes to Māori and other Pacific peoples, but thought that friendly relations would develop through the connection with New Zealand. 'The Samoan is certainly not ready to fraternise with his Maori cousin as yet,' he wrote in his report to Ngata, 'in fact has a hearty contempt for all other island peoples; but I think some day a Polynesian consciousness will emerge.'[62]

Ultimately, both men saw the future of New Zealand rule in the Pacific lying in a combined 'Ministry of Polynesian Affairs' or, better yet, within a Department of Native Affairs with jurisdiction over both the Cook Islands and Sāmoa. They believed staff should gain experience working in Māori communities and be trained in anthropology. The government agency should be linked to an Institute of Polynesian Research based in the University, and fund ethnological research. Ngata went as far as applying for funding to the Rockefeller Foundation and trying to lure Buck back to New Zealand to a Chair.[63] This government agency should, he argued, work with the museums which could collect and display a 'representative' sample of the material culture of the different Island groups under New Zealand administration, both for the general public and the training of officials.[64]

Conclusion

The relationship of Ngata and Buck, New Zealand and its Pacific possessions, and anthropology and government is extremely complex and defies the simple analytical frameworks of imperial, political, and postcolonial approaches employed in much previous research. These educated and successful Māori leaders wove together museums, ethnology, and politics as they moved inside, outside, and alongside European structures in a constant process of negotiation with Western society and local peoples in Aotearoa and Te Moana nui a Kiwa. While this chapter has only begun to explore this topic, and does not consider the Pasifika response, or trace the associations very far along the networks into the Pacific, it has demonstrated the value of rethinking the nature of colonial relations in New Zealand's Pacific empire. In contrast to seeing the world as structured like a language, reducing relations to either/or contrasts of power and knowledge, it can be understood as a continuous unfolding and emerging of human and non-human agency. Seen in this way, the colonial social appears messy and complex but full of potential, a tricky two step in which agents weave their way between government and communities, European and Polynesian, and subject and object.

As Cooper reminds us, postcolonial studies of history often overlook 'the ways in which colonized peoples sought – not entirely without success – to build lives in the crevices of colonial power and to deflect, appropriate, or reinterpret the teachings and preachings thrust upon them'.[65] There was a tendency, after the Māori sovereignty movement of the 1980s, to view Āpirana Ngata and Peter Buck as 'selling out' to the majority culture. Yet in the 1920s and 1930s a post-assimilationist Māori consciousness emerged from several interrelated networks that were competing, crossing, and converging around heritage, science, government and race. Buck saw himself as bicultural, and valued both sides of his family history, in ways which defy simplistic analyses of Māori and Pākehā identities. Ngata moved both inside and outside government, working for the state but also with and for his own people, in a delicate act of compromise that eludes any critique conducted in black and white terms. At the same time, sympathetic Pākehā such as Keesing and Best, while products of their time and shaped by its prejudices, could act in ways that would benefit Māori and Pacific agendas.

[63]

Admittedly, Buck and Ngata were not rebels seeking liberation from the yoke of colonial culture, but neither did they simply go along with assimilation. Both were committed to the survival of Māori and Pacific Island peoples and the maintenance of their culture, what they called 'the efforts to save the worthiest in our past while seeking elements in the new culture applicable to our conditions'.[66] Their historical research, and their political and economic work as leaders and scholars, was ultimately directed at the problems of the present. It aimed to construct a Polynesian past as a platform for the future, through pride in the achievements of ancestors who Buck called the 'Vikings of the sunrise'.[67] As Condliffe pointed out, Buck and Ngata also wanted to show Europeans this glorious past in order to prove their ability to stand tall in modern society: 'The Maori, they protested, were no Calibans to serve as menials, but men and women fully equal in mental capacity and honour to their Pakeha compatriots.'[68]

Acknowledgements

The research for this chapter was conducted as part of an Australian Research Council funded project, 'Museum, Field, Metropole, Colony' (DP110103776). I am a partner investigator in an international team headed by Professor Tony Bennett from the Institute for Culture and Society at the University of Western Sydney. I would also like to thank Fiona Cameron and my research assistant Arawehetu Berdinner.

Notes

1   Alexander Turnbull Library, Wellington (hereafter ATL), MS-papers-0189-078, 'Rarotonga ramblings', by Te Rangihīroa MP (Peter Buck), Various MSS re journey to Rarotonga.
2   ATL MS-papers-0189-078, 'Rarotonga ramblings', by Te Rangihāroa MP (Peter Buck), Various MSS re journey to Rarotonga.
3   The term 'native' was widely used in New Zealand in this period, and changed after the Second World War, so the Department of Native Affairs became Maori Affairs in 1949.
4   Frederick Cooper, 'Postcolonial studies and the study of history', in Ania Loomba, Suvir Kaul, Matti Bunzl, Antoinette Burton, and Jed Esty (eds), *Postcolonial Studies and Beyond* (Durham NC and London: Duke University Press, 2005), pp. 401–22.
5   Andrew Pickering, *The Mangle of Practice: Time, Agency, and Science* (Chicago and London: University of Chicago Press, 1995).
6   Conal McCarthy, '"Empirical anthropologists advocating cultural adjustments": The anthropological governance of Āpirana Ngata and the Native Affairs Department', *History and Anthropology*, 25:2 (2014), 280–95.
7   Damon Salesa, 'New Zealand's Pacific', in Giselle Byrnes (ed.), *The New Oxford History of New Zealand* (Melbourne: Oxford University Press, 2009), pp. 149–72; Sean Mallon, Kolokesa Mahina-Tuai, and Damon Salesa (eds), *Tangata o le moana: New Zealand and the People of the Pacific* (Wellington: Te Papa Press, 2012); Tony

Ballantyne, *Webs of Empire: Locating New Zealand's Colonial Past* (Wellington: Bridget Williams Books, 2012).

8   Damon Salesa, 'Half castes between the wars: Colonial categories in New Zealand and Samoa', *New Zealand Journal of History*, 34:1 (2000), 98–116.

9   Edward Said, *Orientalism*, revised edn (New York: Penguin, 1995); Rod Edmond, *Representing the South Pacific: Colonial Discourse from Cook to Gauguin* (Cambridge: Cambridge University Press, 1997).

10 Tim Barringer and Tom Flynn (eds), *Colonialism and the Object: Empire, Material Culture and the Museum* (London and New York: Routledge, 1998).

11 David Scott, 'Colonial governmentality', *Social Text*, 43 (1995), 191–220. For the source of Foucault's famous phrase, see Michel Foucault, *Dits et écrits IV* (Paris: Gallimard, 1994), p. 237.

12 George Steinmetz, *The Devil's Handwriting: Precoloniality and the German Colonial State in Qingdao, Samoa, and Southwest Africa* (Chicago: University of Chicago Press, 2008).

13 Linda Tuhiwai Smith, *Decolonizing Methodologies: Research and Indigenous Peoples* (Dunedin: University of Otago Press, 1999); Toon van Meijl, 'Historicising Maoritanga: Colonial ethnography and the reification of Maori traditions', *The Journal of the Polynesian Society*, 105:3 (1996), 311–46.

14 Frederick Cooper, *Colonialism in Question: Theory, Knowledge, History* (Berkeley: University of California Press, 2005).

15 Amiria Henare, *Museums, Anthropology and Imperial Exchange* (Cambridge: Cambridge University Press, 2005); Conal McCarthy, '"Our Works of Ancient Times": History, colonisation and agency at the 1906–7 New Zealand International Exhibition', *Museum History Journal*, 2:2 (2009), 119–42; Sarah Longair and John McAleer (eds), *Curating Empire: Museums and the British Imperial Experience* (Manchester: Manchester University Press, 2012).

16 James Belich, *Paradise Reforged: A History of the New Zealanders from the 1880s to the Year 2000* (Auckland: Allen Lane & Penguin, 2001), p. 189.

17 Conal McCarthy, *Exhibiting Māori: A History of Colonial Cultures of Display* (Oxford and New York: Berg, 2007).

18 Bruno Latour, *Reassembling the Social: An Introduction to Actor-Network-Theory*, Clarendon Lectures in Management Studies (Oxford: Oxford University Press, 2005); Sarah Byrne, Anne Clarke, Rodney Harrison, and Robin Torrence (eds), *Unpacking the Collection: Networks of Material and Social Agency in the Museum*, One World Archaeology (Santa Fe: Springer, 2011).

19 Pickering, *The Mangle of Practice*, p. 5.

20 Andrew Pickering, 'Material culture and the dance of agency', in Dan Hicks and Mary C. Beaudry (eds), *The Oxford Handbook of Material Culture Studies* (Oxford: Oxford University Press, 2010), p. 195.

21 Ranginui Walker, *He Tipua: The Life and Times of Sir Apirana Ngata* (Auckland: Viking, 2001).

22 Apirana Ngata, 'Anthropology and the government of Native races in the Pacific', in James Allen (ed.), *New Zealand Affairs* (Christchurch: Institute of Pacific Relations New Zealand Branch, 1929), pp. 22–60.

23 Archives New Zealand, Wellington (hereafter ANZ), MBER ACIH 16068 MA51/2 22.

24 ANZ, MBER ACIH 16068 MA51/2 22.

25 ATL, MS-papers-8051, Letter from Elsdon Best to T. W. Downes, Whanganui n.d. [ca. early 1920s].

26 Felix M. Keesing, *The Changing Maori* (New Plymouth: Thomas Avery & Sons, 1928), p. 182.

27 M. P. K. Sorrenson (ed.), *Na to Hoa Aroha: From Your Dear Friend: The Correspondence between Sir Apirana Ngata and Sir Peter Buck 1925–50. Vol. 2: 1930–32* (Auckland: Auckland University Press, Maori Purposes Fund Board, 1987), pp. 110–11.

28 M. P. K. Sorrenson, 'Ngata, Apirana Turupa 1874–1950', *Dictionary of New Zealand Biography*, 1996, www.dnzb.govt.nz/, accessed February 2015. Apirana

Ngata, 'Maori land development', *Appendices to the Journal of the House of Representatives*, Wellington, 1931. For the construction of tribal identities, see: Angela Ballara, *Iwi: The Dynamics of Māori Tribal Organisation From c. 1769– c. 1945* (Wellington: Victoria University Press, 1998).

29   M. P. K. Sorrenson (ed.), *Na to Hoa Aroha: From Your Dear Friend: The Correspondence between Sir Apirana Ngata and Sir Peter Buck 1925–50*. Vol. 3: 1932–50 (Auckland: Auckland University Press, Maori Purposes Fund Board, 1988), p. 77.

30   Peter Buck, *Samoan Material Culture* (Honolulu: Bishop Museum Bulletin 75, 1930); *An Introduction to Polynesian Anthropology* (Honolulu: Bishop Museum Bulletin No. 187, 1945).

31   M. P. K. Sorrenson (ed.), *Na to Hoa Aroha: From Your Dear Friend: The Correspondence between Sir Apirana Ngata and Sir Peter Buck 1925–50*. Vol. 1 (Auckland: Auckland University Press, Maori Purposes Fund Board, 1986), p. 237.

32   J. B. Condliffe, *Te Rangi Hiroa: The Life of Sir Peter Buck* (Christchurch: Whitcombe & Tombs, 1971), p. 152.

33   ANZ, ACIH CGA 8280 IT1W2439/131-112/3/1, Letter, Ayson to Secretary Cook Islands, Ethnology Bernice P. Bishop – Museum Honolulu 907/1924), 17 October 1926.

34   Condliffe, *Te Rangi Hiroa*, p. 152.

35   Sorrenson, *Na to Hoa Aroha*, Vol. 1, p. 48.

36   Sorrenson, *Na to Hoa Aroha*, Vol. 2, p. 212.

37   ATL, MS-papers-0148-015, 'Andersen: Papers: Material relating to AN and Peter Buck', Letter, Peter Buck to J. C. Andersen, 19 November 1934.

38   Sorrenson, *Na to Hoa Aroha*, Vol. 1, p. 116.

39   Ngata, 'Anthropology and the government of Native races'.

40   Sorrenson, *Na to Hoa Aroha*, Vol. 2, p. 18.

41   ANZ, C565 996 Ref No AAOP 6018, 'M. R. Jones Papers: file on correspondence between Ngata and Keesing' 1928–31, Letter, Ngata to Keesing, Fiji, 22 May 1930.

42   Sorrenson, *Na to Hoa Aroha*, Vol. 3, p. 88.

43   Sorrenson, *Na to Hoa Aroha*, Vol. 3, p. 160.

44   Sorrenson, *Na to Hoa Aroha*, Vol. 2, p. 42.

45   'Pacific culture: The island races: Intensive study: Dr Buck's visit', *Evening Post* [Wellington], (4 February 1936), n.p.

46   Sorrenson, *Na to Hoa Aroha*, Vol. 1, p. 162.

47   Michael Field, *Mau: Samoa's Struggle Against New Zealand Oppression* (Auckland: Reed, 1984).

48   Patricia O'Brien, 'Ta'isi Olaf Nelson and Sir Maui Pomare: Samoans and Maori Reunited', Seminar Stout Research Centre, Victoria University of Wellington, 19 September 2012.

49   Ngata, 'Anthropology and the government of Native races', pp. 42–3.

50   Condliffe, *Te Rangi Hiroa*, pp. 158–9.

51   Sorrenson, *Na to Hoa Aroha*, Vol. 1, p. 61.

52   Sorrenson, *Na to Hoa Aroha*, Vol. 2, pp. 104–5.

53   Sorrenson, *Na to Hoa Aroha*, Vol. 2, pp. 198–9.

54   Sorrenson, *Na to Hoa Aroha*, Vol. 2, p. 41.

55   Felix M. Keesing, *The Changing Maori*, and *Modern Samoa: Its Government and Changing Life* (London: Allen & Unwin/Institute of Pacific Relations, 1934).

56   Sorrenson, *Na to Hoa Aroha*, Vol. 2, pp. 210–11.

57   ANZ, AAOP 6018, 'M. R. Jones Papers: File on correspondence between Ngata and Keesing', 1928–31.

58   Sorrenson, *Na to Hoa Aroha*, Vol. 1, pp. 187–9.

59   Sorrenson, *Na to Hoa Aroha*, Vol. 2, p. 197.

60   Sorrenson, *Na to Hoa Aroha*, Vol. 2, p. 198.

61   On this point, see Salesa, 'Half castes between the wars'.

62   ANZ, Keesing, Container Code C565 996 Ref No AAOP 6018, 'M. R. Jones Papers: File on correspondence between Ngata and Keesing' 1928–31, 'Some notes on Samoa 1931'.

63   Sorrenson, *Na to Hoa Aroha*, Vol. 1, p. 170.

64 Sorrenson, *Na to Hoa Aroha*, Vol. 3, p. 77.
65 Cooper, 'Postcolonial studies and the study of history', p. 403.
66 Sorrenson, *Na to Hoa Aroha*, Vol. 2, p. 42.
67 Peter H. Buck, *Vikings of the Sunrise* (New York: Frederick A. Stokes & Co., 1938).
68 Condliffe, *Te Rangi Hiroa*, p. 215.

PART II

Imperial mobility

CHAPTER FOUR

Travelling the Tasman world: travel writing and narratives of transit

Anna Johnston

The Australasian part of the British world was dominated by seven English colonies, opined Sir George Smyth Baden-Powell in 1872: 'five on the "Big Island," and two on the adjoining "insulae"' of Tasmania and New Zealand'.[1] Like many nineteenth-century travellers, Baden-Powell encountered the antipodean settler colonies consecutively as his journey progressed through the region. Each colony appeared as an independent location, detached from nascent Australian and New Zealand nationalisms. Shipping routes mapped the British world: Gravesend–Rio de Janeiro–Sydney; Hobart–Auckland; Sydney–Batavia–India; Swan River–Cape Town; San Francisco–Sydney–Auckland. While many important studies have analysed travel writing within national historical and literary contexts – most notably, in New Zealand studies, Lydia Wevers' superb *Country of Writing*[2] – this chapter analyses travel writing by explicitly moving across the Tasman Strait to ask a series of questions about the role of the antipodean settler colonies in the British imagination, about the similarities and distinctions emergent in what would later become separate Australian and New Zealand cultures, and about how imperial ideas were explored in travel writing concerning the trans-Tasman world.

Ideas about empire, 'race', and 'whiteness' were tested in distinctive ways in settler colonies. By reading and interpreting trans-Tasman travel writing, we can see how particular variants of Britishness – and, as a consequence, of settler subjectivity – emerged through the colonial narratives that both asserted and resisted relationships with the imperial centre. The nineteenth-century settler colonies lured travellers keen to witness novel antipodean societies and exotic landscapes, while the burgeoning infrastructure of empire made travel increasingly accessible as the century progressed.[3] The prospect of emigration, and of geopolitical domination, meant that the settler colonies attracted considerable interest from both British travellers and armchair readers. From the 1860s onwards, many travellers searched for and celebrated 'Greater Britain' (in Charles Dilke's term)[4] and the spread of Anglo-Saxon peoples and sensibilities. A plethora of travellers posited New Zealand and Australia as 'New Homes for the Old Country', to borrow Baden-Powell's book title.[5] These locations promised modernity, space, and opportunity for Britons who were dissatisfied with the rapid industrialisation throughout Europe.

Among the Australasian colonies, New Zealand held a special place in the minds of imperial travellers. Its geographic distance was belied by its cultural similarity, and many travellers who found the mainland Australian colonies uncomfortably replete with brash and self-confident colonists saw New Zealand as an alternative to overt rejections of British heritage. Even New Zealand's distance was at times an advantage. Alice Anne Montgomery, Duchess of Buckingham and Chandos, describes how the inspiration for her 1893 voyage to Australia and New Zealand began when she watched her cousin's wife

> making blue cotton pinafores for her little girl to wear on board ship, and talking of their voyage to New Zealand as others would talk of a trip to Paris. "You see," she said, "it does not seem so long as you suppose: first one stops at Gibraltar, then at Malta, Brindisi, Suez, Aden, and Ceylon; and the only long part is from Ceylon to Albany in King George's Sound, and that is only 10 days. After reaching Australia, one feels one has almost arrived at New Zealand, although it is quite a little voyage to get there from Melbourne."[6]

Montgomery's travel trajectory serves to remind us that empire was powered not only by steam routes and privileged elite postings, but also by personal and domestic motivations, inflected by gender, family, and domesticity as much as by politics. For many female travellers, it was easier to feel 'at home' in New Zealand than the Australian colonies – perhaps due to a perception of the ongoing nature of gender imbalance that typified the early penal colonies. In 1889, Katherine E. Bates, writer, traveller, and spiritualist, declared: 'I think most English people will feel, as I did, far more at home in New Zealand than in Australia. There is less pretension and more simplicity of life, and the result is that people are more genial and natural.'[7] Gender made a difference to the way that late imperial travellers such as Bates saw emigration prospects and evaluated colonial environments: 'Were I a man, with strong physical or mental endowments, I would certainly choose Australia as the best theatre for the exercise of them; but I would not spend an unnecessary penny in the country.'[8] Disingenuously, Bates declares that only those who are sympathetic to a topic should write about it: then, having demonstrated 'that I am absolutely and hopelessly disqualified as a critic on matters colonial, what remains for a thoroughly consistent *woman* to do but herewith commence, or rather continue, her criticisms on the subject'.[9]

For other travellers, climate and geography made New Zealand a natural choice both for the British emigrant and intra-colonial retirees. 'J. D.', writing about his medical leave from a civil service post in India, notes his profound dislike and distrust of 'the Continental curative process'. Coupled with a love of the sea, this resulted in his ninety-day and 19,000-mile round voyage in 1885 to see 'some of the curiosities of topsyturvydom and the wonders of Maoriland'.[10] In accord with Anthony Trollope, J. D. finds New Zealand to be 'the cream of the English colonies. Its climate is well suited to the Anglo-Saxon constitution, and is undoubtedly healthy on the whole ... One of the most striking natural features of the colony, and one which undoubtedly gives it a marked superiority over Africa and Australia, is the abundance of water.'[11] Like many late-nineteenth-century travellers, J. D. emphasises the shared Anglo-Saxon heritage and culture to be found in the settler colonies, and particular environmental conditions sympathetic to English populations.

New Zealand's distinctive place in this travel discourse forms the kernel of analysis in this chapter, which shows how New Zealand's situation inside imperial travel narratives might illuminate the complex and shifting understandings of race, empire, and global networks of connection during the 1860s–90s. Drawing evidence from a comprehensive survey of English language travel writing about the Australasian region encompassing the full nineteenth century, this chapter maps the geographic imaginings of imperial travellers as they encountered the antipodean settler colonies. Large numbers of travellers moved across the region – my broader study identifies over 500 book-length texts specifically covering the Australian colonies published in the nineteenth century – for a variety of purposes: leisure, business, emigration, health, family reunion, and curiosity, amongst others. The travel accounts I discuss in this chapter focus on the period from the late 1860s onwards, when New Zealand became a staple destination of the itinerary of Britons travelling to Australia and beyond. Like their many fellow travellers, these writers were of mixed social status, both men and women, and while some were professional writers, for others an account of a trip to the colonies would be their only publication. Although often repetitive, even the most naïve accounts were rarely ill-informed, for their authors read previous travel accounts, especially on the long voyage south; frequently other travel writers are mentioned, argued with, or used as authorities on colonial matters. Many travel accounts were drawn from diaries undertaken while travelling, and the literary skill and aesthetic ambition in the transformation of textual forms varies considerably. Some travel books evolved from letters written back home to friends and family; others compiled letters that had been published in local newspapers back home as they travelled. Few of the writers discussed would be familiar to readers; rather, across the spectrum, these accounts of trans-Tasman travel reveal a vernacular rendering of the large questions posed by the British Empire as the century progressed. The dense intertextuality of these texts complicates a developmental account of a history of ideas about race and culture, given that travelling readers engaged with a back catalogue of travel writing that stretched back to earlier colonial periods. Many writers established their textual authority by seeking to update older accounts. Nevertheless, late imperial and metropolitan ideas about the potential decline of empire – concomitant with observations of nascent colonial independence – ensured that as the century progressed, identifying British-ness in the settler colonial world became a common preoccupation, as did surveying the ways in which settlers identified themselves against Britain. Could the Empire simply continue to expand, until it encompassed the whole globe? What would white European settlers create in new temperate colonies? What relationships would settlers maintain with their fellow Britons, and with the idea of empire? Tamara Wagner's proposition to read settler colonial and metropolitan writing in tandem to reveal 'a new appreciation of genre formation on an increasingly global scale' is compelling. As Wagner argues of Victorian settler narratives more broadly, complex and shifting representations of the settler world 'transformed the idea of home itself – arguably the most central idea in Victorian culture – and the modes of reproducing it'.[12]

The settler colonial environs 'discovered' by imperial travellers provided unsettling evidence of the multiple 'nineteenth-century worlds' existing in overlapping yet non-synchronous times and spaces. These earlier global interests, heavily influenced by empire, inform our current worldview. Keith Hanley and Greg Kucich argue that today's globalisation debates have their roots in the nineteenth century, especially with the 'stunning advances in ... transportation and communication networks that physically linked parts of the planet' and that prefigured our contemporary global consciousness and sense of worldwide connectedness.[13] Nineteenth-century travel writing evinces the benefits of those technological advances for curious metropolitans, but it also reveals the complex knowledge gathered through new forms of mobility; knowledge that could both confirm and question the triumphalist rhetoric of modern Britain. The 'Greater Britain' aspirations of late imperial political pundits sought to foreclose some of these surprising multiplicities by ways of older geopolitical affiliations and ideologies: empire, race, and blood.

Greater Britain and settler colonialism

Settler colonial studies avows an interest in mythologies (James Belich's term), narratives, and stories (Lorenzo Veracini uses these terms interchangeably in his 'theoretical overview' of settler colonialism),[14] yet the field uses these terms very loosely and with little engagement with the vast body of scholarship that analyses narrative forms and their socio-cultural impact. As Dror Wahrman asks, rhetorically: 'What enabled the reproduction of metropoles across this Anglo world, what tied its many parts together, and what unified it as the triumphant force in Belich's Great Anglo Divergence? Much of the answer must lay [sic], it seems to me, in the realms of language and culture.' Cultural history and literary studies methodologies are conspicuously absent in the current iterations of settler colonial studies, even though, as Wahrman suggests, if these disciplines 'cannot produce the remains of the veins and sinews of this global nineteenth-century multi-headed English-speaking hydra, then it probably never lived'.[15]

Nineteenth-century travel writing provides an ideal vehicle to test globalised settler colonial models, because it maps the transcolonial and mobile consciousness through which New Zealand and Australian settler colonial entities and identities were forged. As a key part of the vast 'floating literature of London' that James Froude found in Sir George Grey's library at Kawau in 1886, published travel writing about Australia and New Zealand burgeoned during the nineteenth century.[16] Colonial writing generally reveals, as Tony Ballantyne suggests, the '"constant, intricate, but mostly unacknowledged traffic" that not only linked Europe and its colonies, but also forged important ties between disparate colonies as well'.[17] Travel writing makes this explicit in its mobile narrators, knowledge, and ideologies. These recent modes of conceptualising empire – from Ballantyne's 'webs of empire' to Alan Lester's 'imperial networks' to Peter Hulme's 'traffic' to James Clifford's 'routes' – are crucial to new understandings of past and present empires, and particularly of the production and circulation of colonial knowledge.[18] Travel texts remind us that 'national' cultures emerged in a dialectical relationship with other colonial cultures as much as with Britain, and that crucial ideas about race, place, and identity were developed across the Tasman region rather than adhering to the centre–periphery models of empire.

Sidney Smith lectured in his mid-century emigration guide *Whether to Go and Whither?* (1849):

We entreat our colonial fellow countrymen to consider their high functions, and solemn responsibilities. They are called by their destiny to lay
in Australia the foundations of an empire, larger and more gifted than
that of all Europe. In New Zealand they are the rulers of a kingdom,
larger and finer than that of the mother country. In Tasmania they possess
another, and more fertile, and sunny Ireland.[19]

In this early invocation of an emergent settler empire, Smith linked
the Cape of Good Hope with New Zealand, Australia, and the Falkland
Islands as settler locations that might constitute 'a new empire, with
the fifth part of the world, and that the finest and richest, for a dominion'.[20] This was not just a 'workable utopia', in Smith's terms, but a
serious racial responsibility.

By the 1880s James Froude found the settler colonies to be Edenic
landscapes 'where the children grow who seem once more to understand what was meant by "merry England"'.[21] While the 'little England'
trope became a cliché in colonial literatures, it performed important
ideological work: it evacuated colonial landscapes of prior Indigenous
cultures and elided uncomfortable questions about the cross-cultural
violence that effected Indigenous removal from the path of triumphant
settler expansion. Earlier travellers such as George French Angas
had found 'Savage Life and Scenes' to be the unsettling underside of
Anglo-Saxon boosterism.[22] These other temporalities and narrative
trajectories troubled imperial travellers, who at times struggled to
reconcile the utopian promise of new settler empires with evidence of
pre-existing Indigenous cultures and peoples.

The colonies of the south were eventually expected to form not a
competing but a complementary force to the imperial metropole. As
Donald Denoon argues, settler societies in temperate zones were initially 'garrison outposts defending the frontiers of European empires
centred on tropical possessions'.[23] Formed by British mobility, these
remote sites came to be seen as 'laboratories' for ongoing reinvention
and transformation – of people, of ideas, of raw materials – for the ulti-
mate renovation of the old northern world.[24] Charles Dilke's boostering
travel narrative, *Greater Britain* (1868), is motivated by 'a conception,
however imperfect, of the grandeur of our race, already girdling the
earth, which it is destined, perhaps, eventually to overspread'.[25] In
his race-based tour of the world, he finds in America, New Zealand,
Australia, and India that conflict with 'the cheaper races' is the main
impediment to the 'universal dominion of the English people'. Informed
by his travel, Froude concludes that 'race distinctions will long continue, that miscegenation will go but little way towards blending races;
that the dearer are, on the whole, likely to destroy the cheaper peoples,
and that Saxondom will rise triumphant from the doubtful struggle'.[26]

Like Anthony Trollope in his *Australia and New Zealand* (1873), Dilke carried with him 'the portable boundary of a racial identity' that he sought to have confirmed in his encounters: 'For the English traveller of Trollope's day, to move inside the portable boundary of the Anglo-Saxon race was to carry one's own "little England" everywhere one went', even if, as James Buzard notes of Trollope, cross-cultural experience often infiltrated permeable racial and cultural categories.[27]

Many travelling commentators were keen to tell the southern settlers their duty, as conceived by metropolitan pundits. In 1885 Froude considered it his role to propagate Thomas Carlyle's theories about England, 'though, of course, translated into the practical, with the metaphorical parts of it toned down'.[28] The 'empire of Oceana' was to 'send the stream of life back into [England's] loaded veins'; '... no longer a small island, but an ocean empire, where her millions and tens of millions would be spread over their broad inheritance, each leading wholesome and happy lives on their own fields, and by their own firesides, hardened into men by the sun of Australia or the frosts of Canada – free human beings in fact, and not in idle name, nor miserable bondsmen any more.'[29]

This is the implied threat of 'Greater Britain' that was only marginally recognised by imperial commentators, and continues to be subsumed by critics. Even Belich's magisterial exposition of 'the Settler Revolution' underplays the force of late nineteenth-century arguments about how Britishness might be condensed or indeed refined in southern settler environments. Under-emphasised, too, is the explicit challenge this posed to metropolitan theories of race and cultural superiority. Belich does note that Britain was 'politically embarrassed' by the racial discrimination exposed by the White Australia Policy and its equivalents around the Dominions: marked by the Federation-era Immigration Restriction Act 1901, Australia's exclusionary immigration law was itself based in 1850s racial ideologies and goldfield tensions. Belich recognises that race-based immigration policies 'underwrote a sense of kinship with Old Britain, creating a further web – of "crimson threads" – to hold the Greater British system together'.[30] He acknowledges settler colonial claims to provide new sources of Anglo-Saxon virility – the 'Better Britons' who were 'preserving British virtues somewhat better than the old' – and in passing mentions settler colonial neo-colonialism (Canadian interests in the West Indies; Australian and New Zealand interests in the Pacific; South African interest in Rhodesia and other protectorates), although the point becomes subsumed by questions of how the settler colonies 'fought for Britain as though they co-owned it', especially in the First World War.[31] The specific, race-based claims made for settler unification with 'Greater Britain' demand further explanation, and in this it is essential to account for the role of culture and language in either supporting, or indeed complicating, the espoused teleology of settler colonialism. Belich marshals 'aggregate facts' to make his arguments (demographic data, trade data, production data, shipping data), yet as Wahrman argues, the cultural context and meaning of these facts is often subsumed by the relentlessly quantitative approach. [32]

Trans-Tasman colonies

Baden-Powell's mapping of settler colonial geographies sees the Australasian colonies as interconnected geopolities. Unlike most nineteenth-century travel texts, *New Homes for the Old Country* (1872) moves fluidly across intracolonial territories, rather than sequentially. Division One surveys Australian, New Zealand, and Pacific colonies, in both geographical and social terms, for eight chapters that range between Sydney, Melbourne, Tasmania, Fiji, New Caledonia, and Lord Howe Island, concluding with New Zealand. Division Two returns to Australia with a focus on 'Ways and Means of Getting About', then working through internal transport across colonial contexts. Division Three focuses on 'Life on the Bush', including station life; cattle camps; and wine, sugar, flax, and meat industries. Division Five addresses Mineral Wealth; Division Six, Natives and Climate; Division Seven, Political Features; still moving flexibly between colonies to address the cohering themes. These organising structures enable the writer to analyse comparatively, and in doing so to conclude that while 'Of all the Australias Tasmania reminds one most of home,' it is New Zealand that is 'perhaps the most remarkable of all our colonies.'[33]

Baden-Powell's imagined geography is notable, because most antipodean travel texts tend to survey the Australian colonies from the west coast to the south east (following the shipping routes), before embarking on a side trip to New Zealand. Depending on the attitude and intentions of the traveller, some colonies receive only passing attention; for example, brief stops at the Swan River colony en route to Adelaide tend to receive cursory coverage, particularly after mid-century when the sheer volume of travel texts forced aspiring authors to consider their contribution within a saturated literary market. Constrained first by particular shipping routes, then by railway lines (and the inevitable troubles of mismatched gauges between the colonies), travellers followed highly regularised itineraries.[34] Some writers distinguished themselves by extended periods of residence 'up country', particularly once the gold rush provided a new market for Australian travelogues, although this textual seam was soon well picked over. As early as 1859, Frank Fowler promised that he would not drag his readers 'for the thousandth time' through the Australian gold fields:

> Bored enough must he be with 'sinkings,' drowsed enough with 'cradles,' and crushed enough with quartz; while profound must be his conviction, after reading those digging chronicles which promise so much and fulfil so little, that all is not gold that glitters – since it may be only mica![35]

Travel further afield could offer some variety, as at the newer Queensland settlements once settlement was opened up from the 1850s, for example. Some travellers saw New Zealand only as a side trip that threw the virtues of the Australian colonies into relief; others, more interestingly, preferred New Zealand to Australia. What these travel texts reveal, then, are the fine discriminations between antipodean locales that were being made on the ground by settler colonists, and the perceptions of these by imperial travellers.

The fallibility of knowledge collected by itinerant observers was acknowledged by local (and sometimes metropolitan) critics and subsequent travel writers. Of particular note was Froude's *Oceana*. Because Froude had a reputation as an eminent historian as well as a professional travel writer, critics, colonists, and readers were excoriating about his shortcomings. One subsequent traveller made explicit Froude's responsibility to his readers: the public 'are too much in the habit of attributing infallibility to a great author, and to take their opinions ready-made from such an authority'.[36] Katherine Bates began her book by noting the colonial reception of Froude: despite his 'fulsome flattery', Froude had 'failed to please everybody ... poor Froude's name in Australasia is as the red rag to the Colonial bull'.[37] Bates goes on to label Australia as a second- or third-rate England, and a caricature of America: she much prefers New Zealand. She is also acutely aware that travel to the settler colonies has already become part of a commercial tourism industry by the late 1880s, and decries the loss of 'old instincts of hospitality' which used to see visitors welcomed by locals and accommodated in private homes. Now, she regrets, the visitor must stay in hotels and, instead of being revered for bringing 'the atmosphere of the dear old country with him, is now spoken of as a "globetrotter" and a "sponge"'. Technologies of communication and of transport have ensured that New Zealand is no longer out of touch with England, so that they can 'dispense with the society of the tourist unless he has some exceptional qualities to recommend him to their notice'.[38] By the late 1880s, then, we can see evident scepticism about the print culture that had thoroughly mapped the British world, especially in the antipodean settler colonies. So, too, the rise of tourism industries augured the kind of ennui that would later feed twentieth-century nostalgia for a pre-modern, and non-globalised, travel culture.

Mobility and cultural difference

Although imperial observers often sought to make clear-cut distinctions between Australian and New Zealand colonies, they frequently found that trans-Tasman mobility seriously tested their assumptions. Travellers typically assume that while they are mobile, the subjects of their attention are fixed in place.[39] Yet, as an example, many found that ex-convicts had moved to New Zealand. Elim Henry D'Avigdor described the New Zealand gold fields as occupied by thousands of diggers, 'mostly fine young fellows from England, and America, and Germany, and Italy'. Age could indicate a doubtful background: 'If you saw a man with a wrinkle on his face or grey hairs, you might be sure that he was some old "lag" escaped from Tasmania ... And those old chaps weren't up to any good ... They were up to tricks they liked better than hard work.'[40] By the late 1880s, reminders of earlier colonial modes were partly titillating for British travellers, but they were also uncomfortable reminders of an unsavoury past for which travelling Britons might need to account. Bates found that those who guarded convicts had similar mobility. Her encounter with John Gale – ex-governor of Pentridge Gaol in Melbourne, whom she finds in Glenorchy at Lake Wakatipu – invokes the horrors of Marcus Clarke's *For the Term of His Natural Life*, given that Gale had served with Captain Price ('made famous under a *nom de plume*' in the novel) and had witnessed his murder at Williamstown. Bates quickly passes over Gale's scepticism at the sensationalist representation, in order to focus on criminality and heredity: 'after an experience of thirty years, he is convinced that crime is as much inherited as drunkenness or insanity ... I have never known one reformation that was both genuine and lasting. It is born and bred in the bone.' Bates' conclusion is frankly eugenicist:[41] '[C]riminals should not be allowed to marry, and so go on providing inmates for asylums and gaols.'[42] Convictism and its aftermath, resurfacing throughout the antipodean colonies, provided not only salacious copy for travel writers but also a disruptive counterpart to the supposed triumphal progression of Anglo-Saxon culture and blood.

The distinctly modern eugenicist rhetoric of the Greater Britain travellers sought to unite the British Empire through images of blood and family. Thus Froude proudly orates: 'The people of England have made the colonies. The people at home and the people in the colonies are one people ... We ourselves – the forty-five millions of British subjects, those at home and those already settled upon it – are a realised family which desires not to be divided.'[43] Yet the history of convict transportation troubled many visitors less prone to speechifying, or with more subversive intentions than proponents of imperial federation. In 1847, George French Angas was astounded at the beauty of Sydney: 'Whatever may be the defects of the convict system, it has done all this. The criminals of Great Britain have built a city that has risen to be the metropolis of the south.'[44] In 1879, such claims were embarrassing: Henry Cornish backed his argument that Western Australia was politically 'the most backward of all the colonies ... on account of the strong convict element in the population'. He asserted that the end of transportation meant a loss of good opportunity for 'erring gentlemen', claiming that some old convicts who were not free to return to the United Kingdom were 'connected by blood ties with very high families in England', often convicted of 'the aristocratic crime' of forgery: 'one cannot regret, for their sakes, that they were sent across the sea'.[45] Baden-Powell was equally unsure that a convict origin could prove beneficial; instead, like many others by late century, he hoped that these traits would simply die out. The convict element, he assured his readers, 'is fast becoming absorbed, and disappearing off the face of the earth, owing to the fact that no convicts have been allowed to land for many years ... The next generation then being brought up, often in England, with every advantage, all traces of convictism are rapidly becoming eliminated.'[46] Others found evidence instead of the continuation of transportation cultures, and were explicit about England's culpability. Fowler located 'the last attenuated remnant of convictism' in the 'rowdy and Bohemian' parts of colonial cities, where

> the most hideous developments of old and new world ruffianism are presented. This is worth recording; because as all such places in Australia owe their origin and, in fact, their population, to convictism, it is not out of place to inform our governing classes at home of the harm they inflict upon a country by making it, even in its infancy, a depôt for the scum and scoundrelism of the old world.[47]

The convict taint could account for the greater comfort in New Zealand, compared to Australian colonies, for the delicate sensibilities of some imperial travellers (provided they ignored evidence of trans-Tasman mobility). On such matters, Dilke was clear: the colonies are dominated by the 'very scum and outcasts' of the Anglo-Saxons. Their economic success – emphasised as statistically impressive in Dilke's boostering narrative – gives rise to a moment of concern: could the mother country be 'overshadowed by America and Australia'?[48] Dilke was quick to counter this idea, though other travellers sometimes found something different in their settler colonial explorations.

Travel writers who had extended residence in the colonies provided considerable evidence to contradict sensationalist accounts of convict life. Kathleen Lambert – who travelled in the Australian colonies in 1843 as a young child, until her marriage returned her to England – published *The Golden South* in 1890 under the pen-name 'Lyth'. She was a staunch defender of the dignity of colonists and used telling anecdotes to persuade her English readers. One relates to a faithful family retainer – that stalwart of Victorian fiction – whose convict origins are unknown to her until she sits reading with him in his dotage. One day, 'he remarked in answer to some question of mine, "You see, Miss, I was lagged very young, so can remember those times well." "What, Sam! were you sent to Australia?" was my shocked question. "Yes, Miss," in an apologetical tone; "but not for a very bad crime; they called it poaching ... ".'[49] Lyth belatedly realises that Sam had long ago been assigned to the family, and had stayed ever since; his character was unimpeachable. To those who slighted Australian colonists because of their origins, Lyth answers directly from her experience: 'In my long sojourn in Australia I have met with some [ex-convicts], and many of their descendants, but, with very few exceptions, have found them kind, generous, and clever, like other folk – in fact, better than many who have emigrated.' She concludes: 'No wonder an Australian is proud of his country, which appears to me the most wonderful example of the determined energy of the Anglo-Saxon race.'[50] Here the old story about a convict stain becomes instead part of a modern narrative of English racial improvement, in ways which would have seriously disturbed proponents of racial purity and moral virtue.

Not only convictism disrupted seamless imperial narratives. The sheer mobility of settlers concerned visitors, who assumed that only they had access to portability and its privileges.[51] Froude finds in Ohinemutu that the 'river of tourists' is flowing, with thirty-five new arrivals at their hotel during his trip, mainly Australians on excursion; he had previously met several of them in Melbourne or Sydney.[52] Froude examines the young Australian tourists with some caution. Noting that they are 'English-born and English in character', he nevertheless confirms his suspicion that 'young Australians, growing in the full sunshine of modern ideas, were less absolutely benefited by those ideas than true believers in them could desire'. Concerned about their conviction of their own embodiment of progress and development, Froude is troubled that colonial youth have been led to believe that 'each age is necessarily wiser and better than the age which preceded it, and therefore that no man, or set of men, had yet existed who could be compared morally or intellectually with themselves'.[53] Froude's concern was not just elderly humbug but a real – and widely shared – conservative concern with the ideologies of colonial improvement. The young Oxford graduate C. E. R. Schwartze was frank, and made the political point clear: he objected to 'the hollowness of the so-called democracy; and of the degrading worship of wealth'. There was also 'the extraordinary habit of self-glorification in which the ordinary Australian loves to indulge, and to that boastfulness which is so apparent among even the best people'.[54]

Expecting to find in the colonies a perfect copy of England and the imperial self, the Greater Britain traveller could be disconcerted to find that Englishness in the colonies had mutated into something slightly different. As Penny Edmonds suggests, 'Rather than being places of Anglo-Saxon triumph, confidence, and sameness ... the colonies were often places of anxiety and bewilderment, uneasy emergent colonial modernities for both newcomers and indigenous peoples alike.'[55] New Zealand's image as a working-man's paradise was lauded by some visitors, and awkwardly glossed by others. D'Avigdor favourably compares working-class cultures in England and the antipodes, noting the generosity and good humour between classes evident in Melbourne. He muses: 'though they say to "new chums" from England, "We are as good as you are," and this assertion appears offensive, yet their behaviour goes a long way to prove it. Are things not what they seem? Are we all wrong in our old world, and is there something in Democracy, after all?'[56] Katherine Bates gained a similar insight, though with the reverse political effects. Discussing New Zealand's franchise with a fellow traveller, she confesses that her experience of a culture in which working interests were integrated had somewhat shaken her anti-Conservative views: '"Yes," he answered, "I am not surprised to hear you say so. In England you are only playing at democracy. Here you see it worked out, and it means mob rule, with the result of ruin to the country."'[57] Bates rejects this cynical analysis, but it is evident that her experience of 'Underbred colonials' challenges her personally and politically.[58]

These modern colonial social formations were not identical across the Australian and New Zealand colonies during the period 1860s–90s, but neither were they entirely distinguishable, especially by itinerant commentators. This too proved unsettling for travellers looking for evidence of the continuity of Anglo-Saxon blood and culture, and finding instead both colonial difference from the metropole *and* intra-colonial difference.

Articulations of difference: conclusions

James Buzard detects in Anthony Trollope's *Australia and New Zealand* the 'uncanny effect' whereby New Zealand, the epitome of the 'little England abroad' trope, is also the site where Indigenous difference – and Māori authority – must be explicitly accounted for in the traveller's narrative.[59] A broad survey of travel writing about the settler colonies confirms Buzard's claim. While it was possible to travel throughout the Australian colonies and not, astonishingly, mention Aboriginal cultures, the same was not true of travel to New Zealand. In part because Māori participated energetically in nascent tourism markets, and Aborigines did not, imperial travellers had to deal with race differently across the Tasman. Travellers almost always visited the Pink and White Terraces – and, after their destruction, Rotorua and the Hot Lakes – and encountered the famous Māori guide Sophia Hinerangi. C. E. R. Schwartze had Sophia as his guide in 1885, and claimed to find the Lakes to be little known: this fact 'enabled us to travel through a comparatively new, and in some places really unknown, territory, and to feel that for once we were "off the line"'. Schwartze was interested in the Māori as well as the scenery – 'To see these strange people in the small remnant of territory which is still their own, should repay any trouble and any inconvenience on the journey' – yet he misses the fact that this is hardly virgin tourist territory.[60] Indeed, Guide Sophia's presence in travel writing had by this time became a cliché: thus Bates comments that she goes to call on 'the famous "Sophia"' at the Terraces, noting that her 'manners in their quiet dignity and self-possession would do credit to any London drawing-room'.[61] Lydia Wevers has acutely analysed the fraught negotiations between Māori communities and travellers over the economies of tourism, noting that an increased tourist trade produced 'a conflict between what travellers regard as an entitlement [seeing sights] and the Maori perceive as a form of intellectual property right' that made cultural difference unavoidable, if uncomfortable, for many travellers.[62]

Outside of particular and unusual mission stations in the 1880s, tourists in Australia simply could not claim the same regularised and commodified access to Aboriginal culture.[63] Aboriginal people and culture were noted by travellers, and in detail by some, but it was also quite common for Indigenous issues to go largely unremarked by imperial travellers. Indeed, despite a long history of conflict between settlers and Aborigines, most often sites that had witnessed settler deaths at the hands of Aborigines were memorialised, rather than the vastly more common sites of white violence against Aborigines. Of course, this is the work of settler myth-making: obscuring the violence that produced settler hegemony, and inserting a new narrative of settler sacrifice and historicity. Gaye Sculthorpe suggests that the late nineteenth and early twentieth centuries marked the beginning of 'a form of tourism focused on Aboriginal people and culture', particularly in relation to domestic travel to sites of Aboriginal reserves or camps.[64] Such tourism often figured the imminent demise of Aboriginal people, in a disturbing rhetoric of replacement. Thus, in his 1886 travel guide *Australian Pictures Drawn from Pen and Pencil*, Howard Willoughby describes the 'favourable circumstances' brought about by government and mission stations, whereby 'full-blood' populations were dying out, and 'half-caste' Aborigines were being distributed through the general population. In this instance, the 'dying race' trope instigates a timely touristic imperative: 'The visitor should not miss the opportunity of inspecting one of the establishments, most of which are easily reached ... [and where] he is sure of a hospitable reception.'[65] Earlier traces of this kind of historical tourism, which share its ghoulish triumphalism, are evident primarily in Tasmania, where the infamous imperial experiment of removing Indigenous people from the path of settler expansion could hardly go unmentioned by most travellers from the 1830s onwards. Yet across the Australian colonies, travellers' accounts often emphasised the suffering of settlers, rather than Indigenes, and a rhetoric of mourning and memorialisation regularly focused on white colonial subjects rather than dispossessed Aborigines.

These distinctions between the settler colonies matter, as Tony Ballantyne argues, because they help to 'explore the dynamics through which specific places developed and the ways in which the nation ... took shape'. They also enable us to see how the settler colonies played an essential role in broader movements: imperial regimes, capitalism, globalisation, and modernity.[66] This is a *distinctive* role, as historians since Denoon have noted, although critics have often found it complex and uncomfortable to discern the particular nature of settler colonial difference given the predominance of eugenicist and racial discourse from the period, even if it was more than just race (or blood) that mattered.

Re-orienting our scholarly attention from the centre to the periphery, as the chapters in this volume do, also reveals new ways of analysing the global implications of imperial thinking. Trans-Tasman alliances and differences shift the dominant assumptions of a view from the metropolitan centre, a lesson as relevant to current scholarship as it was in the nineteenth century. Evidence from the colonial peripheries suggests that a new 'geomodernity', in Laura Doyle and Laura Winkiel's terms, can be traced from the 1860s: for instance, a settler modernity that was rather less interested in England than the English might have hoped. Doyle and Winkiel propose 'geomodernity' as 'a locational approach to modernisms' engagement with cultural and political discourses of global modernity'. This is, they suggest, a way to foreground 'an uneven, often racialized global modernity'.[67] The ideas underpinning the Greater Britain travellers, vastly popular in the metropole, often looked quite different in the settler colonies. Luke Gibbons situates late nineteenth-century Ireland as part of a series of *'alternative* or *discrepant* modernities, no less intent on determining their own futures as their dominant Western counterparts but not necessarily following in their footsteps'. For Gibbons, 'peripheral modernities' often built from old imperial structures, through which distant cultures, 'though underdeveloped and remote from each other … were yoked together through the exigencies of empire and propelled into a strange, violent proximity'. These could be seen in Paul Gilroy's articulation of the 'Black Atlantic', in colonial political economies, or, for Gibbons, in the enormous outflows of Irish emigration.[68]

Concerted efforts to yoke together blood and race as part of a renovated late nineteenth-century white empire remind us just how important New Zealand and other settler colonial possessions were to the British, even as those possessions sidled towards political independence. Considering the trans-Tasman settler colonies as a distinctive case study of such a 'peripheral modernity' casts new light upon the importance of the settler world, but also upon the new, rough, and improvisational global formations that tried to imagine and regulate it.

Notes

1 George Smyth Baden-Powell, *New Homes for the Old Country. A Personal Experience of the Political and Domestic Life, the Industries, and the Natural History of Australia and New Zealand*, 2 vols (London: Richard Bentley & Son, 1872). George, politician and author, was the elder brother of the Scouting Baden-Powell.

2 Lydia Wevers, *Country of Writing: Travel Writing and New Zealand, 1809–1900* (Auckland: Auckland University Press, 2002).

3 See Frances Steel, *Oceania Under Steam: Sea Transport and the Cultures of Colonialism, c.1870–1914* (Manchester: Manchester University Press, 2011).

4 Charles Wentworth Dilke, *Greater Britain: A Record of Travel in English-Speaking Countries During 1866 and 1867* (London: MacMillan & Co., 1868).

5 Baden-Powell, *New Homes for the Old Country*, pp. 1, 2.

6 Alice Anne, Duchess of Buckingham and Chandos, *Glimpses of Four Continents: Letters Written During a Tour in Australia, New Zealand, and North America, in 1893* (London: John Murray, 1894), pp. vii–viii.

7 E. Katherine Bates, *Kaleidoscope: Shifting Scenes from East to West* (London: Ward & Downey, 1889), p. 72.

8 Bates, *Kaleidoscope*, p. iv.

9 Bates, *Kaleidoscope*, pp. ix–x.

10 J. D., *Ninety Days' Privilege Leave to Australia, Tasmania, and New Zealand, 1885* (Allahabad, India: Pioneer Press, 1886), p. 2.

11 J. D., *Ninety Days'*, p. 101.

12 Tamara S. Wagner, 'Introduction', in Tamara S. Wagner (ed.), *Victorian Settler Narratives: Emigrants, Cosmopolitans, and Returnees in Nineteenth-Century Literature* (London: Pickering & Chatto, 2011).

13 Keith Hanley and Greg Kucich, 'Introduction: Global formations and recalcitrances', *Nineteenth-Century Contexts*, 29:2–3 (2007), 76, citing Malcolm Waters.

14 Lorenzo Veracini, *Settler Colonialism: A Theoretical Overview* (Houndmills: Palgrave Macmillan, 2010). See in particular chapter 4.

15 Dror Wahrman, 'The meaning of the nineteenth century: Reflections on James Belich's Replenishing the Earth', *Victorian Studies*, 53:1 (2010), 96.
16 James Anthony Froude, *Oceana: Or England and Her Colonies*, new edn. (London: Longmans, Green, & Co., 1886), p. 264.
17 Tony Ballantyne, 'Rereading the archive and opening up the nation-state: Colonial knowledge in South Asia (and beyond)', in Antoinette Burton (ed.), *After the Imperial Turn: Thinking With and Through the Nation* (Durham, NC: Duke University Press, 2003), p. 104.
18 Alan Lester, *Imperial Networks: Creating Identities in Nineteenth-Century South Africa and Britain* (London and New York: Routledge, 2001); Peter Hulme, 'Postcolonial theory and early America: An approach from the Caribbean', in Robert Blair St. George (ed.), *Possible Pasts: Becoming Colonial in Early America* (Ithaca, NY: Cornell University Press, 2000).
19 Sidney Smith, *Whether To Go and Whither? Or, The Cape and The Great South Land. Being a Practical View of the Whole Southern Fields of Settlement, with Full Information for Intending Emigrants* (London: John Kendrick, 1849), p. xxv.
20 Smith, *Whether To Go*, p. vii.
21 Froude, *Oceana*, p. 15.
22 George French Angas, *Savage Life and Scenes in Australia and New Zealand: Being an Artist's Impressions of Countries and People at the Antipodes*, 2 vols (London: Smith, Elder, & Co., 1847).
23 Donald Denoon, *Settler Capitalism: The Dynamics of Dependent Development in the Southern Hemisphere* (Oxford: Clarendon, 1983), p. 3.
24 See Ann Laura Stoler, *Race and the Education of Desire: Foucault's History of Sexuality and the Colonial Order of Things* (Durham, NC: Duke University Press, 1995), p. 15.
25 Dilke, *Greater Britain*, p. vii.
26 Dilke, *Greater Britain*, p. 407.
27 James Buzard, 'Portable boundaries: Trollope, race, and travel', *Nineteenth-Century Contexts*, 32:1 (2010), 9.
28 Froude, *Oceana*, p. 133.
29 Froude, *Oceana*, pp. 329, 132–3.
30 James Belich, *Replenishing the Earth: The Settler Revolution and the Rise of the Anglo-World, 1783–1939* (Oxford: Oxford University Press, 2009), pp. 466–7.
31 Belich, *Replenishing the Earth*, p. 467.
32 Wahrman, 'The meaning of the nineteenth century', p. 96.
33 Baden-Powell, *New Homes for the Old Country*, pp. 57, 9.
34 See Steel, *Oceania under Steam*.
35 Frank Fowler, *Southern Lights and Shadows: Being Brief Notes of Three Years' Experience of Social, Literary, and Political Life in Australia* (London: Sampson Low, 1859), pp. 5–6.
36 Elim Henry D'Avigdor, *Antipodean Notes Collected on a Nine Months' Tour Round the World* (London: Sampson Low, Marston, Searle, & Rivington, 1888), pp. 9–10.
37 Bates, *Kaleidoscope*, p. iii.
38 Bates, *Kaleidoscope*, p. 72.
39 Julia Kuehn and Paul Smethurst (eds), *Travel Writing, Form, and Empire: The Poetics and Politics of Mobility, Routledge Research in Travel Writing* (New York and London: Routledge, 2009).
40 D'Avigdor, *Antipodean Notes*, p. 47.
41 The link between travel practices and eugenicist thought are intriguing. I examine elsewhere the link between Francis Galton's African travels and his later coining of the term 'eugenics'. Anna Johnston, '"Greater Britain": Late imperial travel writing and the settler colonies', in Richard D. Fulton and Peter H. Hoffenberg (eds), *Oceania and the Victorian Imagination: Where All Things Are Possible* (Farnham: Ashgate, 2013).
42 Bates, *Kaleidoscope*, pp. 66–8.
43 Froude, *Oceana*, p. 13.

44 Angas, *Savage Life and Scenes*, p. 189.
45 Henry Cornish, *Under the Southern Cross* (Madras: 'Mail' Press, 1879), pp. 31–2.
46 Baden-Powell, *New Homes for the Old Country*, p. 30.
47 Fowler, *Southern Lights and Shadows*, p. 44.
48 Dilke, *Greater Britain*, p. 407.
49 'Lyth', *The Golden South: Memories of Australian Home Life from 1843 to 1888* (London: Ward & Downey, 1890), p. 164.
50 'Lyth', *The Golden South*, pp. 15–16.
51 John Plotz, *Portable Property: Victorian Culture on the Move* (Princeton, NJ: Princeton University Press, 2008).
52 Froude, *Oceana*, p. 253.
53 Froude, *Oceana*, pp. 238–9.
54 C. E. R. Schwartze, *Travels in Greater Britain* (London: Cassell & Co., 1885), p. 111.
55 Penelope Edmonds, '"I Followed England Round the World": The rise of trans-imperial Anglo-Saxon exceptionalism, and the spatial narratives of nineteenth-century British settler colonies of the Pacific Rim', in Leigh Boucher, Jane Carey, and Katherine Ellinghaus (eds), *Re-Orienting Whiteness* (New York: Palgrave Macmillan, 2009), p. 109.
56 D'Avigdor, *Antipodean Notes*, p. 26.
57 Bates, *Kaleidoscope*, p. 77.
58 Bates, *Kaleidoscope*, p. 65.
59 Buzard, 'Portable boundaries', p. 15.
60 Schwartze, *Travels in Greater Britain*, p. 119.
61 Bates, *Kaleidoscope*, p. 99.
62 Wevers, *Country of Writing*, p. 185.
63 See, for example, Peter Carolane, 'Parallel fantasies: Tourism and Aboriginal Mission at Lake Tyers in the late nineteenth century', in Amanda Barry, Joanna Cruikshank, Andrew Brown-May, and Patricia Grimshaw (eds), *Evangelists of Empire? Missionaries in Colonial History* (Melbourne: University of Melbourne eScholarship Research Centre, 2008).
64 Gaye Sculthorpe, 'When whitefellas go walkabout', in Sylvia Kleinert and Margo Neale (eds), *The Oxford Companion to Aboriginal Art and Culture* (South Melbourne: Oxford University Press, 2000), p. 391.
65 Howard Willoughby, *Australian Pictures Drawn from Pen and Pencil* (London: Religious Tract Society, 1886), pp. 175–6.
66 Tony Ballantyne, *Webs of Empire: Locating New Zealand's Colonial Past* (Wellington: Bridget Williams, 2012), p. 264.
67 Laura Doyle and Laura Winkiel (eds), *Geomodernisms: Race, Modernism, Modernity* (Bloomington: Indiana University Press, 2005), p. 3.
68 Luke Gibbons, 'Peripheral modernities: National and global in a post-colonial frame', *Nineteenth-Century Contexts*, 29:2–3 (2007), 272.

CHAPTER FIVE

Law's mobility: vagrancy and imperial legality in the trans-Tasman colonial world, 1860s–1914

Catharine Coleborne

This chapter adds to our understanding of 'New Zealand's empire' in two ways: first, by suggesting that by the 1860s, New Zealand was forging a legal culture of its own inside an existing imperial world of law and legality; and second, by offering a new focus on the legal regulation of colonial mobility. Mobility has been explored by demographers, migration scholars, and geographers, and in the context of historical studies of social class movement.[1] This chapter deploys the concept of mobility to examine the history of vagrancy in colonial New Zealand, and the laws that were introduced to contain it. By privileging the themes of population movement, colonial transience, and the occupation of new social and physical space, the chapter examines the way that undesirable forms of movement were made visible by laws and the criminalisation of the transient poor, also examining the role of law and order in the formation of New Zealand's identity as a colonial power.

Bringing legal-historical sources into view to draw attention to law as part of the broader history of New Zealand's 'empire', the chapter draws from a slice of data: a sample of just over 200 cases of vagrants sentenced in New Zealand in the late nineteenth century whose details were reported in the *New Zealand Police Gazette* (*NZPG*). It also refers to the *New Zealand Parliamentary Debates* (*NZPD*), newspapers, and other contemporary sources, to show the range of ways in which the history of past unwanted mobility might be uncovered. Geographer Tim Cresswell suggests that it is mobility which 'lies at the centre of the vagrant's career'. It was the vagrant's 'mobility that necessitated new laws, regulations and forms of surveillance'.[2] Viewed from this angle, mobility itself, embodied in the vagrant, was the problem. Since the late eighteenth century in Britain, vagrants as 'vagabonds' had been categorised as a separate 'class' of the very poor, given the threat posed by unmoored, mobile people in a society deeply concerned with structured inequality, and practices of the provision of local, parish welfare to the deserving poor.[3]

With one eye on the imperial context for New Zealand's own development as a polity, this chapter therefore draws attention to both the question of mobility, and also the negative meanings of mobility which came from an early modern world concept of 'settlement', and seeped into the colonial worlds of new settlers.[4] How these social, cultural and legal 'transpositions of empire' came to command authority in new places tells us a great deal about the way that colonial law makers were always already embedded inside imperial worlds of meaning.[5] Moreover, the particular and specific articulations of settler colonialism, or imperialism 'on the ground', meant that new colonial laws surrounding vagrancy, in particular, contained stronger and somewhat harsh provisions for the sentencing of convicted vagrants. In addition, these laws foregrounded colonial relationships across ethnic lines. Colonialism, then, encouraged a more deliberate legal strategy for containing populations of the mobile: strategies that contemporaries themselves hotly debated.

In the 1860s New Zealand was in the process of creating a culture of empire that turned on its status as a 'becoming nation' of the British Empire; and at the same time, it reached across the Tasman Sea to form common cultures of legality in the trans-colonial world, a process which had been ongoing during the colonisation period. Although scholars point out that mobility was desirable for some, but barred for others – only some groups enjoyed the 'perfect liberty of locomotion',[6] in the words of one contemporary – few have analysed the complexities in the legal-historical construction of the mobile populations across distinct sites.[7] To put it another way, mobility relied on stasis for its very definition. In the settler–colonial context of these places, mobility was frequently treated as the implied condition of unsettling populations: of Indigenous, itinerant, or racial 'others'. Yet it was settler–colonial mobility which formed the colonial world; this was a world that operated across multiple connecting points and networks, as scholars show.[8]

Law and its personnel traversed New Zealand's empire. This study of the regulation of mobility might best be understood within this regional trans-colonial world which was actively engaged in acts of shaping its own forms of imperial and colonial rule *across* what would later become national boundaries and borders.[9] Focusing its attention on New Zealand, this chapter shows how New Zealand's empire was also a trans-colonial space, one traversed by the mobile peoples and laws of the region.

The laws of vagrancy

Law was a particularly important aspect of the ways in which the colonial world was structured. Laws defining and containing vagrancy represent something of the imperial world from which they sprang.[10] The concept of vagrancy has a long history inside British imperial law.[11] Histories of vagrancy include wandering mendicants; nomadic peoples; vagabonds and robbers; strangers; those struck out of society including lepers; tramps; and children vulnerable to institutional care, among many other types of vagrant peoples. The legal practices that controlled these forms of wandering included ordinances before the twelfth century, and stronger forms of legislation by the 1500s. Strong interest in the meanings of these laws was generated by the late nineteenth century, and by the very subject of vagrancy as a crime.[12]

Deeply articulated legal cultures of empire, as Lauren Benton suggests, 'travelled with imperial officials, merchants, sailors, soldiers, sojourners, settlers, captives, and even pirates', meaning that the ideas and beliefs about the containment of movement were derived from those who had been policing movement in other contexts before their arrival in the colonies.[13] Not only did the laws and practices of imperial Britain lay 'the foundation for the Australian legal system', thereby enforcing British control and hegemony, they also 'enabled British settlers to carry with them many of the laws of England'.[14] This legacy is relevant to New Zealand, because like the Australian colonies, the antecedents of New Zealand's modern vagrancy laws can, then, be situated within a genealogy of repressive statutes.[15] Blackstone's *Commentaries on the Laws of England*, for example, when describing vagrancy, quoted from 'ancient' statutes, reinforcing the notion of vagrants as a specific social class: referring to persons who slept all day, were awake all night, frequented drinking establishments, and belonged in no place.[16] As legal historian Alex Castles points out, however, Blackstone also identified that new colonies would come to set out specific legal provisions for different aspects of social life.[17]

Law was also a 'central mechanism' of the colonial project, integral to the creation of knowledge about people and populations, allocating control, and constructing social difference.[18] At the same time as mobile peoples and their various forms of mobility characterised Australian and New Zealand colonial worlds, laws, too, were mobile, moving with immigrants – who themselves occupied 'transient spaces' – and were amplified in the process of their translation into new settings.[19] This 'increasingly complex field of social governance' evident in settler polities included settler attitudes towards crime, welfare and poverty, land ownership, property, labour, and the regulation of private life.[20] The colonies became an exceedingly complex field for social reform and social welfare initiatives between the 1860s and 1870s in Australia – especially Victoria – and in New Zealand. In the absence of a Poor Law, a web of social institutions and welfare measures existed.[21] Responding to the very poor was not just a matter of policy and practice, but cut right into the heart of the social fabric of new settlements and their populations.[22]

Vagrancy laws in both colonial New Zealand and across the Tasman derived from the Vagrancy Act of 1824 (UK). In Britain, this law followed in the wake of decades of the Enclosure Acts of the eighteenth century, and the continued implementation of enclosure well into the nineteenth century, which forced many people off the land, leaving them homeless and destitute. The end of the Napoleonic War (1803–15) had also precipitated the greater mobility of peoples. Drawn to the urban areas for factory labour, many of these people were forced away from rural lands, including waste lands where they had been gleaners, and they lived in utterly appalling circumstances. There was a 'vagrant underworld' in Britain from 1815, situating vagrancy within an unsettled world of industrialising, post-war restlessness.[23] The 1824 Act was designed to rationalise the many different criminal laws relating to vagrancy which had become inadequate over a long period of time. In addition, practices of removing paupers under existing Poor Laws, and of supporting 'passing vagrants' with parish funds, both of which meant that vagrant and wandering people were given assistance to be relocated back to their own places of origin, had become expensive, and were also open to frequent abuse.[24]

Without a history of poor laws, and with only fledgling systems of outdoor relief and charity, colonial governments could not apply this 1824 law directly to the colonies. However, the law did become a model for the colonial legislature.[25] Offenders were divided into three categories: 'idle and disorderly persons'; 'rogues and vagabonds'; and 'incorrigible rogues'. This was a flexible law, one used to arrest people on a mere *suspicion* of being somehow 'disorderly', and in this way was distinct from other criminal laws. There were two specific differences which set the colonial legislation apart from its imperial model from the 1830s. A clause modelled on imperial legislation about 'consorting with gypsies' translated as associating with Aborigines in New South Wales in 1835.[26] Similarly, as the chapter explains below, the New Zealand legislation of 1866 contained a provision to prosecute vagrant Europeans who were viewed to be consorting with Māori or 'aboriginal natives'.[27] The relationship between vagrancy and the regulation and control of convicts and ex-convicts was also expressed in the New South Wales legislation, illustrating the specific needs of that colonial legal context.[28] In the Australian colonies, a convict class circulated and was viewed as a source of 'social instability and vice', and Aboriginal peoples were perceived to pose different threats to life and property.[29] The introduction of vagrancy laws across the Australian colonies can be read in light of the origins of New South Wales as a penal colony, with historians drawing links between the policing of unwanted movement and cycles of poverty, need, and settlement.[30]

Historically, then, the vagrancy laws are regarded as 'a bundle of diverse offences'.[31] By this, historians mean that such laws tend to elide separate forms of disorderly status under one piece of legislation and, indeed, contemporary observers in New Zealand agreed, pointing out that the law introduced in 1866 was all-encompassing. In most places around the British Empire, vagrancy was viewed as a criminal offence and policed accordingly. In 1835, the first colonial act for the prevention of vagrancy in New South Wales also applied to Port Philip. In 1852, Victoria introduced its own law, one year after becoming a separate colonial entity with its own government. This law proscribed over 100 offences, as Davies points out, including limiting the movement of people who had no visible means of support, begging, consorting, occupying public spaces at night without lawful excuse, and so on. Those arrested were often, though, older, ill, poor, unemployed, as well as juveniles and prostitutes. The 1852 Act was reported across the Tasman in New Zealand newspapers in the common practice of syndicating press stories, but also because there was an interest in the way the Australian colonies managed their populations and legal controls over them.

Fears about colonial movement persisted from the 1850s era into the 1870s and beyond, and were reflected in travellers' narratives as well as in the press. This was a trans-Tasman story, one amplified by the movement of ex-convicts and other mobile people already suspected as criminals, as Englishman Elim D'Avigdor pronounced under his pseudonym 'Wanderer'. The 'Wanderer' remarked on the New Zealand class of 'professional unemployed' by the 1890s.[32] Earlier, *Glimpses of Life in Victoria*, published anonymously in 1872, but thought to be penned by colonist and squatter John Hunter Kerr, includes a chapter titled 'Travellers'. In the Australian colonies, this chapter recounts, a considerable number of people who wandered in search of work or who were 'impelled by a wild disposition', frequented the bush. Some were 'idle vagabonds', others more respectable, but the problem for contemporaries lay in distinguishing between the 'loafers' and the genuine workers. This problem of the so-called 'vagabonds' who abused the hospitality of the locals who fed them led this writer to agree with a 'very stringent law against vagrants', a new colonial law which had its origins in English legislation of the previous two centuries. Considered as a group – a separate 'class' of person – wanderers were regarded as 'a thankless set'.[33] The attitudes expressed towards wanderers and transients in the colonies echoed the much earlier anxieties about vagrants that had circulated among the English population of the early modern era, and arguably well into the eighteenth and nineteenth centuries. The vagrant presented a challenge to the social order of things, because he or she 'broke with the accepted norms of family life'.[34]

In New Zealand, the Vagrant Act was passed in 1866 after three readings, and many suggested changes in wording, not all of which were implemented. Like the 1824 Act in Britain, and its Australian colonial counterparts, the New Zealand law dealt with beggars, prostitution, drunkards, and thieves under the three categories of 'Idle and disorderly persons', 'Rogues and vagabonds', and 'Incorrigible rogues', with the proscribed sentences following conviction set at one month, three months, six months, twelve months, or two years, depending on repeat offending and the severity of the offence. Interestingly, Spiller, Finn, and Boast devote no time at all to New Zealand's Vagrant Act of 1866, despite the fact that it was enforced only twenty-six years after the official colonisation of New Zealand, and therefore represents only one of a few pieces of legislation imported from British Law. Arguably, this should have placed some emphasis on its enactment, especially when coupled with its controlling purpose and the wide reaction to it. Several earlier vagrancy ordinances existed before the 1866 law in New Zealand, as Richard Hill's histories of policing show.[35]

Concern about the potential infringement of individual freedoms embodied in the law was voiced in the *NZPD*, as well as in the press, before the bill was passed into law.[36] In February of 1865, the *New Zealand Herald* mocked the legislation, commenting that

> in reality it is an Act enabling every person in the Province to take into custody every other person on some vague suspicion that they have sometime or other used insulting language, worn a pair of slippers after dark, or carried a riding-whip or walking-stick, or other weapon for offensive or defensive purposes.[37]

Other newspaper articles and editorials followed suit, also lamenting the inability of the legislation to really achieve what it intended, which was to prevent crime before it happened. Interestingly, one major critique stemmed from the idea that this legislation was 'a transcript of an Imperial act', meaning that it did not fit its purpose in the colony.[38] Later, in the 1880s, religious leaders continued to object to the scope of the act, and suggested amendments to the Contagious

Diseases Act instead of using the existing vagrancy law to deal with prostitution.[39]

The law was also important because it was suggestive, as argued by Miles Fairburn, as legislation which illustrated the several 'constraints on chaos' that were imposed by central government in nineteenth-century New Zealand.[40] Fairburn's analysis shows that vagrancy laws in New Zealand were used to regulate the influx of gold prospectors at a time of social upheaval, with the heavy rate of prosecution declining after the 1880s (and an amendment to the act which abolished habitual drunkenness as a definition for the offence).[41] There was a popular revulsion towards the wanderer or vagrant. The vagrant was, historically, 'feared and loathed', and invested with negative social meanings.[42] The idea, expressed in the second clause of the Act, that Europeans found 'lodging or wandering in company with any of the aboriginal natives of New Zealand' spoke to the anxieties in 1866 about law and order on the frontier in the context of land alienation, and acquisitions of Māori land by the Crown. There was a link between the colonial use of 'shaming words' and specific linguistic forms to describe vagrancy.[43] Part of this fear stemmed from the horror of 'downward mobility' as well as the quick transition from early settlers to identify all newcomers as strangers and outsiders, in both small New Zealand towns and communities and in the colonial cities.[44] These fears were, like the laws that came to manage them, part of the mobile imperial world of which New Zealand's empire was part.

Between 1899 and 1900, of the 200 people arrested for vagrancy in New Zealand, sixty-five were given a relatively stern three-month jail sentence.[45] Their convictions, listed in the *NZPG*, provide us with some sense of what the vagrancy laws of the 1860s enabled the colonial authorities to achieve by the turn of the century. The policing of women and men in public places for wandering, idling and stopping, being offensive, or predation and acts of solicitation for prostitution was, by then, commonplace. Roughly equal numbers of men and women were sentenced, and many had numerous prior convictions for vagrancy. These recidivist offenders, having collected a variety of scars, tattoos, and wounds, became known over time to the police in their various locales. Most of the women were designated as prostitutes; the male vagrants were from different walks of life.

Among those sentenced were the Danish labourer, William Holst, aged 52, who had only one leg and was tried in Wanganui for vagrancy and drunkenness; Isaac Keighly, a partly-blind cabinet maker tried in Auckland as a 'rogue and vagabond'; and Carrie Corbett, aged 37, who was tried in Wellington for vagrancy and theft. Many others, too, were sentenced for shorter periods. Although some vagrants also ended up inside social and medical institutions, including the Auckland Hospital for the Insane, those tried in the courts and sent to prison were in the majority. A network of welfare and carceral institutions contained this mobility and unauthorised 'stopping', however, and colonial authorities tended to medical and legal solutions for this problematic 'movement' of peoples.

Specific clauses in the New Zealand vagrancy laws, as noted earlier, sought to prevent forms of casual interaction between Māori and Pākehā, showing that these laws, unlike their imperial models, to some extent turned on a colonial preoccupation with managing relationships across the racial divide.[46] Very few Māori were prosecuted for vagrancy themselves, as newspaper reports reveal. Yet by the early years of the twentieth century, other concerns about Māori surfaced, such as the practice of Tohungaism (Māori spiritual and physical healing), which led to the prosecution of some Māori as vagrants, as in the case of Wiremu Te Whitu, arrested in Takapu and charged at Huntly in 1904.[47]

The regulation and control of women working as prostitutes presents insights into the different forms of mobility for colonial women around the British Empire.[48] Of the 200 people arrested between 1899 and 1900 under the Vagrant Act, seventy-eight were women. The vast majority, fifty-five, were arrested for acts of prostitution. Their sentences were typically short and presumably designed to remove them from the streets and from the negative influences of their trade, including alcohol. Around half of the women arrested for prostitution under the Act had several previous convictions. In one extreme case located through newspaper research, Christina Lawson was arrested repeatedly for vagrancy from the 1880s in New Zealand, attracting 181 convictions by 1907 for prostitution and drunkenness.[49]

Reminding us of the relative fluidity and mobility of 'identity' in the colonial world, many of those arrested used 'aliases', possibly to avoid detection. Without passports or identity cards, these subjects were often scrutinised by police and details about their bodily markings, including tattoos, scars, and characteristics, taken down and put on record. One function of the *NZPG* was to aid policing work: the information these publications contained was shared not just around New Zealand but also across the Tasman in the Australian colonies. Red hair, baldness, burn marks, broken fingers, a dent in the forehead, lost testicles, prominent lips: all of these physical characteristics came to define vagrants arrested more than once. Some became known to the police: their recognisable features, along with their patterns of movement and stasis, now gave them away to law enforcers.

The question of vagrancy: mobile peoples and mobile laws

If the laws of New Zealand derived from the imperial world, so did the attitudes towards vagrancy itself. By the 1890s, a 'hardened' view of the casual poor had begun to characterise debates in Britain. Many of the attitudes towards the very poor also travelled with immigrants and new settlers across the British world from the late eighteenth century and well into the nineteenth century. The very poor who were left behind by the outcomes of rapid industrialisation and imperial labour markets were no longer the focus of so much sympathetic social and political commentary. They were now regarded with suspicion, as argued by Gareth Stedman Jones, like criminals; their poverty was in fact increasingly criminalised.[50] There was an increased moralising of the conditions of the 'casual poor', and the prevalence of the view that the poor were social outcasts who posed a threat; in fact, Jones draws attention to the changing identities of the casual poor in this age of imperialism, which was also an age of mobility.[51] In this era, we can see in the records of institutionalised people the effects of this hardening on labouring men in Britain: institutionalised men suffered from an 'intense fear of poverty and deep anxiety about their economic future'.[52] This partly derived from new codes of masculine behaviour for labouring men.[53]

This idea of a 'hardening' fits with Fairburn's thesis about the 'moral panic' over vagrancy in New Zealand: there was a strong sense that immigrants would bring with them old world problems. When this attitude collided with the realities of seasonal and transient work for men, contemporaries faced the difficulty of social classification: some men looked vagrant even if they were not. In addition, it was increasingly emasculating and unrespectable for men to rely upon welfare. The poor, the different, and the transient became outcasts. This was true for James Cox, whose 'days of darkness' spent as a vagrant due to unemployment in the early 1890s coloured the rest of his life. In a rare first-hand account of vagrancy, Cox recounts his severe depression and poor health, and detailed his own movement around the North Island.[54] The account of his mobility reminds readers of the sheer physical feat of being a swagger, a wandering man in search of work, shelter, and food, in all weather: Cox trekked for several months. He was at the mercy of the generosity of others, wore out his shoes and feet, had little privacy, and experienced privation of spirit. As Fairburn notes, he was not the only man who lived in this way in the 1890s or at other points in New Zealand's colonial past.[55]

Vagrancy as an 'activity' or experience was not restricted to the lives of wandering men looking for work in rural areas during these years of economic depression. Increasingly it became a problem for the urban centres, illustrating the more conspicuous populations of the poor and vagrant in cities from the 1880s onwards. In 1914, Aucklanders were still witnessing the habitats of vagrants: a photograph published in the *Auckland Weekly News* (*AWN*) depicted the dwelling place of a woman 'for several months' among the toi-toi growing in the Auckland Domain. This 'unfortunate woman' had made a place for herself to stop at night, and ventured out, speculated the press, for 'food and clothes' during the day. She was arrested by the police, and the curious dwelling place photographed for the readers of the *AWN*.[56] Arguably this highlighted the popular concern about the colonial-born population slipping into habits of idleness and pauperism, and provided more evidence that the vagrancy law was a useful tool to maintain social order.

Conclusions

By reflecting on the ways in which colonists, settlers, and immigrants to New Zealand imagined controls over the unauthorised mobility of some people and how these concerns expressed themselves in laws, this chapter has suggested that we might also find out more about how the law worked to define a colonial 'category of legal person', particularly since the textual constructions of 'the vagrant' embodied ideas about his or her identity. Locating and analysing just some of the legal-historical sources for the New Zealand history of vagrancy, this chapter has briefly illustrated the marginalisation, regulation, and criminalisation of the many people who upset the imperative to settle in New Zealand. It has also uncovered fresh sources of knowledge about the local effects of mobility within a wider framework of empire.

If, as Cresswell argues, it was the mobility of the vagrant that acted as a 'critique' of established moral geographies, we might also say that the mobility of the imperial laws that modelled categories of social identity for the colonies also carried with them these deeply embedded notions of moral codes for behaviour.[57] These in turn were articulated in colonial contexts against new and existing populations, including Indigenous peoples. As Benton argues, the very familiarity of settlers and colonists with 'a complex legal order' and its attendant rules, procedures, and rhetoric helped to form colonial hegemonic relationships; furthermore, the 'constant referencing of other legal authorities', she suggests, arguably 'intensified in colonial settings'.[58]

The focus suggested by this chapter promises to reveal new insights into the anxieties and imperial world views held by New Zealand as settlers scoped out their own sense of who belonged in a settled society. At the same time, it provides glimpses of the ways mobility was utilised, resisted, and negotiated in the margins of settler society, where Indigenous and colonised peoples retreated – both by choice and force.

Acknowledgments

I acknowledge the excellent research contributions made by Dr Debra Powell and Chelsie Foley. I am also grateful for the provision of research funding from the Contestable Research Fund, the Faculty of Arts and Social Sciences, University of Waikato, 2012–13.

Notes

1 Tim Cresswell and Peter Merriman (eds), *Geographies of Mobilities: Practices, Spaces, Subjects* (Surrey and Burlington, VT: Ashgate, 2011); John Urry, *Mobilities* (Cambridge and Malden, MA: Polity, 2007); Miles Fairburn, 'Vagrants, "folk devils" and nineteenth-century New Zealand as a bondless society', *Historical Studies*, 21:85 (1985), 495–514.

2 Tim Cresswell, 'The vagrant/vagabond: The curious career of a mobile subject', in Cresswell and Merriman (eds), *Geographies of Mobilities*, p. 251.

3 Jeremy Seabrook, *Pauperland: Poverty and the Poor in Britain* (London: C. Hurst & Company, 2013), pp. 67–8.

4 David Rollison, 'Exploding England: The dialectics of mobility and settlement in early modern England', *Social History*, 24:1 (1999), 1–16.

5 Shaunnagh Dorsett and Ian Hunter (eds), *Law and Politics in British Colonial Thought: Transpositions of Empire*, Palgrave Studies in Cultural and Intellectual History (Houndmills and New York: Palgrave Macmillan, 2010).

6 Marilyn Lake and Henry Reynolds, *Drawing the Global Colour Line: White Men's Countries and the International Challenge of Racial Equality*, Critical Perspectives on Empire (Cambridge: Cambridge University Press, 2008), p. 43.

7 Examples of this approach can be found in recently edited issues of the critical legal studies journal *Law Text Culture*; see Volume 15 (2011), 'Under the Eye of the Law: Mobile Peoples in the Pacific', edited by Nan Seuffert and Tahu Kukutai, work which emerged from a University of Waikato research project.

8 Graeme Davison, John William McCarty, and Ailsa McLeary (eds), *Australians 1888* (Sydney: Fairfax, Syme & Weldon, 1987), p. 230. See also Alan Atkinson, *The Europeans in Australia: A History, Volume Two: Democracy* (Melbourne and New York: Oxford University Press, 2004), p. xiv.

9 See for example Durba Ghosh and Dane Kennedy, *Decentring Empire: Britain, India and the Transcolonial World*, New Perspectives in Asian History (Hyderabad: Orient BlackSwan, 2006).

10 Lauren Benton, *A Search for Sovereignty: Law and Geography in European Empires, 1400–1900* (New York: Cambridge University Press, 2010), p. 3.

11 C. J. Ribton-Turner, *A History of Vagrants and Vagrancy, and Beggars and Begging* (Montclair, NJ: Patterson Smith [Chapman & Hall, 1887], 1972).

12 The global history of vagrancy and homelessness *Cast Out: Vagrancy and Homelessness in Global and Historical Perspective* includes chapters about legal attitudes towards vagrancy in particular historical periods and places; see A. L. Beier and Paul Ocobock (eds), *Cast Out: Vagrancy and Homelessness in Global and Historical Perspective*, Ohio University Research in International Studies, Global and Comparative Studies Series 8 (Athens: Ohio University Press, 2008).

13 Benton, *A Search for Sovereignty*, p. 3. See also Lauren Benton, *Law and Colonial Cultures: Legal Regimes in World History, 1400–1900*, Studies in Comparative World History (New York: Cambridge University Press, 2002).

14 Alex C. Castles, *An Australian Legal History* (Sydney, Melbourne, Brisbane and Perth: The Law Book Company, 1982), p. 1.
15 Gerard Curry, 'A bundle of vague diverse offences: The vagrancy laws with special reference to the New Zealand experience', *Anglo-American Law Review* 1 (1972), 523–36.
16 Curry, 'A bundle of vague diverse offences', pp. 523–4. On Blackstone's *Commentaries*, see Wilfred Prest, *William Blackstone: Law and Letters in the Eighteenth Century* (Oxford: Oxford University Press, 2008).
17 Castles, *An Australian Legal History*, p. 17.
18 Sally Engle Merry and Donald Brenneis (eds), *Law and Empire in the Pacific: Fiji and Hawai'i*, Advanced Seminar Series (Santa Fe: School of American Research Press, 2004), pp. 6–10; Benton, *A Search for Sovereignty*, p. 137.
19 Penelope Edmonds, 'The intimate, urbanising frontier: Native camps and settler colonialism's violent array of spaces around early Melbourne', in Tracey Banivanua Mar and Penelope Edmonds (eds), *Making Settler Colonial Space: Perspectives on Race, Place and Identity* (Houndmills and New York: Palgrave Macmillan, 2010), p. 144.
20 Mark Finnane, 'The limits of jurisdiction: Law, governance, and Indigenous peoples in colonized Australia', in Dorsett and Hunter (eds), *Law and Politics in British Colonial Thought*, p. 154.
21 Stephen Garton, *Out of Luck: Poor Australians and Social Welfare*, The Australian Experience (Sydney: Allen & Unwin, 1990); Margaret Tennant, *Paupers and Providers: Charitable Aid in New Zealand* (Wellington: Allen & Unwin/Historical Branch, 1990); and Richard Kennedy (ed.), *Australian Welfare History: Critical Essays* (Melbourne: Macmillan, 1985), p. 32; Christina Twomey, *Deserted and Destitute: Motherhood, Wife Desertion and Colonial Welfare* (Melbourne; Australian Scholarly Publishing, 2002), p. 34.
22 Margaret Tennant, *The Fabric of Welfare: Voluntary Organisations, Government and Welfare in New Zealand, 1840–2005* (Wellington: Bridget Williams Books, 2007).
23 Lionel Rose, *'Rogues and Vagabonds': Vagrant Underworld in Britain 1815–1985* (London and New York: Routledge, 1988), pp. 1–2.
24 Rose, *'Rogues and Vagabonds'*, pp. 4–5.
25 On the development of colonial laws in Australia and New Zealand see: Bruce Kercher, *An Unruly Child: A History of Law in Australia* (St Leonards: Allen & Unwin, 1995), pp. 124–53; Peter Spiller, Jeremy Finn, and Richard Boast, *A New Zealand Legal History* (Wellington: Brookers, 1995), p. 85.
26 Susanne Davies, 'Vagrancy and the Victorians: The Social Construction of the Vagrant in Melbourne, 1880–1907', unpublished PhD thesis, University of Melbourne, 1990, p. 131.
27 Section 2 (2), The Vagrant Act 1866, New Zealand.
28 Davies, 'Vagrancy and the Victorians', pp. 131–3.
29 Davies, 'Vagrancy and the Victorians', p. 129.
30 Julie Kimber provides a useful historiographical overview of different colonial Australian vagrancy laws; see Julie Kimber, 'Poor Laws: A historiography of vagrancy in Australia', *History Compass*, 11:8 (2013), 537–50.
31 Curry, 'A bundle of vague diverse offences', pp. 523–36.
32 'Wanderer', 'The professional unemployed', in Cherry A. Hankin (ed.), *Life in a Young Colony: Selections from Early New Zealand Writing* (Christchurch, Sydney and London: Whitcoulls, 1981), pp. 213–19.
33 John Hunter Kerr, *Glimpses of Life in Victoria By 'A Resident'*, Introduced by Marguerite Hancock (Melbourne: Melbourne University Press, 1996 [1876]), pp. 163–4.
34 A. L. Beier, *Masterless Men: The Vagrancy Problem in England 1560–1640* (London and New York: Methuen, 1985), p. 51.
35 Richard Hill, *Policing the Colonial Frontier: The Theory and Practice of Coercive Social and Racial Control in New Zealand, 1767–1867*, Part 2 (Wellington: Historical Branch/Internal Affairs, 1986), p. 681.

36 *NZPD* 1864–66, Friday 10 August 1866, p. 868; Friday 3 August 1866, p. 809.
37 'The Vagrant Act, 1865: A medley', *New Zealand Herald* (8 February 1865), p. 4.
38 'The Vagrant Act', *New Zealand Herald* (23 February 1865), p. 4.
39 'Deputation to the mayor', *New Zealand Herald* (3 October 1882), p. 6.
40 Miles Fairburn, *The Ideal Society and its Enemies: The Foundations of Modern New Zealand Society 1850–1900* (Auckland: Auckland University Press, 1989), p. 195.
41 Fairburn, *The Ideal Society*, p. 248.
42 Fairburn, 'Vagrants, "folk devils"', p. 50.
43 Fairburn, 'Vagrants, "folk devils"', p. 50.
44 Fairburn's idea about the horror of downward mobility is amplified by Nan Seuffert in 'Civilisation, settlers and wanderers: Law, politics and mobility in nineteenth century New Zealand and Australia', *Law Text Culture*, 15 (2011), 21.
45 The discussion of the data is based on a Microsoft Word Access Database of 200 individuals found in the *New Zealand Police Gazette* between 1899 and 1900.
46 In Melbourne, Victoria, Aboriginal people came to be identified among the 'inconvenient', 'wanderers', and 'nuisances'. Vagrancy laws, as Penelope Edmonds shows, were used to prevent fraternisation between newcomers to Melbourne and women in Aboriginal camps; see Edmonds, 'The intimate, urbanising frontier', p. 138.
47 'Arrest of a Tohunga', *Wairarapa Daily Times* (17 September 1904), p. 5.
48 Philippa Levine, *Prostitution, Race and Politics: Policing Venereal Disease in the British Empire* (New York and London: Routledge, 2003), pp. 184–7. In colonial Melbourne, Edmonds also shows that vagrancy and prostitution were categories deployed in the policing of the streetscape, and that both were 'produced through [the] complex colonial relations' characteristic of a settling population'; see Edmonds, *Urbanizing Frontiers: Indigenous Peoples and Settlers in 19th-Century Pacific Rim Cities* (Vancouver: University of British Columbia Press, 2010), p. 244.
49 Various articles about Lawson describe her recidivism, including 'Been in all Dominion Gaols', *Dominion* (5 February 1912), p. 4.
50 Gareth Stedman Jones, *Outcast London: A Study in the Relationship Between Classes in Victorian Society* (London and New York: Verso, 1971).
51 Jones, *Outcast London*, p. 329.
52 Akihito Suzuki, 'Lunacy and labouring men: Narratives of male vulnerability in mid-Victorian England', in Roberta Bivins and John V. Pickstone (eds), *Medicine, Madness and Social History: Essays in Honour of Roy Porter* (Houndmills and New York: Palgrave Macmillan, 2007), p. 118.
53 Suzuki, 'Lunacy and labouring men', p. 127.
54 Miles Fairburn, *Nearly Out of Heart and Hope: The Puzzle of a Colonial Labourer's Diary* (Auckland: Auckland University Press, 1995), pp. 58–73.
55 Fairburn, *Nearly Out of Heart and Hope*, p. 72.
56 W. Beattie, 'The unknown abode', *Auckland Weekly News* (15 October 1914), p. 50. Auckland Libraries, Sir George Grey Special Collections, AWNS-1914 1015-50-7.
57 Cresswell, 'The vagrant/vagabond', p. 251.
58 Benton, *Law and Colonial Cultures*, p. 264.

CHAPTER SIX

'The world's fernery': New Zealand, fern albums, and nineteenth-century fern fever

Molly Duggins

Through fern fever, an aesthetic science in which ferns oscillated between specimens, decorations, and souvenirs, the New Zealand land-scape was transformed into a worldwide phenomenon in the latter half of the nineteenth century. While Australasian ferns were lauded abroad as curiosities and commodities, in the colonies they were embraced as cross-cultural landmarks entangled in notions of locality, identity, and industry, with the endemic *Cyathea dealbata*, or silver tree fern, taking on emblematic proportions as a national symbol in New Zealand (Figure 6.1). Promoted as a world set apart, with a unique indigenous landscape and as a modern and accessible tourist attraction, New Zealand was represented as the 'Pacific's wonderland' in natural history and travel literature. This coalesced in *The South Pacific Fern Album*, ca. 1889, a luxury gift-book combining pressed New Zealand fern specimens with an illustrated letterpress introduction, produced by Mary Ann Armstrong (1838–1910) and published in Melbourne in ca. 1889.[1]

Subscribing to a genre of commercial New Zealand fern albums com-piled in the colonies between the 1870s and 1890s, *The South Pacific Fern Album (SPFA)* was geared to entice the botanical collector, colonial tourist, and armchair traveller of empire alike. Such albums embodied the vibrant New Zealand fern industry that evolved in tandem with the commodification of natural history in the mid- to late nineteenth century, engaging in multi-directional botanical exchanges through trade and exhibition. Marketed as a collection of living ferns, New Zealand supplied a range of world-wide gardens and herbaria with fern specimens through a network of colonial nurserymen and fern dealers. This scientific and horticultural trade mirrored New Zealand's export industries of farming and agriculture, forestry and mining, which took the fern, and its association with a fast-disappearing pristine wilder-ness, as its trademark.[2] As a promotional medium, the fern became a

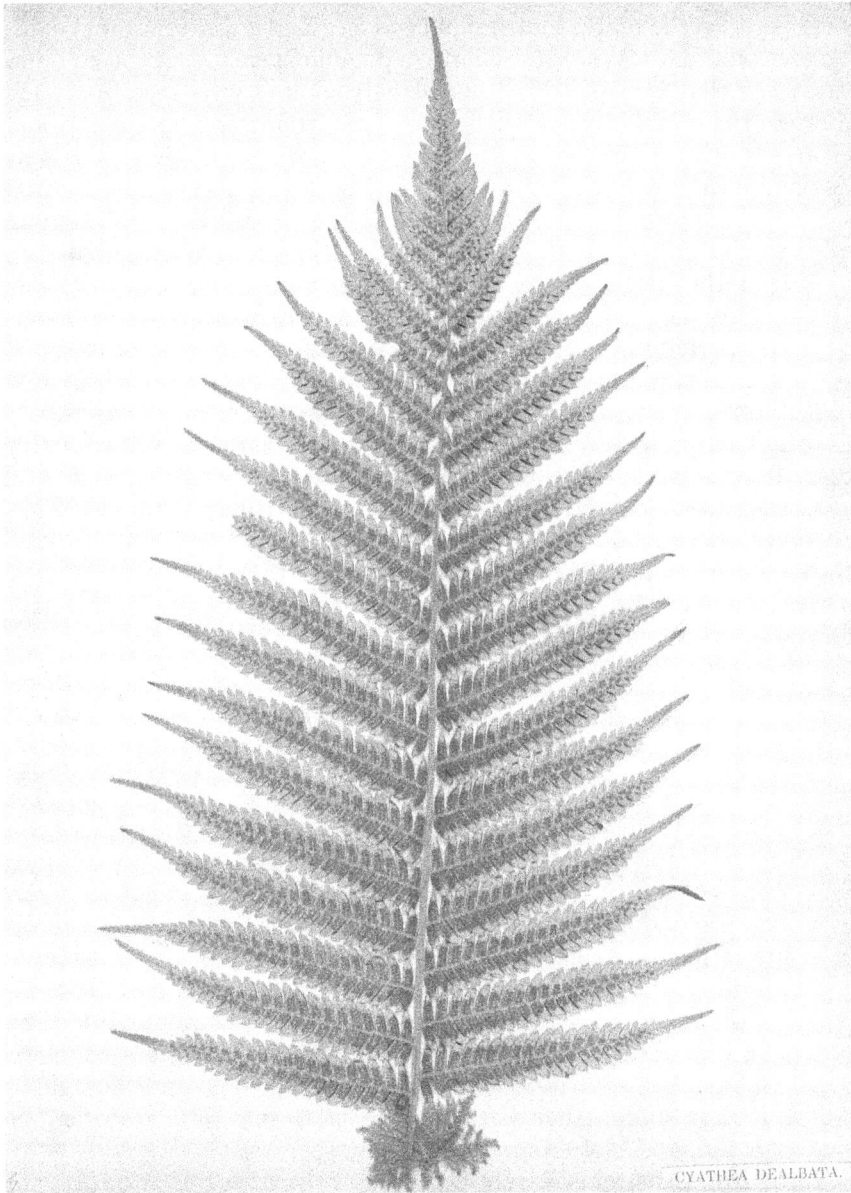

CYATHEA DEALBATA.

6.1 *Cyathea dealbata*, fern specimen on paper, 'Ferns of Australasia', ca. 1900, Mary Ann Armstrong (State Library of Victoria, H94.11/7).

focal point in the representation of New Zealand at international exhibitions, where it was subsumed into a popular spectacle of the colonial landscape that catered to an increasingly mobile visual economy fed through the circulation of media, mass entertainment, and a national form of tourism.[3] Embracing the fern as a transnational motif, the New Zealand fern industry ultimately contributed to a developing colonial sphere of modernity through scientific, aesthetic, and commercial migrations that were both global in outlook and locally oriented.[4]

Within the pages of the *SPFA*, nestled among its ornamentally arranged fronds, the image of New Zealand as an exotic paradise is cultivated into that of the 'world's fernery', anchored in the international aesthetic value of the fern.[5] Focusing on the *SPFA* and the commercial fern album genre within the context of the New Zealand fern industry, in this chapter I assess such albums as portable variants of the fernery that disseminated New Zealand ferns through trade, tourist, and exhibitive networks. Beyond their significance as mobile repositories, however, these albums were also engaged in constructing a romantic colonial nationalism through enacting the fernery's collapse of the indigenous New Zealand landscape into an intimate and interactive form of modern spectacle.

The New Zealand fern industry

Dubbed 'pteridomania' by the British clergyman and naturalist Charles Kingsley in 1855, fern fever was fed by the invention of the Wardian case, a portable sealed glass container that enabled the cultivation of ferns in smog-filled city spaces and the transportation of fern specimens around the globe.[6] Available from country vendors, urban hawkers, professional collectors, and nurseries, live ferns were collected in ferneries, rockeries, and botanic gardens, while pressed ferns were arranged and displayed in herbaria and albums. From the handmade to the machine-made, fern-inspired imagery complemented the profusion of patterns that defined mid-Victorian design, and the fern motif was applied to furniture, cast ironwork, textiles, ceramics, glass, and souvenirs embellished with pressed specimens, fern transfers, or spatter-work, which often featured foreign species.[7]

Ferns from Australasia were especially valued on the international market for their size, abundance, diversity, and connection to the remote antipodes. One of the most popular exhibits at the London International Exhibition of 1862, which was the first to include a significant collection of fern specimens and decorations, was Eugene von Guérard's *Ferntree Gully in the Dandenong Ranges* (1857), a lush and shadowed Australian landscape dominated by tree ferns that inspired fern tourism in the colonies and an export industry of specimens.[8] 'Universally praised for their elegance of form', according to the New Zealand missionary and naturalist William Colenso, tree ferns were recommended by Ferdinand Baron von Mueller, director of the Melbourne Botanic Gardens, as 'ideal garden ornaments'.[9] They were sent to stock gardens and glazed ferneries as antipodean sentinels in the English countryside, as well as to enhance collections in Europe, Asia, and America, thereby revealing the imperial transfer of plants as more than a unilateral endeavour.[10]

By the 1860s, elaborate nursery displays of Australasian ferns attempted to bring von Guérard's image to life, as epitomised in the Tropical Fernery at J. Backhouse & Son's, which William Robinson in 1864 declared formed 'a sight which it would be difficult to persuade a Maori had not been bodily transferred from the Antipodes'.[11] In addi-tion to contributions from British horticulturalists and gardeners, such ferneries were supplied by a growing number of colonial nurserymen and fern dealers, including Arthur Yates in Auckland and Sydney, George Matthews in Dunedin, and Adams & Sons in Christchurch, for whom the intercolonial and international exportation of New Zealand ferns and tree ferns had 'become quite an important branch of business', according to the *Otago Witness* in 1878.[12] As Paul Star has argued, this colonial commercial network offered a significant coun-terpoint to metropolitan botanical exchange, often circumventing the imperial centre to engage directly with foreign markets.[13]

At later exhibitions large-scale ferneries provided some of the most spectacular displays. Complete with artificial rockwork, the fernery of the New Zealand Court at the Colonial and Indian Exhibition in London in 1886 was the largest of the colonial ferneries and was filled with tree ferns exported from New Zealand, in addition to specimens culled from local botanical gardens and nurseries.[14] Catering to an urban London audience of cosmopolitan consumers familiar with such manufactured spectacle, it transformed the New Zealand landscape into a three-dimensional promotional postcard that highlighted the wilderness and natural resources of the colony.

Colonial fern fever was not derivative of this British craze but a reciprocal and complementary phenomenon. The collection and display of ferns held special significance in the Australasian colonies, where the plethora of local species became a symbol of pride. In the wake of Joseph Dalton Hooker's *Flora Novae-Zelandiae* (1851–53), a number of books on New Zealand ferns were locally published to cater to the amateur colonial pteridomaniac, and collections of ferns were displayed at colonial exhibitions, featuring at the New Zealand exhibi-tion held in Dunedin in 1865. Open-air ferneries were established in

Australia from the 1870s and New Zealand from the turn of the century and took pride of place in colonial exhibitions, such as that at the New Zealand and South Seas Exhibition in Dunedin in 1889. This was described in the press as 'a splendid advertisement for the beauty of the native ferns of New Zealand', and was the subject of fervent proposals for its preservation after the closing ceremony.[15]

To these constructed sylvan retreats was added a conventionalised New Zealand tourist circuit that emerged towards the end of the New Zealand Wars, centred upon the fern and Māori. Beyond intercolonial travel, increased steamship operations meant that visitors could reach New Zealand directly from Britain in forty to forty-five days, with alternate routes via New York, San Francisco, and Honolulu.[16] Guidebooks such as *Maoriland: An Illustrated Handbook to New Zealand*, issued by the Union Steamship Company of New Zealand Ltd in 1884, provided information on popular ferny districts, the tourism of which revived local Indigenous material culture.[17] A range of botanical guides and souvenirs were produced to support this industry – from collections of pressed specimens to scenic photographs of ferns and fern-decorated handicrafts that were available in situ, as well as from larger towns and ports.

Colonial commercial fern albums produced from the 1870s form a distinct subset of this genre; they offered the experience of a virtual tour through the assemblage of fern varieties collected throughout the islands and provided a tactile medium through which to intimately connect with the New Zealand landscape. Experienced through the revelatory process of turning the page and fingering fronds, crosiers, mosses, and lycopods, these albums evoked the sensory spectacle of wandering down a fernery path bordered by densely textured specimens. Through the inclusion of preserved mature fronds displaying spores capable of germination, they also functioned as portable nurseries, adding to the circulation of plants that traversed the spaces of empire. Luxurious bespoke volumes governed by a strong ornamental component that appealed to a genteel audience caught up in the fad of collecting natural history, they embraced the commodity status of the fern and were produced not only to enrich the amateur botanist's cabinet, but also to adorn drawing room tables as souvenirs of the colony.

Three of the most notable New Zealand album manufacturers were Eric Craig, Herbert Dobbie, and Thomas Cranwell. Born in Scotland, Craig (1829–1923) arrived in New Zealand in 1852, and was a collector, publisher, and dealer of natural history who opened a curiosity shop in Princes Street, Auckland, in the 1870s. Advertised as 'the best place in all the Australasian colonies for shells, ferns, & curios', his depot sold Māori and Pacific Island artefacts as well as ferns.[18] Located near the Auckland Museum building and Queen Street booksellers, who carried sets of specimens and fern albums, it was part of an Auckland tourist route dedicated to New Zealand collectables.[19] Enlisting various local suppliers to supplement his collections, Craig sold ferns mounted in sets from 12 to 152 varieties, in albums with mottled kauri wood covers, boxes, or on cardboard, as well as packets of fern 'seeds' and live plants in Wardian cases intended for an export market.[20] In a catalogue published in Birmingham featuring 140 New Zealand varieties for sale, he offered to exchange New Zealand ferns for foreign species, which he then sold in boxes with 'up to 300 varieties'.[21]

Craig also published two editions of an album with cyanotype illustrations of ferns that were partial facsimiles of an earlier volume, *New Zealand Ferns: 148 Varieties Illustrated* (1880), by Herbert Boucher Dobbie (1852–1940).[22] A fern enthusiast from Middlesex, Dobbie arrived in Auckland in 1875 and was bewitched by the number of local varieties, describing the Waitakare Ranges as a fern fairyland and later constructing a fernery at his home, Ruatotara.[23] Composed of 104 plates of ferns inscribed with their names and localities produced through the cyanotype process, which created white silhouettes on a blue background, Dobbie's album honed in on the decorative potential of the indexical value of the ferns at the expense of their scientific usefulness, omitting details of venation and fructification.[24] Reminiscent of Anna Atkins's *Cyanotypes of British and Foreign Flowering Plants and Ferns* (1854), his blue books focus on the sheer surface value of the fern, rendered in mechanically precise detail, fetishising its essential form.[25]

The decorative appeal of the fern was similarly exploited by Thomas Cranwell, a singing teacher from Lincolnshire, who migrated to New Zealand in 1862. By 1875 Cranwell was based in Parnell and was advertising ferns mounted on cardboard – from twelve shillings per set of twenty-four sheets – and 'handsomely bound books of ferns' as the 'best presents for England', which were available from 'the principal Booksellers'.[26] To distinguish his fern albums from others on the market, Cranwell collaborated with Anton Seuffert (1815–87), a cabinet-maker from Bohemia who immigrated to Auckland in 1859. Seuffert established a reputation for creating showpieces and gifts for dignitaries, made from native woods; with elaborate marquetry depicting Māori material culture and New Zealand flora and fauna, these items were exhibited and sold overseas.[27] He crafted inlaid wooden album covers and boxes for Cranwell's sets of ferns, favouring rare and distinctive species such as *Hymenophyllum*, or the filmy fern, and the detail of his designs suggests that he may have used dried ferns as templates.[28]

The commercial fern work of Craig, Dobbie, Cranwell, and Seuffert was supplemented by New Zealand fern albums, gift-books, and handicrafts produced by women who drew upon the aesthetic overlap between amateur natural history and artistic practices to become active collectors, artists, and exhibitors. Few women, however, engaged in the New Zealand fern industry as a significant and sustained business venture. The fern work produced by Mary Ann Armstrong is distinctive in this regard. Capitalising on the aesthetic appeal of the New Zealand fern as a growing emblem of the colony and a Pacific grand tour souvenir, she created fern albums, pictures, greeting cards, as well as photographs and prints of scenic views and Māori culture embellished with fern collages, in addition to meticulously mounted and scientifically labelled specimens. While her male colleagues stressed their role as professional collectors and mounters, Armstrong distinguished herself as a botanic fern artist to become 'a household word in the Colonies'.[29]

Mary Ann Armstrong, botanic fern artist

Mary Ann Armstrong, née Newey (1838–1910), immigrated to Victoria from Birmingham in January 1853 in the SS *Wandsworth*. She settled at the gold fields in Bendigo, where she married Charles Clarke Armstrong (1835–1923), a coach runner and fruiterer, also from Birmingham, in 1858 (Figure 6.2).[30] Relocating to New Zealand in the early 1860s with their sons, William and Charles Clarke, Jr, the Armstrongs took up residence in Dunedin, engaging in a variety of ventures, including hotel management, to support their growing family that would total thirteen children. The Christmas editions of the *Otago Daily Times* in 1866 and 1867 describe the family shop on Princes Street, decorated with ferns, evergreens, and flowers, as 'an especial object of attraction' and a 'perfect picture', suggesting Armstrong's early proclivity and skill for fern arrangement.[31]

To supplement the family income, Armstrong began to sell collections of pressed New Zealand ferns 'For Book, Post or otherwise', with 'Choice collections already arranged' from the family home in Dowling Street in the early 1870s.[32] These early collections include sets of eight dried ferns mounted on cardboard, scientifically labelled by hand and arranged in the florilegia tradition into bouquets anchored with roundels of mosses or lycopods, which evoked a subtle sense of landscape – as visible in her *Cyathea Dealbata* arrangement in Figure 6.1.[33] They often display Armstrong's business label, a convention of commercial fern albums of this era, stating that the enclosed specimens were 'Mounted and Botanically Named by Mrs. C. C. Armstrong, Dunedin'. In 1877 Armstrong exhibited at the Annual Camellia Show at the

6.2 Mary Ann Armstrong (1838–1910), ca. 1890
(courtesy of Richard Daffey, Melbourne).

Horticultural Hall in Victoria Street, Melbourne, where a reviewer declared her pressed ferns were 'very suitable for home presents or for the drawing room table', thus emphasising their export potential and decorative appeal, the two most common attributes of the New Zealand fern industry.[34]

Interestingly, her prepared specimens were also praised for their self-germinating properties:

> A still further advantage they possess is that being gathered at a particular season they have attached to them the sporules or seeds, and these, it is found readily germinate, so that with proper soil and suitable conditions of temperature and moisture, it is not difficult to propagate from them.[35]

An alternative to shipping live ferns in Wardian cases – a service offered by a number of her competitors, including Craig – Armstrong's fern albums were thus promoted as miniature mobile nurseries. The preserved specimens had the added benefit of easily surviving transfer, providing the opportunity for fern enthusiasts abroad to cultivate their own exotic New Zealand ferneries.

[109]

Following her success in Melbourne, Armstrong contributed a number of fern exhibits to intercolonial and international exhibitions in order to promote her commercial work. One of her earliest exhibits, a small collection of dried New Zealand Ferns 'in natural colours', was displayed under her husband's name alongside the work of Eric Craig at the Sydney International Exhibition in 1879, where it received special commendation.[36] At the Melbourne International Exhibition the following year, Armstrong exhibited under her own name and was awarded a first order of merit for her 'collection of Victorian wild flowers and New Zealand ferns'.[37] She expanded her repertoire at the New Zealand International Exhibition, held in Christchurch in 1882, to include 'ferns and flowers framed in various devices; some arranged to represent scenery with Helen's babies playing about', as well as 'photographs of New Zealand scenery, and of Maoris, mounted with ferns'.[38]

Her inclusion of Helen's babies refers to a comic novel of that name by the American journalist and author John Habberton, devoted to the 'innocent, crafty, angelic, impish, witching, and repulsive' boys Toddie and Budge. First published in Boston in 1876, the book inspired a series of sheet music and a play adapted by Garnet Walch which was performed at the Theatre Royal in Melbourne in 1877 and on Broadway in 1878. In referencing Helen's babies in her exhibition entry, Armstrong appealed to a colonial audience versed in popular American entertainment, effectively situating New Zealand fern fever within a context of transnational cultural networks created through an internationalising media. Similarly, her addition of New Zealand scenery and Māori suggests the emergence of local tourism fixated on an exoticised Indigeneity as a by-product of industrialisation, increasing global trade, and settler revisionism intent on colonial promotion.[39] Within her arrangements, ferns become referents for the Indigenous, conflating a romanticised vision of traditional Māori culture with the primeval New Zealand landscape.

An extant album of Armstrong's New Zealand ferns from the mid-1880s provides an example of what her Christchurch exhibition entry may have looked like.[40] Composed of twelve pages of mounted and named fern specimens, the album features a series of photographs of the Hot Lakes District by the New Zealand photographer Frank Arnold Coxhead (1851–ca. 1919), including views of Wairoa, the White and Pink Terraces of Rotomahana before and after the eruption of Mount Tarawera on 10 June 1886, and Ohinemutu. Following the well-publicised tour of the Duke of Edinburgh in 1870 to promote the region – recently the location of Māori resistance led by Te Kooti Arikirangi Te Turuki (ca. 1832–93) – tourists flocked to the Hot Lakes

6.3 'White Terrace Rotomahana N. Z.', albumen print and fern specimens on paper, 'New Zealand Ferns', 1886–87, Frank Arnold Coxhead and Mary Ann Armstrong (courtesy of Hans P. Kraus Jr, New York).

District.[41] There they confronted a sublime landscape of steam and gas rising from volcanic ash; enjoyed the therapeutic quality of the springs at Rotorua; witnessed 'Maoris at home'; and searched for rare ferns at the Terraces, the silica-covered sides of which were encrusted with ferns, dragonflies, and other items in a tantalising form of ready-made souvenir, and which were supplemented by local handicrafts.[42]

Exploiting this market, Armstrong's album incorporates Cox's photographs in fern collages that function as signs of the exotic 'other', entangled in what Frances Loeffler has described as the discourse of 'tropicality' associated with this district.[43] In a page displaying a photograph of the White Terrace, reproduced in Figure 6.3, a section of a frond sliced down its stem and turned on its side forms a miniature forest, a fragment of the landscape that stands for the whole, embodying the dense fern growth in the foreground of the scene. While Armstrong's frame extends the sensory experience of this tropical hot-spring country, it also functions on an aesthetic level, whereby the persistent romantic view of the antipodean forest is combined with the revival of Gothic architecture and design.

Associated with ruins, the fern was seen as both a complement to crumbling stonework and, through its delicate complexity of form, as a metaphorical Gothic ornament in its own right.[44] Placing emphasis on their formal qualities of line and colour, Armstrong transformed her pressed ferns from botanical specimens into artistic mediums, the crosiers of which resemble scrollwork, while the central fronds evoke a pointed arch. Embellishing the remains of Rotomahana, she moulds the fern into an alternative cultural landmark of the New Zealand landscape, enmeshed in both historical and contemporary aesthetic values.

Increasingly ambitious in scope and design, Armstrong's fern work expanded to incorporate stationery as well as albums and collage arrangements, including a set entitled 'The New Zealand Native Fern, A Novelty for Friends at Home and Abroad'.[45] She also produced postcards with fern transfers, which, along with her other fern work, were sold through retailers in Gisborne and Dunedin.[46] Her 'framed fern pictures and books of ferns mounted and named' were awarded the Albert Edward Prince of Wales Executive President Medal at the Colonial and Indian Exhibition in London, 1886, and were presented to the Prince of Wales for his residence at Sandringham.[47] Exhibited in the New Zealand Court, which featured a fernery designed to resemble a 'semi-realisation of a New Zealand fern gully', Armstrong's entry transformed this large-scale installation into a portable distillation of the colony, an emblematic ornament for the imperial drawing room par excellence.[48]

By 1888 Armstrong had relocated to Melbourne, where she was committed to continuing her fern work on a larger scale. In addition to exhibiting pressed fern collections at the Melbourne Centennial Exhibition of 1888 – which were awarded a bronze medal and a first order of merit – Armstrong also had a stand at which she and one of her daughters demonstrated the process of preserving ferns.[49] Her son, Charles Clarke, Jr, who had remained in Dunedin as a scenic photographer and fern artist specialising in artificial fern work, was also engaged in collecting and exporting New Zealand ferns from Gisborne to Victoria where, according to an 1889 advertisement in the *Poverty Bay Herald*, they found a 'ready market'.[50] The imports included dried specimens and 'fern pictures', and were sold by various auction houses in Sydney and Melbourne. Addressed to amateurs, gardeners, nurserymen, florists, and others, auction advertisements emphasised the choice variety of these specimens – including the popular *Todea superba*, known as 'Prince of Wales feathers' – which were 'packed for transmission (if required) to Europe'.[51]

With a steady stream of specimens flowing in from New Zealand, Armstrong embarked upon a new commercial project involving the production of a set of albums on the ferns of Australasia which, in addition to pressed specimens, included a letterpress introduction. Together with Jeremiah Twomey, a Melbourne-based journalist and publisher of the *Farmer & Grazier* (and Armstrong's future son-in-law), she established the New Zealand Fern Company to promote and sell the series. Begun in Melbourne in 1889, the *SPFA* in scope and scale represents both the culmination of Armstrong's career and that of the nineteenth-century New Zealand fern industry. Combining the display tactics of the fernery with the political picturesque rhetoric of the late nineteenth-century atlas in a gift-book unlike any other fern album on the market, it was distinguished by an international style and was marketed to a cosmopolitan audience, presenting New Zealand's resources and industry, history, and culture, cloaked under the mantle of a romantic botanical tourism.

The South Pacific Fern Album

The album was introduced in 1889 in an article from the Melbourne *Argus* that was reprinted in several colonial newspapers:

A project which deserves encouragement is the gathering of the different varieties of ferns of Australasia and New Zealand in a systematic manner in order to place interesting collections upon the English and American, as well as the Australian, markets. The work has been taken in hand by the New Zealand Fern Company, who have secured the services of Mrs C. C. Armstrong, formerly of Dunedin, for the preparation and arrangement of samples, and also a staff of fern-gatherers, who are at present in Auckland, New Zealand, where there are extensive fern districts ... The company intend to devote their attention principally to the issue of the 'South Pacific Fern Album', which, in addition to a complete collection of ferns, will contain descriptions of the ferns, and the localities in which they are found, as well as illustrations by means of the photolithographical process.[52]

Time-intensive and laborious, the creation of the *SPFA* was a mammoth project that 'entailed much expense and trouble', according to Twomey in the introduction.[53] Its full title, *The South Pacific Fern Album: New Zealand Section*, suggests a series of albums devoted to various Australasian regions; however, there is no evidence that other editions were produced. A notice in the *Launceston Examiner* from 1890 indicates that 100 copies were prepared, yet by 1893 an advertisement in the *Maitland Mercury* reveals that the album was selling in a limited edition of thirty copies by the London publishers Sampson, Low, Marston & Co., priced at the expensive sum of three guineas.[54]

Composed of eighteen to twenty plates of mounted ferns accompanied by printed labels and often flanked by decorative unnamed fronds, the album would have required the collection of an immense number of specimens to produce the 100 copies proposed in the *Examiner*. Led by Charles Clarke, Jr, into the 'remotest parts of the interior' of the North Island from a base at Poverty Bay on the east coast, the fern gathering was declared 'the most arduous portion of the undertaking'.[55] Once gathered, the specimens were prepared onsite by a young Māori woman, whose duty it was 'to attend to the drying of the ferns when collected in the cottage'.[56] They were then shipped to Melbourne for arrangement by Armstrong, whose reputation for fern work was marketed as the strongest selling point for the album.

George Thomson, author of *The Ferns and Fern Allies of New Zealand*, published in 1882, is quoted in the introduction of the *SPFA* as praising Armstrong's remote arrangement of the specimens, to assuage any fears regarding their quality or freshness:

> I have seen specimens of her work which would only require the dew upon the fronds to convince one that they had just been gathered from their native haunts though they were at the time thousands of miles away from where they had been gathered.[57]

Samples of these arrangements, along with fern-decorated Christmas cards by Armstrong, were displayed at Twomey's offices at Phoenix Chambers, 11 Market Street, Melbourne, to advertise the album, the title page of which featured reproductions of her medals awarded for fern work.

Beyond the scale of its production, the *SPFA* was distinguished from other colonial commercial fern albums by its illustrated letterpress introduction that was divided into two sections. Part I includes an overview of the fern, a scenic tour of fern localities in New Zealand, the economic and medicinal uses of ferns, and their role in traditional Māori culture, while Part II is devoted to the description and distribution of each genus and species. Its expansive programme, composed of text, images, and specimens, demonstrates a familiarity with the exhibitions frequented by Armstrong that were geared to endorse colonial production and progress, culture and scenery. Such exhibitions, as Peter Hoffenberg has argued, were agents of the 'new imperialism' that evolved in the late nineteenth century and were instrumental in propagating a shared cultural British heritage as well as emerging nationalisms through propagandistic displays.[58]

In its construction of a promotional, picturesque vision of New Zealand, the *SPFA* also resembles the illustrated colonial atlases produced around the time of the Australian Centenary in 1888. This is exemplified in the *Picturesque Atlas of Australasia* (1886–88), featuring the New School of wood engraving imported from America, which combined artistic and technical innovation to create a dynamic scrapbook of imagery engaged in assembling a nationalist iconography for an outward-looking colonial society.[59] The *Picturesque Atlas* provided a likely source of inspiration for the *SPFA*, which was published in its wake and targeted a similarly international audience, with extant copies held in public and private collections in Australia, New Zealand, the United Kingdom, and North America.

Intended more 'for those who admire the beauty of nature's productions than for those skilled in botany', the *SPFA*'s introduction takes the form of a perambulating picturesque tour, following the route of 'the tourist – whose path would generally be that of the botanist'.[60] Highlighting the peculiar natural wonders of New Zealand, which is described alternately as a 'Garden of Ferns' and a 'Wonderland of the South', the introduction jumps from the Bay of Islands to the Hauraki Gulf, the Hot Lakes District, and Poverty Bay – fern localities 'associated with some historical or romantic incident', which according to Twomey, 'adds to the pleasure of passing through them'.[61] Expounding upon the mystery, primeval nature, tropical lushness, and proliferation of the fern in verdant valleys, mountain gorges, river banks, and dark recesses, it proclaims the fern as emblematic of New Zealand, describing the colony as 'the land of the Maori and the Moa, and may we say of the fern'.[62]

As in Armstrong's earlier photographic album of the Hot Lakes District, the fern and Māori are conflated in a discourse of exotic otherness that overshadows the significant historic and symbolic role of the fern in traditional Māori culture. While the *SPFA* anecdotally addresses the Māori culinary, medicinal, and mythological significance of the fern, it focuses its attention on a sensationalised aspect of contact history: a relic from the 'Te Kooti Massacre' at Poverty Bay in 1868 that was discovered on one of the New Zealand Fern Company's fern-gathering expeditions.[63] Found embedded in a tree branch by Charles Clarke, Jr, while he was erecting a trig station on the heights of Nagatapu, a stirrup-iron – attributed to a member of Te Kooti's entourage, who was supposedly shot in the act of repairing it – was reported in the local press as an evocative souvenir of the New Zealand Wars.[64] It was later exhibited in Twomey's Melbourne office as a curiosity and an advertisement for the *SPFA*, symbolising the New Zealand Fern Company's penetration of the secluded, exotic bush.[65]

The image of an untouched wilderness dominates the pictorial programme of the *SPFA*, which includes engravings of ferns and exotic scenery. Some of these may be based on photographs taken by Charles Clarke, Jr, while others are by Melbourne illustrators Charles Turner and George Treeby, who worked under the pseudonym of G. Bron, suggesting that Twomey solicited contributions from local artists.[66] A few of these illustrations appear in contemporary colonial atlases, including a cockatoo vignette by Turner from *The New Atlas of Australia* (1886) and a view of a native climbing a giant tree fern, which is similar to an engraving in the *Picturesque Atlas of Australasia*.[67] The *SPFA* not only borrowed illustrations but also the illustrative style of montage that distinguished these atlases. Integrated with the letterpress, its composite imagery showcased both the aesthetic worldliness of colonial graphic design and the technological sophistication of the late nineteenth-century Australian printing industry.[68]

Appealing to a modern eye conditioned to process spectacle through a fragmented and multiple focus, montage was also an intimate vehicle that personally appealed to the viewer, drawing upon a culture of collecting that was widely disseminated through album-making practices. Throughout the introduction of the *SPFA*, montage functions as a visual accompaniment to the picturesque tour, enveloping the New Zealand fern and, by extension, the antipodean landscape in a constructive narrative based on the synthesis of image, emblem, and text.[69] This composite layout is revealed in a page devoted to the 'primeval forests of Australasia': Turner's vignette of cockatoos borders a column of text resting above a photolithograph by Treeby, depicting the giant tree fern, *Dicksonia billardieri* (Figure 6.4).[70]

Thrusting out of the foreground on a diagonal, its colossal trunk bisects and flattens the scene, reflecting the influence of Japanese prints

GIANT TREE FERN *(Dicksonia billardierii).*
(FROM AN ORIGINAL PHOTO.)

6.4 'Giant Tree Fern (*Dicksonia billardierii*)', engraving, *South Pacific Fern Album*, ca. 1889, George Treeby (State Library of Victoria, 587.3 T93).

on the Aesthetic Movement, while dwarfing a fashionably attired touring couple on a rustic wooden bridge similar to those constructed in contemporary ferneries. Indeed, Treeby's illustration is reminiscent of the scenes of urban leisure that dominated colonial atlas imagery, subscribing – as Erika Esau has suggested – to an 'iconography of cosmopolitanism' employed in contemporary American illustration and in European Impressionist art filtered through magazine reproductions.[71] Treeby's tourists encounter a forest cordoned off and framed, aestheticised through picturesque discourse and preserved through photography, much as the reader encountered the album page as a curated space that strove to present a productive vision of the colonies blending together art, science, culture, and technology in a manner reflective of contemporary exhibition design.

A number of copies of the *SPFA* also contain two hand-coloured lithographs of picturesque views by C. Troedel & Co., adorned with artistically arranged pressed fronds similar to the descriptions of decorated Christmas cards available for purchase from Twomey's office.[72] Reminiscent of the scenic photographs from the commercial views trade employed in Armstrong's earlier album of New Zealand ferns, these lithographs represent both an exotic wilderness and a domesticated landscape, displaying alternately a dense forest scene untouched by human presence, and a solitary traveller journeying along a rustic bush road. As in Armstrong's previous collage compositions, the ferny frames generate a multifaceted sense of vision that embraces the particular and the general, in an aesthetic assemblage intended to evoke an antipodean fern land complicit with the introduction's overarching narrative of a Pacific wonderland.

Armstrong continued to produce fern work on a reduced scale in Melbourne after the *SPFA*, compiling an album entitled *Ferns of Australasia*, ca. 1900. This item, held in the State Library of Victoria, includes a large frond of *Cyathea dealbata*, mounted to showcase its silver underside (Figure 6.1).[73] While the majority of specimens in this album, as in the *SPFA*, are decoratively arranged two or three to a page, the silver tree fern, due to its size and striking colour, is displayed in isolation as an evocative icon of the New Zealand landscape. Described in the *SPFA* as 'the well-known and much-admired "Silver Tree Fern" of the settlers', it emerged as an outward-looking nationalist symbol and industrial trademark in the late nineteenth century.[74] It drew promotional power from its connectedness to Indigenous culture and nature as one of the few fern species that was widely known by its Māori name of *Ponga*, which resonated with a romanticised, pristine wilderness. Infused with a political picturesque engaged in what Loeffler has described as 'legitimizing the settler presence and inscribing its status as an indigenized community, existing in harmony with the land', the *SPFA* ultimately fetishises the indigenous New Zealand landscape, circulating preserved ferns through international networks as an emblem of modern settler culture and progress.[75]

The paradise of the fern?

In the *SPFA*, Twomey decrees New Zealand 'the paradise of the fern', claiming, '... there is not a portion of the colony, from end to end, in which these lovely plants may not be found in more or less profusion'.[76] However, by the time the album was produced in the late 1880s and early 1890s, the New Zealand landscape was undergoing a drastic industrial transformation through agriculture, forestry, and mining. This shift is acknowledged in the *SPFA*'s introduction, which laments the surface of the land 'torn and hacked by the pioneer's axe, and desecrated by the ruthless steam engine', while admitting that 'the face of the country is rapidly changing, and its wealth of flower and foliage is giving way to the more prosaic paddock and farm land'.[77] Besides the environmental impact of agricultural and industrial progress, fern fever also took its toll. The *SPFA* reveals that in Auckland, local varieties were 'greatly utilised by the residents of the city in rockeries and grottoes'.[78] Through their overuse as private and civic decorations, the ferns growing around Dunedin were depleted by 1915 according to a report by George Thomson, who became a founding member of the Dunedin and Suburban Reserves Conservation Society.[79]

New Zealand defended its title of 'Land of the Ferns' through increasingly spectacular displays geared to a global audience.[80] This was epitomised in the fernery at the New Zealand International Exhibition of Arts and Industries, held in Christchurch from 1906 to 1907. In this display, hundreds of native ferns, mosses, and lycopods were featured around a central pool crossed by a bridge constructed from tree fern trunks, reminiscent of Treeby's rustic overpass in his touristic image of a primeval forest in the *SPFA*.[81] Popular with the exhibition's nearly two million visitors, the fernery transformed the South Island into a Pacific wonderland that belied the ecological effects of burgeoning industry.

Increasingly absent from the local landscape, New Zealand ferns were enshrined in ferneries and exhibitions, herbaria and albums, where they functioned just as much as odes to industry and economy as they did to aesthetic science.[82] In this chapter, I have argued that colonial commercial fern albums produced from the 1870s to the 1890s represented a significant means of botanical exchange that enacted a reversal of ecological imperialism.[83] Shaped by trade, exhibition, and design, the New Zealand fern industry was a global phenomenon in which fern specimens, live and preserved, criss-crossed the empire and beyond as vegetal emissaries of the Pacific's wonderland, a primeval and exotic landscape turned modern tourist attraction. New Zealand fern albums played a crucial role – not only in feeding this transnational craze, through their intimate and accessible format that evoked a condensed form of spectacle – but also in demonstrating the cosmopolitanism of late colonial visual culture.

Defined by its international style and outlook, the *SPFA* represents perhaps the most sophisticated fern gift album produced in the colonies at the height of the nineteenth-century New Zealand fern industry. The album brought the romantic discourses of colonial tourism and nationalism into the home, where they could be processed on an intimate level. Responding to the robust export trade of New Zealand ferns, which transformed the colony into 'the world's fernery', the *SPFA* functioned as a combined herbarium, nursery, and virtual tour of specimens and scenic views that hinged upon sensory experience. Embracing the fluid aesthetic currency of the fern in late nineteenth-century visual culture, the *SPFA* ultimately combined contemporary exhibition strategy with cosmopolitan illustrative design, to present New Zealand not as an isolated Pacific wonderland, but as a 'Greater Britain' shaped by international industrial and cultural networks, reinforcing its place not only within the empire but also on the world's stage.[84]

Notes

1   Mary Ann Armstrong and Jeremiah Twomey, *The South Pacific Fern Album* (Melbourne: J. Twomey, ca. 1889), p. 14.
2   Frances Loeffler, 'Pteridomania: A Visual History of the Fern in New Zealand', MA thesis, Victoria University of Wellington, 2006, p. 86.
3   Robert Dixon, *Photography, Early Cinema and Colonial Modernity: Frank Hurley's Synchronized Lecture Entertainments* (London and New York: Anthem Press, 2012), p. 214.
4   Dixon, *Photography*, p. xvii; Erika Esau, *Images of the Pacific Rim: Australia and California 1850–1935* (Sydney: Power Publications, 2010), p. 17.
5   Armstrong and Twomey, *The South Pacific Fern Album*, p. 15.
6   Charles Kingsley, *Glaucus; or, The Wonders of the Shore* (London: Macmillan & Co., 1855), p. 4.
7   Sarah Whittingham, *Fern Fever: The Story of Pteridomania* (London: Frances Lincoln, 2012), pp. 71–2.
8   Tim Bonyhady, *The Colonial Earth* (Victoria: Melbourne University Press, 2000), pp. 104–7.
9   Loeffler, 'Pteridomania', p. 14; Julia Horne, *The Pursuit of Wonder: How Australia's Landscape was Explored, Nature Discovered, and Tourism Unleashed* (Carlton, Victoria: Miegunyah Press, 2005), p. 265.
10 Paul Star, 'New Zealand's biota barons: Ecological transformation in colonial New Zealand', *Environment and Nature in New Zealand*, 6:2 (2011), 3.
11 Whittingham, *Fern Fever*, p. 103.

12 'News of the week', *Otago Witness* (4 May 1878), p. 15.

13 Star, 'Biota barons', 6.

14 *Colonial and Indian Exhibition, Catalogue of New Zealand Exhibits* (London: William Clowes & Sons, 1886), p. 107; Whittingham, *Fern Fever*, p. 103.

15 Whittingham, *Fern Fever*, p. 159; 'The New Zealand and South Seas Exhibition. The closing ceremony. A review', *Otago Witness* (24 April 1890), p. 18.

16 *Colonial and Indian Exhibition*, p. xvi.

17 Amira J. Henare, *Anthropology and Imperial Exchange* (Cambridge: Cambridge University Press, 2005), p. 189.

18 Advertisement of 1891, reproduced in Jeanne Goulding, 'Early Publications and Exhibits of New Zealand Ferns and the Work of Eric Craig', in *Records of the Auckland Institute and Museum*, 14 (1977), p. 69.

19 Loeffler, 'Pteridomania', pp. 69–70.

20 Goulding, 'Early Publications', p. 69. A packet of Craig's fern 'seeds' is in the collection of Tim McCormick, Sydney.

21 Eric Craig, *Catalogue of Ferns and Lycopodiums in the Herbarium of Eric Craig, Princes Street, Auckland* (Birmingham: Chas. Stocker, Summer Row, ca. 1890). Goulding demonstrates that this catalogue had a wide distribution to overseas herbaria and Craig's specimens can still be found in a number of American collections. See Goulding, 'Early Publications', p. 75.

22 Eric Craig, *New Zealand Ferns: 167 Varieties Illustrated* (ca. 1888), and *New Zealand Ferns: 172 Varieties Illustrated* (ca. 1892).

23 Herbert Boucher Dobbie, *New Zealand Ferns: 148 Varieties Illustrated* (Auckland, 1880), p. 1. Collection of Hans P. Kraus Jr, New York; Whittingham, *Fern Fever*, p. 159.

24 Whittingham, *Fern Fever*, p. 83.

25 Loeffler, 'Pteridomania', p. 50.

26 Cranwell's advertisement appears in *Ferns Which Grow in New Zealand and the Adjacent Islands, Plainly Described by H. E. S. L.* (Auckland: Reed & Brett, 1875).

27 *Colonial and Indian Exhibition*, p. 57.

28 Loeffler, 'Pteridomania', pp. 64–5.

29 'Special advertisements', *Poverty Bay Herald* (3 December 1885), p. 2. A label from an album in the State Library of Victoria, entitled *Ferns of Australasia*, ca. 1900, designates her as a 'botanic fern artist'.

30 I am extremely indebted to Richard Daffey, great-grandson of Mary Ann Armstrong, for sharing with me his extensive family research on the Armstrongs. For more biographical information on Mary Ann, see Molly Duggins, 'Mrs. C. C. Armstrong', *Design and Art Australia Online*, www.daao.org.au/bio/mary-ann-armstrong/, accessed 12 August 2013.

31 'Inveniam viam aut faciam', *Otago Daily Times* (25 December 1866), p. 4; 'Inveniam viam aut faciam', *Otago Daily Times* (25 December 1867), p. 4.

32 'Ferns', *Otago Daily Times* (18 October 1873), p. 3.

33 See, for instance, Mrs. C. C. Armstrong, 'New Zealand Ferns', (Dunedin, ca. 1885), New York Public Library, Stuart 13837.

34 'The Annual Camellia Show', *Argus* (24 August 1877), p. 7.

35 'The *Argus*. Published daily', *Argus* (24 September 1877), p. 5.

36 *Sydney International Exhibition: Official Record* (Sydney: Thomas Richards, Government Printer, 1881), p. 1008.

37 'Australian news', *Wanganui Herald* (21 March 1881), p. 2.

38 M. Mosley, *New Zealand International Exhibition, 1882: Record, Containing Retrospect of the Colony, Sketch of Exhibitions, Complete Description of Exhibits* (Christchurch: James Caygill, 1882), p. lxx.

39 Loeffler, 'Pteridomania', p. 105.

40 Mary Ann Armstrong, 'New Zealand Ferns', 1886–87, collection of Hans P. Kraus, Jr, New York.

41 Henare, *Anthropology and Imperial Exchange*, p. 190.

42 Armstrong and Twomey, *The South Pacific Fern Album*, pp. 25–6.

43 Loeffler, 'Pteridomania', p. 8.
44 David Elliston Allen, *The Victorian Fern Craze: A History of Pteridomania* (London: Hutchinson, 1969), p. 20.
45 The Hocken Library, University of Otago, Dunedin, holds a set of Armstrong's stationery, UVPF A.
46 Betty Malone, 'Mary Ann: Personal Recollections', collection of Richard Daffey. Malone was the granddaughter of Armstrong.
47 *Colonial and Indian Exhibition*, p. 59; Whittingham, *Fern Fever*, p. 85. Advertisements for her fern work suggest that she had also sent an exhibit to the *Exposition Universelle* in Paris in 1878. 'Ferns! ferns! ferns!', *Poverty Bay Herald* (29 March 1884), p. 3.
48 Whittingham, *Fern Fever*, p. 32.
49 *Official Record of the Centennial International Exhibition, Melbourne, 1888–1889* (Melbourne: Sands & McDougall, 1890), p. 1061. This demonstration was not without mishap. The *Sydney Morning Herald* reports that a small fire was started at the stall by Miss Armstrong, who accidentally lit a box of safety matches. 'Fire at the Melbourne Exhibition', *Sydney Morning Herald* (26 November 1888), p. 7.
50 *Poverty Bay Herald* (1 October 1889), p. 2. The advertisement gives a sense of the value of these shipments: 'During the last quarter Mr Armstrong shipped ferns hence to Australia valued at £110.'
51 'Large variety of New Zealand ferns', *Sydney Morning Herald* (16 July 1885), p. 1.
52 'The preparation of ferns', *Argus* (23 October 1889), p. 11.
53 Armstrong and Twomey, *The South Pacific Fern Album*, p. 9.
54 'Current topics', *Launceston Examiner* (12 July 1890), p. 4; *Maitland Mercury & Hunter River General Advertiser* (14 October 1893), p. 4.
55 Armstrong and Twomey, *The South Pacific Fern Album*, p. 13.
56 Armstrong and Twomey, *The South Pacific Fern Album*, p. 13.
57 Armstrong and Twomey, *The South Pacific Fern Album*, p. 9.
58 Peter Hoffenberg, *An Empire on Display: English, Indian, and Australian Exhibitions from the Crystal Palace to the Great War* (Berkeley: University of California Press, 2001), pp. 3–4.
59 Tony Hughes-d'Aeth, *Paper Nation: Picturesque Atlas of Australasia, 1886–1888* (Melbourne: Melbourne University Press, 2001), p. 224.
60 Armstrong and Twomey, *The South Pacific Fern Album*, pp. 1, 16.
61 Armstrong and Twomey, *The South Pacific Fern Album*, pp. 16, 21–6.
62 Armstrong and Twomey, *The South Pacific Fern Album*, p. 15.
63 Armstrong and Twomey, *The South Pacific Fern Album*, pp. 16–17.
64 'Published every evening', *Poverty Bay Herald* (20 October 1885), p. 2.
65 Undated *Herald* newspaper clipping from the scrapbook of Jeremiah Twomey, collection of Richard Daffey.
66 The *Examiner* reveals that commercial photographs were also sent to Twomey for consideration. 'Current Topics', p. 4.
67 *The New Atlas of Australia* (Sydney: John Sands, 1886), p. 42; Andrew Garran, ed., *Picturesque Atlas of Australasia* (Sydney: Picturesque Atlas Publishing Co., 1886), p. 305.
68 Esau, *Images of the Pacific Rim*, p. 123.
69 Hughes-d'Aeth, *Paper Nation*, pp. 216–18.
70 Armstrong and Twomey, *The South Pacific Fern Album*, 9.
71 Esau, *Images of the Pacific Rim*, pp. 124, 126.
72 Illustrated in Robyn Stacey and Ashley Hay, *Herbarium* (Cambridge: Cambridge University Press, 2004), p. 144.
73 Despite her prolific collection and production over a twenty-year period, there is no evidence that she discovered any new species. However, she did contribute information on existing species, including the *Phylloglossum drummondii*, which she discovered in the Canterbury districts. Armstrong and Twomey, *The South Pacific Fern Album*, p. 7. Armstrong passed away on 2 July 1910 and is buried in Melbourne General Cemetery beneath a headstone inscribed with ferns.

74 Armstrong and Twomey, *The South Pacific Fern Album*, p. 3.
75 Loeffler, 'Pteridomania', p. 105.
76 Armstrong and Twomey, *The South Pacific Fern Album*, pp. 14, 20.
77 Armstrong and Twomey, *The South Pacific Fern Album*, p. 15.
78 Armstrong and Twomey, *The South Pacific Fern Album*, p. 16.
79 Loeffler, 'Pteridomania', p. 99.
80 Henry Field, *Ferns of New Zealand and Its Immediate Dependencies, with Directions for Their Collection and Cultivation* (London: Griffith, Farren, Ockden, & Welsh, 1890), p. 1.
81 J. Cowan, *Official Record of the New Zealand International Exhibition of Arts and Industries Held at Christchurch, 1906–1907: A Descriptive and Historical Account* (Wellington: Government Printer, 1910), pp. 165–8; Whittingham, *Fern Fever*, pp. 205–6.
82 Loeffler, 'Pteridomania', p. 83; James Belich, *Paradise Reforged: A History of the New Zealanders from the 1880s to the Year 2000* (Auckland: Allen Lane & Penguin, 2001), pp. 29–30.
83 Star, 'Biota Barons', p. 12.
84 Armstrong and Twomey, *The South Pacific Fern Album*, p. 16.

PART III

New Zealand's Pacific empire

CHAPTER SEVEN

From Sudan to Sāmoa: imperial legacies and cultures in New Zealand's rule over the Mandated Territory of Western Samoa

Patricia O'Brien

On 26 December 1898, British forces were under pressure on a small sand and shingle island in the Blue Nile. Known as the Battle of Rosaires, this attack was one of the last actions in Britain's fight to subdue the long-standing Sudanese insurrection against the British-backed Egyptian occupation.[1] In the intense fighting, machine guns and several British companies tried to dislodge 'fanatical' dervishes who had taken refuge on the island (see Figure 7.1). The intense fighting killed many; others drowned swimming the Nile.[2] The brunt of British casualties were taken by the Xth Soudanese, commanded by Major Charles Fergusson, who was 'severely' wounded and mentioned five times in dispatches for his heroism in the battle.[3] For Fergusson, the Sudan left an indelible mark. It became the lens through which he refracted imperial polemics three decades after the Battle of Rosaires, when he presided over another insurrection against imperial rule, this time in the Pacific.

After the Sudan, Fergusson's military career took him to Ulster and then on to the Western Front during the First World War. His 1924–30 appointment as Governor-General of New Zealand capped off a distinguished military and imperial career (see Figure 7.2). Both his father, Sir James Fergusson (1873–74) and his father-in-law, Lord Glasgow (1892–97) had served as New Zealand governors.[4] The first years of his term were relatively uneventful: he travelled extensively around New Zealand and also took in a tour of 'Greater New Zealand' – its island dependencies – in May 1926, of which he wrote that the 'reception accorded me by residents and natives alike was most satisfactory'.[5] He wrote effusively of Western Samoa, lavishing praise on General George Spafford Richardson: a 'born administrator of native races, and a man of high ideals, of wide vision of the highest order', a man who had achieved 'extraordinary success'.[6] Richardson's devotion to the Sāmoans as shown in Figure 7.3 was likened to that of a father

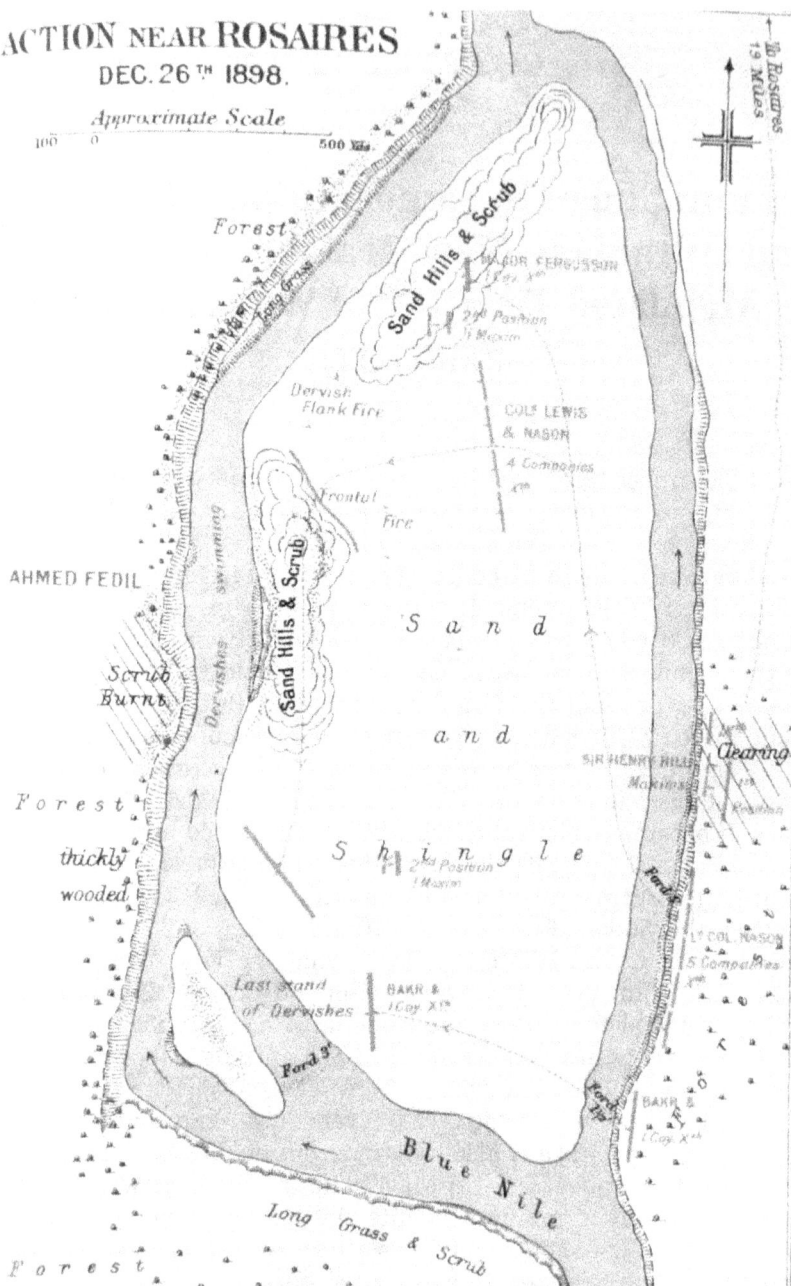

7.1 'Action near Rosaires', map from Winston Churchill, *The River War: An Historical Account of the Reconquest of the Soudan* (London: Longman Green and Co., 1899) Volume 2, opp. p. 344.

7.2 Sir Charles Fergusson. Crown Studios Ltd., negatives and prints,
ref: 10x8-2185-F
(Alexander Turnbull Library, Wellington, New Zealand).

to his children. This message was encapsulated in a widely distributed
photograph, ca. 1925, of the administrator holding the hand of a young
Sāmoan girl who gazes up at him, as does a little boy who is supposedly
hoisting the Union Jack.[7] The photograph attempted to visually represent (albeit awkwardly) the paternalism embedded in New Zealand's
Samoan colonial enterprise.

Yet Fergusson had to concede that Richardson's 'great determination'
had not won over everyone. There were detractors among the European
community, people who had 'battened on the natives in the past and
have looked at Samoa and its people from the point of view of exploitation and their own enrichment', and who were also disgruntled by
the local prohibition on alcohol.[8] Without fully realising it, Fergusson
had identified the nascent anti-colonial movement that would erupt
six months later, drawing him, New Zealand, and Britain into another
imperial trouble zone: the Mandated Territory of Western Samoa.

Fergusson played a critical and behind-the-scenes role in the
Sāmoan troubles until his term ended in January 1930. Unlike his

[129]

7.3 Portrait of General George Spafford Richardson with Samoan children. Rutherford, Alexander Mathieson, 1915–. Photographs of Samoa.
Ref: PA1-o-446-61-2
(Alexander Turnbull Library, Wellington, New Zealand).

father, Sir Charles's vice-regal duties were supposed to be confined to 'ceremony, constitution and community'.[9] New Zealand's 1907 shift from colonial to dominion status curbed vice-regal powers. Fergusson was to act as the line of communication between New Zealand and British governments, reporting on, but not interfering with, domestic political affairs that included governing Sāmoa. Yet New Zealand's continuing deference to Britain, the office of Governor-General, Fergusson's friendships with key personalities in the New Zealand government, and his extensive imperial experience – especially in the Sudan – emboldened Fergusson to overstep the limits of his role on numerous occasions.

In governing all its Pacific dependencies, New Zealand was an empire within an empire, but with Sāmoa there was the additional layer of imperial oversight in the form of the League of Nations' Permanent Mandates Commission (PMC). This chapter tracks the role Fergusson played in exerting British influence from its imperial centre to its colonial peripheries: to New Zealand and then to Sāmoa. It also shows how he and the New Zealand government managed British rule of Sāmoa with the PMC, and the Governor-General's consistent advocacy for the maintenance of imperial prestige in Sāmoa through the use of violence.

Between 1926 and 1930, international opinion about New Zealand's execution of its imperial duties plummeted, almost entirely as a result of its handling of the Sāmoan troubles. In 1930, the *Chicago Tribune* charged New Zealand with being 'unjust' and 'roughly handling' Sāmoans, and this from a nation 'supposed to represent the best grade of British emigration'.[10] Only four years earlier, at the Imperial Conference held in London in October 1926, Australian Prime Minister Stanley Melbourne Bruce had asserted that New Zealand's 'eighty years of previous experience in governing Polynesians' had served them well in their rule over Sāmoa.[11] Unlike South Africa and Australia, which governed the Mandated Territories of South West Africa and New Guinea respectively, New Zealand had received less negative attention for its rule over Sāmoa. Australia had consistently attracted negative international attention for its conduct towards New Guinea, and towards its own Aboriginal peoples.[12]

The seemingly abrupt change in opinion about New Zealand's imperial capabilities ignored its longer troublesome history in the Pacific, not least of which was the 1918 influenza epidemic that had killed over 20 per cent of Sāmoa's population. Many Sāmoans held New Zealand accountable for this calamity and afterwards grew increasingly critical of its administration.[13] Within months of Bruce's flattering views, resistance erupted in Sāmoa. This followed the formation, in March 1927, of the Samoan League, known as the Mau, which resulted from two meetings held on 15 October and 12 November 1926, when Sāmoans and Europeans met in Apia to discuss concerns about General Richardson's administration. Richardson tried to have the second meeting stopped. While noting that 'freedom of speech and honest criticism of the Government are not barred in any way; they are British privileges to which no exception can be taken', he considered that Sāmoans were being drawn into political affairs that concerned only Europeans and this was 'disturbing the peace, order and good government of the Territory'.[14] He wanted Sāmoan and European affairs to be separate; ignoring this directive would be considered an act of defiance. Despite his strong disapproval, the meeting continued and organisers asked, '[can] the interests of Samoans and Europeans ... be separated, or are they identical?'[15]

Richardson reacted to this perceived insubordination by issuing a swathe of banishment orders to Sāmoans who participated in the meeting. He also began threatening the Europeans involved with exile from Sāmoa, though this would first require the New Zealand Parliament to amend the 1921 Samoa Act that was the legal foundation of New Zealand's Sāmoan administration. Richardson's harsh response prompted the formation of the Mau, which adopted non-violent civil disobedience, petitioning and publicity as their main tactics.[16]

Parliamentarians confronted Sāmoan resistance during debates in June and July 1927 as they debated legalising exile from Sāmoa without trial by amending the Samoa Act. Parliamentary speeches covered a range of routine subjects as well as stirring and passionate ones, such as British Empire, race, and New Zealand history.[17] Many parliamentarians clung to the government line, encapsulated by Minister for External Affairs William Nosworthy's statement, 'I can stand in this house and say confidently that there is nothing wrong with the Samoa Administration'.[18] Prime Minister Gordon Coates argued that exile and banishment without trial were standard powers in 'the United States of America, France, Germany, Spain and then the British countries of South Africa, Australia, India and Egypt'.[19] Other MPs strenuously disagreed with the government's depiction of New Zealand's Sāmoan administration. In the words of Opposition leader and ardent supporter of the Sāmoan cause, Harry Holland:

> Has it come to this: that whoever dares to criticize the Administration of Samoa is to be met with a sentence of deportation? This is not to the credit of New Zealand: it constitutes an outrage upon every principle of British liberty, and is the reason to-day why there is so much resentment throughout New Zealand and other countries because of what we are doing in Samoa.[20]

Some parliamentarians remembered with unease New Zealand's history of exiling Māori leaders without trial. The turbulent and violent history surrounding Te Kooti Arikirangi Te Turuki was a case in point, including his exile without trial to the Chatham Islands in 1866, his 1868 escape back to New Zealand, and his prosecution of a draining war that lasted four years. This was in the minds of Holland and his fellow members William Lysnar, Edwin Howard, Peter Fraser, and Sir Māui Pōmare.

Both Howard and Pōmare also recalled the bloody consequences for Taranaki Māori resistance.[21] 'Looking back right through history to the Native wars we have had ... especially the trouble at the foot of Mount Egmont, we can trace it all back to bad mistakes in administration', Edwin Howard told Parliament on 19 July 1927.[22] In 1881 a military attack on the non-violent community of Parihaka in Taranaki had resulted in the capture of the community's leaders, Te Whiti O Rongomai and Tohu Kākahi, their exile to the South Island, and then the extensive confiscation of Māori lands. As well as providing a salient lesson on exile without trial, Parihaka was also a precedent for non-violent resistance, a philosophy and anti-imperial tactic the Sāmoan

Mau would follow.[23] Despite these evocations of New Zealand's troubled colonial past, Parliament did amend the Samoa Act to make exile from Samoa without trial lawful.

The government refused to acknowledge any genuine grievances against its administration. When Sir James Parr, New Zealand's High Commissioner to London, addressed the PMC in June 1928, following the 1927 petition, he stated that the 'Mau of present-day is quite a recent matter. Before the natives had been drawn into consultations and public meetings with the whites, the Samoans had had no idea whatever of raising the demand for self-government.'[24] Parr's portrayal of the sudden emergence of the Mau and calls for 'Samoa for Samoans' was misinformed and misleading. Sāmoans had been protesting colonial rule since 1908, when the German governor put down an armed revolt in Sāmoa by exiling its leaders to Saipan in the Mariana Islands. (Germany governed Sāmoa from 1900, until New Zealand's military occupation in 1914.) Parliamentarians were well aware of this event, which they took as a legitimate precedent for exile from Sāmoa without trial.[25] The 1908 uprising had its origins in the erosion of Sāmoan authority and the imposition of taxes: their demands were for greater Sāmoan autonomy. Europeans, too, wanted self-government: as they put it in a 1910 petition sent to the Reichstag, their 'chief desire' was to have 'those who pay the rates' also 'control the expenditure'.[26]

After 1918, and with a heightened sense of grievance following the influenza epidemic, Sāmoans continued to press New Zealand for self-government. Yet the 1921 Samoa Act ignored these aspirations and made 'no provision of any right of the people of Samoa to have a voice in the government of the country'. In 1923 the legislation was amended to allow for the election of three 'Europeans' to the Legislative Council, who would serve with six appointees.[27] New Zealand adopted the German model of creating a Fono of Faipule – an advisory body of Sāmoan chiefs – but this disrupted Sāmoan systems of power and became a leading cause of discontent.[28] There were also economic dimensions to the friction. Sāmoans were engaged in a boycott of European food and goods, which had escalated in price, while values for local products remained low.[29] In 1922 Richardson's predecessor, Administrator R. W. Tate, signed the Samoan Offenders Ordinance, which aimed to control 'certain Samoan customs'. Many Sāmoans saw this ordinance as 'vicious' as it permitted 'a sequence of banishments and degradations without trial of sacred and high Chiefs'.[30] When Richardson became administrator in 1923, he faced an already tense situation. By applying the ordinance in more egregious ways and exacerbating other tensions, he inflamed the discontent that culminated in the formation, or more accurately, the *reformation* of the Mau in early 1927.

7.4 Portrait of Ta'isi O. F. Nelson reproduced in N. A. Rowe, *Samoa Under Sailing Gods* (London: Putnam, 1930).

Initially New Zealand linked the emergence of the Mau to Germany's re-entry into international affairs. In September 1926 Germany joined the League of Nations, raising fears that it intended to regain its former colonies.[31] New Zealand authorities felt quite certain the Mau was a German plot to 'discredit New Zealand in the opinion of the world' and so support 'the demand for the transfer of the Mandate for Western Samoa from His Majesty the King in his right of government of this Dominion back to Germany'.[32] A proposed visit to Sāmoa and other ex-German Pacific colonies by the former governor, Dr Erich Schultz, and other officials in April 1927 amplified these fears.[33] The New Zealand Government also explained the Mau as a plot by self-interested and greedy Europeans. One of these 'Europeans', who maintained he was 'Samoan by birth, blood and sentiment', was Ta'isi O. F. Nelson, depicted in Figure 7.4.[34] New Zealand consistently singled him out as the éminence grise of the Mau.

Ta'isi was Sāmoa's richest man, who owned forty-five trading stations and over one hundred copra sheds.[35] From 1924 he became one of the three elected members of the advisory Legislative Council. Richardson held him in the highest esteem, claiming him as a friend, seeking his counsel and declaring in September 1926: 'I should be quite prepared to introduce him with confidence to any society in any part of the world to fitly represent yourselves.'[36] After Ta'isi chaired the two public meetings in late 1926, however, Richardson's admiration evaporated. In 1927 Ta'isi became chairman of the Citizens' Committee – the 'European' branch of the Mau – and drove the international campaign to highlight New Zealand's maladministration. But the Mau constituted much more than Ta'isi, although New Zealand refused to see it. When the great majority of Sāmoans allied themselves with the Mau, New Zealand officials accounted for this by arguing that 'Natives in the movement are Nelson's dupes' or, as Richardson would phrase it, 'so simple are the minds of the Natives ... they can be led by the nose to a keg of beef – and be galled by the wily half caste with his glib tongue in the vernacular'.[37]

That Ta'isi had German relatives by marriage, 'one of whom fought for Germany in the Great War', had entertained Germans, and was supported by them in Legislative Council elections, seemed conclusive evidence that further condemned him.[38] But stopping the German visit in 1927 did not quell the Mau and this conspiracy theory had to be abandoned. In July of that year William Nosworthy drafted an angry letter to Ta'isi, charging the Mau with attracting 'world wide attention' that threatened New Zealand's reputation.[39]

There was intense discussion in New Zealand about how to combat the Mau's non-violent resistance and civil disobedience tactics. Force, the traditional method of dealing with Indigenous resistance, was not as easily applied in the face of such a stance. The League of Nations added more complexity to this question of combating non-violent resistance. Officially the PMC made ambiguous statements on this issue and New Zealand was deferential to the PMC's position on the use of force. There were competing and confused sovereignties over Sāmoa, between New Zealand as a deputised power to Britain and the unclear role of the PMC. Did New Zealand, Britain, or the PMC have the greatest authority over Sāmoa? The Mau exploited these unclear jurisdictions. They also provided a platform for the Governor-General.

In his advice to the New Zealand government about the Sāmoan protest, Fergusson drew on his imperial experience. He noted that both Sāmoa and the Sudan were hampered by the 'ennervating effect' of climate.[40] Their problems, too, he saw as 'similar': both had 'a large native race ruled by a handful of Europeans, mainly by moral force'. Fergusson also believed that the 'native mind' had universal characteristics, regardless of geography: it 'never responds to nor appreciates conciliation', which 'is invariably interpreted as weakness'.[41] His advocacy of 'firm' colonial action was a vital part of the growing call, within the New Zealand government, the League of Nations and Britain, from early 1928, to use force against the Mau.

Fergusson began airing his views on Sāmoa in December 1927 to his trusted confidant, Sir Francis Bell, leader of the Legislative Council and conservative powerbroker. 'I am doing a most improper thing I suppose in writing to you, but you are an old friend and advisor and I think I may do it safely.' Fergusson was 'worried about Samoa and the Prime Minister's attitude about it'. He feared that Coates did not fully trust and support Richardson, even though the latter had been exonerated by the recently released findings of a Royal Commission into his administration. It was imperative, Fergusson continued, to publicly 'disgrace the agitator' [Ta'isi] and fully support Richardson, as 'the native mind is a queer thing and the only way to impress it is to take a strong line and show strength and firmness'.[42]

Buoyed by the commission's findings, Richardson launched a crackdown on the Mau. In January 1928, Ta'isi and two other Europeans were deported, an act New Zealand thought would quickly deflate the Mau. Instead, the civil disobedience campaign escalated. New Zealand sent two warships to Apia Harbour in February 1928 and a stand-off between New Zealand forces and the Mau lasted through March. During this period of heightened tension the option of violence was discussed.[43] Instead of resorting to force, Coates replaced Richardson as administrator, effective from 31 March 1928, giving him a face-saving appointment to the League of Nations where he would answer questions from the PMC about his administration in mid-1928. Ta'isi would also travel to Geneva to present a petition protesting his exile as well as one signed by 7,982 of a possible 9,325 Samoan taxpayers.[44] Not permitted to formally address PMC hearings, Ta'isi made private representations to some commissioners.[45]

Fergusson was not pleased with the government's course of action in March 1928. He wrote to Bell that the news about the termination of Richardson's appointment 'gave me a rather sleepless night'. This action would be a 'surrender to the malcontents'; 'the next administrator ... will never be trusted ... [and] the Government will never again regain its prestige'. He went on,

> to give in now is only to put off the evil day when you will have to fight it out. I quite see that to send troops is a serious matter, but it seems to me that having said publicly that you are going to see the thing through, to give in now is absolutely fatal ...

'I need hardly say,' he added, 'that I have no wish to interfere or be troublesome.'[46]

Fergusson also expressed his views to Coates in mid-March. 'I do not want to go one step beyond what is right or constitutional in proffering advice or expressing my views but I feel that you should at least know what they are.' He was concerned that the 'moral effect of our armed forces has been lost owing to the natives having become alive to the fact that they have been forbidden to use force ... our bluff has been called and exposed ... Imperial troops have been publicly derided and brought into contempt.' He was gravely concerned that the open defiance of the Mau, now led by Tupua Tamasese Lea'lofi – who assumed the Mau leadership after Ta'isi's exile – was not being met with 'firmness and decision'. He ended by telling Coates that 'the immediate arrest of Tamasese and the dispersal of the Mau from Apia at all costs are essential steps to be taken'.[47]

Responding eight days later, the prime minister assured Fergusson that he had 'carefully weighed' his views. Intelligence from Apia stressed that the navy could not have arrested Tamasese 'by force of arms' without the 'possibility of injuring and perhaps killing a large number of natives'. The commodore in command was 'deeply impressed with the difficulty of applying naval force to ignorant and childlike natives who have offered no violence on any occasion'. Coates acknowledged that he too feared 'our prestige has suffered' and that although the government would 'remedy the position by force if this is the only way', it felt they had acted appropriately against the Mau on their 'pacific course'.[48] What Coates did not admit here – although Richardson would reveal it to the PMC in June, asking them 'not to record in the Minutes what I wished to say' – was that New Zealand had taken care not to 'prejudice' the PMC's opinion of New Zealand by using force in March.[49]

The new administrator, Colonel Stephen Allen, was introduced to the public in one newspaper profile as a 'disciplinarian' who excelled in the New Zealand Expeditionary Force and had developed an 'enigmatic' reputation for his wartime feats. He warned the 'recalcitrant natives to abandon their present attitude', for it 'would be a thousand pities if the necessity to use force should arise'. 'Law rests upon force and duty is still duty however unpleasant it may be ... should further clemency fail, the regrettable alternative must be faced.'[50] To back up this warning, a new military police force of seventy-four, made up ideally of 'unemployed returned soldiers', would support Allen's administration.[51] Figures 7.5 and 7.6 both illustrate the public newspaper reportage.

As part of New Zealand's anxious preparations for the June 1928 PMC hearings, Coates said that the government would oversee 'another period of patience' in the hope that this may 'facilitate an amicable settlement' against the Sāmoans' passive resistance.[52] Comments

7.5 'Reinforcement for the administration police at Samoa; the departure from Auckland last Saturday morning', staff photographer, *Auckland Weekly News*, 26 April 1928 (Auckland Libraries, Sir George Grey Special Collections, AWNS-19280426-38-3).

7.6 'Keeping the peace in New Zealand's mandated territory at Samoa', photograph by A. J. Tattersall, *Auckland Weekly News*, 13 September 1928 (Auckland Libraries, Sir George Grey Special Collections, AWNS-19280913-40-3).

during the hearings gave the government heart that their approach would meet with PMC approval. Richardson was particularly gratified when his military reputation was cited and the anticipated hostility of the German commissioner, Dr Ludwig Kastl, did not eventuate.[53] Sir James Parr reported back to Wellington that the commissioners accepted New Zealand's explanation, that 'all of these evils were due to Nelson and his friends'; or as British commissioner Lord Lugard phrased it, the slogan 'Samoa for Samoans really means government of Samoa and the natives by 5 or 6 commercial residents on the beach', led by that 'blighter' Nelson.[54] Parr and Richardson were also heartened by commissioner Dr William Rappard's statement, 'the tutor who does not punish his ward when the ward is insubordinate is ... not doing his duty', and Kastl's argument that New Zealand's policy of tolera-tion must now be abandoned and replaced by firmer measures.[55] The Belgian and Spanish commissioners 'agreed largely with Mr Kastl', Parr explained, but pointed out that 'the Mandates Commission could not advise the use of forcible or military measures'.[56] The consensus from commissioners was that 'deference for the League should not prevent the mandatory power ... from carrying out its first duty, which was the maintenance of order'.[57]

New Zealand took the PMC's ambiguous statement on force as tacit endorsement: 'it is safe to say,' Parr told Coates, 'that a stiffer attitude to the Mau will not be disapproved at Geneva.'[58] After the favourable findings from the PMC, two other periods of heightened tension again raised the question of the use of force. In November 1928, Allen again sought to arrest Tupua Tamasese and alerted the government that in 'executing [the] warrant now some bloodshed will almost certainly occur'.[59] Coates replied that 'any action to be taken is left to your dis-cretion'.[60] Tupua Tamasese was arrested and then sentenced to a term in Auckland's Mount Eden prison. However, this tactic did not quell the movement: in March 1929 the Mau refused to pay a new personal tax and tensions again escalated.

An infuriated Fergusson wrote a strongly worded letter to the new Prime Minister, Joseph Ward, on 17 March 1929. In his eyes, the Mau were acting as they always had done 'in carrying out Nelson's parting advice to stick to their passive resistance ... and all would come right in their favour'. He claimed that

> in dealing with natives ... you must look on them and treat them as children – be kind, be just, be tactful; but above all be strict, never allow rules to be broken with impunity ... never threaten without carrying out the threat, if cause is given.

This 'fundamental principle' had been neglected and 'led up to the present impasse ... but there comes a time when the situation has to be faced, and then the enforcement of discipline and law and order becomes a difficult and painful necessity'. All the proposed actions discussed with Allen had the same flaw: weakness. Non-payment of taxes, frequent in the Sudan, was dealt with by descending on a village and 'seizing the headman' and 'distraining on the inhabitants', Fergusson explained.

'Payment was taken in kind, in corn or cattle or produce and a fine inflicted.' The 'headman remained in custody till the fine was paid ... if there was active resistance, then heads would get broken and possibly then the village was burnt'. Fergusson reminded Ward that the League of Nations 'has expressed its opinion pretty strongly that the fault of New Zealand in the past has been its want of firmness ... and it has practically called upon New Zealand to carry out its task of enforcing law and order'. 'The opinion by men who are one and all experts in dealing with native races' was 'ample justification in the eyes of public opinion for standing no more nonsense in Samoa'.[61] To Fergusson's great frustration, New Zealand revoked the tax after Allen was recalled to Wellington for meetings with the Ward government, which concluded that, given the size of the population and the opposition to the tax, even loyal Sāmoans would not pay up without the use of 'hard and stern means'.[62]

The government was still unclear about the league's position. At the June 1929 PMC hearings Parr was to convey that the government would 'coerce the disaffected Samoans by force of arms should this be unavoidable' and that 'a section of the Samoans' also believed that force was 'the quickest way of concluding present difficulties'. Despite all their 'recalcitrance' the Mau had 'never been threatening and ... the movement, unfortunate and mischievous as it undoubtedly is, has been conducted ... with some dignity and restraint'. In 1928, Parr had tried to obtain from the PMC 'a definite indication to the extent to which force should be applied', but only received the 'opinion in general terms that authority must be enforced'. For the 1929 PMC meetings he was instructed to

> state that if the Permanent Mandates Commission find themselves unable to agree with the wisdom of the course adopted and consider the application of force essential the New Zealand Government, while of course maintaining their view of the position, would be grateful if the Commission would in intimating this fact in their report specify the manner in which, and the degree to which they consider force should be applied.

Parr was to venture into this terrain only if the PMC obviously favoured force; this discussion could also be conducted in private meetings with members. Parr did raise the issue of force and got a similar official response to that of 1928.[63]

It was not the question of force, however, that gave Parr a 'most difficult time' at the 1929 PMC hearings, but trying to square previous annual reports and Richardson's 1928 evidence with the Vershaffelt, Park, and Berendsen (VPB) Report of January 1929. This report undermined New Zealand's previous stance and instead, to New Zealand's embarrassment, supported one of the Mau's chief criticisms

[140]

of the administration: extravagance.[64] After the PMC's censure of New Zealand's administration, the Mau issued another petition to King George in mid-November 1929, requesting that the administration of Sāmoa be transferred to the British Colonial Office.

Before he left New Zealand in 1928 to take up his post in Sāmoa, Allen had a lengthy meeting with Fergusson, who, as he reported to Coates, 'gave me a good deal of advice that will be of use I think'.[65] In late June, Allen told the prime minister about the 'battle of Malautu' one month earlier, when Mau members suffered wounds during scuffles with New Zealand forces intent on arresting a Mau agitator, Leota. The incident 'shook them up badly' and nearly sparked a defection of supporters from the Mau.[66] Allen predicted that if another similar incident occurred, the Mau would dissolve quickly: 'if by chance they resist arrest and there is some bloodshed I believe it [the Mau] will go quickly, especially if we find any good chance to arrest the leaders'. Coates should 'expect something of this sort to happen'.[67]

Allen's scenario for 'bloodshed' was remarkably close to the events of 28 December 1929. A large procession of men was heading for the Apia waterfront to greet returning deportee A. G. Smyth (who had been exiled from Sāmoa along with Ta'isi the previous January) and Ta'isi's lawyer, Alfred Hall Skelton. The latter was in Sāmoa to collect testimony for an upcoming libel action brought by Ta'isi against *New Zealand Herald*. When New Zealand forces tried to arrest two Mau members in the procession, the result was what has become known as the Black Saturday Massacre. The coronial inquiry into the 'riot' found that Constable William Abrahams was attacked and killed, along with eight Sāmoans.[68] This triggered a response from New Zealand forces that included machine gun and rifle fire from three sharpshooters, both from a second-floor balcony. The Chief Judge, J. H. Luxford, found that the machine gun was 'fired for its moral effect' but did not cause any of the casualties, whereas the rifle fire resulted in fatal injuries. Despite concluding that rifle fire was unnecessary, he determined that the New Zealand action was 'justified' owing to the circumstances of the 'affray'.[69] Allen reported to Wellington that the show of force had a 'great' immediate effect on the Mau. He was 'rather sorry Tamasese was killed, and would have preferred it to be Faumuina [Faime Mulinu'u] ... one really bad ruffian Tuia was shot' and perhaps the man who had killed Abrahams. Apart from that 'there was no one else killed of any particular importance'.[70] Fergusson told Ward that now that salutary 'bloodshed has ... taken place', New Zealand needed to 'maintain its authority and prestige'.[71]

One month after the massacre, in his final quarterly report to the Secretary of State of the Dominions (Lord Passfield), and at the end of his term as Governor-General, Fergusson recounted the events of and following 28 December, which had successfully broken the 'stalemate'. He again noted the centrality of Ta'isi: 'upon him justly falls the odium of misguiding ... this backward though lovable Samoan people'. Since the 'disloyal movement' had started in late 1926, New Zealand had 'been pursued by a most perverse fate' in its policy towards the Mau. In his view, the movement 'could have been nipped in the bud had firm action been taken during the first six months', or on subsequent occasions of heightened tension, but Coates had not been convinced 'that aggressive action was the best solution'. 'My own part in the Samoan drama,' Fergusson wrote, 'may be at variance with the modern conception of the function of a Governor General' but 'the suggestions ... I ventured ... were not without encouragement ... So fortified by these assurances and by the knowledge that the Government have now taken a course of action in line with my own conclusions, I am unrepentant.'[72]

Complex global and historical frames affected this imperial episode. The question of applying force against the non-violent Mau bedevilled New Zealand authorities for some years; when they did resort to force, it was with the knowledge that both the PMC and Britain would quietly approve. The PMC's attitude to force was a considerable factor in New Zealand's decision-making, as was the British approach so strongly, if secretly, advocated by Fergusson. There is irony here. In their petitions of 1919 and 1929, the Sāmoans had requested that the administration of their country be transferred to the British Colonial Office. They saw Britain as the superior, more professional and experienced colonial power. As Fergusson's conduct shows, however, colonial experience could cut two ways. His Sudanese experience not only normalised violence as a governing tool, but taught him that its application was indispensable in dealing with 'child-like' races. In 2002 the New Zealand government rightly accepted responsibility for the 1929 massacre and apologised. Yet the agents behind this event extended beyond the New Zealand government. Governor-General Charles Fergusson exerted a great deal of influence on events leading up to the massacre. He collapsed the geographical and temporal distance between the Battle of Rosaires in the Sudan in 1898 and the Black Saturday Massacre in 1929 on the streets of Apia, and thus drew clear lines of imperial practice and attitude between these seemingly disconnected episodes of British imperialism thirty-one years apart.

Acknowledgements

I acknowledge the generous support of the Stout Trust and the Stout Research Centre as well as the invaluable assistance of Lydia

Wevers, Tamasailau Suaalii-Sauni, and Rachel Buchanan. I thank Sanjay Subrahmanyam, Tony Brunt, librarians at the National Library of New Zealand, especially Roger Swanson, and archivists at Archives New Zealand, particularly Donal Raethel. I also thank the Ta'isi āiga, especially Tui Atua Tupua Tamasese Ta'isi Efi and Masiofo Filifilia, as well as my own āiga for their continuing devoted support of my work.

Notes

1   Winston Churchill, *The River War: An Account of the Reconquest of the Sudan*, MobileReference.com, 2010, pp. 353, 215, 102.

2   Churchill, *The River War*, MobileReference.com, chapter 18. Churchill often used the adjective 'fanatical' to describe the Sudanese rebels. See, for example, pp. 17, 25, 27.

3   Churchill, *The River War*, MobileReference.com, pp. 405–6; Map from Churchill, *The River War: An Historical Account of the Reconquest of the Soudan* (London: Longman Green & Co., 1899), Vol. 2, opp. p. 384; Archives New Zealand (hereafter ANZ), G48/6 R19162155,'Brief Sketch of His Excellency's Career'. Richard Toye, *Churchill's Empire: The World That Made Him and the World He Made* (New York: Henry Holt, 2010).

4   John Wheeler-Bennett, 'Fergusson, Sir Charles, of Kilkerran, seventh baronet (1865–1951)', rev. Roger T. Stearn, *Oxford Dictionary of National Biography*, Oxford University Press, 2004, www.oxforddnb.com.proxy.library.georgetown.edu/view/article/33111, accessed 3 October 2013.

5   National Archives, London (hereafter NA), DO 35/4, Charles Fergusson to Prime Minister Gordon Coates, 21 June 1926, p. 8.

6   NA, DO 35/4, Charles Fergusson to Prime Minister Gordon Coates, 21 June 1926, p. 8.

7   Alexander Turnbull Library, Wellington, New Zealand (hereafter ATL), Photographs of Samoa, PA1-0-446-61-2, 'Portrait of General George Spafford Richardson with Samoan children'; ATL, PA1-0-446-61-2, Alexander Mathieson Rutherford, 'Photographs of Samoa'.

8   NA, DO 35/4, Charles Fergusson to Prime Minister Gordon Coates, 21 June 1926, p. 8.

9   *Te Ara: The Encyclopedia of New Zealand*, http://www.teara.govt.nz/en/ gover nors-and-governors-general/page-1, accessed 15 July 2013.

10 'The white man's burden', *Chicago Tribune* (4 February 1930), n.p.

11 'Australia's mandates: Care of Natives', *Argus* (25 October, 1926), p. 17.

12 Patricia O'Brien, 'Reactions to Australian colonial violence in New Guinea: The 1926 Nakanai Massacre in a global context', *Australian Historical Studies*, 43:2 (2012), 191–209.

13 Malama Meleisea, *The Making of Modern Samoa: Traditional Authority and Colonial Administration in the History of Western Samoa* (Suva: Institute of Pacific Studies, 1987); Mary Boyd, 'Coping with Samoan resistance after the 1918 influenza epidemic', *Journal of Pacific History*, 15:3 (1980), 155–74.

14 ATL, Bell Family Papers Series 3, Sir Frances Henry Dillon Bell (hereafter BP], 5210-159, 'Administrator Richardson's letter read to Public Meeting of Citizens', 12 November 1926, in Joint Samoan Petition Inquiry Committee Report, August 1927, p. 20.

15 ATL, BP 5210-159, F. Nelson, Chairman, in 'Transcript of Public Meeting of Citizens', 12 November 1926, in Joint Samoan Petition Inquiry Committee Report, p. 20.

16 J. W. Davidson, *Samoa Mo Samoa* (Oxford: Oxford University Press, 1967); Mary Boyd, 'The record in Western Samoa to 1945', in Angus Ross (ed.), *New Zealand's*

Record in the Pacific Islands in the Twentieth Century (London: Longman Paul, 1969).

17 See New Zealand Legislative Council and House of Representatives Parliamentary Debates (hereafter NZPD) Vol. 212, 23 June–27 July 1927.

18 William Nosworthy (Ashburton), NZPD Vol. 212, 19 July 1927, p. 669.

19 Prime Minister Gordon Coates, NZPD Vol. 212, 22 July 1927, p. 831.

20 Harry Holland (Buller), NZPD Vol. 212, 22 July 1927, p. 839. Nicholas Hoare, 'Harry Holland's Samoan complex', Journal of Pacific History, 49:2 (2014), 151–69.

21 Holland, William Lysnar (Gisborne), Edwin Howard (South Christchurch), Peter Fraser (Wellington Central), and Maui Pomare (Western Māori), NZPD Vol. 212, pp. 897, 676–7, 678, 686, 928.

22 Howard, NZPD Vol. 212, p. 678.

23 For further discussion of connections between Parihaka and the Mau see Patricia O'Brien, 'Ta'isi O. F. Nelson and Sir Maui Pomare: Samoans and Māori reunited', Journal of Pacific History, 49:1 (2014), 26–49. The Sim Commission's 1926 and 1927 hearings into nineteenth-century Māori land confiscations should have refreshed more parliamentarians' history. As a child, Maui Pomare lived at Parihaka when it was attacked in 1881. Hazel Riseborough, Days of Darkness: Taranaki 1878–1884 (Wellington: Allen & Unwin, 1989), chapter 6; Rachel Buchanan, The Parihaka Album: Lest We Forget (Wellington: Huia Publishers, 2009), pp. 145–51.

24 Sir James Parr to Permanent Mandates Commission Hearings, 21 June 1928. Richardson tried to link the Mau in the Mandated Territory with the one in American Samoa that he stated had been in existence for 'approximately ten years'. ANZ, IT1 267 EX 25/14 R17961849, Proof copy of 'Proceedings of Fourteenth Meeting of the Permanent Mandates Commission June 1928', pp. 110–11.

25 Peter Hempenstall and Noel Rutherford, Protest and Dissent in the Colonial Pacific (Suva: Institute of Pacific Studies, 1984), pp. 26–32. See speeches in NZPD Vol. 212, pp. 835, 863, 889, and 896.

26 Government Printer, Wellington, 'Petition forwarded by certain residents of Western Samoa on the 4th February 1910 to the High President of the German Parliament in Berlin', appended to Mandated Territory of Western Samoa Report of Visit by Hon. W. Nosworthy, 1927, pp. 44–6, http://atojs.natlib.govt.nz, accessed 7 March, 2013.

27 O. F. Nelson, The Truth About Samoa: A Review of Events Leading up to the Present Crisis (Auckland: O. F. Nelson, 1928), p. 8.

28 For a history of the Fono of Faipule under German rule, see Hempenstall and Rutherford, Protest and Dissent, p. 22.

29 ANZ, IT1 EX79/2/1 R17962644, E. P. Lee, Minister for External Affairs, to O. F. Nelson, 15 January 1921, p. 1.

30 Nelson, The Truth, pp. 8–11.

31 O'Brien, 'Reactions'.

32 ANZ, G48 38 S/17 R19162280, Nosworthy to External, 12 June 1927; ANZ, IT1 37 EX 1/23/8, part 6, R17961291, draft of Nosworthy to Chairman of Citizen's Committee [O. F. Nelson], 12 July 1927.

33 See various documents in ANZ, G48 35 EX S/3(1), R19162267, such as Prime Minister Coates to Charles Fergusson, 15 March 1927.

34 ANZ, IT1 EX79/2/1 R17962644, O. F. Nelson to Prime Minister Massey, 8 January 1921, p. 1.

35 BP 5210-159, 'Evidence before Joint Samoan Petition Inquiry Committee', p. 37.

36 Ibid., p. 34.

37 ANZ, G48 38 S/17 R19162280, Nosworthy to External, 12 June 1927; ATL, BP 5210-068, Richardson to Bell, 11 July 1928.

38 ANZ, G48 35 EX S/3(1), R19162267, George Richardson, 'Secret Memorandum on German Propaganda', 13 January 1927, and the cancelled memorandum for the Governor General from Prime Minister Coates, 15 July 1927.

39 ANZ, IT1 37 EX 1/23/8, part 6, R17961291, draft of Nosworthy to Chairman of Citizen's Committee [O. F. Nelson], 12 July 1927.

40   ANZ, AAEG W3240 950, box 55, R17709025, Fergusson to Ward, 23 February 1929.
41   ANZ, G48 EX S/17 (1), box 40, R 19162282, Fergusson to Ward, 17 March 1929.
42   BP 5210-067, Fergusson to Bell, 13 December 1927.
43   See ANZ, AAEG W3240 950, box 28, part 5, R17708949, Berensden to Coates, 15 February 1928 as well as other documents in this file ca. mid-February 1928.
44   *NZ Samoa Guardian* (27 June 1929), p. 4 states that 7,982 taxpayers signed the 1928 petition to the League out of 9,325 possible taxpayers who were defined as Samoan men over age 17; Davidson, citing the *NZ Samoa Guardian* suggested this number of petitioners was exaggerated, p. 133.
45   Susan Pedersen, 'Samoa on the world stage: Petitions and peoples before the Mandates Commission of the League of Nations', *Journal of Imperial and Commonwealth History*, 40:2 (2012), 231–61; Gerald Chaudron, 'The League of Nations and imperial dissent: New Zealand and the British Labour Governments, 1924–31', *The Journal of Imperial and Commonwealth History*, 39:1 (2011), 47–71.
46   BP 5210-067, Fergusson to Bell, 3 March 1928.
47   ANZ, AAEG W3240 950, box 29, part 6, R17708952, Fergusson to Coates, 13 March 1928.
48   ANZ, AAEG W3240 950, box 29, part 6, R17708952, Coates to Fergusson, 21 March 1928.
49   ANZ, AAEG W3240 950, box 28, part 7, R17708950, Richardson to Berensden, 3 July 1928.
50   ANZ, AAEG W3240 950, box 29, part 6, R17708952, 'Samoan Affairs: New Administrator', 27 March 1928 (newspaper article with no publication recorded).
51   ANZ, AAEG W3240 950, box 29, part 6, R17708952, Coates to Allen, 26 March 1928.
52   ANZ, IT 1, box 267, R17961849, Coates to Parr, 25 May 1928.
53   ANZ, IT 1 box 267, R1796184, 'Proceedings of Fourteenth Meeting of the Permanent Mandates Commission June 1928', Richardson's military reputation cited p. 97; ANZ, AAEG W3240 950, box 28, part 7, R17708950, Richardson to Bell, 11 July 1928.
54   ANZ, IT 1 box 267, R17961849, Parr to Coates, 5 November 1928; ANZ, AAEG W3240 950, box 28, part 7, R17708950, Richardson to Coates, 28 July 1928.
55   ANZ, G48 35 EX S/3 (1), R19162267, Parr cablegram to Prime Minister's Department, 25 June 1928; ANZ, IT 1 box 267, R17961849, Parr to Coates, 5 November, 1928.
56   ANZ, IT 1 267, R17961849, Parr to Coates, 5 November, 1928.
57   ANZ, IT1 267, R17961849, Proof copy in 'Proceedings of Fourteenth Meeting of the Permanent Mandates Commission', p. 136.
58   ANZ, G48 35 S/3 (1), R19162267, Parr cablegram to Prime Minister's Department, 25 June 1928.
59   ANZ, G48 35 S/3 (1), R19162267, Allen to External Affairs, 14 November 1928.
60   ANZ, G48 35 S/3 (1), R19162267, Coates to Allen, 18 November 1928.
61   ANZ, G48 40 S/17 (1), R19162282, Fergusson to Ward, 17 March 1929.
62   ANZ, G48 40 S/17 (1), R19162282, Fergusson to Ward, 17 March 1929.
63   ANZ, G48 40 S/17 (1), R19162282, 'Notes on Western Samoa for the use of the representative of New Zealand at the League of Nations and the Permanent Mandates Commission', 1929, pp. 8–9. See Pedersen, for discussion of the 1929 PMC meetings, pp. 250–1.
64   ANZ, AAEG W3240 950, box 65, part 9, R17709062, Parr cablegram to Prime Minister, 18 November 1929.
65   ANZ, AAEG W3240 950, box 29, 311/3/7, part 6, R17708952, Allen to Coates, 11 April 1928.
66   ANZ, AAEG W3240 950, box 28, part 7, R17708950, Allen to Coates, 28 June 1928; for the official account of the 'battle of Malautu' see ANZ, AAEG W3240 950, box 28, R17708950, part 7, R17708950, Allen to Coates, 29 May 1928.
67   ANZ, AAEG W3240 950, box 28, R17708950, Allen to Coates, 28 June 1928.
68   Figures for Sāmoans killed differ. The 1930 Annual Report said eleven Sāmoans died. The monument at Vaimoso says nine Sāmoans were killed, Tupua Tamasese and

eight compatriots. The inquest investigated the deaths of William Abraham, High Chief Tamasese, Tapu, Faumuina of Safotu, Savai'i, Ainoa, Vele, Migao, Tu'ia, and Leota. See Michael Field, *Black Saturday: New Zealand's Tragic Blunders in Samoa* (Auckland: Reed, 2006).

69 National Library, Wellington, New Zealand, 'Coroner's Finding in the Inquest Respecting the Fatalities in Western Samoa', 1930, pp. 15, 16; http://atojs.natlib. govt.nz, accessed 1 October 2013.
70 ANZ, AAEG W3240 950, box 65, part 9, R 17709062, Allen to Ward, 8 January 1930.
71 ANZ, G48 S/17 (1), box 40, R19162282, Fergusson to Ward, undated handwritten letter; Ward responded to his letter on 4 January 1930, giving the date of Fergusson's letter as 2 January.
72 NA, DO 35/331/8, Fergusson, 'Report for Quarter ending 31 December 1929', 28 January 1930.

CHAPTER EIGHT

'Fiji is really the Honolulu of the Dominion': tourism, empire, and New Zealand's Pacific, ca. 1900–35

Frances Steel

New Zealand's colonial history is not confined to its own archipelago but stretches east and north into the vast Pacific. Many studies of 'New Zealand and the Pacific' address territorial ambitions and annexations, and the modalities and trajectories of direct rule.[1] As familiar as we are with the limitations of perceiving empire exclusively through geopolitical and 'hard power' lenses, it is instructive to recall at the outset here that even geopolitical imaginings were not formed merely from maps or by imperial cartographic practices. Regular travels beyond New Zealand and into the wider region lent knowledge and substance to these imaginings and helped sustain them. Empires, as John M. MacKenzie reminds us, were not just shaped by war, economic exploitation, and settlement; they were also empires of travel.[2]

Travel was not the sole domain of a small number of leading figures and officials. Rather, it involved hundreds of people who pursued a range of projects and itineraries, among them, and notably after 1900, increasing numbers of tourists. The beginnings of a tourist traffic between New Zealand and other islands in the Pacific forms the basis of this chapter. I examine how the industry became a source for the spread of new geographical and cultural perceptions of New Zealand's neighbourhood and new, non-peripheral imaginings of New Zealand's role in the Pacific. In short, I look to the ways in which tourism fashioned new frameworks for ordering relations between New Zealand and its neighbouring islands, including those beyond its sphere of formal sovereignty.[3]

Key to these changing perceptions was shipping. Colonial tourism has a maritime history, but questions of transport have sat largely at the margins of the existing historiography.[4] The steamships ferrying tourists from New Zealand into the wider Pacific carried diverse passenger lists and cargoes. For this reason, the tourist traffic cannot be seen as a wholly distinctive form of mobility, but entangled with the more 'mundane' and routine circulation of people and goods between islands. Maritime operations propelled the material sinews of an informal New Zealand empire in the Pacific, of which leisured mobility was one important strand, yet tourism was itself envisaged by its promoters to advance other ends. In the first part of the chapter I examine the ways in which tourism dovetailed with empires of trade and empires of settlement.

Shipping directs us to histories of connection. I adopt an oceanic lens in this chapter to also offer new perspectives on the tourism history of the wider Pacific basin. Histories of tourism – with notable exceptions, such as Ngaire Douglas's pioneering 1996 study, *They Came for Savages* – tend to be written of discrete nations and islands, of favoured destinations in isolation. This reflects the touristic value of the novel, the unique, and the exceptional.[5] Yet shipping routes and the mobility of tourists along them linked island ports. Historical studies of travel and tourism form an increasingly important part of colonial New Zealand's cultural and political history.[6] Just as commercial interests began to capitalise on New Zealand's natural 'wonders' and develop a domestic tourism industry, so too did they look into the Pacific with an eye to stimulating a new traffic.

The quotation in the title of this chapter – 'Fiji is really the Honolulu of the Dominion' – is drawn from the impressions of Auckland visitor E. Napier to Fiji in 1926.[7] It would be more accurate if it pinpointed Suva, Fiji's port capital, as the spatial equivalent of Honolulu, rather than the Fiji Islands as a whole. Napier's impressions suggest a comparative, mirror-image framing. 'If you look at a map of the Pacific,' another observer remarked, 'Fiji appears the natural hub of the south-central Pacific, as Hawaii is of the north-central.'[8] Both groups of islands lay proximate to larger countries of white settlement, but unlike Hawai'i's relationship to the United States, Fiji was not incorporated formally within New Zealand's Pacific empire, despite ongoing agitation for annexation from prominent leaders in New Zealand and pockets of disaffected white settlers in Fiji into the early twentieth century. In this sense it is not a neat parallel. Yet British influence in Fiji emanated from the proximate Dominions. As traveller Marjorie Appleton remarked on leaving Suva for Auckland in the late 1930s, 'I afterwards realised that New Zealand had in fact come out as far as Fiji to meet us'.[9]

The long shadow cast by America's extra-territorial push into the Pacific mediated white settler attitudes towards Fiji. Other scholars have examined the entangled colonial histories of Fiji and Hawai'i, notably through the racial politics of land title and citizenship, given the similar historical experiences of plantation economies and indentured Asian labour.[10] I consider how they were a part of a connected colonial history involving leisure and labour, and through a maritime network. The second half of the chapter examines the impact of American seaborne imperialism in the interwar years, as notions of a 'British' vis-à-vis an 'American' sea collided. In all these ways, then, I hope to connect the rise of tourism to a more archipelagic and trans-colonial historiography of the Pacific, one that accords due weight to New Zealand as a regional power in its own right, but as it sought to negotiate, accommodate, and contest the projections of others.

'A great national work': early tourism development in Fiji

On the basis of its location and perceived value as a gateway into the eastern Pacific, Fiji was the prominent focus of early New Zealand and Australian political and economic interest. As the *Otago Daily Times* declared in 1870, 'whoever rules at Fiji will command the trade of the islands in the South Pacific'.[11] Following the decline of the Victorian and Otago gold rushes and the outbreak of war in northern New Zealand, in the late 1860s many recent British immigrants regarded Fiji as a site of investment and on-migration. Britain annexed Fiji in 1874 yet Australia supplied much of the capital for its economic development, notably through the Colonial Sugar Refining Company.

Introduced in the early 1870s, the first steamship services to Fiji linked Sydney, Melbourne, and Auckland. In 1881 the Union Steam Ship Company of New Zealand (USSCo) – emerging as the key shipping provider between New Zealand and other Pacific ports – extended its domestic coastal operations, offering routes to Suva from Australasian ports, and later expanding its island trades to encompass Tonga, Sāmoa, and the Cook Islands. These services were primarily for the carriage of cargo and mail, but increasing passenger traffic was also envisaged. To this end USSCo offered a series of dedicated cruise tours from the 1880s. The first of these was a winter excursion to Suva in 1883. It was advertised as an opportunity to gain more knowledge about the colony, which was known only as the place of the 'sweet banana and luscious pineapple' and as a 'model Crown Colony which shared with New Zealand the divided attentions of our late ceremonious Governor, Sir Arthur Gordon'. Yet Fiji had 'made great strides' since British annexation, the *Otago Daily Times* observed, 'and the growing importance of its trade cannot but be a matter of much interest to New Zealand, which from its proximity should be in the best position to secure it'.[12] USSCo manager James Mills was on board, accompanied by 'several of the leading mercantile men of Dunedin'. In Suva he used the opportunity to inform commercial and pastoral interests of the company's intention to improve shipping services within Fiji and to Australasia.[13]

This tour was followed in 1884 by two round-trip cruises between Fiji, Tonga, and Sāmoa. Again, the value of a cruise was expressed through the prospects of enhanced trading relations markedly bearing some overtones of an informal empire of trade. 'It is clearly the policy of the colony to throw out tentacles Pacific-islands-wards,' the *New Zealand Times* remarked. 'Every business man of New Zealand who can find time should go make the tour.'[14] The long-standing appeal of the islands lay in the 'richness and variety of their tropical beauty', but as the Australasian colonies grew in importance 'the political and commercial value of these neighbouring Islands' correspondingly increased.[15] The cruise revealed to the 'financial companies' and 'enterprising merchant firms' of New Zealand a realm of islands 'teeming with future wealth', one passenger enthused, asserting, therefore, that USSCo was doing 'a great national work'.[16]

Tourism appeared to provide a foundation for increasing New Zealand engagement in the Pacific. Dedicated cruises were, however, expensive and took ordinary passenger steamers out of their regular trades. While company directors felt sure that 'being somewhat of a novelty' the island excursions would be well supported and become 'very popular and also very profitable', public interest soon lapsed. It was not until the end of the century that cruising was revived briefly, with two tours offered in 1898 and 1899. These itineraries extended further into the eastern and western Pacific islands.[17] USSCo offered package tours only intermittently in the early twentieth century, often to coincide with special events such as the coronation ceremonies in Fiji in 1902. The company also encouraged people to take tours independently, making use of their regular shipping services to travel between island ports. To this end, it hired Irish travel writer and journalist Beatrice Grimshaw to pen a series of travel guides, in which, ironically, she denounced steamships, ports, and the sociability of group travel, encouraging readers to venture into the interior to discover 'authentic' island life.[18]

It was the trans-Pacific lines, with larger passenger lists and higher expectations of service and hospitality en route, which gave added impetus to tourism promotion and development. The fact that New Zealand and American shipping interests were both engaged in these long-distance trades at about the same time is significant. The Pacific Mail Steamship Company of New York operated a mail route between San Francisco and Sydney on a regular basis from 1875. This called at Honolulu and initially at Galoa Harbour at Kadavu in southern Fiji. From 1885 USSCo assumed operation of the service, one that now bypassed Fiji, in conjunction with the American Oceanic Steam

Ship Company, managed by the son of Hawaiian sugar magnate Claus Spreckels. From 1893 another route, opened by Australian shipowner James Huddart, linked Sydney and Vancouver via Brisbane, Suva, Honolulu, and Victoria. It was known as the Canadian Australian Line (CA Line) or the 'All Red Route', in that the service linked British territories. A branch line between Suva and Auckland connected this trans-Pacific route to New Zealand until 1911, when USSCo assumed operation of the service and Auckland replaced Brisbane as a port of call. The route might now induce tourists to 'do the Pacific in a systematic manner', the Australian superintendent for immigration proposed in 1913, while also observing that tourism was 'frequently the forerunner of increased trade'.[19]

Ostensibly 'All Red', this route touched at Honolulu. Annexed by America in 1893, the Hawaiian Islands were incorporated as a territory in 1900. Trade in sugar and pineapples remained the principal industries, but the widespread circulation of Hawaiian motifs on the United States mainland, through music, postcards, photographs, travelling performances, and film, raised the prospects of enhanced tourism. There were enthusiastic predictions that tourists would be 'THE leading crop of the future'.[20] The Hawaii Promotion Committee (HPC) was established by former annexation leaders in 1903 to improve publicity in order to promote tourism, white settlement, and investment. Tourism was not an end in itself, as Christine Skwiot makes clear in her account of the US tourism empire in Hawai'i and Cuba. It was also encouraged with hopes that well-off tourists would stay and become planters, expanding the white middle class. This would strengthen America's imperial foothold in Hawai'i just as it fostered Hawaiian integration into the US economy. As the HPC worked to attract 'gentleman farmers', the Hawaii Immigration Board sought to increase the white labouring class so as to counter 'Asiatic competition', transforming Hawai'i, as President Theodore Roosevelt declared, into 'the right kind of island'.[21]

With Honolulu and Suva linked by the CA Line, passengers could not but be struck by the contrasts in the development of those two ports. One man from Nelson remarked in 1905 that while he could see the potential for the establishment of factories in Suva, 'I would not live in this hole for £2000 a year!' In Honolulu he advised readers to 'arrange to get off here and go on by the next boat – you would find it well worthwhile'.[22] His remarks illustrate the close relationship between sightseeing and prospecting, as not all passengers were travelling explicitly for leisure. They also indicate that published travellers' accounts served as a form of publicity beyond the work of official promotion agencies, and not always to a port's benefit. Comparative assessments were also found in editorial columns. Honolulu has 'palatial hotels, magnificent streets, beautiful homes, electric lights, motor cars, surf bathing, and bands to play each mail steamer in and out', complained the *Fiji Times* in 1909, 'and Suva, with every natural facility excelling Honolulu, a big weed-overgrown, paint-wanting village, practicing a cheese paring municipal economy that looks upon parks as luxury and roads as a special concession to private influence!' Unless Suva cleaned up its environment, the writer feared, 'Fiji will find herself left aside by the world's stream of traffic'.[23]

The quality of accommodation was a key measure of a port's attractiveness. On the early cruises passengers did not lodge ashore, but slept on board ship for the duration of the itinerary. On trans-Pacific passages the provision of good accommodation in port might induce passengers to break their journey and await the arrival of the next ship, stimulating the expansion not only of tourism and allied activities ashore but also of cruise capacity and traffic. Existing guest houses and hotels at Pacific ports usually doubled as drinking establishments, catering mainly for expatriate male workers rather than married couples, families or women. They offered very rudimentary facilities and single occupancy was uncommon. Sleeping quarters were more like dormitories, with curtains or flimsy partitions dividing each cubicle.[24] In Suva, the McDonald's Hotel was regarded as the best guest house. But as the USSCo island inspector, R. K. McLennan, wrote to his head office in Dunedin in 1903: 'it is clean and the table is fair, which is the best that can be said of it'. The 'proprietress is not a model hostess', he continued. 'Often, I am told she will not take in ladies or children on any condition.' Complaints about the current lodgings 'have a deterrent effect upon their friends proposing a similar trip – especially ladies'.[25] The prospect of increasing numbers of white women travelling in the Pacific demanded more attention to the gendered concerns of privacy and comfort, at sea and ashore. Moreover, USSCo engaged in trans-Pacific shipping partly to entice Americans further south into the Pacific, beyond Hawai'i. Many American passengers, when made aware of the lack of facilities in Suva, reportedly chose to travel by the San Francisco route to Australia which did not call at Fiji.[26]

Fearing that the lack of decent hotels in Suva would reflect poorly on the company, USSCo lobbied the Fiji government for approval to erect a new hotel and eventually secured a fifty-year lease of a harbour-front site in 1909 with right of renewal for twenty-five years. The chosen site was originally a canoe landing spot for the Indigenous inhabitants of Naiqasiqasi, the original Suva village. When the colonial capital moved to Suva the Indigenous residents were relocated to Suvavou or 'new Suva', a site on the opposite side of the harbour, in order to clear the area for the construction of the Government House. The hotel would be located centrally in the town's administrative quarter. It was anticipated that 'the objectionable class of customers' would continue to patronise guest houses at the opposite end of town near the wharves, while the 'desirable class' would make the hotel their meeting place, given its proximity to the cricket grounds and the Town Hall.[27]

Designed by Dunedin architects Salmond and Vanes, the Grand Pacific Hotel opened in 1914, shortly after the outbreak of the First World War. A thirty-bedroom, two-storied building with a chalk-white façade, it was advertised as 'the coolest building in Suva'.[28] To complete the picture of tropical comfort, USSCo engaged an Indian staff directly from Calcutta, believing that those Indians who already worked as servants in Fiji were 'practically useless' and that if not indentured specifically for domestic service they would be 'particularly unreliable'.[29]

The early years of operation were marred by a leaking roof, poor patronage, and staff conflict. Even before the end of the war thousands of Americans booked passages to tour the battlefields of Europe, rather than making excursions to the South Seas.[30] Neither was local patronage immediately forthcoming, and managers were soon pondering how best to popularise the hotel 'without bringing down its "social standing" and incidentally augment the revenue'.[31] Within three years USSCo seriously considered selling the building at great loss to the Fiji government, with proposals to convert it into a boarding school for European children. While this did not come to pass, staffing difficulties, low occupancy rates, and expensive maintenance continued to trouble them. This experience discouraged USSCo from extending its hotel-keeping to other islands, and the company declined a request from the New Zealand administrator for Western Samoa in 1923.[32]

More broadly, Suva struggled to maintain an inviting image, battling the ongoing expense of tourism promotion and infrastructure and the indifference of colonial officials. There were sections of Fiji's European society opposed to public funds being spent on the passenger liner trade. Such criticisms had been raised intermittently in preceding decades, with USSCo being accused, for instance, of taking its earnings out of the colony, unlike more 'productive' sectors of the economy. In 1922 the Suva Council of Planters petitioned for the subsidy granted to the CA Line (£5,000 per annum) to be redirected to a cargo service via India and Singapore.[33] Even Fiji's governor remarked that USSCo chose Suva for their hotel project rather than a New Zealand port purely to save money and to avoid interference from their own government. This upset company managers, for such attitudes confirmed 'the peculiar ideas our Island friends have at times on such matters. This no doubt arises through their being cut off to a certain extent from busy centres.'[34] This conflict was not unique to Fiji, as officials in other tropical colonies also perceived plantation wealth as the best evidence of a stake in the future.[35]

The relationship between tourism, trade, and settlement gradually unravelled in Hawai'i. The vision of the island group as a 'happy white republic governed by and for free whites' foundered in the face of lack of interest from the 'right' kind of immigrants from the US mainland.[36] The last overt attempt to market tourism as a route to white settlement occurred in 1914. The Hawaiian Tourist Bureau replaced the HPC in 1919. The Bureau, as Skwiot outlines, embarked on a new campaign, pitching Hawai'i as a 'royal resort' devoted to the pleasures of the modern haole (white) aristocracy. It was now imagined as a place where they 'ruled and recreated, not where they toiled and procreated'.[37] To this end the Bureau commanded an annual budget of $125,000 in the 1920s.[38]

In 1923 the European Settlement League established the Fiji Tourist Bureau, effectively a one-man band under John Herrick. It was modelled on Hawai'i's bureau, given the latter's modern and attractive advertising material was admired in both Fiji and New Zealand (the Hawaii Tourist Bureau later asserting that tourism was 'the industry that advertising built').[39] The Fiji Bureau published a monthly gazette for distribution on steamers and at regional shipping offices, pitching Fiji as 'the Riviera of the Southern Seas'.[40] Within a few months the Bureau reported that 'a number of dairymen from New Zealand' had arrived to inspect land with a view to settlement, having made use of the Bureau 'with much benefit'.[41] Throughout the 1920s, articles published in New Zealand newspapers promoted Fiji's prospects, notably the infant dairy industry and canning factories, under titles such as 'Come to Fiji'.[42] Unlike in Hawai'i, leisured and economic mobility continued to be closely analogous, as expounded in promotional and anecdotal evidence, if not through more concrete statistics.

Yet Fiji was still a poor cousin to Hawai'i with respect to its visibility in New Zealand as a desirable tourist destination. The Fiji Comptroller of Customs visited New Zealand shortly after the establishment of the Tourist Bureau to report on how Fiji was being marketed there. He returned disappointed. There was little information to be had and USSCo tended to favour passengers who planned to stay at the Grand Pacific Hotel. He observed a large traffic between New Zealand and Hawai'i on account, he believed, of the amount of advertising done by the Hawaii Tourist Bureau, whose pamphlets were revised every few months.[43]

Just as New Zealanders were being enticed along the All Red Route into the Pacific, New Zealand was also part of the route's appeal, with Auckland a key trans-Pacific port of call. A triangulation between New Zealand, Hawai'i, and Fiji developed, which tended to marginalise Fiji. As one article in a 1930 edition of the *Hawaii Magazine* put it: 'After Hawaii – New Zealand.'[44] This emergent hierarchy was also pronounced in debates over which archipelago could rightly claim the title 'Paradise of the Pacific' in its promotional material. The Hawaii Tourist Bureau requested that New Zealand officials desist in 'appropriating our trade name'. As publicity officer George Armitage argued in 1932, 'Hawaii certainly originated the name and has made it world famous through millions of dollars of advertising and promotion'.[45] The use of 'paradise' went as far back as early European settlement, New Zealand observed, but Armitage retorted that it was also used to 'describe countries long before New Zealand and Hawaii were discovered … I never saw the phrase used by New Zealand until it became so well known in connection with Hawaii that the two were synonymous. We hope, therefore, that you will devise some other phrase for your advertising.'[46]

Beyond this jockeying for brand identity and official commitment of funds, issues around shipping again came to illustrate the ways in which the histories of tourism 'playgrounds' were interlinked. In the interwar years geopolitical realignments in the Pacific witnessed British maritime activity (that is, USSCo) largely overshadowed by a handsomely subsidised American seaborne imperialism, encroaching beyond Hawai'i and further south to Fiji, New Zealand, and Australia. Whereas the immediate post-Second World War period is readily understood as one of increasing American domination, which lay 'new protocols for the forms and modalities of empire in the Pacific', as Damon Salesa observes, New Zealand's Pacific empire was already confronting American domination in the interwar years, a period I now turn to discuss in more detail.[47]

'Travel British': patriotic mobility in the interwar years

The Matson Steam Navigation Company (Matson Line) absorbed the Oceanic Steam Ship Company as a subsidiary in 1926. It then announced plans to build a new hotel at the beach-front area of Waikiki, scheduled to open in time for the launch of its new steamer, the *Malolo*, in 1927. The 400-room Royal Hawaiian Hotel was a far more elaborate affair than Suva's Grand Pacific Hotel. Built with the backing of plantation company Castle & Cooke (one of Hawai'i's 'Big Five' industries), construction was estimated at $3.5 million. The opening simulated a coronation ceremony that, as Skwiot argues, 'staged the succession of a haole aristocracy to a court at Waikiki'.[48] Lavish public spectacles to legitimate white acquisition of land and power at the expense of the Indigenous elite could not have the same purchase in Fiji, where Fijians retained ownership of over 80 per cent of their lands.

Comparative assessments of Honolulu and Suva became more pronounced. J. H. McDonald, head of a Canadian timber delegation visiting New Zealand in 1930, remarked to an audience of Auckland Rotarians that to compare the relative position of Honolulu under the American flag and Fiji under the British, 'Honolulu is the only child of a millionaire, while Fiji is the twenty-seventh child of a working bricklayer'.[49] Rumours circulated of Matson's plans to erect a 'palatial hotel on the lines of its Waikiki edifice' in Suva, for Oceanic had introduced a call at Suva between Pago Pago (American Samoa) and Sydney in 1925.[50] This did not eventuate, yet American investment was often portrayed as the key to a prosperous future for Fiji: if the islands just lay closer to the continent, American visitor Arthur Floyd remarked enthusiastically, 'one can only guess what a wonderful resort Fiji would be ... hotels would spring up on all sides and property values go sky-rocketing'.[51]

The promise of Fiji's emergence as a tourist destination, however, now appeared to hold grim forebodings for New Zealand and USSCo. Matson's services were diverting Australian passengers away from USSCo vessels. Sydney residents could now enjoy a two-week trip to Fiji: five days each way 'on a comfortable liner' and four days ashore, an excursion which 'has become a great attraction'.[52] The premier British shipping firm P&O also introduced cruises from Australia to Fiji in the early 1930s, partly in the hope of checking Matson's growing appeal in the western Pacific.[53] Matson seemed to hold the belief 'that any trade is open to them', but USSCo hoped that competition in the US trades to the Philippines would make them 'a little more inclined to see the other man's point of view'.[54]

Such guarded optimism was short-lived. In 1931 Matson interposed a call at Auckland between Suva and Sydney. Matson had consistently denied any interest in New Zealand up to this point, but now stressed that such a call was needed in order to encourage American tourists to venture across the Pacific, for Australia was not an attractive enough destination in itself.[55] USSCo had no objections to Matson bringing American tourists to New Zealand, but it regarded its trans-Tasman incursion as an unwarranted encroachment on an 'all-British' trade, all the while America kept British boats out of its coastal trades. The incorporation of Hawai'i as a territory and coastal port of the United States in 1900 had forced USSCo out of the Sydney–San Francisco route, for under American navigation legislation only American companies could ship between domestic ports. To circumvent these restrictions, USSCo launched a new itinerary, shipping from Sydney to San Francisco via Wellington, Rarotonga, and Papeete (Tahiti) rather than Hawai'i. Matson's decision to enter the Auckland–Sydney route was also troubling because the American government supported its maritime industry with large subsidies, perceived by USSCo as an aggressive national and naval policy in the Pacific, rather than solely as a commercial one. Matson initially declared that it was only interested in the trans-Pacific through-traffic and would not carry trans-Tasman passengers, but it soon reversed its decision, apparently in response to numerous requests from Auckland residents.[56] Its ships carried no cargo from Sydney or Suva to New Zealand, however, because Auckland waterside workers refused to handle it.[57]

Some commentators, perhaps overlooking or misunderstanding the unequal trading environment, supported Matson's activities and argued that New Zealand's prosperity was intimately entangled with American developments, particularly the growth of tourism. As Postmaster General J. B. Donald contended: 'If we wanted to stop progress let us stop the Matson steamers.'[58] As if in confirmation, Matson's passenger superintendent visited Auckland in 1932, announcing an imminent campaign in the USA to promote New Zealand as a tourist destination. 'The era of the Pacific is definitely started', he remarked, while not omitting to stress that New Zealand had the most to gain.[59]

Beginning in 1930, USSCo launched an intensive propaganda campaign to exclude Matson from carrying passengers between Australia and New Zealand. It distributed pamphlets to newspaper editors, corrected misinformed statements in the press (company managers often calling authors into their offices to be 're-educated'), and attended election campaigns to challenge politicians to state their position on the issue. Yet because Suva, Auckland, and Sydney were not under the jurisdiction of a single government, it would take a multilateral agreement to legislate against American shipping. Both the Australian and New Zealand governments were initially reluctant to act, hoping Britain would take the lead.

Matson's shipbuilding programme heightened the Union Company's anxieties. In the preceding decades American passengers used Oceanic's ships to complete the crossing from San Francisco to Honolulu, then often transferred to the more comfortable Union liners to New Zealand and Sydney. The prospect of modern Matson ships to replace its anti-quated fleet – subsequently built at the height of the Great Depression through a government loan fund of $250 million to aid merchant ship-building – would change the playing field dramatically. The *Mariposa* and the *Monterey*, touted as 'the new sovereigns of the Pacific', captured three-fifths of the trans-Pacific passenger traffic by 1935. Private correspondence between USSCo officials attests to a climate of dismay as many Australian and New Zealand passengers, including prominent commercial figures, supported 'buy British' campaigns yet failed to 'travel British'. For one branch manager, it was 'mortifying that people of the English race should patronise an American line'.[60] Some passengers even wrote to USSCo, accounting for their decision to take a Matson ship. A former director of New Zealand's Northern Steam Ship Company asserted 'he was not doing this of his own volition, but his wife wished to travel by the vessel'.[61]

Back in Fiji, USSCo recognised that its attitudes towards Suva needed to change. There was growing local dissatisfaction with the regularly late arrival of USSCo ships, and their failure as a result to meet the contractual requirement of six hours' daylight in port. A comparison tabled by the Suva Chamber of Commerce indicated that in eight previous visits, Union Company vessels stayed for only an average of 4.2 hours, whereas Matson vessels averaged six hours.[62] Irregular ship arrivals hampered the provision of official hospitality to important passengers. Relations deteriorated when the late arrival of one ship threw into disarray the governor's plans to welcome the English cricketers in 1933.[63] The Suva branch manager reported that 'we are getting "digs" from all quarters comparing Matsons and ourselves'. He felt that masters of CA Line vessels 'have never taken the position seriously as regards Suva and invariably have classed it as a small port to which the least possible time and attention should be given'.[64] When Matson's passenger agent visited Suva to promote the development of shore activities for excursionists, it was said that USSCo had 'done nothing' by way of tourist publicity for Fiji, a statement it roundly refuted.[65] With the introduction of Matson's new superliners, passengers also made unfavourable comparisons with the Grand Pacific Hotel, its rooms perceived as smaller than cabins. Expectations of unwavering service were also transposed from ship to shore, leading the Suva branch manager to decry 'the travelling public of today' as 'spoilt' and 'over-catered for'.[66]

In the 1930s America's 'uneconomic competition' in the Pacific sufficiently agitated the highest players in British shipping circles to give rise to what became known as 'the Pacific problem'. Faced with a global depression in the shipping sector, the volume of overseas trade contracted, whereas the merchant fleets of most maritime countries, except Britain, expanded. The Pacific was now felt to be the domain wherein imperial shipping was most under threat.[67] The situation came to a head in 1936 when USSCo terminated its Sydney–San Francisco service. The company received an annual subsidy of £34,500, whereas estimated annual losses in this trade amounted to £50,000. The Matson Line, by contrast, was estimated by Britain to receive over £200,000 annually in state subsidies.[68] In the same year New Zealand passed the Protection of British Shipping Bill to restrict trans-Tasman passenger shipping to British vessels. It could not be made law until Australia carried similar legislation. In 1937 the Australian cabinet ruled out taking action in this direction, acquiescing to American protests.[69] A committee appointed to enquire into Britain's waning maritime supremacy in the Pacific recommended a new programme of ship-building, but the outbreak of the Second World War disrupted renewal plans.[70] The post-war climate was even more challenging and, faced with ongoing operating losses and government reluctance to increase subsidies, the CA Line was terminated in 1953. This signalled the end of USSCo's engagement in trans-Pacific shipping. The company did not renew the lease for Suva's Grand Pacific Hotel on its expiry in 1959.

Conclusions for New Zealand's empire

To understand the historical meanings of New Zealand's empire in the Pacific, we need to look beyond the islands of formal political influence. Territorial claims and direct rule do not capture the full scope of New Zealand's aspirations and endeavours in the region. Arguably, tourism enters the realm of informal imperialism, one of cultural and commercial influence, of images and markets, not easily accounted for by frameworks which centre on the state and key political officials. If, as Salesa remarks, we need to 'recognise the traffic that constituted the New Zealand Empire', we need to turn to the sea.[71] An examination of historical shipping routes highlights the everyday commercial activity that was central to making a maritime empire 'work', just as it opens up to a far more expansive vision of New Zealand's Pacific, stretching across to Vancouver and San Francisco.

The maritime infrastructure, services, and mobilities of the nascent tourism industry gradually imparted a sense of entitlement 'in what should be our own territory', as the USSCo managing director remarked with particular reference to Fiji.[72] The political and economic transformation of Honolulu had appeared to offer a model worth emulating in Suva. Over time, however, America's Pacific empire represented far more than a powerful symbolic overlay, the touchstone of glamour, sophistication, and the promise of handsome profits. Matson's interwar expansion beyond Hawai'i was perceived as out of place, an aggressive and unwarranted American encroachment to be challenged and resisted.

The New Zealand government, along with its Australian counterpart, was slow to protect USSCo's interests. New Zealand appeared to look sanguinely enough at the American incursion and, indeed, many

New Zealanders seized the opportunity to travel by Matson's new luxury liners; British race patriotism did not appear to extend to the sea. In this sense New Zealand lay as a pivot between Britain's formal empire and America's informal commercial empire in the Pacific. Following shipping through the lenses of travel and tourism can shed light on the ways in which these 'soft' tissues of inter-island and international connections played out against the background of high politics and hard power in an age of competing imperialisms in the Pacific world.[73]

Notes

1 For example, Angus Ross, *New Zealand Aspirations in the Pacific in the Nineteenth Century* (Oxford: Clarendon, 1964); Angus Ross (ed.), *New Zealand's Record in the Pacific Islands in the Twentieth Century* (Auckland: Longman Paul for the New Zealand Institute of International Affairs, 1969); Damon Salesa, 'A Pacific destiny: New Zealand's overseas empire, 1840–1945', in Sean Mallon, Kolokesa Māhina-Tuai, and Damon Salesa (eds), *Tangata o le Moana: New Zealand and the People of the Pacific* (Wellington: Te Papa Press, 2012), pp. 97–122.

2 John M. MacKenzie, 'Empires of travel: British guide books and cultural imperialism in the 19th and 20th centuries', in John K. Walton (ed.), *Histories of Tourism: Representation, Identity and Conflict* (Clevedon: Channel View Publications, 2005), p. 19.

3 Dennis Merrill observes a similar relationship between tourism and geopolitical imaginings in *Negotiating Paradise: U.S. Tourism and Empire in Twentieth-Century Latin America* (Chapel Hill, NC: University of North Carolina Press, 2009).

4 For a more general discussion, see Shelley Baranowski, 'Common ground: Linking transport and tourism history', *Journal of Transport History*, 28:1 (2007), 120–4.

5 Ngaire Douglas, *They Came for Savages: 100 Years of Tourism in Melanesia* (Lismore: Southern Cross University Press, 1996). Unsurprisingly, as the focus of sustained American political, commercial, and cultural transformation, the wealth of scholarship has concentrated on Hawai'i. For example: Jane C. Desmond, *Staging Tourism: Bodies on Display from Waikiki to Sea World* (Chicago: University of Chicago Press, 1999); Heather A. Diamond, *American Aloha: Cultural Tourism and the Negotiation of Tradition* (Honolulu: University of Hawai'i Press, 2008).

6 Lydia Wevers, *Country of Writing: Travel Writing and New Zealand, 1809–1900* (Auckland: Auckland University Press, 2002); Margaret McClure, *The Wonder Country: Making New Zealand Tourism* (Auckland: Auckland University Press, 2005); Margaret Werry, *The Tourist State: Performing Leisure, Liberalism, and Race in New Zealand* (Minneapolis: University of Minnesota Press, 2011); Peter Alsop, Gary Stewart and Dave Bamford, *Selling the Dream: The Art of Early New Zealand Tourism* (Nelson: Craig Potton Publishing, 2012).

7 'Fiji's charm', *Auckland Star* (19 July 1926), p. 11.

8 Paul McGuire, *Westward the Course: The New World of Oceania* (Oxford: Geoffrey Cumberlege, 1942), p. 70.

9 Marjorie Appleton, *East of Singapore* (London: Hurst & Blackett, 1942), pp. 9, 23.

10 Sally Engle Merry and Donald Brenneis (eds), *Law and Empire in the Pacific: Fiji and Hawai'i*, Advanced Seminar Series (Santa Fe, NM: School of American Research Press, 2004).

11 Editorial, *Otago Daily Times* (24 June 1870), p. 2.

12 'Excursion to Fiji', *Otago Daily Times* (21 May 1883), p. 2.

13 'The Fiji trade', *Otago Daily Times* (13 July 1883), p. 2.

14 Alexander Turnbull Library, Scrapbook, MSY-5843, *New Zealand Times* (11 March 1884) [no title or page].
15 Alexander Turnbull Library, Scrapbook, MSY-5843, 'Winter Excursion to the South Sea Islands', 1 March 1884.
16 'The Wairarapa's cruise in the Pacific', *Te Aroha News* (9 August 1884), p. 6.
17 For an extended discussion of the first cruises see Frances Steel, 'An Ocean of Leisure: Early cruise tours of the Pacific in an age of empire', *Journal of Colonialism and Colonial History*, 14:2 (2013), http://muse.jhu.edu/journals/journal_of_coloni- alism_and_ colonial_history/v014/14.2.steel.html, accessed 31 May 2014.
18 Beatrice Grimshaw, *Three Wonderful Nations* (Dunedin: USSCo, 1907); Beatrice Grimshaw, *In the Strange South Seas* (London: Hutchinson and Co., 1907).
19 'Attracting immigrants: Pacific tourist route', *Auckland Star* (26 August 1913), p. 7.
20 Cited in Adria L. Imada, *Aloha America: Hula Circuits Through the U.S. Empire* (Durham, NC: Duke University Press, 2012), p. 156.
21 Christine Skwiot, *The Purposes of Paradise: U.S. Tourism and Empire in Cuba and Hawai'i* (Philadelphia: University of Pennsylvania Press, 2010), p. 67, pp. 71–3.
22 'Notes on the Vancouver route to America', *Evening Post* (27 May 1905), p. 13.
23 'The Canadian-Australian mail service', *Fiji Times* (3 March 1909), p. 2.
24 Douglas, *They Came for Savages*, pp. 61–2, 100.
25 Hocken Collections, University of Otago, Dunedin (hereafter HC), USSCo Records, AG-292-005-001/069, McLennan to Holdsworth, 19 September 1903.
26 National Archives of Fiji, Suva (hereafter NAF), CSO, 04.4558, Duncan to colonial secretary, 16 November 1904.
27 HC, USSCo Records, AG-292-005-001/086, McLennan to Holdsworth, 25 September 1908.
28 *A Day in Suva* (Dunedin: USSCo, 1921), p. 22.
29 Wellington City Archives, Wellington (hereafter WCA), USSCo Records, AF080:210:3, Morgan to Mills, 28 August 1913.
30 HC, USSCo Records, AG-292-005-004/142, Mills to Holdsworth, 30 August 1915.
31 WCA, USSCo Records, AF080:211:2, Hughes to Eva, 15 October 1915.
32 WCA, USSCo Records, AF066:7:5, Falla to Richardson, 10 November 1923.
33 NAF, CSO, 22.2446, 23 May 1922.
34 WCA, USSCo Records, AF080:211:1, Eva to Hughes, 24 March 1915; Hughes to Eva, 17 April 1915.
35 Frank F. Taylor, *To Hell with Paradise: A History of the Jamaican Tourist Industry* (Pittsburgh: University of Pittsburgh Press, 1992), p. 74.
36 Skwiot, *The Purposes of Paradise*, p. 86.
37 Skwiot, *The Purposes of Paradise*, p. 77.
38 Imada, *Aloha America*, p. 156.
39 Archives New Zealand (hereafter ANZ), TO1-121-6/25, Agencies, Hawaii Tourist Bureau Annual Report 1928.
40 'Fiji as a tourist resort', *Fiji Tourist Gazette* 3:26 (1926), pp. 6–7.
41 'Our Fiji letter', *Auckland Star* (22 June 1923), p. 7.
42 '"Come to Fiji": A resident's advice', *Evening Post* (14 August 1928), p. 10.
43 NAF, CSO, 23.1921, 21 May 1923.
44 ANZ, TO1-121-6/25, Agencies – Hawaii Tourist Bureau, A. H. Messenger to George Armitage, 2 June 1930.
45 ANZ, TO1-121-6/25, Agencies – Hawaii Tourist Bureau, Armitage to Clinkard, 3 March 1932.
46 ANZ, TO1-121-6/25, Agencies – Hawaii Tourist Bureau, Armitage to Clinkard, 20 June 1932. The magazine, *Paradise of the Pacific*, was established in Hawai'i in 1888.
47 Damon Salesa, 'New Zealand's Pacific', in Giselle Byrnes (ed.), *The New Oxford History of New Zealand* (Melbourne: Oxford University Press, 2009), p. 165.
48 Skwiot, *The Purposes of Paradise*, p. 104.
49 'Boosting Fiji', *Fiji Times* (12 April 1930), n.p.
50 For example, *Evening Post* (27 July 1926), p. 8.

51 'Fascinating Fiji', *Fiji Times* (9 April 1926), p. 2.
52 'Tourist traffic', *Fiji Times* (1 June 1926), p. 3.
53 WCA, USSCo Records, AF080:331:6, James to Aiken, 7 July 1933.
54 HC, USSCo Records, AF-292-005-002/002, Back to Hughes, 9 August 1929.
55 HC, USSCo Records, AG-292-005-004/181, Holdsworth to Aiken, 17 October 1928;
    WCA, USSCo Records, AF066:7:1, Aiken to Carter, 10 June 1929.
56 WCA, USSCo Records, AF080:85:1, Back to Aiken, 8 July 1931.
57 'Bananas from Fiji', *Auckland Star* (19 March 1932), p. 7. Sydney waterside workers
    could not be induced to follow suit, believing others would simply handle cargo in
    their place; 'Matson Line', *Sydney Morning Herald* (31 March 1932), p. 10.
58 'Competition good', *Auckland Star* (21 August 1931), p. 8. It was noted privately that
    Donald spoke out of turn, as cabinet had not yet issued a statement of its position.
    He also had interests in island trading, so was not an impartial commentator. See
    WCA, USSCo, AF080:85:2, Aiken to Soutar, 21 August 1931 and Millward to Aiken,
    2 September 1931.
59 'Flow of tourists', *Auckland Star* (2 April 1932), p. 11. This advertising was later
    celebrated by the New Zealand Trade and Tourist Commissioner in Sydney as
    'splendid ... it really has life in it'. ANZ, TO1-121-6/42/1, Agencies, San Francisco
    – Matson Navigation Corporation, 27 August 1932.
60 WCA, USSCo Records, AF080:88:1, Cato to General Manager, 22 November 1934.
61 WCA, USSCo Records, AF080:88:1, Cato to General Manager, 22 November 1934,
    AF080:86:5, Carter to Aiken, 8 November 1932.
62 British Library, India Office Records, IOR/L/E/7/1469, File 6008(ii), Legislative
    Council, Address by M. Fletcher, Governor, 13 May 1930. From 1928 USSCo was
    required to forfeit £32 in respect of each hour of daylight short of six hours.
63 WCA, USSCo Records, AF080:169:2, Hancock to Irons, 7 April 1933; AF080:169:3,
    Hancock to Matthewson, 29 August 1935.
64 WCA, USSCo Records, AF080:169:2, Hancock to Wheeler, 27 September 1933.
65 WCA, USSCo Records, AF080:87:1, Hughes to Hancock, 3 May 1933.
66 WCA, USSCo Records, AF080:241:6, Hancock to Falla, 9 May 1934; AF080:88:4,
    Hancock to General Manager, 14 April 1936.
67 Archives and Libraries Canada, RG25, Vol. 1790, file no 318 AD, Memorandum
    on the Shipping Situation, July 1934. See also Frances Steel, 'Lines across the sea:
    Transpacific passenger shipping in the age of steam', in Kirsten McKenzie and
    Robert Aldrich (eds), *The Routledge History of Western Empires* (London and New
    York: Routledge, 2013), pp. 315–29.
68 'Losses in the Pacific: The cost of new ships', *The Times* (16 April 1936), p. 12;
    'Shipping in the Pacific: The American subsidy', *The Times* (2 July 1936), p. 10.
69 National Archives of Australia, Canberra, CP4/2-67, Transpacific Shipping services
    (b) USA Pacific Shipping.
70 Imperial Shipping Committee, *The Possibilities of a British Passenger and Cargo
    Service Between Western Canada and Australia-New Zealand* (London, 1936).
71 Salesa, 'New Zealand's Pacific', p. 172.
72 WCA, USSCo Records, AF080:169:2, Wheeler to Hancock, 11 September 1933.
73 Research for this chapter was supported by the Australian Research Council
    Discovery Early Career Researcher Award scheme (project number DE120101731).
    I would like to thank G. Balachandran and the editors of this collection for their
    comments on earlier versions of this chapter.

CHAPTER NINE

Empire in the eyes of the beholder: New Zealand in the Pacific through French eyes

Adrian Muckle

> If I have used the word empire to characterise New Zealand's colonial domain, this is undoubtedly a very big word for it. This empire is Lilliputian.[1]

There is a long tradition of French writing on New Zealand and, in turn, of commentary on French perceptions of New Zealand and its people. In New Zealand much of this commentary appears in works celebrating formal and informal ties between the two countries. Such studies balance or moderate the discussion of old rivalries (such as the race to colonise New Zealand) and more recent tension (notably during protests over France's nuclear testing and the bombing of the *Rainbow Warrior*) by also exploring histories of cultural exchange and constructive cooperation. Insofar as these studies also aim to establish a better understanding of France's presence in the region, the French Pacific (or the francophone Pacific) also looms large.[2] These studies of New Zealand and France do not, however, provide any notable exception to the observation by historian Damon Salesa that New Zealand's Pacific empire 'has rarely been taken seriously by New Zealand's historians'.[3] Most include a discussion of the most famous of all French observers, André Siegfried, for example, but none comments on what Siegfried wrote about New Zealand's Pacific imperialism.[4] Yet that New Zealand was 'both powerful as an imperial envoy' and had its 'own sovereign role in Pacific nations' – as suggested in the editors' abstract for this collection – was patently clear to Siegfried, who clearly described the distinction and tension between New Zealand as a part of the British Empire and as an aspiring colonial and imperial power in its own right at the end of the nineteenth century. In the middle of the twentieth century, developments in 'New Zealand's empire' also preoccupied France's Plenipotentiary Minister in Wellington, Noël Henry. New Zealand's 'colonial domain' was 'Lilliputian' in Henry's eyes, but its lessons for France ought not to be ignored, he argued.

Complementing Salesa's mapping of the 'empire-state' and the attempt to widen the frame of New Zealand history to encompass metropole and colony,[5] this chapter addresses a blind spot in the history of France–New Zealand relations: the ways in which French diplomatic observers saw New Zealand as a colonial and imperial power in the Pacific between ca.1900 and ca.1955.[6] The blind spot in question owes its existence in part to the much greater attention levelled at relations after the establishment of the French nuclear testing site in French Polynesia in the 1960s, and also to the absence of high-level bilateral relations between the two countries before 1945. France's diplomatic representation in New Zealand began in the nineteenth century, but was limited to consular affairs, while higher level diplomacy was handled by officials in London and Paris. New Zealand's external relations with France were handled almost exclusively through British diplomatic channels and, except during the Second World War, the same was true of its relations with France's Pacific territories. As this chapter goes on to show, however, the French diplomatic archive reveals more than passing interest in New Zealand's Pacific aspirations and activities. At the beginning of the twentieth century and in the two post-war decades in particular – 1919–29 and 1945–55 – they reveal heightened interest in New Zealand as an emerging member of an 'imperial family'.

Two voices dominate the French diplomatic archive on which this study is based: that of the longest-serving inter-war consul, Paul Adolphe Serre (1923–31); and that of Minister Plenipotentiary, Noël Henry (1952–55). Focusing on what they saw and what they sought to compare, this chapter contributes to an obscure(d) history of inter-imperial observation and an examination of a 'politics of comparison' based on 'the value of looking comparatively at circuits of knowledge production, governing practices, and indirect as well as direct connections in the political rationalities that informed imperial rule'.[7] It examines the ways in which New Zealand's colonial or imperial activity was meaningful to a particular category of French observer and explores in particular the appeal to a shared imperial or colonial experience.

New Zealand and Sāmoa observed

In the 1890s, French interest in New Zealand's imperial aspirations grew apace with New Zealand's calls for a 'Pacific federation', an idea which emerged alongside the question of Australasian Federation and which 'posed an alternative to it after 1900'.[8] France's initial concern was not so much New Zealand's ambitions, but the potential power of a federated Australia – with or without New Zealand – and the stance that it might take in relation to the New Hebrides.[9] But as the likelihood of New Zealand joining the Australian Federation diminished, the question of how to interpret the respective imperial interests of the two countries became more acute. Foreshadowing the likely conclusions of the 1901 Royal Commission regarding Federation, the French consul, Courte, reported that: 'The political idea of a Polynesian island federation may only be touched upon lightly in this report, but … morally it will exercise a certain weight in the balance.'[10] Citing the same Commission's view 'that imperial unity may be even more encouraged by the existence in our seas of two British Powers instead of one', André Siegfried identified a 'duality of policy' and two distinct but complementary 'currents of imperialism': a 'greater imperialism' that was bringing the colonies into the orbit of the larger Empire, and 'a local imperialism, the product of exclusivism and of racial pride, which seems to be becoming more and more characteristic of Anglo-Saxon colonials'. Together they were characterised as 'jealous and never-sleeping watchdogs, who mount guard at the entrance to these seas', but there were differences in the character and intensity of their policies: 'New Zealand prides herself on her imperial policy; but at the same time she also claims to have her private attitude to Oceania. Following Australia, she gives herself up willingly to a colonial jingoism that might be called Australasian imperialism.'[11]

In the following decade, French observers remained alert to 'Anglo-Saxon' ambitions or jealousies, especially in regard to the New Hebrides, but New Zealand's own Pacific policies or practices were of little concern. In 1900 the annexation of the Cook Islands did not concern Paris since it had been under British protection since 1888, and ongoing talk that Tonga might be transferred from British to New Zealand control was seen in a similar light in 1911.[12] That New Zealand might join the Australian Commonwealth seemed increasingly unlikely given the 'difference in mentality between the two peoples' and their diverging 'aspirations', reported the consul in 1912; Australia wanted to be strong and independent, while New Zealand sought to promote Empire so as to be protected in times of danger. It would take a 'major upheaval or an imminent national danger such as the yellow peril' to bring them together.[13] Only when challenged by the Islanders themselves did the conditions of New Zealand's colonial rule attract attention. A rare consular note on the Cook Islands followed Chief Justice Robert Stout's investigation of complaints against the administration in 1911. Echoing Stout, the consul observed that the

Cook Islanders 'have only accepted British suzerainty on the condition of retaining their local administration in its integrality ... today, they too aspire to be a "self-governing Dominion" and seem less than enthusiastic at their annexation to New Zealand'.[14]

At the end of the First World War France paid renewed attention to the Pacific region. The war itself (notably the deployment of NZ troops in France but also the use of New Caledonia as a staging post for the seizure of German Samoa in 1914) had provided new opportunities for diplomatic exchange and cooperation. The heightened interest can be traced in a visiting mission to Australia and New Zealand in 1919,[15] in the French colonial inspectorate's 1922 survey of France's Pacific territories, and in *La Revue du Pacifique* (1922–37), one of the voices of France's Oceanian lobbyists.[16] French concerns, as summarised by the latter, were several. In addition to a concern to assess the economic and political situation in France's territories, and their regional linkages after a period of wartime isolation, there was interest in the fate of Germany's Pacific possessions. The Oceanian lobby was dissatisfied that France had not profited from the seized German territories despite facilitating their occupation.[17] There was also concern about renewed lobbying by the Presbyterian churches, in Australia and New Zealand, for France's involvement in the New Hebrides condominium to be ended, and the support such statements had been given by New Zealand's Premier, William Massey, at the Imperial Conference in 1921.[18]

With the shared mandate of Nauru as its new northern limit, and Sāmoa at its centre, post-war developments in 'New Zealand's immense island domain' attracted especial interest.[19] Digesting the international press, *La Revue du Pacifique* noted in 1922 that New Zealand had commenced its 'first effort at governing beyond its own shores', that already there had been complaints that it was not up to the task of colonial administration in the tropics, that affairs in Sāmoa were deteriorating, and that Sāmoans had petitioned to be placed directly under British rule. Bringing New Zealand itself into the frame, it also commented on New Zealand's finances, improving Māori natality, and on the lavishly produced official yearbook for 1921–22 with its detailed description of the island territories, notably the Cook Islands which had much in common with 'French Oceania'.[20] These and subsequent observations are mostly unremarkable, but in the aggregate particular concerns become evident.

Significantly, policies towards immigrant and mainly Asian indentured labour emerge as a key point of difference in colonial or imperial style. In 1922, while inspecting France's Pacific territories, colonial inspector Charles Revel was scathing of the 'imprudent' steps taken by New Zealand in Sāmoa in restricting the importation of Chinese labour; 'their abject fear of the "yellow"' had led, he reported, to 5,000 'coolies' being sent home without any guarantee that Sāmoan labour could replace them.[21] In 1924, both France's consul in New Zealand, Serre, and the Governor of New Caledonia, Arboussier, reported that labour issues were central to renewed criticism by the Presbyterian churches in Australia and New Zealand of the French presence in the New Hebrides and calls for the archipelago to be placed entirely under British control.[22]

With its new responsibilities in Sāmoa, New Zealand's own position on indentured labour was not beyond reproach, however. Several years earlier, as he prepared for New Zealand's takeover of Sāmoa, Prime Minister William Massey had sought to defend indentured labour, as carried out 'under the British flag', from being labelled as 'slavery'.[23] As New Zealand debated the recourse to indentured immigrant labour in Sāmoa in the early 1920s, Serre highlighted what he saw as the hypocrisy of the New Zealand Methodist mission's apparent support for indenture and of New Zealand's antipathy to indentured Asian labour more generally. For Serre, attempts 'to maintain the purity of the Samoan race' were a lost cause in view of the ample evidence of racial mixing. Moreover, such a stance seemed untenable in view of other priorities:

> The Australians and New Zealanders claim to be resolute in their fight against the infiltration of Asians which, in their view, is polluting the beautiful British race as much as the admittedly less beautiful native races! But that which is still possible on the continents of the Pacific is no longer possible in the archipelagos, notably in the Marquesas, where foreign labour is as indispensable as the mixing of blood if the effects of depopulation are to be countered.[24]

While the surprise expressed at Australasian hostility towards Asian races hints at a more tolerant 'French Way', the interest in this issue also reflected the concerns of France's colonial lobbyists and their campaign for the recruitment of labour from Indochina.

La Revue du Pacifique's interest in New Zealand's Pacific waned, but Serre continued to report on Sāmoa until the 1930s. That the principal prism for his reports was Sāmoa's status as a mandate – together with France's own position as a mandatory power – rather than the implications for France's Pacific territories is a useful reminder that New Zealand's intervention in Sāmoa was as much a foray into international relations, involving the establishment of the Department of External Affairs, as it was an exercise in colonial administration.[25] In 1923 Serre proposed to keep France's office at the League of Nations abreast of 'the polemics that the exercise of the mandates might generate in New Zealand'.[26] Reporting on the '[s]erious troubles' that had developed by July 1927 – as the Sāmoan protest movement, the Mau, gained strength – Serre noted that the daily newspapers had published 'numerous articles in which France had been given a rough time concerning the mandate that it exercises in Syria' (where it had faced a revolt since 1925) and that '[n]ow it is New Zealand's turn to have some difficulties'.[27] Developments in Sāmoa seemed 'as complicated as in Syria', he wrote, and he commented that the:

> problems in the mandated territories (whether Syria or Samoa) arise from the fact that those fishing in troubled waters hope to create discord among the great powers who distribute the mandates. Furthermore, they have deluded themselves as to the power of the League of Nations. If Syria and Morocco were French, and if Western Samoa were New Zealand's, there would be fewer agitators.

Underlying such comments was an assumption that New Zealand and France were both pursuing annexation as the endgame: 'tutelage means possession at some time in the future. This is what we think in relation to Cameroon and Togo in particular, and this is how they think, in New Zealand, in the case of Samoa.'[28] So long as France's Pacific territories were excepted, New Zealand's lingering aspiration 'to administer all the island groups between New Zealand and Hawai'i' was not mocked. A year earlier, following the annexation of Tokelau in 1926, Serre had remarked with admiration that while the late Prime Minister Massey's imperialism had been cautious, Coates, 'younger and full of energy, has not been afraid to expand New Zealand's responsibilities in the Pacific'.[29]

Serre's emphasis on the predicaments shared by mandatory powers betrayed the existence of what might be called a community of racial sympathy, interest, and interpretation. This was evident from his first meeting with Massey in 1923. Commenting on his great interest 'in ethnographic questions', Serre related that Massey had 'identified me as of the Saxon type (!)', prompting him in turn to insist that he was of 'the Gallic type now so rare in France' and that the two were 'both Celts and well placed to get on with each other'.[30] In his subsequent reports on Sāmoa, Serre aligned himself with the administration's interpretation of the Mau movement. He poured scorn on the leaders of the movement, notably the part-Sāmoan businessman, Olaf Nelson. His racial prism was especially strong; Serre reported that the administrator, Richardson, as a 'pure White', albeit 'a little hasty', had been acting in the best interests of Sāmoans who had failed to appreciate his actions and had been led astray by 'half caste Caciques or Whites "indigenised" through their marriages to Samoan women'.[31]

[168]

Ultimately, if one were to distil a general picture of New Zealand's colonial administration from the more than a dozen reports that Serre wrote on Sāmoa – as was required of those who received them in Paris, Geneva, Tahiti, New Caledonia, and the Intelligence Services – then it was largely a sympathetic portrait which accepted the self-claims and interpretations of New Zealand officials that the administration was progressive and well-meaning and that Sāmoans had been led astray by Olaf Nelson and other half-castes. To these might be added Serre's more critical assessments – many of which were shared more widely: that the administration had been let down by its inexperience; that civilian rather than military administrators had been required; and that the government had been hamstrung by its preoccupation with public/ electoral opinion and had therefore not acted soon enough with the force required. In some respects these assessments were echoed by the Permanent Mandates Committee itself, which 'criticised New Zealand for lenience, not severity'.[32]

Letting down the imperial family: 'la bombe du 19 mars 1953'

In the next post-war decade, 1945–55, New Zealand's efforts to divest itself of its 'colonies' troubled France much more than had their original acquisition and generated much greater interest in them than previously. At the close of the Second World War and on the back of wartime cooperation, the development of direct diplomatic relations between Wellington and Paris, and the establishment of the South Pacific Commission, allowed for a greater level of French attention to New Zealand's Pacific presence. The spur to greater bi- and mul-tilateral diplomatic engagement was the Canberra Pact of January 1944 – a key statement of Australian and New Zealand foreign policy in the region. Instructions issued to the French Embassy in London in December 1944 stressed that France's invitation to New Zealand to step up diplomatic relations be couched in terms of the recent invita-tion issued to Australia – as well as 'the brotherhood of arms' in North Africa – and 'the community of interests bringing the two countries together in the Pacific'. It was, furthermore, 'desirable that this con-secration of the goodwill that New Zealand has ceaselessly displayed with regard to France, especially since June 1940, should enter into action at the moment when [France's] provisional government is being sounded out with regard to its participation in the "South Seas Conference", which the two South Pacific Dominions propose to call in early 1945'.[33]

The invitation was influenced in large part by the assessment of the Canberra Pact as an act of 'Australasian regionalism' and 'a turning point in the political history of Australasia'. An early French report on the Pact concluded that the young 'white colonies' had attained their 'majority' and were 'claiming what they consider to be their natural rights based on their geographical position'. The unprecedented convergence of New Zealand and Australian policy required a rethinking of the ideas that had dominated since 1912; both Paris and London were surprised that the two neighbours had overcome their 'differences in mentality and their diverging views in matters of domestic policy' to formulate a common foreign policy.[34] They also could not be ignored because, although the Pact had affirmed France's position in the region, there had been a resurfacing of annexationist ideas (notably in Keith Murdoch's *Melbourne Herald*, 18 February 1944) and renewed talk of a 'Pacific Federation'. The French report on the Pact noted that the latter had been publicly aired by New Zealand's Deputy Prime Minister and representative on the Pacific War Council, Walter Nash. It also outlined a 'secret' New Zealand report on the 'Future of the South Pacific Islands' which it attributed to 'H. F. van Haast, unofficial adviser to the New Zealand government'. Haast, the report claimed, had recommended the purchase of France's territories, the disbandment of the condominium in the New Hebrides, the abolition of the mandates, and had demanded a 'South Pacific island federation under the protection of the British Empire or under Anglo-American control'.[35]

The language of imperial family was still more explicit in a later report on 'the position of New Zealand within the framework of a Franco-British alliance'. In 1946, diplomat Armand Gazel noted that for England 'the time has come for the members of the imperial family who have reached their majority to participate more in their own defence and in that of the Empire'. Addressing questions about the status of the Dominions within any future Franco-British alliance, Gazel suggested that regional pacts might be needed so as to extend to 'all of our Empire the advantages of the British alliance'.[36] At play in this period was an awareness that the level of France's own commitment to the region remained uncertain and that in matters of regional post-war Pacific security the ties of empire were not as strong as they had been before the war.

In the following years, France's wariness of direct and indirect challenges to its sovereignty and interests would guide its engagement with the emerging South Pacific Commission as well as with New Zealand's post-war plans for Sāmoa. In 1946–47 it was especially concerned by the potential precedent established by New Zealand's presentation, to the United Nations Trusteeship Council, of a Sāmoan petition requesting immediate self-government, and the special UN visiting mission that New Zealand proposed to invite in response. While defending the need for a special mission (which would allow New Zealand to have more influence over its membership), Prime Minister Peter Fraser endeavoured to reassure French officials that New Zealand would not object to the visit being regarded as one of the 'periodic' visits provided for under the Trusteeship system, and that New Zealand had 'no desire to take any action which would be a source of embarrassment to the French government'.[37]

Six years later, however, Prime Minister Sidney Holland unwittingly dropped what came to be referred to as a 'bomb' on France, in the form of his March 1953 statement on preparations for self-government and for a constitutional convention in Sāmoa.[38] Causing alarm among French officials, the 'bomb' resulted in three reports by France's senior diplomat in Wellington, Noël Henry, examining 'New Zealand's tutelage of Western Samoa', 'New Zealand's colonial Empire', and the possible measures by which New Zealand's plans for Sāmoa might be countered.[39] The reports show that France's own policies in the Pacific were not developed in isolation from thinking about wider French imperial and metropolitan problems.[40] They are also indicative of the way that New Zealand's post-war Pacific plans were perceived by France as a threat to solidarity among the imperial powers in the Pacific region.

New Zealand had not directly challenged France's colonial interests and France had no direct interest in Sāmoa, but Henry's concern was 'the danger of contagion and the example set' by Holland's announcement. Not only might it have 'disagreeable repercussions' by awakening demands for similar reforms in France's Pacific territories, but the possibility that the interests of the European and 'Euronesian' minority would be subject to the Sāmoan majority risked exposing France to criticism for its reluctance to allow similar developments in Tunisia and Morocco, which were also home to 'two differently evolved societies'.[41] The fear of contagion in France's Pacific territories quickly subsided, but the precedent remained. Leon Pignon, France's representative at the UN Trusteeship Council, considered that 'the danger is in the method'. Henry concurred that since 1946 'New Zealand has accustomed us to imprudent initiatives ... which threaten to unleash a most unfortunate agitation in our overseas possessions'. The danger was 'in the word rather than in the thing':

> It happens that New Zealand, lost at the end of the world, at the extremity of the southern oceans, has forgotten that it lives with others on the same planet. No country is more insular than she is. She is certainly well disposed towards France, even extremely so. But if we ignore her, as we do too often, we risk seeing her create the most serious difficulties even if she does not really wish to cause them.[42]

If New Zealand had attained its 'majority', in French eyes, it was now in danger of walking out on the imperial family and required all the more attention.

A particular feature of New Zealand's empire that troubled Henry as he cast his eye about for potential brakes on Sāmoa's advance to self-government was 'the profound indifference of New Zealand public opinion to the problems of the Pacific'. Looking for signs of division as potential leverage, Henry regretted the lack of press coverage and debate following the March 1953 announcement and the April 1953 visit by the Trusteeship Council: 'New Zealand public opinion shows itself to be radically indifferent to these matters.' He explained to Paris that since the events of 1929 in Sāmoa, and the 'reparation' that had followed the 1935 election of the Labour government, 'it has become the custom to not let this thorny issue become a subject of partisan debates'. Unless something serious occurred, New Zealand's parliament would not intervene until after the constitutional convention when presented with amendments for approval.[43] Historians may have played down the degree of public interest in New Zealand's empire,[44] but Henry's comment suggests that the path towards independence for Sāmoa did not generate the same level of debate as the various calls for annexation half a century earlier. In 1955, bemoaning the same public indifference to Pacific issues, Henry informed Paris that New Zealand 'does not have any imperialist mentality'; the only issue that appeared to raise any imperialist spirit or sympathy was the situation in Indochina.[45]

As with Serre's reports several decades earlier, Henry's observations were bound up with comments on New Zealand's metropole, implicit appeals to a sense of racial or imperial community, and attempts to draw parallels with France's own colonial predicaments. Surveying the possible local and international repercussions of the March 1953 proposals, Henry had 'no doubt but that at the bottom of their hearts [Māori] consider the New Zealanders to be intruders', but the population balance meant that the New Zealand government had nothing to fear and that it would never face the same problems that France was confronting in North Africa.[46] New Zealand seemed oblivious to the double standard of promising self-government to Sāmoans but not to Māori.

Reviewing the findings of the 1953 UN visiting mission to Sāmoa, Henry argued (much to the surprise of the official who annotated the report's margins) that there were significant similarities between New Zealand's actions in Sāmoa and France's actions in North Africa: both powers had worked in the spirit of trusteeship, though New Zealand had achieved better results; both had been involved in a 'civilising mission' that was not yet complete; both still had much to do in terms of development and to put a modern state in place unless the territories were to be left to return to their 'former anarchy'; and both faced growing populations and therefore expenses. However, there were, he conceded (to the relief of the marginal scribe), two critical differences: nearly everyone in Sāmoa was Christian, and the European minority was so small that there really was only one community and no need for a bipartite development or special measures to prevent a more evolved minority from oppressing a less evolved majority (as Henry feared for North Africa).[47]

Henry's broader-ranging analysis of 'New Zealand's colonial Empire' – a term encompassing 'metropolitan dependencies' such as the Chatham Islands as well as the Cook Islands, Tokelau, Niue, and the Ross Dependency – drew attention to some of the problems that faced New Zealand as an imperial power, as well as the lessons that it provided for France in its handling of colonial citizenship and migration. The first lesson for France in the New Zealand solution to these problems was the need to respect the 'exigencies' of distance; each of New Zealand's colonies – even each island, in the case of the Cook Islands – was treated as a separate political entity. The 'Lilliputian' empire was united to some degree by its mainly Polynesian and Christian populations (and almost non-existent European population), but its isolation and dispersal militated against centralising imperatives.[48]

The second lesson was that 'the New Zealand colonial political system is graduated as a function of the degree of evolution of the islanders'. After Sāmoa, the Cook Islands were at the top of the scale, with an 'embryo' of representative government, followed by Niue and Tokelau. While all their inhabitants were citizens with 'equal access to public employment, provided that the candidates meet certain criteria', there were 'certain restrictions' on electoral rights (notably the absence of representation in Wellington), migration to and from the islands, and the right to trial by jury. Henry noted that Niueans had recently confirmed their 'savagery' and therefore their placement towards the bottom of the scale, by the murder of the Resident Commissioner, Larsen. Like Serre before him, Henry was sympathetic to the New Zealand administration's interpretation of such events, but the system was not beyond reproach; he observed that Larsen had exercised the combined functions of administrator, judge, and prison officer, and that the perpetrators would not have been sentenced to death if they had had the right to a jury of 'pure Polynesians'.[49] Nevertheless, for Henry, the New Zealand model of citizenship, with its graduated or hierarchical distribution of political rights, presented an admirable example for France as it grappled with questions about the rights of its own colonial citizens:

This diversity in the institutions must reflect the status of the inhabit-ants. Common citizenship cannot be absolute. To affirm that it can be is nothing but hypocrisy ... It is pushing the notion of citizenship to the point of absurdity to claim that it prevents the regulation of the circula-tion of people: vagabondage must not be raised to the level of a national institution. Feeding the army of crime and revolution by throwing Algerians out on to the footpaths of Paris will have tragic repercussions for France.

New Zealand had its colonial priorities right, according to Henry. What 'natives' needed above all was development; citizenship was meaningless for the hungry, he wrote:

New Zealand has understood. She has not multiplied industrial culture at the expense of agriculture; basically she has preoccupied herself with cultivating the land. She is fighting against the "shanty towns".

She has reaped what she has sown. Her colonies are calm. Let us hope that a false humanitarianism, an unrealistic messianism and unfortu-nate initiatives such as in Samoa do not cause her to miss out on the rewards of her generous and enlightened actions and do not compromise her fate ... with those of others.[50]

Henry's wish was not, however, to be fulfilled in the terms in which he saw it; preparations for Sāmoan self-government proceeded, and his own suggestion that France might block or slow down the process by engineering pressure on New Zealand to deliver greater democracy or universal suffrage – so as to create a backlash from the Sāmoan chiefs – was not realised.[51]

This brief overview of French perceptions of New Zealand's empire ends on the eve of the 1960s, during which the two countries' postco-lonial paths would diverge significantly. In that decade, France's Pacific territories would lose much of the autonomy they had attained by the end of the 1950s, while New Zealand stepped up moves towards the formal political decolonisation of Sāmoa in 1962 and the Cook Islands in 1965. With the development of French nuclear testing, by 1966 the New Zealand critique of France's Pacific colonialism would grow.

Over the previous half-century, New Zealand's colonial or imperial activity had been meaningful in sometimes surprising ways to the likes of Serre and Henry. New Zealand's empire was diminutive or 'Lilliputian', but it was not isolated from larger issues or questions. Its Sāmoan 'troubles' might help deflect attention from France's own colo-nial problems; its empire formed a 'microcosm' from which lessons for France's own territories might be drawn. They had been occasionally admiring of New Zealand's colonial administration, and often sympa-thetic in regards to the challenges it had faced, but in Henry's case they were also highly concerned at the prospect of a retreat from colonial administration and imperial responsibility. New Zealand's decolonisation attracted much greater concern and interest than its original expansion and lingering annexationist or even federationist desires. Indeed, as steps towards Sāmoan self-government quickened, French officials rallied to counter New Zealand's apparent positioning of itself as the 'spokesperson of Polynesia' in debates over the future participation of Indigenous representatives in the South Pacific Conference.[52] The various reports examined here also draw attention to questions beyond the scope of this chapter that further analyses would do well to explore: that of Australia's shadow in shaping the way New Zealand's Pacific aspirations and activities were perceived, and that of the role of New Zealand public opinion (or its possible absence) in shaping the end of its so-called empire. More importantly, they might usefully highlight some of the tensions, contradictions, compromises, and hypocrises entailed by colonial rule.

Acknowledgements

The Faculty of Humanities and Social Sciences at Victoria University of Wellington for a Faculty Research Grant, and Steven Loveridge for Research Assistance. Unless otherwise indicated, translations from the French are my own.

Notes

1 Archives du Ministère des affaires étrangères, Courneuve, Paris (hereafter MAE), Asie-Océanie, Nouvelle-Zéalande (hereafter AO, NZ), Mandats, E275-5, no. 301/AS, N. Henry to Ministre des affaires étrangères, Wellington, 16 septembre 1953.
2 Notably John Dunmore (ed.), *New Zealand and the French: Two Centuries of Contact* (Waikanae: Heritage Press, 1990); *Le Colloque d'Akaroa 16–19 août 1990* (Waikanae: Heritage Press, 1990); and John Dunmore (ed.), *The French and the Maori* (Waikanae: Heritage Press, 1992); [Anon. (ed.)] *60 Years Ago ... Celebrating the Anniversary of Diplomatic Relations between New Zealand and France* ([Wellington, 2005]).
3 Damon Salesa, 'New Zealand's Pacific', in Giselle Byrnes (ed.), *The New Oxford History of New Zealand* (Melbourne: Oxford University Press, 2009), pp. 149–51.
4 For example, David Hamer, 'André Siegfried's View of New Zealand', in Dunmore (ed.), *New Zealand and the French*, pp. 112–15; and Rognvald Leask, 'André Siegfried and the discovery of the New Zealand democracy', in [Anon. (ed.)], *60 Years Ago*, pp. 55–60.
5 Salesa, 'New Zealand's Pacific', pp. 149–51.
6 Cf. Mervyn Norrish, 'Political relations between New Zealand and France', in Dunmore (ed.), *New Zealand and the French*, pp. 155–64; Steven Hoadley, *New Zealand and France: Politics, Diplomacy, and Dispute Management* (Wellington: New Zealand Institute of International Affairs, 2005).
7 Ann Laura Stoler, 'Tense and tender ties: The politics of comparison in North American history and (post) colonial studies', *Journal of American History*, 88:3 (2001), 831.

8 Philippa Mein Smith, 'New Zealand', in Helen Irving (ed.), *The Centenary Companion to Australian Federation* (Cambridge: Cambridge University Press, 1999), p. 401.

9 MAE, Océanie, Nouvelle-Série 1, NZ (1899–1912), Vossion to Ministre des Affaires étrangéres, no. 21, Sydney, 23 septembre 1900.

10 MAE, Océanie, Nouvelle-Série 1, NZ (1899–1912), Courte to Ministre des Affaires étrangères, no. 3, Wellington, 5 mars 1901.

11 André Siegfried, *Democracy in New Zealand*, trans. E. V. Burns (Wellington: Victoria University Press, 2nd edn, 1982 [1914]), pp. 349–50.

12 MAE, Océanie, Nouvelle-Série 1, NZ (1899–1912), Ministre des Colonies to Ministre des Affaires étrangères, Paris, 16 juillet 1900); MAE, Océanie, Nouvelle-Série 1, NZ (1899–1912), Le gérant du consulat de France to Ministre des Affaires étrangères, no. 92, Auckland, 27 septembre 1911.

13 MAE, Océanie, Nouvelle-Série 1, NZ (1899–1912), Le gérant du consulat de France to Ministre des Affaires étrangères, Auckland, 23 janvier 1912.

14 MAE, Océanie, Nouvelle-Série 1, NZ (1899–1912), Le gérant du consulat de France to Ministre des Affaires étrangères, no. 88, Auckland, 21 septembre 1911.

15 For a note on this mission see: Mervyn Norrish, 'Political relations between New Zealand and France', p. 157.

16 A key voice was the Comité de l'Océanie française, which had been promoting French interests in the region, and commenting on developments in New Zealand and Australia, since 1905. See Robert Aldrich, *The French Presence in the South Pacific, 1842–1940* (Honolulu: University of Hawai'i Press, 1990), pp. 237–72, 278–81.

17 E. Pelleray, 'La question des Nouvelles-Hébrides', *La Revue du Pacifique*, 1 (1922), 56–75: 73–4, http://gallica.bnf.fr/ark:/12148/bpt6k55453427, accessed 10 November 2013.

18 Pelleray, 'La question des Nouvelles-Hébrides', p. 65.

19 Formerly Western Samoa, but referred to in this chapter as Sāmoa.

20 *La Revue du Pacifique*, 3 (1922), 75–9.

21 Centre des archives d'outre-mer, Aix-en-Provence (hereafter CAOM), Contrôle 828, Revel to Ministre des Colonies, Sydney, 10 juillet 1922. This figure appears to be an exaggeration; New Zealand reported to the LON in 1921 that there had been 2,200 Chinese labourers in Sāmoa in 1914 and that all but 832 had been repatriated by 1920; since then 500 more had been recruited.

22 CAOM, Contrôle 829, Serre to Ministre des Affaires étrangères, no. 68 [ca. May 1924]; CAOM, Contrôle 829, Arboussier, 'Menées presbytériennes aux Nouvelles-Hébrides', Nouméa, 28 avril 1924. Cf., for example, 'Under two flags', *Auckland Star* (26 May 1924), p. 9.

23 W. Massey in *New Zealand Parliamentary Debates*, Vol. 185, 1919, p. 517. I thank Nicholas Hoare for bringing this reference to my attention.

24 MAE, AO, Australie-Mandats C, Serre to Ministre des Affaires étrangères, no. 185, Auckland, 14 novembre 1923.

25 Gerald Chaudron, *New Zealand in the League of Nations: The Beginnings of an Independent Foreign Policy, 1919–1939* (Jefferson, NC: McFarland, 2012), pp. 21–2.

26 MAE, Service français de la Société des nations (hereafter SDN), 242QO, no. 625, Serre to Ministre des Affaires étrangères, no. 114, Auckland, 28 juillet 1923. For further context, see Chaudron, *New Zealand in the League of Nations*.

27 MAE, AO, Australie-Mandats C, Serre to Ministre des Affaires étrangères, no. 73, Auckland, 31 juillet 1927. Serre's counterpart in Melbourne welcomed Australian reports which showed that 'New Zealand shares with us the fate of being under the rod' of Australian criticism and hoped that the information would be of use to France's delegation at the LON. See: MAE, SDN, 242QO, no. 625, Turck to Ministre des Affaires étrangères, no. 32, Melbourne, 12 août 1927.

28 MAE, AO, NZ, E276, Serre to Ministre des Affaires étrangères, no. 107, Auckland, 22 octobre 1927.

29   MAE, AO, NZ, E276, Serre to Ministre des Affaires étrangères, no. 27, Auckland, 21 mars 1926.

30   MAE, AO, NZ, E276, Serre to Ministre des Affaires étrangères, no. 12, Auckland, 1 mars 1923.

31   MAE, AO, Australie-Mandats C, Serre to Ministre des Affaires étrangères, no. 95, Auckland, 31 août 1927.

32   See Joseph V. Wilson, 'New Zealand's participation in international organisations', in T. C. Larkin (ed.), *New Zealand's External Relations* (Wellington: NZ Institute of Public Administration, 1962), p. 63; and Frank Henry Corner, 'New Zealand and the South Pacific', in Larkin (ed.) *New Zealand's External Relations*, p. 139.

33   MAE, AO, NZ, E275-1, Pleven to Ambafrance Londres, Télégramme, Paris, 4 décembre 1944.

34   MAE, AO, NZ, E275-1, 'Note: Accord de Canberra du 21 janvier 1944' [n.d.].

35   MAE, AO, NZ, E275-1, 'Note: Accord de Canberra du 21 janvier 1944' [n.d.]. Heinrich Ferdinand von Haast (1864–1953) was a member of the New Zealand Round Table Group. He was an advocate of 'the Federation of the British Commonwealth in matters of foreign policy and defence' and authored many of the Group's quarterly contributions and pamphlets. The 'secret' document referred to in the French report may well be one of these documents. See: [New Zealand], 'Dr. Von Haast – An Appreciation', *The Round Table*, 170 (1953), 193–4.

36   MAE, AO, NZ, E275-1, Armand Gazel to Ministre des Affaires Etrangères, Wellington, 18 avril 1946. On France's post-war policy more generally, see Sarah Mohamed-Gaillard, *L'Archipel de la puissance? La politique de la France dans le Pacifique Sud de 1946 à 1998* (Bruxelles: Peter Lang, 2010), pp. 171–97.

37   Archives New Zealand, R20106565, P. Fraser to A. Gazel, PM/311/10/3, Wellington, 12 April 1947.

38   MAE, AO, NZ, E275-1, N. Henry, Note au sujet du Samoa occidental sous tutelle néozélandaise, 18 mai 1953; cf. Mary Boyd, 'The record in Western Samoa since 1945', in Angus Ross (ed.), *New Zealand's Record in the Pacific Islands in the Twentieth Century* (Auckland: Longman Paul for the New Zealand Institute of International Affairs,1969), pp. 222–4.

39   The third was ostensibly a review of the report issued by the 1953 UN visiting mission to Sāmoa.

40   Robert Aldrich, *France and the South Pacific Since 1940* (Honolulu: University of Hawai'i Press, 1993), pp. 60–4.

41   MAE, AO, NZ, E275-1, N. Henry to Ministre des Affaires Etrangères, no. 180/AS, Wellington, 18 mai 1953; MAE, AO, NZ, E275-1, N. Henry, Note au sujet du Samoa occidental sous tutelle néozélandaise, 18 mai 1953.

42   MAE, AO, NZ, E275-1, N. Henry, Note au sujet du Samoa occidental sous tutelle néozélandaise, 18 mai 1953.

43   MAE, AO, NZ, E275-1, N. Henry, Note au sujet du Samoa occidental sous tutelle néozélandaise, 18 mai 1953.

44   Salesa, 'New Zealand's Pacific', p. 153.

45   MAE, AO, NZ, E275-1, N. Henry to Ministre des Affaires étrangères, no. 46, Wellington, 10 mai 1955.

46   MAE, AO, NZ, E275-1, N. Henry, Note au sujet du Samoa occidental sous tutelle néozélandaise, 18 mai 1953.

47   MAE, AO, NZ, E275-5, N. Henry to Ministre des Affaires étrangères, no. 304/AS, Wellington, 16 septembre 1953.

48   MAE, AO, NZ, E275-1, N. Henry to Ministre des Affaires étrangères, no. 301/AS, Wellington, 16 septembre 1953.

49   MAE, AO, NZ, E275-1, N. Henry to Ministre des Affaires étrangères, no. 301/AS, Wellington, 16 septembre 1953. The death sentences were not carried out. See Dick Scott, *Would a Good Man Die? Niue Island, New Zealand and the Late Mr Larsen* (Auckland: Hodder & Stoughton and Southern Cross Books, 1993).

50   MAE, AO, NZ, E275-1, N. Henry to Ministre des Affaires étrangères, no. 301/AS, Wellington, 16 septembre 1953.

51 MAE, AO, NZ, E275-5, N. Henry to Ministre des Affaires étrangères, no. 304/AS, Wellington, 16 septembre 1953.

52 Centre des archives diplomatiques de Nantes (CADN), Délégation française à la Commission du Pacifique Sud, 27 POI/1, no. 2, R. de Bercegol de Lile to Ministre des Affaires étrangères, no. 34/AM, Wellington, 10 janvier 1957. Cf. Mohamed-Gaillard, *L'Archipel de la puissance?*, p. 257.

CHAPTER TEN

War surplus? New Zealand and American children of Indigenous women in Sāmoa, the Cook Islands, and Tokelau

Judith A. Bennett

During the Second World War, troops of the United States occupied most of the South Pacific island groups. Of New Zealand's dependencies, all but Niue saw a rapid build-up of their bases. With the Japanese in retreat by 1943, many influential Americans advocated that expenditure of their 'blood and treasure' should warrant post-war territorial security in the region for the United States. The New Zealand as well as the Australian government feared the Americans would stay on after the war. This threatened New Zealand's Pacific possessions. Away from these high politics, but entwined in them, this powerful ally also left a legacy of part-American children across the islands, including New Zealand. New Zealand's stance on these outcomes of intimacy was framed not only by its own societal values and those of the islands' peoples, but also within a wider lens that encompassed both wartime and post-war dependency on the United States.

As early as the 1850s New Zealand had dreamt of being a South Pacific power. A succession of governors and prime ministers supported or tried to pressure Britain to expand its imperium and make the region a 'British Lake' to counter the French in Tahiti and New Caledonia. In 1888, Britain accepted the Cook Islands as a Protectorate to forestall the French, and passed its administration to New Zealand and then full responsibility for the Cook Islands (1901) and Niue (1904), and later, Tokelau (1926). Following Germany's defeat in the First World War, Britain willingly agreed to New Zealand's control of Sāmoa – very different from 1899 when it had stymied the colony's imperial ambitions by allowing Germany to have the west and the United States the east.[1]

These territories were effectively Britain's cast-offs but, as far as New Zealand was concerned, they were her colonial dependencies, even though their legal status was varied: the Cook Islands, Niue, and Tokelau were 'part of New Zealand' but were administered separately.

Their people had the same rights as New Zealanders, but were not always recognised as British subjects, while New Zealand's administration of Sāmoa was under the scrutiny of the League of Nations.[2] These dependencies soon proved of little economic value, but certainly by the 1930s, New Zealand considered itself responsible for improving the education and health of the people along with the productivity of the islands, though the Depression – and, in Sāmoa, the Mau resistance – hindered progress.[3]

War comes

As war in Europe began in 1939, Cook Islanders remained 'intensely loyal to the British Crown'.[4] Except for wanting their own member in the New Zealand Parliament in 1925, they were largely content with local representation on the Island Council along with oversight of the Māori Minister for Native Affairs in the New Zealand government.[5] In 1941, a small local reserve force formed. New Zealand had posted radio operators plus an occasional soldier as coastwatchers on eleven Pacific islands by 1942, though on Rarotonga, Cook Islanders did this.[6] From 1941 in Tokelau, local people carried out coastwatching and relayed reports to Fiji.[7]

In Sāmoa, New Zealand was unprepared for war in two critical ways. First, Sāmoans regarded themselves 'as a separate nationhood' and felt little loyalty to New Zealand, an outcome of administrative mishandling of the 1918–19 influenza epidemic, the Mau resistance, and other peaceful protests.[8] Second, New Zealand's adherence to the League of Nations' principles forbade construction of fortifications. At Britain's request, defensive preparations focused on Fiji and Tonga. The Sāmoan administration formed a local defence force of Europeans and afakasi (half-castes), numbering about 175, who guarded German internees and manned coastwatching posts. A lone New Zealand Army warrant officer led a small reserve force; such was the extent of New Zealand's defence preparation when the war with Japan broke out on 7 December 1941.[9]

Once the new imperial power of the United States entered the war, its forces rapidly fortified several South Pacific islands. Almost two million Americans were involved in the Pacific, doubling the population and more on some islands. Across both Western and American Samoa the US Marines were soon to number ten thousand.[10] In 1942, the 'exhilarating days' of the occupation began:

> On 27 March Apia harbour presented an amazing sight. There lay the 'President Garfield' and other huge transports, in their war blue-grey, with thousands of US Marines and masses of equipment sliding down their high sides. Our local Defence Force looked, felt gratefully over-

whelmed, and melted away. It was so overrun with Americans that no-one remembers whether the order to dismiss was ever given.[11]

Under the 'unity of command' not only were there designated lines of command between the US forces, but all allied military forces in the region also came under the Supreme American commander.[12] For New Zealand, this meant a considerable abnegation of sovereignty. New Zealand in terms of men and materials was very much the junior partner, while Britain and France were similar because they had virtually no forces in the Pacific theatre. While operational command was relatively defined, just where the civilian administration's authority began and the Americans' ended was not always clear and was subject to negotiation.[13] Official policy at high levels of administration and the military often concealed the untidy reality of everyday relations among servicemen and civilians.

Societies and socialising

Young Americans, far from home and all its moral, racial, and gender strictures, soon found that New Zealand's Pacific islands were as beautiful as the images in the Hollywood movies. And the women, while not quite the film star Dorothy Lamour, were pleasing.[14] The men quickly made their interests clear, as one Sāmoan woman recalled:

> There were so many of them. In the afternoons you see some of them lying out in the front of the fale [house] in the evening sun waiting for the truck to come and they all run after it to get on. We were next door to Apia Park and I saw them come to the fence and whistle to my older sister and girl cousins while they were doing their chores. Our parents were not impressed. I was not allowed to play outside or get too close to the fence.[15]

Soon, some young Americans developed intimate relationships with Indigenous women in Sāmoa, the Cook Islands, and most of the South Pacific command zone. Even Tokelau's Atafu atoll with its 370 inhabitants saw friendships develop between the local people and twenty-six to forty Americans based there in 1943 to run a navigation station.[16]

Long before the war, across New Zealand's Polynesian empire, Indigenous gender relations, while not uniform, displayed commonalities. Generally, women were respected for their role in reproduction and the wider society. Marriage was highly valued for its creation of relationships and family affiliations. Children were welcomed and, if out of wedlock, accepted by the wider family, though in Sāmoa often with shame if the family was ambitious for a strategic marriage for its virgin daughters. The Cook Islands had a very hybrid population, primarily from European admixtures dating back to the early nine-teenth-century visits of whalers and traders, a few of whom stayed on. Sāmoa had a similar history, but with a large Indigenous population the ratio of foreign genes was lower.[17]

In colonial times this intermingling continued in Sāmoa, though under the Germans and the early New Zealand administrators and their staff there was an aversion to people of mixed ancestry. The Germans in 1912 even went so far as to forbid interracial marriages. Though the Sāmoans had no inherent discrimination towards part-Sāmoans, some by the 1920s were less tolerant of those Apia-bound afakasi who lacked means and reputation. Few women of this group were socially accept-able to the polite society of parochial New Zealand officials. Although the administration disapproved of marriages between New Zealand civil servants and Sāmoan women, it largely ignored their sexual rela-tionships, if discreet.[18] The Cook Islands, however, was simply too small, its expatriate residents too few, and its peoples too mixed for such pretensions.

At home, New Zealand Pākehā society was extremely intolerant of ex-nuptial female sexuality. Any resultant offspring were given up for adoption by strangers or became a well-hidden family secret. The errant mother and even the child elicited public and often family con-demnation, rather than compassion, a reaction similar to that of white American society.[19]

American needs

The military worked with the civil administration to maintain its support and that of the Indigenous people, whose contribution as labour was significant because it freed the military to pursue their mission and saved them money.[20] Military command needed its fight-ers to be healthy in body and mind. Venereal disease (VD) had to be controlled because this could disable the infected and cause problems for partners in the islands and at home. Although servicemen were not punished for becoming infected, they were court martialled if they tried to conceal infection. Treatment with the relatively new sulpha drugs was usual, but by 1940 some cases displayed resistance. Until late 1943 there was no fast-acting penicillin. Thus the military supplied prophy-lactics, mainly rubber condoms.[21]

Though it is useful to see the relationship between the metropole and the colony as parts of 'one analytic field', the New Zealand government applied some policies in the Islands that would not have been accept-able domestically, even during the emergency.[22] Its co-operation with the United States extended to one specific aspect of intimate relations.

American medical units reported all Island women suspected of consorting with infected servicemen to the administration. Colonial doctors, or, in the Cook Islands, military medical officers, examined and treated such women, with or without their consent, a common pattern in all islands with US bases.[23] For the infected 'who failed to comply with the regulations' on Aitutaki, 'steps were taken to segregate' them.[24] Yet the New Zealand government did not require this of her home population, though it could compel known prostitutes to be treated.[25] Other than this, and putting some areas out of bounds, there was little else done to keep the military apart from Indigenous women in the Cook Islands and Sāmoa. In Atafu, Tokelau, the Sāmoan pastor imposed a curfew at dusk for villagers and for the Americans to return to their camp, but there were other times when young people might meet. Without a resident New Zealand official the administration knew little, other than that seaplanes from the US base on Kanton visited weekly to purchase curios.[26]

When the US Army arrived on Aitutaki in November 1942 to construct an airfield, 1,000 Americans found themselves on a small atoll.[27] The people were welcoming. American doctors reporting on VD observed, 'the women are not immoral – they are amoral'.[28] Despite occasional 'prostitution', most men had regular girlfriends. Women knew about the venereal risk and stayed with one partner; if he went with another, his first dropped him for fear of infection. Medical personnel controlled the infected, and reduced VD incidence from the high levels recorded some months after the troops arrived.[29]

The main value of these women, in the eyes of military command, was for the mental health of the servicemen: 'native girls were of a fairly high type and ... that helped morale a great deal'.[30] In the Pacific theatres more than any others, Americans were prone to neuropsychiatric disorders. Even in the benign bases in Polynesia, behind the battlefields, the rate was high due to boredom, lack of knowledge of overall war strategy, and long tours of duty. Anyone stationed in the Islands for more than eighteen to twenty-four months was especially vulnerable. There were no big cities and very few white women because most had been evacuated to New Zealand in late 1941 and early 1942, though some returned in 1943–44.[31] In Sāmoa, male officers monopolised the few Red Cross women and military nurses. Enlisted men had virtually no opportunities for meeting white women socially, and here and elsewhere resented it.[32] A scant fifteen African American nurses were in the South West Pacific theatre in New Guinea.[33] Thus in the Polynesian South Pacific, the military supported fraternisation with local women and their families because it relieved the scourge of 'isolation, separation from normal family ties, the dullness of existence, and the strangeness of surroundings' for the men.[34]

Other than controlling VD, the colonial government's and the military's only other concern with intimacy was to prevent marriages between servicemen and Indigenous women. No American servicemen were permitted to marry Indigenous women, who could not immigrate to the USA, let alone find a state that did not bar such marriages. If a woman of mixed ancestry had more than 51 per cent 'white blood', permission might be forthcoming. Colonial administrations, including New Zealand's, ensured that local island clergy understood this.[35] For military commanders, Indigenous women had their uses for the men for social and sexual solace, yet clearly would be abandoned when the units left the islands.

Penrhyn was another US Army base in the Cook Islands, a fuelling depot for small ships.[36] The initial 1,000 US Army personnel who arrived in November 1942 'were kept fairly segregated from the native population'.[37] Even so, the goods, employment, and entertainment of the Americans attracted the resource-poor islanders. One mother encouraged her daughter to 'take a walk with a soldier' but the young woman refused, as she had her own Island lover. The Catholic priest complained of the Americans bringing women into their camp for immoral purposes.[38] It seems that airmen unofficially flew in certain women from Tahiti and Honolulu for sex work.[39] The Americans left about ten children on Penrhyn. With a population of just over a quarter that of Aitutaki, these few children reflected Penrhyn's small number of young women, rather than avoidance of the popular Americans.[40]

Such relationships were not as mechanistic as command might have preferred. Intimations of personal attachments occasionally appear in colonial records, especially in the Cook Islands where administrators provided more detail than elsewhere. On the confined atolls of Aitutaki and Penrhyn, they could hardly have ignored what was going on because they, the Americans, and villagers were close together. Although the few administrators discouraged wild parties and relations between very young girls and the Americans, they seemed accepting of what was the inevitable, including a few cases of men paying for sex. They reported warm, intimate relationships between the respective peoples. Incidents of violence towards women emanated from jealous Island men, rarely the Americans. Divorces increased, however, as they did in most places under occupation.[41]

Modernity had come to the Cook Islands, to be embraced as much as the American men. An expanded medical service, improved radio communications, movie shows, electricity, regular shipping, new roads, land transport, novel foods, Sears Roebuck catalogues, increased savings accounts among those working for the United States, and a spike in government revenue, all opened up new vistas.

Isolated administrators, like the Islanders, came to depend on the Americans for a higher standard of living. They little questioned the domestic arrangements between the Americans and the local women.[42] This interdependency permeated to the highest level. As late as mid-1944, the resident commissioner advised the New Zealand government:

> After discussion with the American medical officers at Aitutaki there appears to be a reasonable chance of ... being cured of filariasis [a mosquito-borne illness] ... we are unusually dependant on the good offices of the American Commanding Officer for the use of his facilities for the cartage and lightering of fruit [for export], and it could be most inadvisable to disturb the existing happy relationship between the civil administration and the United States Forces.[43]

In spite of American attractions, the Cook Islanders had no wish to secede from New Zealand. Ethnic ties between the respective Indigenous peoples were strong. The Cook Islands over decades had a long association with Māori members of the New Zealand Parliament; their languages and some tribes were related, their young people visited back and forth, and a chiefly woman – Makea Tui Ariki Takau Love – in 1928 had married an eminent Māori leader – Lt Colonel E. Love.[44] At the height of the occupation in 1943, the people submitted a dozen complaints to a New Zealand delegation. They voiced no claims for support for the Americans' children, but a desire for the Island men to serve with the forces overseas, for representation in the New Zealand Parliament, as well as freer access for young women to domestic work in New Zealand.[45] When the administration imposed duty on sales of US surplus in 1944, upsetting Aitutaki people, one man did ask in a public meeting if they would be better off under the United States, but nothing came of this.[46]

While New Zealand had not differentiated among Island women who were suspected of VD infection, its response to the need for wartime male labour was more nuanced. The Cook Islanders' request to join the New Zealand Army overseas was consistently declined, primarily to funnel men to the insalubrious French island of Makatea to maintain supplies of phosphate for New Zealand's farms in order to supply fresh vegetables to the American Pacific forces. No phosphate could be mined in British Banaba and Nauru because the Japanese occupied these until the end of the war. New Zealand hired fifty Tokelauan men to work on plantations in Sāmoa, since Sāmoans were working for the Americans. In late 1943, New Zealand's support for American appeals for labour for the Solomon Islands saw the Sāmoans refuse because money was easier to earn at home. New Zealand did not pressure them, just as it had decided against imposing tighter controls on wartime inflation and luxury imports because it feared 'political repercussions'.[47] Sāmoa's consistent challenges to New Zealand tempered imperial demands.

In Western Samoa the impact of modernity was more extensive temporally and geographically than in the Cook Islands. It was a time of high wages, many *malaga* (tours around villages) for entertainment and celebration, major church donations, and novel experiences. Americans were generous and egalitarian in their interactions with Sāmoans, unlike New Zealanders. Life was exciting, especially for the young: 'Politics hibernated ... [w]ith millions of added dollars, life became a soaring balloon. Employers were patient, exasperated or ceased to care. Schools closed because teachers wandered off to American employment.'[48] Despite the small 'sisterhood' of the 'beach', most women were loyal to their partners, savouring the American reciprocal benefits and hopes for eventual marriage. A chief offered his daughter, Matua, to the naval historian James Michener. Michener's superior was being investigated for extending the Upolu transinsular road to the house of this woman, a sister of the part-Sāmoan entrepreneur, Aggie Grey. Even so, if the parents and family did not support the relationship between a woman and an American, she was particularly vulnerable to social criticism and shame, as was the case, for example, with the daughters of village pastors pregnant to Americans. Intimacy also had a sordid and opportunistic side: a few Sāmoan men even offered their wives. One village pastor was expelled from his congregation, allegedly for procuring prostitutes for Americans.[49]

By 1944, gonorrhoea rates were under control in Sāmoa but still worrisome. The US medical officer noted that: 'Professional prostitution is uncommon on the island, although the warm reception rendered US servicemen by civilians and the somewhat promiscuous habits of the Samoans remain a barrier to completely effective control.'[50] Overall though, US command's interest in intimate relationships was limited. Occasionally, in regard to Western Samoa and the Cook Islands, commanders noted cohabitation and transient 'romances'.[51] This temporary aspect inherent in a mobile military force was reinforced by the legal strictures against marriage throughout the war. Many romances were sincere but only a few determined men, who found the money to return to the post-war Pacific, married their sweethearts.[52]

Coloured views

Racism, imperialism's handmaiden, permeated both military and colonial thinking. African American troops thought themselves superior to the 'natives', an opinion their white commanders did not share.[53] The commander of the Sāmoan and Wallis Islands, General Charles Price, considered Sāmoan women to be 'primitively romantic'. Like most of his countrymen he regarded 'negros' [sic] as inferior, therefore would not allow African Americans into the Sāmoan Islands, as they would produce undesirable offspring.[54] The New Zealand administrator did not want African Americans in the Cook Islands since they might be a malign influence, but in August 1943, he deferred to the New Zealand government and accepted their presence on Aitutaki with local American assurances that their numbers would soon be reduced.[55] By November, with the base completed, about half the Americans were evacuated, including all African Americans, to the relief of the resident agent.[56] Yet the women of Aitutaki did not discriminate. They ignored white servicemen who told them not to attend 'black dances'. One recalled the whites' disapproval on another occasion. A group of African Americans was sighted in the distance, and a white serviceman quipped: 'Look, the black fish are coming down the reef.' The young women retorted: 'That's alright, we don't mind.'[57]

American high command showed no concern for the fate of the part-American children. Herbert Priday, an Australian war correspondent with the American forces, wrote *The War from Coconut Square*. His book portrayed allied cooperation and interactions with the Indigenous people. Nonetheless, the book had to face the American censors. In the original typescript he wrote regarding Aitutaki:

> To discourage romances from going too far, the US Army in its wisdom made it clear to the administration that marriages between members of the Forces and island women would not be approved. However, in the case of children born of American fathers – I am told these are not numerous – it was established policy to get the father voluntarily and in agreement with the girl and her family and the NZ representative, to pay for the support of the child until 12 years of age. To this end a trust fund was opened with the Resident Agent. As $300 was considered sufficient to fulfil this obligation, the GIs paid up like gentlemen, finding that with almost complete lack of opportunity to spend money on the island this sum could be built up quickly.[58]

The censors allowed only the first sentence to remain. The United States regarded interracial miscegenation as singularly undesirable.[59] Such portrayals, conveying to the American public descriptions of young white American manhood cohabiting with women of colour and producing 'half-castes' or 'nigger' babies, would have damaged domestic morale and domestic relations.[60] Although the remaining Aitutaki chapter was published, the implication that some relationships were affectionate and some men responsible languished in the military archives, the fate of this 'fund' is unrecorded.[61]

In the Cook Islands, the New Zealand resident agent and the commander displayed some fleeting interest in the American children who numbered around eighty, including about seventy on Aitutaki. In late 1943, Aitutaki's resident agent, H. Hickling, settled some claims for child support by the arrangements that Priday described. Some mothers were reluctant to claim support since many had benefitted by the Americans' generosity and loved their partners. Still, the men would soon depart. In mid-1944 Foss Shanahan, assistant secretary of New Zealand's war cabinet, wanted to know the outcomes of such arrangements. The resident agent confirmed that some men had entered into voluntary agreements to pay support, but once they left the islands nothing more was forthcoming. The US commander suggested that claims then be sent to commanders where the men were stationed.[62]

No more was heard of this, in either New Zealand or the United States, despite Public Law 625/77th Congress of the United States 1942 and 1943 amendments.[63] This provided for dependent children, legitimate or not, to be maintained by a serviceman father and by the US government. The evidence acceptable to the American officials was: legal adoption of the child by its putative father; admission of paternity by the father; a judicial order to contribute to the child's support; or a judicial decree that the enlisted man was the putative father. Court orders could not be made if the man had left the country. Even if he were still present, there was some doubt that a New Zealand court had standing in the United States. Moreover, if it did, the commanding officer of the man's unit could get him to pay his contribution by threatening disciplinary action, but that lapsed once he was out of the service. All military-deducted family allowances stopped six months after the cessation of hostilities. Further legal action was hamstrung by the prohibition against releasing the civilian address of any serviceman involved in a paternity suit. The bureaucratic procedures were imperfectly researched by the legal advisors of the government of New Zealand, whereby many hundreds of servicemen's children, Pākehā and Māori, were left fatherless. The government displayed no enthusiasm for pursuing it further. For American children in the islands as well as in New Zealand, this legislation was so hedged that it was never tested.[64]

Legacies

In Western Samoa, one group displayed concern for the future of such children. Fourteen American citizens from the business community and the clergy petitioned the US secretary of state in June 1945 for a resident consul, revealing the way in which both the military and the colonial government ignored 'over eight hundred children' and co-operated to keep their fathers and mothers apart:

> The situation of these children is, in many instances, deplorable. There should ... be someone here ... to represent them and protect them when necessary. Many of the fathers of these children wished to marry the women who became their mothers, but this was not in a single instance permitted by the military officers in command. Now, many of the fathers wish to return, marry the women, and support their children, but up to date no single father has been permitted to land. Also many of the women, of good family and character, have expressed their wish to join their unmarried husbands in America, but, without a consul here, this, so far, has been impractical.[65]

No record exists of the secretary's response. Both the US and the colonial governments left it to the Island society to address this, just as they did in the Cook Islands. New Zealand had never been especially concerned with Islanders' family arrangements, other than trying, with some success, to lower infant mortality.[66]

After all the occupation's excitements, Sāmoan women suffered great shame when their American partners left.[67] Abandoned by their lovers for others, a few women committed suicide.[68] Jealous Sāmoan men vented their feelings in a well-known song, *Sosola uma o seila i Meleke*, deriding naïve young women for consorting with Americans, as one verse tells:

> *Sosola uma o seila i Meleke*
> *Tiai oe i le alatele*
> *Nofonofo solo i le auala tele*
> *ma si ou foga ua tau malepe*
> *ua uma foi aso o le faapepe pepe*
> *i talane o le tama mai Meleke*
> *ua uma ona ou faiatu aua e te mateletele*
> *ua iu lava ina e tu sameme.*

> (Sailors have all run away to America
> Abandoning you on the road
> You sit by the roadside
> With your face crying.
> Over were the days of romancing
> Next to the boys from America.
> I have warned you
> Don't be arrogant
> You will end up with nothing.)[69]

Mothers and foster-fathers, grandparents, or near relatives raised such children. Most were accepted and had good lives.[70] A New Zealand schoolteacher recalled: 'They were known as *Malinis* ... [i]n a class of chubby, full-blooded youngsters their pale bodies looked strangely naked, but they were as lovingly cared for as the others.'[71] Not all families were as loving. Several children suffered from being called names such as malini (marine) or maligi and far worse. They missed their fathers. Some, though loved, lived in poverty, limiting their access to education.[72]

In the Cook Islands, however, as in other eastern Polynesian societies, women were not burdened with feelings of societal shame. Children had happy childhoods, although several recalled disruptions in their lives as consequences of not having their biological fathers.[73]

Beyond fleeting concern in the occupied Cook Islands, the New Zealand government did not try to help the mothers to obtain American assistance. As post-war life resumed, no claims emerged from Indigenous mothers in these societies where all, no matter how created, belonged to some family. The government, reflecting the moralistic attitudes of pre-war New Zealand society, offered no support to its own illegitimate war children, whether Māori or Pākehā, let alone those in its territories. The mothers could deal with their illegitimates.[74] New Zealand had wider concerns about the USA that may well have reinforced this hands-off attitude; it shared with Australia a fear that the Americans would claim rights to maintain their bases in the South Pacific.

Politics' frame

Throughout 1943, President Roosevelt, naval command, and senators favoured a permanent US strategic presence across the region in return for its outlay of men and money. New Zealand acted to avoid any basis for US claims in its empire. In Sāmoa, New Zealand paid for all US war damage, purchase of land for airfields, and leases, as it did in Atafu. In the Cook Islands, although the administration's judge and the US commander had agreed on payments by the Americans, the New Zealand government intervened and paid.[75]

New Zealand and Australia, with established regional territorial and commercial interests, were not prepared to relinquish sovereignty beyond the war. By late 1943, they negotiated the Canberra Pact. Signed in January 1944, this document demanded, among other matters, the withdrawal of United States from all but its own territories after hostilities ceased. This was a bold declaration to the United States as well as to Britain, which needed to keep the Americans fighting to regain the latter's phosphate islands of Nauru and Ocean Island still occupied by the Japanese. Although by 1946 all was to change with American control of Micronesia, when the war was drawing to a close, New Zealand's concerns about Americans remaining in the South Pacific bases persisted.

Within this frame, had the New Zealand government pressed for child support during the war, not only might this have further provoked the US government, but also it might have provided some justification for continuing interest in the Islands. Such an outcome, as New Zealand realised, might be appealing to Islanders who had experienced the Americans' bounty.[76] More significant politically, New Zealand realised that its survival had been due to the United States and did not want to alienate its powerful friend in the post-war world.[77]

As for the progeny of young Americans, a senior New Zealand public servant captured his government's attitude: 'it is estimated that approximately 800 children remain as "souvenirs" of the American invasion' in Western Samoa,[78] a remark of unconcerned disdain. New Zealand worked hard to hold its territories, but once the Americans left, it was disinclined to acknowledge any responsibility to such children at home or in its empire in championing their cause with the United States. In the purview of New Zealand social morality, it was the women's and the families' problem, at home and in the dependencies. In the tectonic political shifts of the Second World War, imperial ambitions soared, but imperial obligations towards the results of the intimacies of the colonised had their limits.

Notes

1 Angus Ross, *New Zealand's Aspirations on the Pacific in the Nineteenth Century* (Oxford: Clarendon, 1964); Angus Ross (ed.), *New Zealand's Record in the Pacific Islands in the Twentieth Century* (Auckland: Longman Paul for the New Zealand Institute of International Affairs, 1969).

2 C. C. Aikman, 'Constitutional development New Zealand's island territories and in Western Samoa', in Ross (ed.), *New Zealand's Record*, p. 310; Archives New Zealand, Wellington (hereafter ANZ), IT121/1/6, Part 3, Resident Commissioner (hereafter RC) to Cook Islands Department, 4 December 1942.

3 Mary Boyd, 'The record in Western Samoa since 1945', in Ross (ed.), *New Zealand's Record*, pp. 132, 137, 177; S. D. Wilson, 'The record in the Cook Islands and Niue 1901–45', in Ross (ed.), *New Zealand's Record*, pp. 24–59.

4 National Archives of the USA, College Park, Maryland (hereafter NAUSA), RG 407, Entry 427, 'Report on Lineout' [Aitutaki], 6 December 1942.

5 ANZ, M101/12, Patrick to Prime Minister, 11 August 1943.

6 O. Gillespie, *The Pacific* (Wellington: Department of Internal Affairs, 1952), pp. 228–38; D. O. W. Hall, *The Coastwatchers* (Wellington: Historical Publications Branch, 1950), pp. 6–7.

7 Peter McQuarrie, *Tokelau: People, Atolls and History* (Wellington: First Edition, 2007), pp. 143–6.

8 ANZ, EA-1, 86/71/7 Pt 1, McKay to Secretary, 5 November 1943; J. W. Davidson, *Samoa mo Samoa: The Emergence of the Independent State of Western Samoa* (Melbourne: Oxford University Press, 1967), pp. 137–8.

9   ANZ, IT1 W2439 69/9/6, War History 1939/45; 'War Against Japan'. www.teara.
    govt.nz/en/1966/wars-second-world-war/5, accessed 12 January 2013.
10 F. O. Hough, V. C. Ludwig, and H. J. Shaw, History of the US Marine Corps in World
    War II, Vol. 1 (Washington DC: US Government Printer, 1958), p. 90.
11 C. G. R. McKay, Samoana: A Personal Story of the Samoan Islands (Wellington:
    A. H. & A. W. Reed, 1968), p. 105.
12 Phillip Meilinger, 'Unity of command in the Pacific during World War Two', Joint
    Force Quarterly, 56 1st Quarter (2010), 152–6.
13 ANZ, IT1 W2439 69/9/6, 'War History 1939/45'.
14 Judith A. Bennett, Natives and Exotics: World War Two and Environment in the
    Southern Pacific (Honolulu: University of Hawai'i Press, 2009), pp. 11–48; Sean
    Brawley and Chris Dixon, Hollywood's South Seas and the Pacific War: Searching
    for Dorothy Lamour (New York: Palgrave Macmillan, 2012).
15 Confidential source cited in Louise Mataia, 'Western Samoa and American Samoa',
    in Judith A. Bennett and Angela Wanhalla (eds), Mothers' Darlings of the South
    Pacific: The Children of Indigenous Women and US Servicemen, World War Two,
    forthcoming.
16 McQuarrie, Tokelau, pp. 147–51.
17 Ernest Beaglehole, 'The mixed blood in Polynesia', Journal of the Polynesian
    Society, 58:2 (1949), 51–7.
18 Paul Shankman, 'Interethnic unions and the regulation of sex in colonial Samoa,
    1830–1945', Journal of the Polynesian Society, 110:2 (2001), 119–47; R. G.
    Crocombe, Pacific Neighbours: New Zealand's Relations with other Pacific Islands
    (Christchurch: University of Canterbury; Suva: University of the South Pacific,
    1992), pp. 18–19.
19 Barbara Brookes, 'Shame and its histories in the twentieth century', Journal of New
    Zealand Studies, 9 (2010), 37–54; Linda Gordon, Pitied But Not Entitled: Single
    Mothers and the History of Welfare (New York: Free Press, 1994), pp. 15–35, 130–2,
    298–9.
20 Bennett, Natives, pp. 133–54.
21 Joel Boone, 'The sexual aspects of military personnel', Journal of Social Hygiene,
    27:3 (1942), 113–24; NAUSA, RG 112, Entry 302, Engelhorn, Medical Report,
    'Aitutaki', 27 July 1944.
22 Ann Laura Stoler and Frederick Cooper, 'Between metropole and colony: Rethinking
    a research agenda', in Frederick Cooper and Ann Laura Stoler (eds), Tensions of
    Empire: Colonial Cultures in a Bourgeois World (Berkeley: University of California
    Press, 1997), p. 15; Angela Wanhalla, 'Maori-American encounters in New Zealand',
    in Bennett and Wanhalla (eds), Mothers' Darlings.
23 Bennett, Natives, pp. 66–7; NAUSA, RG 112, Entry 1012, Thompson, 'Venereal
    Disease-South Pacific Area', October 1945.
24 ANZ, IT 122/5/2 Part 1, Hickling, 'US Forces in Aitutaki', 10 November 1943.
25 Nancy M. Taylor, The Home Front, Vol. 2 (Wellington: Historical Publications
    Branch, 1986), pp. 1033–4.
26 McQuarrie, Tokelau, pp. 149–50, 153.
27 NAUSA, RG 112, 'Organization of Armed Forces in the South Pacific Area'.
28 NAUSA, RG 112, Entry 1012, Thompson, 'Venereal Disease-South Pacific Area',
    October 1945.
29 NAUSA, RG 407, Entry 427, 'Report on Lineout' [Aitutaki], 6 December 1943; ANZ,
    IT 122/5/2 Part 1, Hickling, 'US Forces in Aitutaki', 10 November 1943.
30 NAUSA, RG 112, Entry 302, Engelhorn, Medical Report, 'Aitutaki', 27 July 1944.
31 McKay, Samoana, p. 105; Philip Snow, The Years of Hope: Cambridge, Colonial
    Administration in the South Seas and Cricket (London and New York: Radcliffe,
    1997), pp. 195, 236; Bennett and Wanhalla (eds), Mothers' Darlings.
32 NAUSA, RG 407, Background to Report [on Morale], 1944; RG 313, Entry 183,
    Historical Narrative, Southwest Pacific, Chapter 11, 'Morale', ca. 1946.
33 'The Army Nurse Corps', pp. 8–9, www.history.army.mil/html/books/072/72-14/
    CMH_Pub_72-14.pdf, accessed 12 January 2013.

34 NAUSA, RG 313, Entry 183, Chapter 11, 'Morale', c. 1945; RG 112, Entry 302, Engelhorn, Medical Report, 'Aitutaki', 27 July 1944.
35 NAUSA, RG 313, Entry P 90-A2, Dallard to Olding, 11 June 1942; Marston to Undersecretary of Justice, 19 December 1942; RG 388, Entry AI 339, Ostrander to Commanding General, 6 July 1943; RG 84, file 811.11, Records, Consular Posts, Suva, Scott to Commissioner of Immigration, 3 March 1946 and enclosure; *Pacific Islands Monthly*, August 1943, 25.
36 NAUSA, RG 112, 'Organization of Armed Forces in the South Pacific Area'.
37 Pacific Manuscripts Bureau, Canberra, microfilm (hereafter PMB) 1033, W. G. Coppell Papers, 'Report on Education in the Cook Islands since 1939', 9 March 1948.
38 PMB 1248, RC Office, Resident Agent (hereafter RA) to RC, 7 May 1946.
39 Rosemary Anderson, '"Amerika koe": The "American children" of the Cook Islands', in Bennett and Wanhalla (eds), *Mothers' Darlings*.
40 ANZ, IT1 287, Ex 38/1/2, Morgan to Government Statistician, 4 October 1945.
41 ANZ, IT 122/5/2 Part 1, Hickling, 'US Forces in Aitutaki', 10 November 1943; W. E. H. Stanner, *The South Seas in Transition* (Sydney: Australasian Publishing, 1953), p. 327; National Archives of the USA, San Bruno (hereafter NASB), Annual Report (hereafter AR), RG 284, Governor's Office, American Samoa, Series No. 5, Judicial Department, 30 June 1943; James A. Michener, *The World is My Home* (New York: Random House, 1992), pp. 48, 70, 76; NAUSA, RG 3888, Entry 44463, Smith, Annex No. 2, G-2 Periodic Report No. 101; Elizabeth Wood-Ellem, *Queen Sālote of Tonga: The Story of an Era, 1900–1965* (Auckland: Auckland University Press, 1999), pp. 200–21.
42 PMB 403, Cook Islands AR, 1942-1944; PMB 1033, 'Report on Education … since 1939'; PMB 1193, Aitutaki Correspondence, RC to Secretary of Dept External Affairs, 26 June 1944, Chief of Police to RC, 9 February 1946, 27 November 1944; PMB 1248, Assistant RA, Penrhyn, to RC, 11 November 1943, 12 May 1944, 30 November 1944, 15 February 1945, 7 May 1946; PMB 1064F, Archives of the Catholic Church, Fr David to Commanding Officer, 'Penrhyn', n.d.; ANZ, IT 122/5/2 Part 1, Hickling, 'US Forces in Aitutaki', 10 November 1943, Tailby to Secretary of Internal Territories, 10 October 1944.
43 PMB 1193, Aitutaki Correspondence, RC to Secretary of External Affairs, 26 June 1944.
44 I thank Rosemary Anderson for pointing out this link. S. L. De Miguel, 'Love, Eruera Te Whiti o Rongomai Love', www.teara.govt.nz/en/biographies/5l17/love-eruera-te-whiti-o-rongomai, accessed February 2015; ANZ M101/12, Ngata to Ayson, 1 September 1932: ANZ IT 102/3/1 Ordinance, Mrs Love, 1941–51.
45 ANZ, M101/12, part 1, Patrick to Prime Minister, 11 August 1943 and enclosures.
46 PMB 1192, RC to Hickling, 22 February 1944 and enclosures, Hickling to RA, 'Rarotonga', 2 May 1944.
47 Bennett, *Natives*, pp. 126–7, 147, 152.
48 McKay, *Samoana*, pp. 112–13.
49 Confidential sources; Michener, *The World*, pp. 38–42; Janette Marie Mageo, 'The third meaning in cultural memory: History, identity, and spirit possession in Samoa', in Janette Marie Mageo (ed.), *Cultural Memory: Reconfiguring History and Identity in the Postcolonial Pacific* (Honolulu: University of Hawai'i Press, 2001), p. 67; Featu'i Ben Liuaana, *Samoa Tula'i: Ecclesiastical and Political Face of Samoa's Independence, 1900–1962* (Malua, Samoa: Malua Press, 2004), p. 277; Stanner, *The South Seas*, p. 327.
50 NASB, RG 313-58-3440, 'Sanitary Report for Upolu', 1944.
51 NASB, RG 313 – 58B-3061, Entry 1012, 'History of Upolu', c. 1945; NAUSA, RG 112, Thompson, 'Venereal Disease-South Pacific Area', October 1945; NAUSA, RG 313, 'Inspection Report, Aitutaki', 28 February 1945.
52 Bennett and Wanhalla (eds), *Mothers' Darlings*.
53 Chris Dixon and Sean Brawley, '"Tan Yanks" amid a "semblance of civilization": African American encounters with the South Pacific, 1941–1945', in Peter Bastian and Roger Bell (eds), *Through Depression and War: The United States and Australia*

(Sydney: Australian-American Fulbright Association and the Australian New Zealand American Studies Association, 2002), pp. 98–102.
54   Price cited in Morris Macgregor, *Integration of the Armed Forces*, 1940–1960 (Washington: Government Printing Office, 1981), pp. 110–11.
55   NAUSA, RG 338, Entry 44463, Garity, 'Report on visit to Rarotonga', 6 August 1943.
56   ANZ IT1 W2439 135, 122/5/2, Part 1, Hickling to Tailby, 15 November 1943.
57   Confidential source, cited in Anderson.
58   Cf. NAUSA, RG 338, Entry 44463, Garity, 'Report on visit to Rarotonga', 6 August 1943.
59   Peggy Pascoe, *What Comes Naturally: Miscegenation Law and the Making of Modern America* (New York: Oxford University Press, 2008).
60   Michener, *The World*, pp. 48–50.
61   NAUSA, RG 313, Entry 183, Priday, 'The Cook Islands', draft manuscript, 31 July 1944; H. E. Lewis Priday, *The War from Coconut Square: The Story of the Defence of the Island Bases of the South Pacific* (Wellington: A. H. & A. W. Reed, [1945]).
62   PMB 1033, 'Report on Education in the Cook Islands since 1939'; ANZ, IT1 W2439 135, 122/5/2, Part 1, Hickling, Report, 'US Forces in Aitutaki', 10 November 1942, Shanahan to Secretary, 24 July 1944, Tailby to Secretary, 10 October 1944.
63   Harry Grossman, 'Allowances for the Dependents of Servicemen', *University of Chicago Law Review*, 11:1 (1943), 65–75.
64   ANZ, EA1 610, 87/12/5, Part 1, Crown Solicitor to Secretary External Affairs, 29 May 1947 and enclosures; NAUSA, RG 200, Box 1, 279, American Red Cross, 1947–1964, 'Minutes, Meeting on Social Case Work Problems', 14 May 1942.
65   NAUSA, RG 84, Part 5, Wellington Legation, 1946; Haubold and others, to Secretary of State, 4 June 1945.
66   Cook and Other Islands Reports, Appendices to the New Zealand House of Representatives, Wellington: Government Printer, 1931, 1933, 1936, 1947, 1940; Boyd, 'The record', p. 212.
67   Mataia, 'Western Samoa', in Bennett and Wanhalla (eds), *Mothers' Darlings*.
68   Marc T. Greene, 'Samoa – Paradise of the South Seas', *The New Zealand Woman's Weekly*, 6 December 1945, p. 46.
69   Translation by Tofilau Nina Kirifi-Alai.
70   Penelope Schoeffel, 'Daughters of Sina: A Study of Gender, Status and Power in Western Samoa', PhD thesis, Australian National University, 1979, pp. 199–200, 210; Mataia, 'Western Samoa', in Bennett and Wanhalla (eds), *Mothers' Darlings*.
71   George Irwin, *Samoa: A Teacher's Tale* (London: Cassell, 1965), p. 87.
72   Mataia, 'Western Samoa', in Bennett and Wanhalla (eds), *Mothers' Darlings*.
73   Judith A. Bennett, 'Bora Bora: "Like a dream"', in Bennett and Wanhalla (eds), *Mothers' Darlings*.
74   Brookes, 'Shame and its histories', 37–54.
75   Judith A. Bennett, 'The American imperial threat to the New Zealand's Pacific dependencies in World War Two', in Ian Conrich and Dominic Alessio (eds), *New Zealand, France and the Pacific* (Nottingham: Kakapo Books, 2011), pp. 42–53.
76   NASB, RG 313-58B-3061, [Michener] History of US Naval Station, Upolu; Bennett, 'The American', pp. 41–57.
77   John Battersby, 'Post-war security policy: the formation of the United Nations', in John Crawford (ed.), *Kia Kaha: New Zealand in the Second World War* (Auckland: Oxford University Press, 2000), p. 293.
78   ANZ ITI W2439, 69/9/6, 'War History 1939/1945'. For numbers, see ANZ, IT1 287, Ex 38/1/2, Inspector of Police to Secretary to the Administration, 12 February 1946 and enclosures. Michener numbered the children at around 2,000. NASB, RG 313-58B-3061, [Michener] 'History of US Naval Station, Upolu, Western Samoa', 1945.

PART IV

Inside and outside empire

CHAPTER ELEVEN

Official occasions and vernacular voices: New Zealand's British Empire and Commonwealth Games, 1950–90

Michael Dawson

Founded in 1930 as the British Empire Games, the Commonwealth Games today are major sporting occasions that offer host cities and nations the opportunity to secure economic benefits and international attention. Historians have traditionally viewed the Games as a fairly successful attempt to encourage political and cultural unity among the increasingly diverse membership of the Commonwealth.[1] More recent scholarship, however, emphasises the multiple and competing economic, cultural, and political interests that have shaped these international gatherings.[2]

As host of this competition in Auckland in 1950, Christchurch in 1974, and Auckland again in 1990, New Zealand has played an important role in shaping this event.[3] In examining these three occasions this chapter acknowledges the Games' success and longevity by documenting a shift in official rhetoric, from an emphasis on imperial solidarity to a more diffuse and inclusive notion of Commonwealth unity. Simultaneously, however, it highlights vernacular expressions and activities that offered alternative and oppositional understandings of the Games.[4] New Zealand's British Empire and Commonwealth Games provided useful opportunities to promote, and at times refashion, official expressions of national, imperial, and Commonwealth identity. However, unscripted voices ensured that these occasions were also imbued with national, regional, and ethnic symbolism that spoke to ongoing tensions in New Zealand and abroad. The Commonwealth Games were thus a dynamic forum in which imperial legacies and changing political realities combined to produce a series of sometimes awkward conversations about the nature of New Zealand and Commonwealth identity.

Auckland's 1950 British Empire Games: 'a family affair'?

I detest the wishy-washy word 'Commonwealth'. It always seems to me to have been invented for those who might want to get out. I prefer the old-fashioned term 'Empire', and it is as citizens of the Empire that I welcome you and wish you the best of luck in your competitions.[5]

With these words, Auckland's mayor, J. A. C. Allum, welcomed participants to the 1950 British Empire Games. This gathering boasted fewer than 600 competitors from just twelve countries but it was recognised at the time as 'one of the biggest sporting events in the world'.[6] At their conclusion Auckland was credited with successfully reestablishing the amateur sporting festival after a twelve-year, war-induced hiatus.[7] As Allum's remarks remind us, the 1950 Games were profoundly shaped by their political context. Post-war reconstruction and anxieties about the future of the British Empire shaped assessments of the event's importance. Indeed, the line-up of competing nations in 1950 reflected important imperial and post-imperial developments: India, a Games participant in 1934 and 1938, did not attend in 1950; Nigeria, moving towards self-government, made its Games debut in Auckland; Malaya also competed for the first time in 1950, amidst the 'Malayan Emergency'.

For organisers, the rationale for the Games was clear. Arthur Porritt, doctor and future Governor-General of New Zealand (1967–72), then the newly-appointed Chairman of the British Empire Games Federation and a towering figure in New Zealand sport, considered the Games 'a real force for good in unifying and strengthening the Empire'.[8] The two city council representatives on the organising committee agreed, and proudly reported that residents in the athletes' village formed 'one great and happy Empire family'.[9] Such views were echoed by the New Zealand press. The Christchurch *Press* repeatedly championed the Games as 'a family affair' that promoted 'the tolerance and understanding that are essential to the continuance of a united Commonwealth'.[10] The *Press* took particular delight in the strong performance of the English team, which had 'shown the Empire and the world that England is still far from being a spent force in international athletics'. At the event's conclusion, the newspaper triumphantly announced that 'The competitors have met together as loyal subjects of the King ... linked in a single Commonwealth by common ideals and principles'.[11] The *New Zealand Herald* offered a similar assessment of the Games' importance. 'British sport', it announced, continued to stand strong against 'nationalism or prejudice'.[12] The Games' 'family' atmosphere, it argued, ensured that it was 'a nursery of friendships'.[13]

The highly regimented opening ceremony provided organisers with an opportunity to reinforce these themes. The *Sydney Morning Herald* reported that '[r]oaring guns, the crash of bands, flags, uniforms, and marching men gave the opening ceremony pageantry and brilliance'.[14] The *New Zealand Herald* enthused that 'From the clean precision of the march-on of the Royal guard of men of the Royal New Zealand Navy, through the showing of the King's Colour, the delivery of the Royal message, and the magnificent parade of the athletes, to the last event of the day, all the accent was on Empire'.[15] The rhetoric of unity and sportsmanship infused media coverage of the competitions as well. Among the most celebrated examples of the Games' friendly atmosphere was the crowd's involvement in a successful campaign to reverse a decision to disqualify Canadian runner Don Pettie for his second false start in the final of the 100-yard dash.[16] Another was the enthusiastic support among fellow athletes and the spectators for competitors from smaller nations who faced additional barriers in reaching competitive levels of performance.[17]

As friendly and welcoming as this 'family affair' was, the emphasis on unity did not undermine the competitive nature of the enterprise. The *Montreal Star* celebrated Canadian athletic success but noted enviously that '[r]ampaging Australian athletes hot-footed to a clear 63-point margin' in the overall team standings.[18] When the Games concluded, the Australian media was quick to celebrate its national success, with the *West Australian* going so far as to report that 'The 1950 Empire Games are over and Australia is the champion country'.[19] In its coverage of the closing ceremony Toronto's *Globe and Mail* acknowledged the event's emphasis on the 'honor of the Empire and the glory of sport' but noted enviously that 'most of the honor and glory – and booty – belonged to Australia'.[20] New Zealanders' sporting expectations also belied a national focus. The *New Zealand Herald* did not expect the host country to compete with 'more populous lands' but was confident that 'a goodly proportion of the chosen team would not be noticeably out of class in the highest company'.[21] New Zealanders' performances did not rival Australians' but New Zealand's media certainly celebrated national success stories, including R. H. Cleghorn's weight-lifting prowess which secured him the title of 'strongest man in the Empire'.[22] Official expressions of imperial unity thus had to share pride of place with nationalist assessments of the Games' results – particularly among the Empire's white dominions, who seemed keen to embrace the Games as a venue for communicating their evolving articulations of colonial nationalism.

Moreover, for New Zealand itself the 1950 Games reflected two internal tensions – one that spoke to questions of national and ethnic identity, and another that highlighted regional divisions. Perhaps most striking is the fact that Māori involvement appears to have been restricted to a musical performance for athletes and officials arriving in Auckland by steamship. Māori did not feature in either the opening or closing ceremonies – an omission brought to the attention of the *New Zealand Herald* by 'Kekerengu', a member of Ngāti-ākarana. Kekerengu expressed 'keen disappointment at the absence of a Maori welcome by the local Maori people to the Empire games Athletes'.[23]

Denied such a role in the Games, some Māori took matters into their own hands and organised alternative opportunities to welcome visiting athletes. At the outset of the Games, for example, rowing competitors were invited to a Māori hāngī near Lake Karapiro.[24] A week later King Korokī and Princess Te Puea Herangi invited New Zealand Prime Minister Sidney Holland to attend a welcome for visiting athletes at Ngāruawāhia. Tuarau Wahanui, a Ngāti-Maniopoto elder, and another speaker, N. M. Paora, welcomed Holland and expressed their hope that a new era in Māori–Pākehā relations was at hand. In reply, Holland observed that the unity demonstrated in Ngāruawāhia 'completed that spirit of unity seen at the Empire Games' and suggested that 'it was fitting that the visitors should be given a demonstration that two peoples could live together without any impediment of language or colour'.[25] Absent from the Games' formal ceremonies, Māori initiatives thus created opportunities for conversations about internationalism and Māori–Pākehā relations to intersect.

The 1950 Games also brought into sharp relief New Zealand's key regional rivalry. Christchurch had fought bitterly to secure the event and appealed the decision to award the Games to Auckland. Christchurch Mayor E. H. Andrews blasted the choice as 'very unfair' and claimed that Auckland was once again using 'its greater numbers to bludgeon Christchurch out of something'. The *Christchurch Star-Sun* took pleasure in reporting that two local 'girls' were protesting the decision by boycotting Auckland – though 'they would not ... go so far as to refuse to go out with Auckland boys'.[26] Resentment continued to linger throughout the Games, as Christchurch media delighted in highlighting organisational failings at Auckland's athletic venues.[27] The Empire Games, from this perspective, were as much a part of ongoing regional battles within New Zealand as they were part of a series of international sporting festivals designed to strengthen the bonds of empire.

Forceful official rhetoric championing imperial unity was widespread during the 1950 Games. But national, ethnic, and regional identities infused vernacular voices that offered alternative understandings of this occasion. Indeed, the 1950 Games provided occasions to celebrate imperial unity *and* moments in which competing white dominion nationalisms flexed their muscles, while racial and regional tensions within New Zealand surfaced awkwardly in public view.

Christchurch's 1974 British Commonwealth Games: 'The Friendly Games'?

Undeterred by its failure to secure the 1950 Games, Christchurch persevered and obtained the right to host the event in 1974. The city did so with a healthy chip on its shoulder, and its supporters delighted in the event's success. But local voices were complemented by outsiders who also found much to praise in 1974 – especially given the political context of the time. Faced with controversies surrounding New Zealand's sporting contacts with South Africa, and questions about the safety and efficacy of large-scale sporting events in light of the Munich Olympics, Christchurch received widespread praise for its organisation and welcoming atmosphere. But the 1974 event is perhaps most interesting for the manner in which it highlights the awkward nature of the Games' movement away from their origins as very formal and relatively ethnically homogeneous imperial festivals. Official pronouncements and supportive commentaries combined to offer a more modern, inclusive and diffuse understanding of the Games' unifying role – reflected most directly in the 1974 unofficial title: 'The Friendly Games'. But here too vernacular expressions of identity provided unanticipated and disruptive messages – particularly when it came to racial tensions and the youthful exuberance of competitors that fitted uneasily with traditional notions of proper comportment.

Between 1950 and 1974 Commonwealth Games membership expanded dramatically. Over 1,200 athletes from thirty-nine countries, many of these nations having recently secured independence from Britain, participated in Christchurch. As the event approached, this expanded Commonwealth was fraught with political anxiety – particularly concerning the issue of apartheid and New Zealand's sporting contacts with South Africa. Prime Minister Norman Kirk's decision to prohibit a 1973 Springbok rugby tour of New Zealand was widely credited with preventing an African nation boycott of the 1974 Games and helped to forge the Games' reputation as both inclusive and politically significant. Abraham Ordia, President of the Supreme Council for Sport in Africa, went so far as to champion the cancellation of the tour as a 'major victory for New Zealand'.[28]

Moreover, amid the backdrop of increasingly critical assessments of the gigantism involved in international sporting events and concerns about the Commonwealth's own awkward legacies of colonialism, many observers saluted the Christchurch Games as a successful and promising alternative. For the assembled media the Games' 'friendly' feeling was illustrated in a number of ways. English journalist John Rodda praised the organisers' decision to award Sylvia Potts – the

New Zealand runner whose chance at a certain gold medal in the 1970 Games had evaporated as she fell just a few feet before the finish line – the distinction of being the final baton runner in the opening ceremonies as symbolising 'the gentle, friendly feeling which the Commonwealth Games generates'.[29] More generally, Donald Saunders of the *Daily Telegraph* suggested that 'Christchurch has proved that it is still possible to promote a big international, multi-racial sporting festival without aggravating political strife or colour consciousness'.[30]

Among editorial writers in New Zealand the emphasis remained on the unifying aspects of the Games, but such sentiments were no longer expressed through a prism of British identity. Hence, the *New Zealand Herald* championed the Games for its ability to bring together athletes, officials and spectators 'from so many parts of the world and ... so many races'.[31] On the eve of the Games the Commonwealth Games Federation supported a Nigerian motion to drop the word 'British' from the Games title (the word 'Empire' had been excised in 1966).[32] In embracing this change the *Herald* noted that this was 'a natural development' and warned that the 'Commonwealth and the Games would be none the stronger for trying to persist with the historic emphasis on the British association'.[33] A sense of a direct, familial relationship among participants had thus been reimagined as a more diffuse affiliation – an inclusive shift from imperial to Commonwealth unity.

For New Zealand, itself, the most tangible expression of inclusion must surely have been the extent to which Māori were now centrally incorporated into the event's festivities. In 1974 'a 400-strong Maori song, haka and poi company' secured a starring role in the opening ceremony – and to good effect.[34] The *Manchester Guardian*'s John Rodda praised their contribution: 'The Maoris danced and sang with that lilting sound which seems to hang like a Pacific Breaker', he noted, while Prince Philip 'was met by a Maori challenge, with all its guttural chanting and swaying bodies, a reminder perhaps of how this country became part of the Commonwealth'.[35] Domestically, the *New Zealand Herald*'s Norman Harris celebrated the Māori display as a wonderful 'public relations exercise' ideally suited to the occasion.[36] In presenting itself to a postcolonial gathering of sporting nations, New Zealand's shifting social and political culture had found room for its Indigenous population. While such tightly scripted performances did not necessarily reflect a formal commitment to a more inclusive cultural identity, their central place in the Games programme would appear to represent a significant departure from the ideals on offer in Auckland in 1950.

However, sports and the public ceremonies that accompany them retain an element of unpredictability. In the case of the Christchurch Games, these unscripted elements highlighted the awkward and contested nature of the manner in which imperial identity was being refashioned. In particular, they revealed a persistent concern that racial animosity had not been eliminated from the competition – or the Commonwealth – and highlighted intergenerational tensions that threatened to lay bare competing ideals of Commonwealth identity.

For many New Zealanders the high point of the 1974 competition was Kiwi runner Richard Tayler's surprise victory in the 10,000 metres. England's world-record holder David Bedford was the pre-race favourite, but Tayler took advantage of a tactical battle between Bedford and three Kenyan runners to pull off a victory that was greeted by a 'crescendo of cheering' and caused businesses to come 'to a standstill', as New Zealanders crowded around television sets to celebrate.[37] Years later this dramatic race was still celebrated as an iconic moment in New Zealand sports history. Recalled less often are the racial tensions that marred the event as the Kenyan and English runners battled for position. John Rodda suggested that 'some of the friendliness disappeared' from the Games as the Kenyan runners 'buzzed round Bedford like wasps in a plot to upset the world record holder'. Moreover, throughout the race the increasingly partisan crowd jeered the Kenyan runners whenever one of them took the lead and attempted to slow the pace. When the event was over Bedford accused the Kenyans of employing 'dirty tactics'.[38]

Even as some commentators attempted to suggest that race was not the determining factor in this controversy, their language suggested that it was indeed the key reference point. Lawrie Kavanagh of the Brisbane *Courier-Mail* summed up the event this way: 'Black men kept pushing white men off the track and white men kept doing the same to black men.'[39] After witnessing a series of similar conflicts in other competitions, Australian journalist Ron Carter offered even stronger rhetoric: 'Blood has dripped on the track ... and venom has poured from athletes and officials.' 'The blood,' he explained, 'has come from the spiked legs of white and black men.' He openly wondered whether he wasn't 'witnessing the dirty Commonwealth Games rather than the Friendly Games'.[40]

Moreover, lingering frustration over the cancellation of the 1973 Springbok tour made headlines throughout the Games. Abraham Ordia faced 'abusive remarks from some New Zealanders' who held him directly responsible for the cancellation of the tour.[41] The *Age* reported that one New Zealander was so upset with the cancellation that he threatened the life of the Games' chief organiser, Ron Scott.[42] Official pronouncements celebrating the Commonwealth Games as a unifying and friendly force for international understanding could be reinforced by instances of genuine sportsmanship and hospitality from the host nation. But there were moments too when racial tensions were laid bare – for these Games generated forthright conversations about the reality and future of the Commonwealth.

If competition and partisan support occasionally disrupted and challenged the official rhetoric of racial equality and unity, the closing ceremonies highlighted tensions between older generations that equated deference to authority and military order with imperial or Commonwealth identity, and younger athletes eager to cast aside prescriptive and restrictive rules concerning public deportment. On paper, the closing ceremonies boasted countless displays of military precision and protocol. But the athletes' desire to celebrate and socialise undermined these plans. As the tension from ten days of competition evaporated, some athletes held an 'impromptu football game', stole headwear from military band members and Games hostesses, rode bicycles around the track, and jumped aboard Princess Anne's Land Rover as it made its way out of the stadium.[43] Two athletes dressed up as a cow, while members of the English team 'dumped a team official on the Queen's dais' where he was 'bound hand and foot'.[44]

For Australian team manager Bill Young, the informal atmosphere of the closing ceremony was 'a disgrace to amateur sport'.[45] The competitors 'molested the flag carriers', he reported, 'snatched their caps from their heads, tried to look under their kilts ... they acted like ignorant mongrels'.[46] For John Rodda, the closing ceremony was an 'embarrassing demonstration', but the cause of this rebellious behaviour was the very formality that other observers sought to preserve. 'Militarism,' he argued, had 'no place in sport.' 'The athletes of today,' he explained, 'do not like this military style and they expressed themselves, unhappily to the point of insult, at the closing ceremony.'[47] Australian journalist Terry Vine was more supportive of what he termed 'a magnificent display of total disarray and shambles'. 'It was,' he reported, 'hearty and gay and healthy, full of the spirit that has marked these as the friendliest of Games.'[48]

These joyous scenes undoubtedly contributed to the event's reputation as the 'Friendly Games', but the accompanying controversy highlighted the extent to which the 1974 Games reflected a very public and awkward move away from the event's origins as a formal and imperial sporting festival. Political interventions and scripted ceremony helped to produce a more modern and, at least potentially, more inclusive notion of Commonwealth unity. But official directives could not prevent racial tensions. Nor could they contain a youthful exuberance that rejected old imperial formalities in favour of more spontaneous forms of interaction.

Auckland's 1990 Commonwealth Games: a 'festival of anti-racism'?

In the late 1970s and 1980s the issue of sporting contacts with South Africa came close to derailing the Games entirely – most clearly in the form of a widespread African and Caribbean boycott of the 1986 Games in Edinburgh, to protest British policy towards South Africa. The African boycott of the 1976 Montreal Olympics to protest New Zealand's sporting ties with South Africa combined with National government support for the New Zealand Rugby Union throughout the late 1970s and early 1980s to ensure that racial and political tensions profoundly shaped New Zealand's relationship with the Commonwealth during this era. Astute diplomacy on the part of the New Zealand government played a key role in preventing another boycott from disrupting Auckland's second opportunity to host the Games in 1990.[49] Auckland secured the right to host the Games in 1984 – just three years after the civil strife surrounding the 1981 Springbok tour of New Zealand had laid bare the host country's ongoing dispute about the relationship between race and sport, and forced many New Zealanders to reconsider traditional expressions of national identity.[50] In this context the 1990 Games provided an opportunity to showcase a 'new' New Zealand. On this occasion official rhetoric endeavoured to explicitly refashion both domestic and international perceptions of New Zealand's national identity. But as was the case with the earlier Games, oppositional and alternative voices ensured that this process was far from straightforward.

The second Auckland Games coincided with the 150th anniversary of the Treaty of Waitangi, an occasion celebrated by a government-sponsored commemorative campaign, 'New Zealand 1990'. Plans for the Fourth Commonwealth Festival of the Arts accompanying the Games fitted closely with the mission of the New Zealand 1990 commission, which focused on inclusion and cultural diversity. The festival committee viewed the Games as an 'opportunity to look beyond ourselves and examine with fresh eyes our place in the world and in the future'. The festival would 'reflect the atmosphere of a Pacific nation' and would 'celebrate those differences that need to be acknowledged and respected'.[51] While the 1974 Games had incorporated the Māori into the opening ceremony, the 1990 Games forcefully underscored their centrality to the nation's history. Māori were key players in the arts festival, and in both the opening and closing ceremonies. Even the design of the athletes' medals incorporated Māori content.[52]

Here again the performance and content of opening ceremonies are instructive. The RNZAF 'aerobatic Skyhawk team' performance ensured a modicum of military content, but the spectacle on offer in

1990 was vastly different from that of 1974.[53] In 1990 the opening ceremony boasted '6000 performers ... including 1200 schoolchildren and a 2000-strong Maori welcoming party'.[54] The ceremony also tipped its collective cap to a more 'hip' New Zealand – going so far as to include five bungee jumpers who 'dangled over the audience' – while the country's progressive political tradition was given tangible representation through the inclusion of '[t]wenty deaf people' as 'sign singers' in the opening ceremony's choir.[55] But the core of the ceremony was a highly coordinated revisionist overview of New Zealand history.

The Press provided a nice synopsis of this historical pageant, which underscored the revisionist elements of its narrative: 'The story starts with the creation of the Pacific Ocean, moves on to the Polynesian migration, the Maori discovery and settlement of *Aotearoa*, then the European *rediscovery* and settlement', before a final phase focused on contemporary Auckland and New Zealand and concluded a celebration that focused on the 'diversity of people and cultures in our land'.[56] The University of Canterbury's Ken Strongman, for one, found much to praise in his television column for *The Press*. The 'cultural diversity of modern New Zealand was cleverly depicted', he argued, suggesting that it was 'almost a relief to have so little prominence given to the English tradition'.[57]

Unlike the one in 1950, this ceremony seemed to acknowledge New Zealand's colonial history without celebrating it – an orientation that fitted well with contemporary assessments of the Games' identity and utility. According to Melbourne's *Age*, the sun had set on the British Empire but the Commonwealth Games still held the power 'to unite nations and peoples in friendly competition'.[58] For *West Australian* columnist Andre Malan, the only thing the participants had in common was the fact that 'they once felt the British heel'.[59] Indeed, Matthew Engel, writing in Melbourne's *Age*, described the 1990 Commonwealth Games as a 'sort of festival of anti-racism, with everyone effectively obliged to swear, not fealty to the Queen, but undying hatred of the South African Government'.[60] Such a reimagining of colonial legacies required a fair amount of selective amnesia (not all members of the Commonwealth had felt the British heel with equal force and, of course, some were active participants in imperial endeavours), but as a strategy for providing the occasion with a unifying ethos it certainly seemed to pay dividends.

At the conclusion of the Games, the *Press's* Rod Dew echoed the views of foreign journalists and triumphantly announced that the 'sporting festival has definitely been restored after the disappointments of the Edinburgh effort four years ago'.[61] But there were elements of New Zealand political culture that disrupted even this new and improved official story of unity. The official refashioning of New Zealand and Commonwealth identity was challenged on two fronts – by Māori activists, and by a sometimes parochial nationalism that fitted awkwardly with the event's internationalist orientation.

As a prominent event sure to secure international media attention, the 1990 Games proved an attractive target for Māori activists seeking leverage in their ongoing struggle to secure political reforms. Indeed, as the Edinburgh Games drew to a close in 1986, the Waitangi Action Committee urged African nations to boycott the 1990 Games to protest 'the nonratification of the Treaty of Waitangi'. 'Boycotting the games will hopefully prove that there is really nothing to celebrate', explained committee member Teitewhai Harawira.[62] Two years later a coalition of Māori and Pākehā activists called for the cancellation of the Games. The former took the name He Taua, meaning challenge or war party, while the latter termed themselves the Auckland Treaty Action Coalition (ATAC). They vowed to disrupt the Games and embarrass the New Zealand government by publicising Māori grievances to the event's global audience.[63]

Neither a boycott nor a major disruption ensued but on the eve of the Games, reports noted that organisers' biggest security concern was 'radical Maori groups, protesting about land grievances' – an issue that made headlines in New Zealand and Australia when police raided the homes of Māori activists in search of weapons.[64] Moreover, the Games did provide an opportunity for the furtherance of a trans-Tasman Indigenous alliance, as He Taua announced plans for a vocal but non-violent protest at the swimming venue to mark Australia Day and to demand rights for that country's Aborigines.[65] As was the case during the 1982 Games in Brisbane that were marked by Aboriginal protests, visitors to Auckland, or indeed readers of international press reports, were forced to acknowledge the host nation's troubling colonial legacy.[66] By the late twentieth century, the participation and political influence of many former British colonies from Asia and Africa had dramatically reshaped the political landscape that informed host countries' attempts to publicly articulate a national identity at the Games. This development informed both organisers' and Indigenous protestors' actions – not only in Brisbane and Auckland, but in Victoria (1994) and Melbourne (2006) as well.

More striking for the international media, however, were forceful expressions of New Zealand national identity. Vernacular expressions of Kiwi nationalism took a variety of forms, and while some followed closely the official ideals on display in the opening ceremonies, others did not. Eager to enhance support from the home crowd, members of the New Zealand swim team purchased 'thousands of leaflets listing

Kiwi chants, cheers and war-cries' in an attempt to help the host country's spectators to compete with the traditionally noisy Canadian and
Australian supporters.[67] Amid this competitive atmosphere even the
haka became a source of tension between the Canadian, English, and
New Zealand swim teams. When Canadian and English swimmers
disrupted the Kiwi team's haka, chaos ensued, with a Canadian flag
tossed into the pool in retaliation and the New Zealanders threatening
to toss Canadian team members into the water if this ritual was inter-
fered with again. Deemed undeserving of a prominent place in the 1950
Games, the haka was now a symbol of national pride to be defended
from other Commonwealth nations during the course of competition.[68]

The most controversial expressions of New Zealanders' national
pride, however, were products of the country's media. One British
commentator noted that the New Zealand media had a tendency to
focus so much on third-place Kiwi performances that it was difficult to
ascertain who had finished first and second in the events.[69] Australian
journalist Garry Linnell offered a particularly harsh assessment of New
Zealand's national broadcaster. Based on its performance in Auckland,
he suggested, TVNZ was 'poised to break the world record for interview-
ing athletes who have come last in their event' at the next Games in
Victoria.[70] Another journalist at the *Age*, Matthew Engel, suggested that
'[a]nyone relying entirely on New Zealand television for their information
may be only dimly aware that fifty-four nations other than New Zealand
are participating' – although he tempered his indignation by admitting,
'I suppose there have not been many weeks in history when the rest of
us have felt overwhelmed by New Zealand's national arrogance'.[71]

Criticism of TVNZ's partisan coverage also came from New Zealanders
themselves. One wrote to the *Herald* lamenting the 'bias which ignored
other athletes from around the world'.[72] Another spoke out against
'Kiwi worship'.[73] In paying tribute to the Auckland Games, the *Press*
displayed some discomfort with exuberant expressions of Kiwi nationalism, admitting that 'the New Zealand audience ... may have seemed
unduly partisan at times'. 'National pride is excusable,' it reminded
readers, 'if it is tempered with regard for others who did well and generally did better than ourselves.'[74] This was a fitting acknowledgement
of the tensions at play as the 'new' New Zealand hosted a competitive
enterprise expected to promote international understanding.

Conclusion

At the close of the 1990 Games an editorial in the *New Zealand Herald*
suggested that the event had provided an uplifting spectacle for a nation
that 'sorely needed a celebration of itself'.[75] In truth, all three Games

hosted by New Zealand proved to be important occasions for delineating, and at times refashioning, the country's national identity. This was a dynamic, awkward and even messy process. Over a forty-year span the New Zealand British Empire/Commonwealth Games, like those hosted elsewhere, offered an increasingly inclusive understanding of Commonwealth membership. Official pronouncements played an important role in this transition, but so did vernacular voices that frequently offered oppositional or alternative viewpoints, including regional interests, youth culture, Māori political activism, and Kiwi nationalism.

The Commonwealth Games consist of a variety of sporting events. But they also boast spectacles of public commemoration and public memory. As such they have served as a venue for competing political, social, and cultural interests and as a site where nations such as New Zealand have publicly refashioned their national identity and their relationship to the British Empire and Commonwealth, as part of an ongoing conversation about legacies of colonialism and their relevance for contemporary political culture.

While reporting on the 1990 Games in Auckland, Australian journalist Gary Linnell attempted to convey to his audience the sheer scale of the Games' transformation since their inception in 1930. It was no easy task. So he turned to George Lucas for inspiration. 'A long time ago in an era of amateurism far, far away,' he wrote, athletes gathered 'to celebrate being a part of the great British Empire.'[76] By 1990 the event had been substantially reimagined as an ultra-modern celebration of cultural diversity and racial equality. The three Games hosted by New Zealand highlight the extent to which this process was the product of both official and vernacular voices.

Acknowledgements

Funding from a SSHRC Standard Research Grant and St Thomas University's Senate Research Committee facilitated the completion of this chapter, as did the fine work of some very dedicated research assistants: Jessica Fenton, Cindy Fraser, Anne Dance, Jamie Horncastle, Ashley Doiron, Hannah-Lee Benbow, and Gwen Parsons. My thanks to Katie Pickles, Cathy Coleborne, Catherine Gidney, and the anonymous assessor for their constructive feedback on earlier versions of the chapter.

Notes

1   Harold Perkin, 'Teaching the nations how to play: Sport and society in the British Empire and Commonwealth', *International Journal of the History of Sport*, 6:2 (1989), 145–55; Brian Stoddart, 'Sport, culture, and postcolonial relations: A preliminary analysis of the Commonwealth Games', in *The 1984 Olympic Scientific*

Congress Proceedings/Sport and Politics, vol. 7 (Champaign, IL: Human Kinetics Publishers, 1986); and Katharine Moore, '"The warmth of comradeship": The first British Empire Games and imperial solidarity', *International Journal of the History of Sport*, 6:2 (1989), 242–51. For a succinct summary of the Games' political development, see W. David McIntyre, *The Significance of the Commonwealth, 1965–90* (London: MacMillan, 1991), pp. 236–43.

2 D. Gorman, 'Amateurism, imperialism, internationalism and the first British Empire Games', *International Journal of the History of Sport*, 27:4 (2010), 611–34; and Michael Dawson, 'Acting global, thinking local: "Liquid Imperialism" and the multiple meanings of the 1954 British Empire and Commonwealth Games', *The International Journal of the History of Sport*, 23:1 (2006), 3–27.

3 Despite a well-developed literature documenting the important place of sport in New Zealand society and its connection to imperial and national identities, the Commonwealth Games have not garnered much interest from New Zealand historians. For a welcome and very recent exception to this trend, see Greg Ryan, 'The turning point: The 1950 British Empire Games as an imperial spectacle', *Sport in History*, 34:3 (2014), 411–30. On New Zealand's consistent involvement in the Games, see Charlotte Macdonald, 'Ways of belonging: Sporting spaces in New Zealand', in Giselle Byrnes (ed.) *The New Oxford History of New Zealand* (South Melbourne: Oxford University Press, 2009), 281, 289; Charlotte Macdonald, *Strong, Beautiful and Modern: National Fitness in Britain, New Zealand, Australia and Canada, 1935–1960* (Vancouver: University of British Columbia Press, 2013), 96, 163. On the place of the Games in New Zealand's divisive debates about sporting contacts with South Africa, see Malcolm Templeton, *Human Rights and Sporting Contacts: New Zealand Attitudes to Race Relations in South Africa, 1921–94* (Auckland: Auckland University Press, 1998) and Trevor Richards, *Dancing on our Bones: New Zealand, South Africa, Rugby and Racism* (Wellington: Bridget Williams Books, 1999).

4 On the interplay between official and vernacular cultures, see John Bodnar, *Remaking America: Public Memory, Commemoration, and Patriotism in the Twentieth Century* (Princeton, NJ: Princeton University Press, 1992), pp. 3–9, 13–20.

5 'Mayoral reception to visitors', *New Zealand Herald* (1 February 1950), p. 8.

6 'Treloar fancied in Empire sprint', *Age* [Melbourne], (4 February 1950), p. 18. The participating nations were New Zealand, Australia, Canada, England, Scotland, Wales, South Africa, Southern Rhodesia, Ceylon, Fiji, Malaya, and Nigeria.

7 'Future of Empire Games', *New Zealand Herald* (28 February 1950), p. 8.

8 'Value of Empire Games', *Press* [Christchurch], (27 January 1950), p. 8.

9 Auckland Council Archives, Auckland (hereafter ACA), ACC 275, F48-231, Loc. 66-2-1, A. Tronson and F. G. Lintott to Mayor and Councillors, 20 February 1950.

10 'A family affair', *Press* (4 February 1950), p. 6.

11 'Empire Games, 1950', *Press* (13 February 1950), p. 6.

12 'The Empire teams arrive', *New Zealand Herald* (21 January 1950), p. 6.

13 'New Zealand and the Games', *New Zealand Herald* (4 February 1950), p. 4.

14 'Australian sprinters, swimmers triumph', *Sydney Morning Herald* (5 February 1950), p. 1.

15 'Records broken at Games', *New Zealand Herald* (6 February 1950), p. 8.

16 'Disqualification of Pettie', *Press* (7 February 1950), p. 6.

17 'Great day for the Australians', *Press* (10 February 1950), p. 8.

18 'Empire Games standings', *Montreal Star* (6 February 1950), p. 27.

19 'Australia's feat', *West Australian* (13 February 1950), p. 13.

20 'Flags, speeches', *Globe and Mail* (3 February 1950), p. 20.

21 'New Zealand's chosen athletes', *New Zealand Herald* (5 January 1950), p. 4.

22 'Weight lifting', *Press* (9 February 1950), p. 6.

23 'Maori complaint', *New Zealand Herald* (17 January 1950), p. 8. Greg Ryan has uncovered at least a passing reference in praise of Māori in the Games' *Official Souvenir*. Ryan, 'The turning point', 424.

24 'Oarsmen to leave Karapiro', *New Zealand Herald* (7 February 1950), p. 8.

25 'Maoris' welcome to Mr Holland', *Press* (14 February 1950), p. 6; 'Maori reception to athletes', *New Zealand Herald* (9 February 1950), p. 8.
26 ACA, ACC 275, F48-231, Loc. 66-2-1, newspaper clippings: 'Southern mayor's comment' *New Zealand Herald* (28 September 1948), n.p.; 'All Auckland ears would burn', *Star-Sun* [Christchurch], (2 September 1948), n.p.
27 'Games and players', *Press* (11 February 1950), p. 4; 'Empire Games swimming', *Press* (11 February 1950), p. 4. For more on these regional tensions, see Ryan, 'The Turning Point', 415–16.
28 'Mr Ordia hails N.Z.'s tour cancellation', *Press* (23 January 1974), p. 16. On the intense public debate surrounding the tour's cancellation, see Templeton, *Human Rights and Sporting Contacts*, Chapter 6; Richards, *Dancing on our Bones*; and John Nauright, '"Like fleas on a dog": Emerging national and international conflict over New Zealand rugby ties with South Africa, 1965–1974', *Sporting Traditions: Journal of the Australian Society for Sports History*, 10:1 (1993), 54–77.
29 'Friendly Games' symbolic start', *Manchester Guardian* (25 January 1974), p. 23.
30 'British papers laud Games', *Press* (6 February 1974), p. 11.
31 'And now to the Games', *New Zealand Herald* (24 January 1974), p. 4.
32 'Future Games not "British"', *Sydney Morning Herald* (28 January 1974), p. 15.
33 'A modern monarchy', *New Zealand Herald* (31 January 1974), p. 6.
34 'Moments of warmth', *New Zealand Herald* (25 January 1974), p. 1.
35 'Friendly Games' symbolic start', *Manchester Guardian* (25 January 1974), p. 23.
36 'Opening ceremony impressed', *New Zealand Herald* (25 January 1974), p. 10.
37 *Games Review: Official Pictorial Review Xth British Commonwealth Games Christchurch, New Zealand, 1974* (Christchurch, Christchurch Press, 1974), p. 2.
38 'Bedford "ambushed"', *Manchester Guardian* (26 January 1974), p. 25; 'Fastest not fast enough', *Globe and Mail* (25 January 1974), p. 26.
39 'Kavanagh's Column', *Brisbane Courier-Mail* (26 January 1974), p. 28.
40 'Are these the not-so-friendly Games?', *Age* (29 January 1974), p. 18.
41 'Ordia silent on RU tour', *Manchester Guardian* (31 January 1974), p. 22.
42 'Games' steroids plea', *Age* (15 January 1974), p. 20.
43 'Closing conduct called "disgrace"', *Ottawa Citizen* (4 February 1974), p. 17.
44 'Riotous, frolicking farewell', *Age* (4 February 1974), p. 22; 'Games finale beat the band', *Brisbane Courier-Mail* (3 February 1974), p. 1.
45 'Closing conduct called "disgrace"', *Ottawa Citizen* (4 February 1974), p. 17.
46 'Games finale a "disgrace"', *Brisbane Courier-Mail* (4 February 1974), p. 14.
47 'Athletes welfare came first', *Manchester Guardian* (4 February 1974), p. 17.
48 'Games finale beat the band', *Brisbane Courier-Mail* (4 February 1974), p. 1.
49 'Gov't policies "prevented Games boycott"', *Press* (5 February 1990), p. 6.
50 On the cultural significance of the 1981 showdown, see Macdonald, 'Ways of Belonging', p. 291.
51 ACA, AWC 306, F26, Festival Auckland 1990 – 4th Commonwealth Festival of Arts, draft discussion paper, n.d.
52 'Auckland festivals focus on the arts', *New Zealand Herald* (15 January 1990), p. 10; 'Ceremony forced to go with flow', *New Zealand Herald* (5 January 1990), p. 2; 'Games medals', *Press* (16 January 1990), p. 15.
53 'Tickets sold out', *New Zealand Herald* (20 January 1990), p. 1.
54 'Opening to put city on stage', *New Zealand Herald* (24 January 1990), p. 3.
55 'Aussie flag flies high', *West Australian* (25 January 1990), p. 1; 'Deaf in Games choir', *Press* (18 January 1990), p. 8.
56 'Pageant promises plenty', *Press* (23 January 1990), p. 26. Emphasis added.
57 'The crowd warmer', *Press* (26 January 1990), p. 11.
58 'Let the Games commence', *Age* (24 January 1990), p. 15.
59 'Couch potato marathon ...', *West Australian* (3 February 1990), p. 98.
60 'Gold, gold, gold ...', *Age* (21 January 1990), p. 11.
61 'Auckland Games set high standard', *Press* (7 February 1990), p. 50.
62 ACA, ACC 425, 5c, Harry Bettis to Cath Tizard, 4 August 1986 [enclosed clipping: '1990 boycott requested', *New Zealand Herald* (1 August 1986)].

63 ACA, ACC 425, 4h, Box 4, 'Coalition to stop Games', *The Sun* [Auckland], (9 May 1988), pp. 1–2.
64 'Auckland wakes up on eve of Games', *Press* (23 January 1990), p. 22; 'An opening that's worth a gold medal', *Sydney Morning Herald* (25 January 1990), p. 1.
65 'Protest aimed at Australian swimmers', *Press* (26 January 1990), p. 40.
66 On Aboriginal protests at the 1982 Commonwealth Games in Brisbane, see Naomi Shannon, 'The Friendly Games? Politics, protest and Aboriginal rights at the XII Commonwealth Games, Brisbane, 1982', in Ian Warren (ed.), *Buoyant Nationalism: Australian Identity, Sport, and the World Stage, 1982–1983* (Melbourne: Australian Society for Sports History, 2004), pp. 1–57.
67 'Cash paid to unite war-cries', *New Zealand Herald*, section 2 (2 January 1990), p. 12.
68 'N.Z. swimmers angry', *Press* (27 January 1990), p. 30. On Pākehā appropriations of the haka, see Steven J. Jackson and Brendan Hokowhitu, 'Sport, tribes, and technology: The New Zealand All Blacks *Haka* and the politics of identity', *Journal of Sport and Social Issues*, 26:2 (2002), 125–39.
69 'N.Z. media parochial', *Press* (3 February 1990), p. 11.
70 'Tunstall tops list', *Age* (1 February 1990), p. 26.
71 'If you forget economics', *Age* (4 February 1990), p. 14.
72 J. Freeman, letter to editor, *New Zealand Herald* (6 February 1990), p. 10.
73 R. Johnston, letter to editor, *Press* (12 February 1990), p. 12.
74 'Success for the Games', *Press* (5 February 1990), p. 12.
75 'It *was* the moment', *New Zealand Herald* (3 February 1990), p. 5.
76 'An opening that's worth a gold medal', *Sydney Morning Herald* (25 January 1990), p. 1.

CHAPTER TWELVE

Australia as New Zealand's western frontier, 1965–95

Rosemary Baird and Philippa Mein Smith

Politically and economically, New Zealand began as an eastern frontier of the British Empire in Australia as an extension of the Colony of New South Wales, until New Zealand became a Crown Colony in its own right in 1841. Between 1788 and 1840 New Zealand was part of 'Australia's empire' because of culture contact, maritime traffic, trade and exchange across the Tasman Sea. By the 1860s New Zealand featured as one of the seven colonies of Australasia. But New Zealand did not join the Australian Federation in 1901. Instead it aspired to a grander future on its own, one that included building its own empire. The Tasman world nonetheless continued to function in the twentieth century. Indeed it was remade and strengthened from the 1960s, with the decline of the British Empire and renewed globalisation, to the extent that in some respects New Zealand has become a de facto seventh state of Australia.[1]

Instead of making a case for Australia's influence on New Zealand because Australia is the larger partner in the trans-Tasman relationship, this chapter offers a case study of the reverse, that is, of New Zealand's influence on Australia, using the concepts of empire and frontier. It positions Australia, in particular its mining and outback regions in Western Australia and the Northern Territory, as New Zealand's western frontier from the 1960s, and thus the furthest western edge of 'New Zealand's empire'. In New Zealanders' imaginations, outback mining zones are envisioned as a frontier region where opportunity coexists with harsh environments and raw civilisations. Furthermore, the large numbers of New Zealanders in these regions have strengthened the cultural and social connections between New Zealand and Australia. To examine this novel proposition, this chapter takes a new approach and investigates the personal experiences of New Zealanders who migrated to western frontier zones in Australia from 1965 to 1995.

Demographic and statistical trends reveal the pervasive and growing presence of New Zealanders in Australian frontier zones during the latter part of the twentieth century. Oral histories and written narratives provide fascinating insights into New Zealanders' new and often confronting experiences in frontier Australia. New Zealanders who moved to Australian frontier zones faced different economic and cultural conditions from those who moved to east coast metropolises. Once they settled in these frontier zones, their relationships – in particular family bonds – intensified Tasman connections in New Zealanders' daily lives and made the idea a cultural reality that Australia's remote north and west were the borderlands of 'New Zealand's empire' in the late twentieth century.

New Zealand migration to Australia

Most historical research on trans-Tasman migration focuses on nineteenth-century population movements, or more recently, the large number of Māori in Australia. Historians of the New Zealand gold rushes, settler society, and labour movements explore the frequent population interchange between Australia and New Zealand. These historians are keenly aware that trans-Tasman migration and connections are integral to Australasian history.[2] Rollo Arnold in particular examined the 'perennial interchange' of trans-Tasman migrants both ways across the Tasman Sea during the nineteenth and early twentieth centuries.[3] By contrast, research examining the personal experiences of New Zealanders who moved to Australia in the years following the Second World War is scarce.[4] A few researchers have studied the situation of Māori in Australia. Paul Hamer, the key researcher in this area, concludes that Māori in Australia often find personal success and freedom but struggle with retaining their culture and language.[5] Australian historians acknowledge the waves of New Zealanders who have moved to Australia since the late 1960s but neglect to explain the phenomenon in any detail.[6] British migrants, rather than New Zealanders, are depicted as Australia's 'invisible migrants'.[7] This gap in Australian immigration history is likely due to New Zealanders' ease in migrating and fitting in to Australian society. New Zealanders speak the same language in a similar accent, often using the same colloquialisms, easing their integration into the Australian community.

New Zealanders' access to Australia is unrestricted and informal because of the Trans-Tasman Travel Arrangement, which allows the citizens of each country to visit, live, and work across the Tasman. Until 1973, the White Australia policy imposed restrictions on the entry of non-white New Zealanders. Only from 1973 could Pacific

Islanders who were New Zealand citizens enter Australia. Passports were necessary to travel to Australia from 1981, ostensibly to deter terrorism and drug trafficking. In the 1990s Australia introduced a special category of visa for New Zealanders because of political concerns about swelling migration (although most travellers are oblivious to this visa). New Zealanders and Australians continue to expect freedom of movement between their two countries, as was the case historically for British subjects.[8] The tightening of New Zealanders' eligibility for social welfare in Australia from June 2001 preserved this principle, even while migrants after that date encountered restricted rights compared to those who moved earlier.[9]

This chapter focuses on the 1960s to 1990s because during this period the predominant flow of people across the Tasman switched from eastwards to New Zealand, to overwhelmingly westwards, from New Zealand to Australia. As Figure 12.1 shows, the migration flows between New Zealand and Australia changed dramatically from 1967. From this point far more New Zealanders migrated to Australia than vice versa. Demographer Jacques Poot notes that 'the cycle has been remarkably regular since the 1960s, with peak net outflows to Australia being recorded toward the end of every decade (1969, 1979, 1989, 2008), with only the late 1990s net outflow not peaking until early in the new millennium'.[10] So dramatic was this change that New Zealanders have become the second largest migrant group in Australia in the twenty-first century, while a significant proportion of New Zealanders now live there. In 2010 the Australian Bureau of Statistics estimated that of every hundred people born in New Zealand, fifteen live in Australia.[11] Demographers provide several reasons for this trend. The first is New Zealand's small economy compared to Australia's larger, minerals-based economy and higher wages.[12] A second factor was the replacement of sea travel by air travel. Third, baby boomers began going on their 'OE' (Overseas Experience) as young adults.[13] Moreover, emigration to Australia required little preparation or savings. Many New Zealanders moved to Australia on short notice and were able to settle without applying for permanent residence or citizenship. Because moving to Australia was affordable and convenient, New Zealand migrants came from a much broader cross-section of society than the typical 'rite of passage' migrant. The geographical closeness of the two nations meant that visits home, return migration, and circular movements were easily achievable and frequent.

Historically, New Zealand migrants to Australia have settled in urban areas, on resource-extraction frontiers, and more recently in favoured tourist areas. Demographer Philip Guest notes that from the 1970s to 1990s there were significant changes to New Zealand

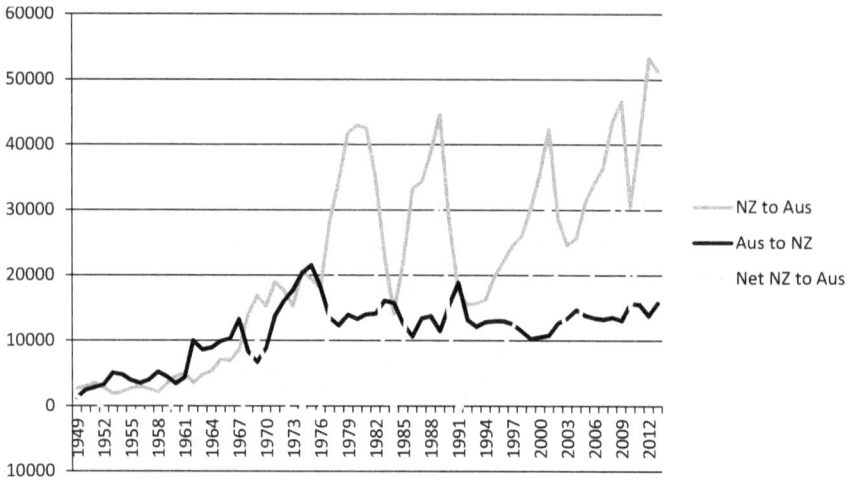

12.1 Trans-Tasman Permanent and Long-Term Migration Flows, Year Ended 31 March 1948–2013 (Source: www.stats.govt.nz, International Travel and Migration).

migrants' areas of settlement. In 1971, New South Wales and Victoria had the largest New Zealand populations. Throughout the 1970s the New Zealand populations of Queensland and the Northern Territory grew rapidly.[14] From 1981 to 1986, Western Australia and the Northern Territory had the largest relative increases in New Zealand-born population, while Queensland – followed by Western Australia – had the largest absolute increases. This shift in geographic distribution generally mirrored trends of Australian-born and overseas-born settlement.[15] In 2010 the Australian Bureau of Statistics reported that 12 per cent of New Zealand-born in Australia live in Western Australia, as opposed to 10 per cent of the Australian-born.[16] Paul Hamer, in his recent work on the 2011 Australian census, points out that New Zealanders, in particular Māori, continue to move to mining areas in large numbers. Between 2006 and 2011 the number of Māori in Western Australia practically doubled, and the number living in the Pilbara grew 119.7 per cent.[17]

New Zealanders on Australia's western frontier

We describe the modern mining regions of Queensland and Western Australia and the outback Northern Territory as a western frontier not only because of their geographical position in the Australian west; these places also have cultural parallels with traditional descriptions of frontier life. On 12 July 1893, a young assistant professor at the University of Wisconsin, Frederick Jackson Turner, memorably gave an address, 'The Significance of the Frontier in American History'.[18] Turner's paper argued that American democracy was formed by frontier experiences. Over the years other historians have developed and appropriated his thesis – that a frontier is a 'region of encounter' – to suit their own needs. For example, Linda Colley builds on his concepts to examine internal, religious and imperial frontiers in British history.[19] Recent scholarship points out that the frontier is a 'contact zone' rather than a linear phenomenon. As Penny Edmonds observes, 'Colonial frontiers did not exist only in the bush, backwoods, or borderlands; they clearly sat at the heart of early town and city building'.[20]

Turner describes the frontier as a 'meeting point between savagery and civilisation'. It is a place where the wilderness strips a person of civilisation, and forces him or her to adjust to the new environment. For Turner, on the frontier the settler's primary labour is to cultivate, settle, and capitalise on land in order to advance his economic and social status. Frontier life is male-dominated and prone to lawless behaviour and vice. It is also productive of individualism, equality, and a distrust of taxes.[21] The nineteenth-century gold rushes in Australia, America, and New Zealand clearly reflect aspects of Turner's description of the American frontier. Furthermore, we argue that New Zealanders' migration to the Australian West from the 1960s onwards provides another, more recent echo of the frontier experience.

In the twentieth century, New Zealanders moved to newly booming resource extraction frontier zones in Australia and arguably participated in modern parallels to these frontier experiences. They moved for personal financial benefit, primarily to profit from the mining industries. Many had new and challenging encounters with Indigenous Australians, inhospitable environments, and tough, masculine, raw communities. Some consciously identified their new home as having a risk-taking, isolationist, frontier spirit.

Financial aspirations

'Go west young man' – a phrase used in discussions of American westward expansion from 1850 onwards – reflected the belief that the American frontier was a place where men willing to work hard in a hostile environment could make their fortunes. Similarly, large numbers of New Zealanders move to Australia because they believe that they will find plentiful job opportunities and high wages. Remote resource extraction locations are often a particular focus of desire. Bruce Ringer moved to Gove, Northern Territory, as a young adult in 1978:

BR   It was a dream, even at Boys' High. I remember sitting in an English class telling the bloke next to me. I said 'It would just be great to go to Australia, work in the mines a couple of years, make a lot of money and come back, and you're set.'

RB   Where do you think you'd heard of that idea that you go to the mines and make a lot of money?

BR   Well it was just general knowledge that you just sort of knew; you could make a lot of money in Australia at the mines. And we didn't know how much or anything like that. It was just you could make money there.[22]

This belief that you could make big money in Australia's frontier regions was shared by other New Zealand migrants.

Financial security justified the hardships of working on the frontier. Murray Hunt, who spent years in Western Australia on mining sites reflected:

> The sacrifice is a little bit of your lifestyle. Go north and earn the big dollars. I've got two BMWs out there. I've got the other car ... I'm not skiting or anything, but it's just ridiculous how easy it all came. Just through basically sacrificing 20 years up north.[23]

A number of New Zealanders reflected that the high wages became addictive. Matthew O'Brien, a gas plant operator in Darwin, spent two weeks on the job, and then two weeks off in Perth with his family. Although it was hard being away from his family the 'good money' was helping them to pay off their mortgage. But he then added, 'the trouble is you earn money you spend it'.[24] For some New Zealanders in frontier zones, the desire to get ahead is never satisfied, and they end up spending years longer in the region than they first anticipated. These economic narratives were almost exclusively male. While women in our sample did move to frontier zones they almost always did so alongside a male partner, and rarely worked in mining-related jobs. But both male and female New Zealand migrants shared a desire to improve their personal financial situation for the sake of themselves and their families.

Challenging encounters

Legends of the American West often congregate around stories and symbols of lawlessness, disruptive encounters with Native peoples, and masculine self-reliance. Similarly, New Zealanders have experienced Australian frontier zones as raw, racist, and rough environments. One of the most confronting issues was the social breakdown among Indigenous Australians and the resulting, seemingly widespread, discriminatory attitudes to them. Most New Zealanders, buttressed by a belief in New Zealand's superior race relations with Māori, were horrified by white Australians' attitudes towards Aboriginal people. Noeline Gentle, who moved to the mining town of Karratha in 1971, felt that the treatment of Aborigines was the 'worst shock' in Australia. She was distressed to learn that the mining company had a policy of not employing Indigenous Australians:

> This was our first contact with a more overt form of racism than what we had experienced growing up in New Zealand. The level of ignorance and racism concerning the indigenous peoples and their culture and history amongst the average Australian then was truly staggering and very sad.[25]

Indeed some New Zealanders (in particular Māori) empathised with Australia's Indigenous people so strongly that they worked in outback frontier regions with Aboriginal groups.[26] Peter Potaka, born in Opotiki and part of a large Māori family, moved to Australia in 1973 with his Pākehā wife. The couple taught in a number of Aboriginal schools near the Simpson Desert and in Alice Springs, and grew to have a real respect for Indigenous peoples' traditional knowledge and survival skills.[27]

New Zealand migrants living in frontier zones also found themselves confronted by the upsetting social breakdown within Aboriginal communities. Even though they were horrified at white Australians' racist attitudes, they were also shocked at what they saw: the homeless, jobless, drunken, and promiscuous lifestyle of many Aboriginal Australians. Bruce Ringer recalled:

> The Aborigines in Gove were a very interesting race. 'Specially round the single men's quarters, around the town, the boys would come in from Yirrkala with the girls and they would nearly just auction them off. It wasn't uncommon to just walk outside the single men's quarters and whistle and they would come in out of the bush and all you'd do is give them a six pack of beer and then you'd have a girl for a night.[28]

Even Peter Potaka, who respected Aboriginal Australians for their bushcraft and hated the comments of some of the white Australians he encountered, had to admit that at times the criticisms were justified.[29] Many New Zealanders in frontier zones held simultaneously sympathetic and critical views towards the Indigenous people.

Australian frontier life, in particular for single men living on mining sites, might also be compared with the American West's stereotype as an uncivilised, lawless, and male-dominated environment. Matt O'Brien worked for several years in a gold mine 'in the middle of nowhere'. His accommodation, a donga, was primitive in the extreme:

> It's like a little shed really. It's like a single man's quarters. And back in them days it was like you had ten in a row. You had a bed and a cupboard

and that was it. All the air con was connected up to everybody else's little donga ... so someone's lighting a cigarette or doing something down one end, it all comes down to the next. And you had to all share toilets and showers and stuff like that.[30]

Life on mining sites had an underbelly of danger. Bruce Ringer recalled, 'Thursday night was always the card night at the single men's quarters. There used to be knifings, stabbings, people were killed playing cards.' While single New Zealand men often grew used to the tough environment, families who moved to the Australian frontier often found the atmosphere unbearable. Matt Clements and Julie Podstolski moved with their three daughters to Kalgoorlie from Sydney in 1997. The move was an 'enormous culture shock'. They found their new home 'isolated', 'grim', lacking in culture, with terrible educational facilities. Julie reflected:

> I used to think that if I was a plant I would have withered up and died in Kalgoorlie ... It really is a man's town. If you go to the airport to pick somebody up, say in Perth ... you can see where people have come from by the way they look. And people that have come from the goldfields, i.e., Kalgoorlie, especially the guys, you just see ... they're not city people at all. They're rough as guts.[31]

Like other Kiwi families, the Clements soon moved to Perth, while Matt commuted to the frontier mining sites. The lifestyle in remote outback towns or mining sites is generally confronting, but monetary rewards have meant that Kiwis continue to move West in search of financial success.

A hostile environment

In Turner's thesis the western settler grapples with, and is in turn shaped by, hostile landscapes and weather patterns. The extreme heat, landforms, and weather in Western Australia likewise impacted on New Zealand migrants. Murray Hunt recalled stepping out of an aeroplane into Port Hedland, Western Australia for the first time: 'I just remember this sudden gust of hot. It seemed like you were walking into a furnace.'[32] Paul McEvedy was astounded by the severe heat at Mount Newman:

> We wore gloves that went all the way down to there [past the elbow] because if ... you'd brush against steel, it was that hot it would take the skin off you, the inside of your arms ... In Mount Newman it'd get to somewhere between 43 and 50 degrees in the heat of summer.[33]

New Zealanders who lived and travelled in remote Australian frontier zones soon developed a healthy respect for their new environment.

New Zealand migrants used words such as 'vast', 'harsh', 'raw', 'huge', 'desolate', 'wide open', 'unchanging', 'stark', 'dry', 'brown', 'sculptural',' coarse', and 'burnt' to describe outback Australia.

A frontier spirit

Some New Zealanders grew to love and identify with their new surroundings, reflected in lyrical descriptions of frontier landscapes. Jennifer Cooper described her reactions to driving through the outback and Nullabor Desert in Western Australia:

> You could drive from horizon to horizon with this arching sky over you. There is no scenery, it's exactly the same. And it's just magnificent in its own way. Space is something that New Zealand hasn't got and space presses on your soul and hooks you in. You stop saying 'Oh another bloody gum tree'. You just say 'this is amazing'. No fences, unlimited space, scruffy growth and bush and red dirt and spinafex and birds, just spectacular. There's something about being out there that grabs you.[34]

For many New Zealand migrants who moved to frontier Australia, the landscape and weather are central to their narratives of new and challenging frontier experiences.

Even New Zealanders who lived in Perth, rather than in mining sites, sensed that there was a different feel to Western Australia. Paul McEvedey, who moved to Perth in 1969, said that Western Australians saw Canberra as trying to steal their mineral treasures and 'were deliberately focused on keeping themselves different from the Eastern States'.[35] Julie Podstolski and Matt Clements, who were particularly imaginative and articulate interviewees, reflected on what they called 'the frontier spirit':

JP It's [Perth] a frontier place. I think there's that general air of optimism here ... like, you can do anything. And Matt in his work finds that if you've got a new idea, people are willing to give it a go whereas in other parts of the world ... they just won't even try ... We seem to be surrounded I think by optimistic souls.

MC I call it a land of gold miners. You know traditionally it was started by the gold rush. People came here for a quick fortune. Basically that has never changed. Now people will very rarely go and try and find bits of gold ... But gold is found in other places: in financial circles, in business. And people still want to go out, have a go, and see if they can make a quick fortune. They go to Kalgoorlie. Instead of looking for gold they go and work for someone who's digging for gold. You know, it's very closely associated with frontier land. An American company that wants to sell a new mining device will try to sell it first in Western Australia to see if it works because somebody will try it here. They won't be able to sell it at home. So there is that mentality and I think that does add a lot to the business potential. You know if you want to do something there is a chance to do it here. That is very attractive, yeah.[36]

While the multitudes of New Zealanders who live in Perth did not directly experience the challenging hardships, mining culture, and interactions with Indigenous Australians, they were still often aware that they were living on the western edge of Australia, in a city that was self-consciously different from the Eastern seaboard cities.

Colonising Australia?

Naturally, many New Zealanders who migrate to Australia do not venture into the frontier zones described above; many choose to settle in urban areas such as Sydney, Melbourne, Brisbane, and the Gold Coast. But the large numbers of New Zealand migrants in Australia, and their continued connections to their homeland, mean that Australia has in some ways become an extension of New Zealand: a 'West Island' in 'New Zealand's empire'.

In recent years migration theorists have increasingly used the concept of 'transnationalism' to describe 'the process by which transmigrants, through their daily activities, forge and sustain multi-stranded social, economic, and political relations that link together their societies of origin and settlement, and through which they create transnational social fields that cross national borders'.[37] But in many ways New Zealanders in Australia do not fit the transnational model. Their continued involvement in New Zealand's political and economic systems is scant. Recent New Zealand governments' attempts to utilise expatriate New Zealand networks and encourage overseas citizens to vote in New Zealand elections have met with limited success.[38] New Zealanders assimilate rapidly, blending in with the local culture. Compared to other migrants in Australia they demonstrate low levels of groupness and rarely join New Zealand political or national organisations.

Rather we conceptualise the movement of New Zealanders to Australia as the latest incarnation of a long history of transcolonial, trans-Tasman mobility and cultural cross-pollination; hence the term 'colonising' Australia. While Australia is not an economic or political colony of New Zealand, the large numbers of New Zealanders living in Australia means there are powerful social and cultural connections between the two nations. New Zealanders' relationships – in particular their family bonds – and their retention of their New Zealand identity mean that, increasingly, they influence (or colonise) Australian society

[222]

and culture and perceptions of Australia – albeit at a personal, informal, everyday level.

There are many small, private ways that New Zealanders link their new 'frontier' lives in Australia with their homeland, New Zealand. Most migrants keep in frequent touch with New Zealand kin and visit New Zealand regularly. Many retain a strong loyalty to New Zealand sport, culture, and products. These connections have the potential to influence subtly the Australian tourism market, education sector, sporting scene, arts, cultural life, and economy.

An interview with Ceris Aorangi Ara Nieuland in Perth typifies many of these informal but strong connections with New Zealand.[39] Ceris, born in 1985, moved to Perth in 1988 (aged 3) with her parents and siblings. Even though she had lived most of her life in Australia, her emotional connections to New Zealand remained strong. She was still close to her New Zealand-based aunties, uncles, and cousins. Ceris reflected: 'it's hard when you live so far away. I mean they're only a phone call away but you just can't go and have dinner or go out together'.[40] In 1995 she and her siblings were sent back to New Zealand for a month to stay with family, and they received many visits in Perth from their New Zealand relatives.

Ceris also participated in a local Māori cultural club in Perth as a child. She believes that her mother took her along to the club for 'the continued connection with our culture':

> I think Mum did it for us and for her as well; so she could socialise with other Māoris and so she could also maintain her culture. And just for us to learn new things. I'm really really happy that she did as well, because I have good memories of practising and performing.

When interviewed, she had recently rejoined a Māori performance group and was enjoying learning new songs, making a traditional *pare* (top), working on her Te Reo pronunciation, and meeting other distant Māori kin. Ceris reflected that belonging to a cultural club had helped her understand and feel comfortable about her Māori identity.

Indeed, Ceris's reflection on her identity as both an Australian and Māori New Zealander revealed some fascinating insights into how New Zealand elements were an integral part of her life in Perth:

> I was born in New Zealand and I am part Māori. And I grew up in Australia so that's what I identify with. I very much feel Australian but at the same time I very much feel like a New Zealander. Sometimes it depends. Like if we're having a hangi or we've got family over then you know it's all very much proud New Zealanders. And then if we've got Aussie friends over we're like 'Oh you know, yeah mate, proud Aussies.' So we just go with however it suits us really. But in saying that, from the heart of it

we're all very proud Māoris; I think because of our ancestors and I think the New Zealand people in general have done really good things in the world and are just generally good people ... it's just nice to be associated with a country that does good things. I feel New Zealand is an environmentally friendly country. I think there's less prejudice, is that the right word, to indigenous people of New Zealand compared to Australia. So that's another reason why we're proud to come from New Zealand as well because it's like 'Well we treat our indigenous people with respect.' And so we have Kiwi key rings. I've got an All Blacks sticker on my car. My brother had like a Tribes sticker on the back of his Ute. And you see it everywhere in Australia too. New Zealanders are just so proud I think generally as people to be New Zealanders. We've got that New Zealand flag there. We've got bits of New Zealand statues around the house and we've got bones. I've got a greenstone that I wear, like paua earrings. I love going down, they have a few Kiwi shops around Perth. I like to just go down and get jewellery or I've got a New Zealand beanie. My sister's got a New Zealand scarf. Just little bits and pieces that we just wear with pride really.

Considering her positive attitude to New Zealand it was not surprising to receive an email from Ceris in 2012, saying that after completing her veterinary training in Perth, she had moved back to New Zealand and was now living and working in the Waikato. She signed off saying, 'it's great to be home'.[41]

Ceris's story illustrates a number of ways in which New Zealand migration to Australia is tightening the bonds between New Zealand and Australia. One of the most obvious is the impact on Australasian tourism. For example, Air New Zealand recently decided to introduce direct flights from Christchurch to Perth. In April 2013 Air New Zealand released a video as part of their advertising campaign for the new route. The company threw in a 'little piece of home' movie night for New Zealanders in Perth, complete with jandals, chilly bins, and Bluebird chips. As part of the evening they flew over an ex-pat's parents for a surprise visit. The video is calculated to tug on the heartstrings, and recognises that it is family connections and nostalgic visits home, as much as tourism, which form the basis for air traffic between New Zealand and Australia.[42]

Also of interest is Ceris's attitude to ethnicity. She strongly identifies herself as a Māori New Zealander. Many Māori and Pacific Island New Zealanders in Australia share this pride in their ethnicity. In addition, many are concerned about their lack of cultural capital and find it difficult to educate themselves and their children in their own language and culture. Like most of the New Zealanders interviewed (Pākehā included), Ceris is also critical of Australia's race relations record and is sympathetic towards the social problems and injustices faced by

Indigenous Australians. Paul Hamer notes that Māori in particular feel a strong kinship with Australia's Indigenous people and often work with, and marry into, Aboriginal communities.[43] As New Zealanders, in particular Māori New Zealanders, become more numerous and enmeshed, there is potential for their views on ethnicity gradually to influence wider Australian society.

Ceris's support of the All Blacks is typical of New Zealanders in Australia. One of the most important ways New Zealanders in Australia publicly identify themselves is by supporting New Zealand sports teams. Almost all New Zealanders interviewed continue to support New Zealand sporting teams at an international level. Loyalty to the All Blacks is near universal, and matches played in Australian centres can at times appear like New Zealand home games. New Zealanders' support for Kiwi teams helps to promote strong ticket sales for Australasian matches. The inclusion of New Zealand teams in Australian sporting franchises – including netball, soccer, and basketball – is also supported by the presence of New Zealand fans in Australia.

Ceris also mentions shopping at a local 'kiwi shop'. Many New Zealand migrants mentioned visiting these shops that sell New Zealand food and memorabilia. While these shops fill a niche, and are hardly representative of the wider market, they highlight the potential for New Zealand migrants in Australia to 'shop Kiwi'. New Zealand products, such as Sauvignon Blanc wines from Marlborough, are potentially more likely to be recognised and purchased in the Australian market.

Conclusions

In this chapter we have linked the concept of the frontier, originating in the United States, with the British-derived idea of 'New Zealand's empire'. As we have explained, the term 'frontier' fits both the landscape and the lifestyle in outback Western Australia and the Northern Territory. For New Zealand migrants, a move to these places meant going as far west as possible, literally and metaphorically. In the process, New Zealanders populated the furthest reaches, westwards, of what may be envisaged as 'New Zealand's empire'.

Over time, New Zealand migrants to the Australian West have found themselves inhabiting a world which in many ways mirrors the historical frontier experience. New Zealanders perceive Australia as the 'lucky country', sending out a siren call of opportunity across the Tasman. But on arrival they face many of the same types of encounters, tests, and hardships as their pioneering trans-Tasman forebears. While large numbers of New Zealanders 'go west' to follow their dreams, most remain inextricably connected to their New Zealand heritage, identity, and homeland. As they settle in their new western frontier zone they subtly influence Australian markets, social attitudes, and culture. Their frequent visits home, and possession of New Zealand goods and artefacts, ways of thinking, practices, and cultural values, mean that they each bring a little piece of New Zealand with them into Australia. In doing so, they silently, little by little, remake Australia as the 'west island' or location of the 'western frontier' within 'New Zealand's empire'.

Notes

1   Philippa Mein Smith, Peter J. Hempenstall, and Shaun Goldfinch, *Remaking the Tasman World* (Christchurch: Canterbury University Press, 2008).
2   For example, on gold fields: Philip Ross May, *The West Coast Gold Rushes* (Christchurch: Pegasus Press, 1967); Patrick O'Farrell, *Vanished Kingdoms: Irish in Australia and New Zealand* (Sydney: New South Wales University Press, 1990); Lyndon Fraser, *Castles of Gold: A History of New Zealand's West Coast Irish* (Dunedin: Otago University Press, 2007). On settler migration: Rollo Arnold, *New Zealand's Burning: The Settlers' World in the Mid 1880s* (Wellington: Victoria University Press, 1994); Jock Phillips and Terry J. Hearn, *Settlers: New Zealand Immigrants from England, Ireland and Scotland, 1800–1945* (Auckland: Auckland University Press, 2008). On labour history: James Bennett, *Rats and Revolutionaries: The Labour Movement in Australia and New Zealand 1890–1940* (Dunedin: University of Otago Press, 2004).
3   Rollo Arnold, 'Some Australasian aspects of New Zealand life, 1890–1913', *New Zealand Journal of History*, 4:1 (1970) 54–76; Rollo Arnold, 'Family or Strangers? Trans-Tasman Migrants, 1870–1920', paper presented at the Australia-New Zealand: Aspects of a Relationship, Proceedings of the Stout Research Centre Eighth Annual Conference (Wellington, 6–8 September 1991).
4   Mein Smith and Hempenstall, 'Living together', in Mein Smith, Hempenstall, and Goldfinch, *Remaking the Tasman World*, Chapter 3.
5   Paul Hamer: *Māori in Australia: Nga Māori I Te Ao Moemoea* (Wellington: Te Puni Kokiri, 2007); 'Māori in Australia: Voting rights and behaviour', *Policy Quarterly*, 4:3 (September 2008) 22–9; 'The Impact on Te Reo Māori of Trans-Tasman Migration' (Wellington: Institute of Policy Studies, Victoria University, July 2010).
6   James Jupp, *Immigration, Australian Retrospectives* (Sydney: Sydney University Press, 1991), and *From White Australia to Woomera: The Story of Australian Immigration* (Cambridge: Cambridge University Press, 2002); John F. Lack and Jacqueline Templeton, *Bold Experiment: A Documentary History of Australian Immigration since 1945* (Melbourne: Oxford University Press, 1995); Eric Richards, *Destination Australia: Migration to Australia Since 1901* (Sydney: University of New South Wales Press, 2008).
7   A. James Hammerton and Alistair Thomson, *Ten Pound Poms: Australia's Invisible Migrants* (Manchester: Manchester University Press, 2005), p. 9.
8   Mein Smith and Hempenstall, 'Living together', pp. 62–4.
9   Mein Smith and Hempenstall, 'Living together', p. 65. For New Zealand migrants' reaction to this policy change, see www.iwinaus.org, accessed 19 September 2014.
10   Richard Bedford and Jacques Poot, 'Changing tides in the South Pacific: Immigration to Aotearoa New Zealand', in Uma A. Segal, Doreen Elliott, and Nazneen S.

Mayadas (eds), *Immigration Worldwide: Policies, Practices and Trends* (New York: Oxford University Press, 2009).

11 Australian Bureau of Statistics, 'New Zealanders in Australia', 4102.0 Australian Social Trends, September 2010, www.abs.gov.au/AUSSTATS/abs@.nsf/Lookup /4102.0Main+Features50Sep+2010, accessed 12 June 2013.

12 John Gould, *The Rake's Progress? The New Zealand Economy Since 1945* (Auckland: Hodder & Stoughton, 1982), p. 118.

13 Jacques Poot, 'Trans-Tasman migration, transnationalism and economic development in Australasia', *Asian and Pacific Migration Journal*, 19:3 (2010), 3.

14 Philip Guest, 'Distribution and mobility of the New Zealand-born in Australia', in Gordon A. Carmichael (ed.), *Trans-Tasman Migration: Trends, Causes and Consequences, Australia Bureau of Immigration Research and New Zealand Immigration Service* (Canberra: Australian Government Publishing Service, 1993), pp. 217–18.

15 Guest, 'Distribution and mobility'; Murray McCaskill, 'The Tasman connection: Aspects of Australian-New Zealand relations', *Australian Geographical Studies*, 20:1 (1982), 17.

16 Australian Bureau of Statistics, 'New Zealanders in Australia', 4102.0 Australian Social Trends, September 2010, www.abs.gov.au/AUSSTATS/abs@.nsf/Lookup/ 4102.0Main+Features50Sep+2010, accessed 12 June 2013.

17 Paul Hamer, 'Māori in Australia: An update from the 2011 Australian Census and the 2011 New Zealand general election', 27 October 2012, http://ssm.com/abstract= 2167613, accessed 13 June 2013.

18 Frederick Jackson Turner, *The Significance of the Frontier in American History*, 1st published 1894, ebook, http://babel.hathitrust.org/cgi/pt?id=wu.89069486553, accessed 2 September 2013.

19 Linda Colley, *The Significance of the Frontier in British History*, British Studies 24 (Austin: University of Texas Press, 1995).

20 Penelope Edmonds, *Urbanizing Frontiers: Indigenous Peoples and Settlers in 19th-Century Pacific Rim Cities* (Vancouver: University of British Columbia Press, 2010), p. 5. On contact zones, see, for example, Katie Pickles and Myra Rutherdale (eds), *Contact Zones: Aboriginal and Settler Women in Canada's Colonial Past* (Vancouver: University of British Columbia Press, 2005).

21 Frederick Jackson Turner, *The Significance of the Frontier in American History* (London: Penguin, 2008), pp. 2–4, 30, 33, 45–6.

22 Bruce Ringer, interview by author, Brighton, Queensland, Australia, 19 September 2010.

23 Murray Hunt, interview by author.

24 Matthew O'Brien, interview by author.

25 Noeline Gentle, written narrative.

26 Paul Hamer notes that Māori often work in and support Aboriginal communities. There is also a significant amount of intermarriage. *Māori in Australia*, pp. 131, 35.

27 Peter Potaka, interview.

28 Bruce Ringer, interview.

29 Peter Potaka, interview.

30 Matt O'Brien, interview.

31 Julie Podstolski, interview.

32 Murray Hunt, interview.

33 Paul McEvedey, interview.

34 Jennifer Cooper, interview.

35 Paul McEvedey, interview.

36 Julie Podstolski, Matthew Clements, interviews.

37 Linda G. Basch, Nina Glick Schiller, and Cristina Blanc-Szanton, *Nations Unbound: Transnational Projects, Post-Colonial Predicaments, and Deterritorialized Nation-States* (Langhorne PA: Gordon & Breach, 1994), p. 6.

38 Alan Gamlen, 'Creating and destroying diaspora strategies', Working Papers, Paper 31, April 2011, Oxford Diasporas Programme, International Migration Institute,

University of Oxford. http://dosen.narotama.ac.id/wp-content/uploads/2012/03/Creating-and-destroying-diaspora-strategies.pdf, accessed February 2015.

39 Ceris is part Māori and it should be acknowledged that, as such, some of her New Zealand connections are related to a specifically Māori experience of connection to land, identity, and culture. However, her case is still representative. Many Pākehā New Zealanders felt an equally strong (even spiritual) connection to New Zealand landscapes, history, sport, identity, and Māori culture.

40 Ceris Nieuland, interview.

41 Personal correspondence, Ceris Nieuland, 29 July 2012.

42 www.youtube.com/watch?v=yy8ofdMCSco, accessed 27 June 2013.

43 Hamer, *Māori in Australia*, pp. 131, 35.

CHAPTER THIRTEEN

Southern outreach: New Zealand claims Antarctica from the 'heroic era' to the twenty-first century

Katie Pickles

With no Indigenous inhabitants, since its discovery by people from elsewhere, Antarctica has been deemed a space ready to be claimed and to have history written upon it. As Elizabeth Leane argues, 'Antarctica's meaning for humans lies in the stories we tell about it'.[1] Antarctica is a place 10,034 kilometres away from New Zealand that few nationals have visited, yet it has occupied a disproportionate place in imperial, national, and individual psyches. This chapter explores and explains that presence. It is concerned with the way nations 'incorporate the Antarctic into their national narratives and claim its frozen wastes as their own'.[2] Such arguments for claiming Antarctica follow from the work of scholars of colonisation and national identity. In particular, I borrow from Edward Said's influential concept of 'the other', which is applied to show how New Zealand's imperial narratives about Antarctica are centrally concerned with New Zealand.[3] Eric Hobsbawn and Terence Ranger's 'inventing traditions' is useful for exposing how histories about Antarctica are made and re-made in order to serve imperial and national identities.[4] Benedict Anderson's concept of 'imagined communities' assists thinking about how wide-ranging peoples across public and private spheres come together to form New Zealand's shared identity.[5] Collectively, perceptions of Antarctica evoke senses of 'elsewhereness', defined by Jeffrey Hopkins as a place where 'the overt manipulation of time and/or space' simulates or evokes experiences of other places.[6]

From the age of high imperialism and the 'heroic era' of the first two decades of the twentieth century, through the Cold War and on to the early twenty-first century, New Zealand's relationship with Antarctica has evolved and strengthened, from a faraway place of little renown to an outreach of New Zealand's imperialism and a part of national identity. Exploration for resource wealth, adventure, strategic geopolitical defence, and scientific research are the major ways in which empires and nations have claimed Antarctica, and New Zealand is no exception. However, importantly, New Zealand's relationship with Antarctica reveals the development of New Zealand as a colonising power in its own right, adapting rather than rejecting British imperial mentalities. Even in the second half of the twentieth century, when New Zealand's foreign affairs were increasingly distinct from Britain, there was considerable evidence of imperial mentalities that displayed much continuity with the past. As New Zealand's status in relation to Britain changed, so too did its relationship with Antarctica. The 1923 decision on the governance of the Ross Dependency, and the 1955–58 Commonwealth Trans-Antarctic Expedition, directly tested New Zealand's overall relationship with Britain, while New Zealand's devolution away from Britain – officially from British colony to dominion status, to member of the British Commonwealth – framed its official claims on Antarctica. As was the general case with New Zealand's international relations, over the course of the twentieth century closer alignment with the United States of America characterised New Zealand's Antarctic endeavours. This chapter positions New Zealand's relationship with Antarctica and suggests that examining the connections between a public sphere history of 'foreign affairs', governance, and diplomacy, and a private sphere of public opinion and popular culture, is vital to understanding how New Zealand and New Zealanders have imagined and constructed Antarctica as a part of a multiple and changing 'imagined community'. Indeed, at times, the New Zealand government has been aware of this, and has actively attempted to foster New Zealand's claim on Antarctica through the public imagination.

An important way that New Zealand has claimed a relationship with Antarctica is through its history as a gateway to the region. Most of the major explorers of the heroic era and beyond have used New Zealand as a stepping stone for exhibitions to and from the South. Russia's Fabian Gottlieb von Bellingshausen; America's Charles Wilkes and Richard Byrd; the United Kingdom's James Clark Ross, Robert Falcon Scott, and Ernest Shackleton; Norway's Carstens Borchgrevink and Roald Amundsen; Japan's Shirase Nobu; Australia's Douglas Mawson; and New Zealand's own Edmund Hillary are the best-known examples. For Anne-Marie Brady, these connections have meant that 'New Zealanders have a stronger sense than the citizens of most other Antarctic players that Antarctica is an intrinsic part of their national history and heritage'.[7]

Christchurch is the New Zealand city with the strongest ongoing history as a gateway to Antarctica. During the heroic era Christchurch welcomed and bade farewell to explorers, most famously Scott,

Shackleton, and Amundsen. David Day has written that when Shackleton left Christchurch's harbour in Lyttelton on the *Nimrod* in 1908, 50,000 people came out on their New Year's Day holiday and sang patriotic songs. The imperial connection to the fore, the ship's second officer, Arthur Harboard, commented that watching the Union Jack fly on the ship's bow made him feel 'proud that we are British, though why I cannot tell'. In an early example of imperial behaviour, the New Zealand government claimed and supported Shackleton, contributing financially to the expedition.[8]

In 1910 Scott stayed on Quail Island in Lyttelton Harbour, and held what was to be his last pre-expedition banquet at Warner's Hotel in Cathedral Square (Figure 13.1). Christchurch claimed Scott and took on his Antarctic endeavours. After his death during the expedition, he was commemorated in a prominent statue sculpted by his widow Kathleen. Importantly, Scott's presence in the region connected New Zealand to the British Empire, as Scott was a fellow British subject. In the early twentieth century, colonial New Zealand was building its own national identity by drawing upon and borrowing British heroes and heroines as role models, and Scott became particularly important because of his physical presence in Christchurch that served to solidify bonds between imperial core and periphery. Claiming Scott and what he stood for, namely British grit, determination, adventure, and the right to explore and colonise new territories, elevated New Zealand's identity as the 'Britain of the South'. In particular, the subtext of death and failure in the face of the awesome power of nature was a feature well understood in the harsh and unpredictable New Zealand landscape and arguably connected Scott to an emerging 'kiwi' settler national identity.[9]

Another connection between New Zealand and Antarctica came through the local New Zealanders who joined the international expeditions. The most famous of these was Frank Worsley of Akaroa, who was Shackleton's navigator from 1914 to 1917. There were others whose stories have fascinated New Zealanders. For example, 'local man' Mr B. R. O'Brien accompanied Admiral Byrd to Antarctica in the 1930s. O'Brien was employed by the expedition to make short wave broadcasts that involved him singing. On his last broadcast he was reported to have sung three Māori folk songs, purportedly to advertise New Zealand. He also returned with a serious diplomatic message: 'Admiral Byrd asked me to convey to New Zealand his very deepest appreciation of the many kindnesses, hospitality, and assistance received in New Zealand, which he considered a great gesture of friendship and goodwill as from New Zealand to America.' Evoking manly heroism, O'Brien added that '[t]he Admiral's fine courage, leadership, and particularly his unceasing consideration for his men, were at all times an inspiration to

13.1 Robert Falcon Scott and his wife Kathleen, on Quail Island
(Alexander Turnbull Library, Wellington, New Zealand).

the whole expedition'.[10] These connections between the United States
and New Zealand over Antarctica would grow during the second half
of the twentieth century.

In the 1920s, New Zealand – out of its close association with
Britain – developed an increasingly separate imperialist mentality of its
own, effectively claiming Antarctica as part of 'New Zealand's empire'.
A significant, yet quiet, change happened in 1923 when the Governor-
General of New Zealand came to administer the Ross Dependency on
behalf of Britain. This relationship was indicative of New Zealand's
status at that time as an emerging nation in control of its internal
affairs, but without the authority to colonise other territories, unless at
the behest of Britain. As Britain controlled the external affairs of New
Zealand, a British government Order in Council was made in London
on 30 July 1923 under the British Settlements Act 1887 that appointed
the Governor-General of New Zealand as the Governor of the Ross
Territory. This Order in Council was published in the *New Zealand
Gazette* on 16 August 1923, and on 14 November 1923 the Governor-
General issued regulations extending New Zealand law to the Ross
Dependency.[11] New Zealand administered the territory for Britain,
rather than on its own. The New Zealand House of Representatives

discussed the situation, noting that while the Governor-General would seek advice from New Zealand ministers, he was also bound to comply with instructions from the Colonial Office in Britain, and 'on behalf of the Empire as a whole and not specially in the interests of New Zealand'.[12]

From 1930, New Zealand began to offer the King advice on the appointment of Governors-General, and after the Statute of Westminster (1931), adopted fully by New Zealand in 1947 and solidified in 1986, New Zealand gained control of its external affairs.[13] The Ross Dependency's governance was caught up in this devolution of power, and the indirect process for New Zealand likely resulted in New Zealand governments being termed 'lethargic' – by Stephen Hicks, Brian Storey, and Philippa Mein Smith – and as 'extremely diffident about the Ross Dependency Claim', by Anne-Marie Brady.[14] Contributing to this diffidence, the real lure of the Antarctic was unclear for the global community, including New Zealand. During the interwar years the issue of the region's resource potential was constantly raised. At the British Colonial Office, Leo Amery mentioned the attraction of oil-rich whales and coal.[15] Australian Mawson's expeditions to the region mentioned the potential for whaling, and for the extraction of gold and other minerals.[16] Science, politics, commerce, and adventure remained entwined, but with no firm direction for the future of the region.

Ideologically New Zealand was trapped in the heroic era, which cast a long shadow over the twentieth century and into the twenty-first, appealing to imperialists, nationalists, adventurers, artists, and scientists alike. Commenting on fiction writing about the place, Elizabeth Leane has argued that 'it is to this era, more than any other, that Antarctic narratives, as well as tourists, want to return'.[17] This was especially the case for New Zealand, where fiction and history often merged together in public and individual imaginations. For example, it was in the years following the Second World War that New Zealand's legendary homegrown latter-day imperial explorer, Sir Edmund Hillary, followed in the footsteps of Scott and Shackleton. In the post-war era New Zealand's participation in Antarctic exploration, and wider afield, as in Hillary's 1953 successful climb of Mount Everest with Tenzing Norgay, was characterised by Commonwealth collaboration, but with Britain still taking the overall lead role.[18]

Throughout the rest of the twentieth century Hillary positioned his life as emanating from the heroic era. As a child he was inspired by Apsley Cherry-Garrard's *The Worst Journey in the World*, an account of Scott's last Antarctic expedition. Hillary wrote that he read Cherry-Garrard's account many times and grew up wanting to go to Antarctica. He recalled that: 'At the Auckland Alpine Club dinner where I announced my engagement to Louise I expressed the view that the Ross Sea Dependency under New Zealand's jurisdiction needed to be explored and that I would love to go on such an expedition.'[19] Alex Moffat-Wood has suggested that in Antarctica 'the lack of indigenous people, the connection with science, and the lack of immediate resource extraction were significant, and in some ways seemed to allow imperial masculinity to rampage guilt free'.[20]

The Commonwealth Trans-Antarctic Expedition of 1955–58, under the leadership of Sir Vivian Fuchs, was a key event for New Zealand, where the nation 'took over' from British control and decided to couch the success of the exhibition in national rather than Commonwealth terms. Overall, polar historians consider that the expedition was befuddled and controversial. With the exception of New Zealand, there was apathy from the other Commonwealth dominions. Canada was busy in the Arctic, and Australia was uninterested.[21] With the goal of completing Shackleton's work to make the first overland crossing of the Antarctic continent, in a new era the expedition was old-fashioned. Of Fuchs' stated objectives, only two related to increased scientific knowledge. The rest concerned politics, strategy, and 'the spirit of adventure' that resonated from the heroic era.[22]

In both the public and private spheres, New Zealand laid claim to Antarctica through the expression of opinions on the obstacles faced by the expedition and the likelihood of failure. It was in fact an 'imagined community' which drove New Zealand's claim on Antarctica. Scholars claim that '[a] few Antarctic enthusiasts in New Zealand were successful in moving their government to assert its long dormant position in the Ross Dependency'.[23] It was the place that Antarctica held in the public imagination that was vitally connected with the official organisation of the tour. Newspapers were harnessed, schools adopted huskies, and individuals could buy 'Share in Adventure' certificates. Edmund Hillary wrote that '[i]n the end New Zealanders raised more money per capita for the expedition than the United Kingdom'.[24] New Zealand's claim to Antarctica had gathered momentum.

With this momentum came success. Hillary led the New Zealand component of the Commonwealth Trans-Antarctic Expedition, successfully completing the first overland crossing of Antarctica via the South Pole on 2 March 1958, with the assistance of three tractors (Figure 13.2). That Hillary did so in a tractor was claimed as indicative of 'kiwi culture' and 'kiwi ingenuity', as mentioned at his 2008 state funeral by then Prime Minister Helen Clark. New Zealand's settler skills were transferable to the colonisation of Antarctica, with tractors as objects of colonisation. In addition, Hillary's friendly rebellion against expedition leader Vivian Fuchs became interpreted as a 'dash

13.2 Hillary, Wright and Ellis on tractors, Commonwealth Trans-Antarctic Expedition, Stan McKay photograph.

for the pole', and a win for New Zealand.[25] Elements of New Zealand's new-found superiority to Britain surface in Hillary's account of the Trans-Antarctic expedition. He describes the British plans as 'amateurish and disorganised'.[26]

During the rest of the twentieth century, as New Zealand developed an increasingly separate identity from Britain, subsequent narratives of both the conquest of Everest and the Trans-Antarctic Expedition increasingly wrote Britain out of the story. For Antarctica, it also set out a new agenda, with Hillary suggesting in 1999 that '[w]e had initiated a wide and continuing programme of scientific research which is being energetically carried on by the New Zealand government to this day'.[27]

In 1959 New Zealand was one of twelve signatories to the Antarctic Treaty, which carved the territory into national regions.[28] Significantly, and clearly, New Zealand was there on its own as a nation capable of its own imperial endeavours. Brady writes that '[t]he Antarctic Treaty was a product of the Cold War and the rivalry between the United States of America and the Soviet Union'.[29] Indeed, the relationship between science and geopolitics was to the fore during the Cold War. In the nuclear age, Antarctica was newly desirable both for its strategic location and its potential minerals. The treaty forbade weapons and mining, and emphasised scientific research. The Antarctic Treaty's primary purpose was to ensure 'in the interests of all mankind that Antarctica shall continue forever to be used exclusively for peaceful purposes and shall not become the scene or object of international discord'.[30] New Zealand's claim to the Ross Sea Dependency led it to become, according to Hugh Templeton, one of the major beneficiaries of the new treaty regime.[31]

Continuing New Zealand's association with Antarctica, from 1955 the United States operated a transport base in Christchurch. This time it was the United States, rather than Britain, which was the superpower using the region as a gateway. During the Cold War the Operation Deep Freeze Base at Harewood was used by those journeying to and from Antarctica by air. The base was at times a controversial site. There were allegations that operations in Antarctica were not exclusively for peaceful research, and that the base made New Zealand a nuclear target. Protests in the 1970s were passionate and Owen Wilkes, a leader who had worked in Antarctica, made connections between science and military pursuits.[32] United States military planes passed though the base, exempt from restrictions.[33] The base was officially on American soil, giving the United States a foothold on New Zealand soil. For many years a Native American totem pole of friendship stood at the entrance to the airport complex, carved in Oregon in 1959 and donated by the United States in appreciation for the hospitality given to personnel of Operation Deep Freeze.[34] Significantly, the base became a part of Christchurch's cultural and popular history, hosting open days and infamous parties. In 1998 the United States Navy officially withdrew from operations in Antarctica and most activity is now under the National Science Foundation.

Day argues that during the Cold War the United States had hopes for Antarctica as a tourist destination.[35] The popular New Zealand fascination with Antarctica prompted Air New Zealand to begin airplane sightseeing trips to the region shortly before the 1979 Erebus tragedy, in which 257 people died when Air New Zealand Flight 901 crashed into Mt Erebus.[36] The crash further cemented Antarctica in the national psyche as a dangerous, foreboding place, reminiscent of narratives of previous loss such as the deaths of Scott and his team. That the Erebus disaster was constructed as a 'national tragedy' strongly served to claim Antarctica as a part of New Zealand.

In recovering from the Erebus disaster, artists, poets, and writers have joined scientists in continuing to create the relationship between Antarctica and New Zealand. For example, Shirley O'Connor found inspiration when she went on the first Mt Erebus memorial flight in 2011, for families affected by the disaster; her husband and brother were victims of the crash. O'Connor did seventeen paintings from photographs.[37] As in the past, artists have been important in the portrayal of Antarctica, with Frank Hurley and Herbert Ponting two famous early photographers. Images and film footage of Antarctica have played an important part in familiarising New Zealanders with a place elsewhere.

In 1996 Antarctica New Zealand became the Crown entity in charge of developing, managing, and implementing New Zealand government activities in Antarctica and the Southern Ocean, particularly in the Ross Dependency. As a Crown entity its range of activities – from arts, media, and youth programmes, to raising public awareness – demonstrate the connection between state and public imaginations of Antarctica, and the deliberate attempt to 'develop a strong awareness of New Zealand's Antarctic heritage among ordinary New Zealanders'.[38] Importantly, women were now increasingly present working in Antarctica, where in the heroic age they had waited for men to return from masculine polar pursuits.

Managing an active New Zealand presence in Antarctica is far from being the sole domain of science and diplomacy. Since 1996, Antarctica New Zealand, in association with Creative New Zealand, has run an Antarctic Arts Fellows scheme. This initiative draws upon high-profile New Zealanders to fuel the place that Antarctica has in the New Zealand imagination by producing art about the region, with the intention of fusing imaginings of New Zealand and Antarctica.[39] Redolent of New Zealand's colonising efforts during the 1920s, in his 2013 book *Civilization: Twenty Places of the Edge of the World*, Antarctic Arts Fellow Steve Braunias includes Apia and Scott Base among a random assortment of New Zealand places, that range 'from Kawakawa in the north, to Mosgiel in the south, and Samoa and Antarctica over the seas'.[40] In attempting to capture the national essence of Scott Base, Braunias eschews the vast and challenging Antarctic landscape in favour of the interior culture of the Base itself:

> Among the happiest sights I saw in my fortnight was morning tea at Scott Base. About a dozen men steamed up a small room with their mugs of tea and coffee, and crowded around a magnificent plate of freshly made sausage rolls. You can take New Zealanders out of New Zealand, but we had arrived at the ends of the Earth and immediately colonized it. We were domestic, suburban, worshippers of tea leaf and pastry, happy to while away the hours at indoor pastimes – all that fortnight, person or persons unknown worked in silence in the library, patiently piecing together a thousand-piece jigsaw of hot-air balloons floating in summer skies.[41]

[237]

His motif of men clinging on to their hold on the continent, battling to control and understand the elements, and themselves, sitting around in enclosed spaces seeking sustenance and home comforts, closely evokes the imperial past.

In 1988 the director of the New Zealand Tourist and Publicity Department, Neil Plimmer, considered that Christchurch was a potential gateway for tourism, and it was hoped that tourism would be more profitable than minerals and of equal importance to science. Day argues that Antarctic exhibits at the Canterbury Museum were upgraded as a way of 'using tourism to reinforce New Zealand's sovereignty', and to contribute towards making Christchurch the 'capital' of Antarctica.[42] Throughout the 1990s such momentum increased, with Christchurch hosting America's National Science Foundation and Antarctica New Zealand.

Around the turn of the twenty-first century there were many markers in Christchurch's landscape that connected Antarctica and New Zealand. A place was retained for the heroic age explorers, with a 'heritage walking trail' that included significant sites around the central city. The tour also included the statue of Scott, 'the great explorer who left the Christchurch port of Lyttelton to sail to Antarctica on his second mission in 1910 and never returned'. Canterbury Museum's Sir Robertson Stewart Hall of Antarctic Discovery celebrated over a century of Antarctic exploration and featured an 'internationally significant' collection of items – many from Scott, Shackleton, Amundsen, and Hillary – as well as Antarctic photographs and archives. The Christchurch Botanic Gardens established a Magnetic Observatory to assist in locating the South Magnetic Pole, one of only three in the southern hemisphere. The observatory was used by early Antarctic explorers and was operated until 1969. Christchurch Art Gallery Te Puna O Waiwhetu exhibited works from Antarctica New Zealand fellows, while the Christchurch Central City Library and Canterbury University both had extensive collections of Antarctic material. Ferrymead Heritage Park in Christchurch featured a restored DC3 plane used in the 1960s for United States Antarctic supply missions, and the city's Air Force Museum had a collection of historic aircraft, including original Beaver and Auster aircraft used in early Antarctic aviation.[43]

In 1992 the International Antarctic Centre, an interactive museum, was opened at Christchurch Airport as a 'major tourist attraction'. It included a penguin encounter, a ride in a Hagglund all-terrain vehicle, a four-season Antarctica weather adventure that included a blizzard, and the chance to play in snow and on ice. There was even an air bridge at Christchurch international airport, 'bearing large images of the ice shelf and emperor penguins – complete with sound effects'.[44] Significantly, Antarctica was 'brought alive' and reproduced in Christchurch. This was elsewhereness at its most explicit. New Zealand's claim on Antarctica included its relocation in the South Pacific.

Meanwhile, in the early twenty-first century, New Zealand official strategic interests in Antarctica concerned conservation, environmental stewardship, biodiversity, and biosecurity. The 2002 New Zealand's revised statement of strategic interests in Antarctica was about a 'commitment to a credible presence in the Ross Dependency', and 'ensuring all activity is undertaken in a manner consistent with Antarctica's status as a natural reserve devoted to peace and science'.[45] In tune with such objectives, the agenda for Christchurch's inaugural 2012 New Zealand IceFest included discussion of international cooperation, collaborative science, research and technology, climate change and the environment, and the future of Antarctica. The festival was an example of strategic interests combined with science and tourism. At the same time, increasing public awareness about Antarctica and promoting the image and identity of New Zealand as an intellectual and logistics gateway to the continent were also on the agenda.[46] Traditionally, Christchurch held a Heritage Week each October to celebrate the city's historic places. After the devastating Canterbury earthquakes in 2010 and 2011, however, much of the built heritage in Christchurch was demolished, so the region's Antarctic heritage was brought in as a substitute. IceFest intended to capture the place that Antarctica held in the New Zealand heritage imagination. At the same time, with most New Zealanders having never visited Antarctica, it offered a sense of escapism, of making people feel elsewhere, ironically, in an often harsh and inhospitable environment.

Serving to solidify the relationship between New Zealand and Antarctica, the festival attempted to reconstruct familiar parts of Antarctica in Christchurch. For example, Christchurch's central park became the 'Hagley Park Ice Station', including a Scott and Shackleton's hut experience and an ice skating rink. In evidence of the invention and inaccuracy involved in such identity building, the Ice Station included an igloo, confusing the Arctic with the Antarctic and suggesting an Indigenous people for Antarctica. While there was romantic and heroic escapism in the festival's activities, the serious intention was that such escapism would encourage more dollars into the country and into the Canterbury region through tourism, diplomatic and trade relations, science and innovation.

The heroic era continued to feature as a backdrop to New Zealand's twenty-first-century imperialism in Antarctica. As well as Scott and Shackleton's hut being reproduced in Christchurch, New Zealand's

Antarctic Heritage Trust is undertaking a five-year hut restoration project at Cape Royds, 'part of its work to protect the legacy of the heroic era of polar exploration from 1895 to 1917'.[47] Foreign objects in Antarctica, such as Shackleton's whisky, left behind during a failed 1907–09 South Pole expedition and found buried in ice under his hut in 2010, have caused much intrigue as out-of-place attempts to colonise the territory. Such cultural imperialism captures New Zealand's transition from colony to nation. In 2013 journalist Deidre Mussen visited the hut and wrote of the decline of the British imperial influence when she found the hut 'packed with memorabilia' from the late 1950s; 'hanging in pride of place are fading photographs of a much-younger Queen and Prince Philip, serving as a reminder of how far we have come'. Mussen wrote: 'These days, Scott Base has a more Kiwi vibe. Large photos of stunning New Zealand locations, rather than reminders of past British links, decorate the walls.'[48]

Twenty-first-century New Zealand imperialism in Antarctica is not limited to extending Britishness. A Māori connection with Antarctica has appeared from the mid-nineteenth century onward, in fiction accounts that have linked Māori origin and travel narratives to the region.[49] At Scott Base's 56th birthday celebrations in 2013 the Union Jacks were gone in favour of a Māori totem pole. A Māori pou whenua was placed at Scott Base by South Island tribe Ngāi Tahu Chief Mark Solomon, in the presence of the New Zealand Prime Minister, John Key (Figure 13.3).[50] In an officially bicultural nation, the placing of a pou

13.3 Unveiling of the Pou Whenua carving at Scott Base.

whenua was advanced by supporters as 'a welcome affirmation of New Zealand sovereignty over its slice of Antarctica'.[51]

Of Māori involvement in Antarctica, Solomon joked that the pou did not mean that Ngāi Tahu was about to lodge a claim on Antarctica: 'I thought I better reassure the Prime Minister that.' Evoking a geographical relationship between the South Island of New Zealand and Antarctica, Solomon said that it was a privilege that Ngāi Tahu, as the southern-most iwi, was asked to carve the pou. The pou, called 'Navigator of the Heavens', was made of native tōtara wood from the West Coast, which he was confident would withstand the rigours of Antarctica's harsh environment, despite it developing several cracks since its arrival on the frozen continent. Solomon's playful attempt at connections paradoxically served to emphasise the distance between the South Pacific and Antarctica. In contrast, Prime Minister Key asserted that the pou was a 'very meaningful addition' to the base. Inventing the relationship between Antarctica and New Zealand, he stated, 'Scott Base has a place in the hearts and minds of New Zealanders even if they haven't visited here. Maori culture is enshrined in who we are as New Zealanders and to have this representation here is a lovely touch.'

Other Māori works of art have been commissioned to literally 'make New Zealand's base on the frozen continent of Antarctica feel more like home'.[52] In 2012 two woven tukutuku panels were made in a project headed by Ngāi Tahu master weaver Ranui Ngarima. Bringing together the major themes of New Zealand's colonisation of Antarctica, and adding in the colonising Māori presence, one panel symbolised Māori ancestors interwoven with New Zealanders who had died in Antarctica, including the 257 passengers and crew killed in the 1979 Mt Erebus plane crash. The other paid tribute to scientific work in Antarctica.[53] The artists articulated their purpose as being 'about the connection of Ngāi Tahu to the Antarctic and the connection between us as Maori and what New Zealand science is doing to enhance our knowledge'. Implicit in this explanation was extending the influence of Antarctica as bicultural New Zealand territory.[54]

New Zealand's southern outreach to Antarctica is a vital part of New Zealand's evolving colonial past. Throughout that history, public sphere governance and private sphere culture have come together to create versions of Antarctica in both the official and the popular imagination. The heroic era was hugely influential in setting the stage for the development of New Zealand's place in Antarctica. Especially in the case of claiming Antarctica, New Zealand has developed a national identity influenced by the British imperial past. As the direct British influence waned, the United States was an increasingly influential part of New Zealand's Antarctic history, especially in the development of Christchurch as a gateway city to Antarctica. The inclusion of biculturalism and a Māori colonising presence at Scott Base is the latest step in claiming Antarctica as a strong part of New Zealand's national identity. New Zealand's Indigenous peoples are included as agents of a revised imperialism.

Overall, New Zealand's claim on Antarctica has displayed continuity, being concerned with often overlapping interests in resource wealth, adventure, strategic geopolitical defence, and scientific research. The current scientific mantra associated with New Zealand's involvement in Antarctica is that it is doing so to advance world-leading research on global change such as global warming, evolution, survival, and biosecurity. From a tentative colony involved in Antarctica as an outreach of the British Empire, in the early twenty-first century New Zealand has developed an imperial mentality of its own, and claims Antarctica as a part of its national identity. As an example of elsewhereness, a process that involves claiming distant landscapes and re-placing them replete with new histories, Antarctica features in New Zealand's imagined community.

Acknowledgements

I am grateful to audiences at the New Zealand Historical Association Biennial Conference, University of Otago, November 2013, and at a seminar at the University of Waikato in March 2014, especially Tom Brooking and Kirstine Moffat, for helpful comments. Eric Pawson suggested the importance of a chapter on Antarctica in this collection.

Notes

1 Elizabeth Leane, *Antarctica in Fiction: Imaginative Narratives of the Far South* (New York: Cambridge University Press, 2012), p. 182.
2 David Day, *Antarctica: A Biography* (Sydney: Knopf, 2012), quoted from dust jacket.
3 Edward W. Said, *Orientalism* (London: Vintage Books, 1979).
4 Eric Hobsbawm and Terence Ranger (eds), *The Invention of Tradition* (Cambridge: Cambridge University Press, 1983).
5 Benedict Anderson, *Imagined Communities: Reflections on the Origin and Spread of Nationalism* (London: Verso, 1983).
6 Jeffrey S. P. Hopkins, 'West Edmonton Mall: Landscape of myths and elsewhereness', *Canadian Geographer/Le Géographe canadien*, 34:1 (1990), 2–17.
7 Anne-Marie Brady, 'New Zealand's Antarctica', in Anne-Marie Brady (ed.), *The Emerging Politics of Antarctica* (Abingdon and New York: Routledge, 2013), p. 148; 'Introduction: Conflict or cooperation? The emerging politics of Antarctica', in Brady (ed.), *Emerging Politics in Antarctica*, pp. 1–9. New Zealand is, of course, but one of many nations and places with direct connections to Antarctica, such as Tasmania and parts of Chile and Argentina.
8 Day, *Antarctica*, p. 134.

9   See Katie Pickles, 'Kiwi icons and the re-settlement of New Zealand as colonial space', *New Zealand Geographer*, 58:2 (2002), 5–16.
10 'Local man returns', *Evening Post* (23 February 1934), p. 10.
11 *New Zealand Gazette*, Vol. II: 2211 (1923), and Vol. III: 2815 (1923).
12 *NZPD*, Francis Bell, 1923.
13 W. David McIntyre, *Dominion of New Zealand: Statesmen and Status, 1907–1945* (Wellington: New Zealand Institute of International Affairs, 2007).
14 Stephen Hicks, Bryan Storey, and Philippa Mein Smith, 'Against all odds: The birth of the Commonwealth Trans-Antarctic Expedition, 1955–1958', *Polar Record*, 49:1 (2013), 50–61, and Brady, 'New Zealand's Antarctica', p. 149.
15 Day, *Antarctica*, p. 180.
16 'Australia's Share', *Evening Post* (16 February 1933), p. 11.
17 Leane, *Antarctica in Fiction*, p. 173.
18 See Peter H. Hansen, 'Coronation Everest: Empire and commonwealth in the "second Elizabethan age"', in Stuart Ward (ed.), *British Culture and the End of Empire* (Manchester: Manchester University Press, 2001), pp. 57–72.
19 Sir Edmund Hillary, *View From the Summit* (Auckland: Doubleday/Random House New Zealand, 1999), p. 124.
20 Alex Moffat-Wood, 'Blizzard City: Built Environment and Civilization in Antarctica, 1911–1961', MA thesis, Victoria University of Wellington, 2012.
21 On Canada's post-war colonisation of the North, see Katie Pickles, 'Forgotten colonizers: The Imperial Order Daughters of the Empire (IODE) and the Canadian North', *Canadian Geographer/Le Géographe canadien*, 42:2 (1998), 193–204.
22 Hicks, Storey, and Mein Smith, 'Against all odds', p. 53.
23 Hicks, Storey, and Mein Smith, 'Against all odds', p. 50.
24 Hillary, *View From the Summit*, p. 127.
25 See Hansen, 'Coronation Everest', p. 68.
26 Hillary, *View From the Summit*, p. 133.
27 Hillary, *View From the Summit*, p. 188.
28 The Antarctic Treaty was signed in 1959 by twelve nations active in Antarctica during the 1957–58 International Geophysical Year (Argentina, Australia, Belgium, Chile, France, Japan, New Zealand, Norway, South Africa, United Kingdom, United States, and USSR). The Antarctic Treaty, New Zealand Ministry of Foreign Affairs and Trade/Manatū Aorere, www.mfat.govt.nz/Foreign-Relations/Antarctica/2-Antarctic-Treaty-System/index.php, accessed 30 June 2014.
29 Anne-Marie Brady, 'Introduction: Conflict or cooperation? The emerging politics of Antarctica', in Brady (ed.), *Emerging Politics in Antarctica*, p. 1.
30 The Treaty entered into force on 23 June 1961 and applies to the area south of 60° South latitude. The Antarctic Treaty, www.mfat.govt.nz/Foreign-Relations/Antarctica/2-Antarctic-Treaty-System/index.php, accessed 30 June 2014.
31 Hugh Templeton, *All Honourable Men: Inside the Muldoon Cabinet 1975–1984* (Auckland: Auckland University Press), p. 99.
32 Elsie Locke, *Peace People: A History of Peace Activities in New Zealand* (Christchurch: Hazard Press, 1992), pp. 279–85.
33 Brady, 'New Zealand's Antarctica', p. 159.
34 Christchurch: New Zealand's gateway to the ice, Media Resources, www.newzealand.com /travel/media/features/nz-regions_christchurch-on-ice.cfm, accessed 30 June 2014.
35 Day, *Antarctica*, p. 512.
36 Brady, 'New Zealand's Antarctica', p. 148.
37 Shirley O'Connor, watercolour artist, www.shirleyoconnor.net, accessed 30 June 2014.
38 Brady, 'New Zealand's Antarctica', p. 151.
39 Antarctica New Zealand, Artists & Writers Programme, http://antarcticanz.govt.nz/ scholarships-fellowships/artists-writers-programme, accessed 30 June 2014.
40 Steve Braunias, *Civilisation: Twenty Places on the Edge of the World* (Wellington: Awa Press, 2012). The places in the book are Hicks Bay, Pegasus; Waiōuru; St

Bathans; Ōhinemutu and Whakarewarewa; Hauraki Plains; Miranda; Scott Base; Apia; St Roskill; Wanganui, Whanganui; Mercer; Winton; Tangimoana; Mosgiel; Wānaka; Greymouth; Collingwood; Wainuiomata; and Maromaku Valley.

41   Braunias, *Civilisation*, p. 105.
42   Day, *Antarctica*, p. 152.
43   Christchurch, New Zealand gateway to the ice, www.newzealand.com/travel/media /features/nz-regions/nz-regions_christchurch-on-ice.cfm, accessed 30 June 2014.
44   Christchurch, New Zealand gateway to the ice .
45   2002 Revised New Zealand Statement of Strategic Interest, Antarctica, Foreign Relations, New Zealand Ministry of Foreign Affairs and Trade/Manatū Aorere, www.mfat.govt.nz/Foreign-Relations/Antarctica/1-New-Zealand-and-Antarctica/1-NZ-Strategy-in-Antarctic.php New Zealand's strategic interests in Antarctica, accessed 30 June 2014.
46   Icefest October 2012 brochure, *Press*.
47   Deidre Mussen, 'NZ reinforces Kiwi connection to Antarctica', *Press* (26 January 2013), A18.
48   Mussen, 'NZ reinforces Kiwi connection to Antarctica'.
49   Leane, *Antarctica in Fiction*, pp. 24–5.
50   Deidre Mussen, 'Ngai Tahu carving unveiled in Antarctica', *Press* (20 January 2013), www.stuff.co.nz/the-press/news/8200978/Ngai-Tahu-carving-unveiled-in-Antarctica, accessed 30 June 2014.
51   Barrie Cook, 'NZ aims for pole position on slice of ice', *Press* (10 June 2013), A15.
52   Samantha Early, 'Artistic treasures Antarctica bound', *Mainland Press* (6 September 2012), p. 1.
53   Deidre Mussen, 'Key, Solomon unveil totara carving at Antarctic base', *Press* (21 January 2013), A7.
54   Samantha Early, 'Artistic treasures Antarctica bound', *Mainland Press* (6 September 2012), p. 1.

CHAPTER FOURTEEN

A radical reinterpretation of New Zealand history: apology, remorse, and reconciliation[1]

Giselle Byrnes

A little over 150 years ago, a crucial battle took place in the western Bay of Plenty in New Zealand. The event was to be a turning point in New Zealand's turbulent civil wars; British colonial ambition was effectively stymied and settler and Indigenous Māori relations were severely ruptured for most of the remainder of the nineteenth century. Te Whawhai o Pukehinahina (the Battle of Gate Pā) was an intense confrontation in which 1,700 British troops were soundly defeated by the military intelligence, intricate defences, and strategic resilience of a combined Māori force of a mere 230 warriors. The conflict, which came to a head on 29 April 1864 and was one of the last acts in the Crown's campaign to alienate large tracts of Māori land for future British settlement, has been well documented.[2] Pukehinahina remains significant, both as a battle site and as an historical moment, chiefly because Māori irregular fighters were victorious in the face of overwhelming odds. They secured a crucial victory against the invading colonial forces based on superior military tactics and skill; Māori also displayed honourable conduct towards the dead and wounded. Pukehinahina was an example of what Māori resistance could achieve: while they may have 'lost' the wars, they decisively won this battle. Pukehinahina (the place and its memory) exists today as an aide-mémoire of the impact the past continues to exert on the present, a wound that is only now beginning to heal.[3]

In 1998 the Waitangi Tribunal, the statutory body charged with examining alleged breaches of the Treaty of Waitangi (1840), commenced its investigation into the Tauranga Moana and western Bay of Plenty claims.[4] Between June 2012 and December 2013 the New Zealand government and Māori representatives signed successive deeds of settlement, with the government issuing public apologies for the loss of land, resources, and economic wellbeing, along with innumerable breaches of the Treaty partnership.[5] In 2014, the city of

Tauranga held a number of public events to remember the battles of Pukehinahina and Te Ranga, with the commemorations seen as an opportunity for the community to acknowledge the past, look forward in unity and lay the ghosts of history to rest.[6]

The importance of this event and its modern commemoration lies not in the Treaty settlements per se, but in the contemporary reinterpretation of events and the way in which, in a highly specific and localised way, twenty-first-century citizens, Māori and Pākehā alike, are reminded of the Crown's imperial ambitions and its role as internal coloniser. Of course, this was not an isolated event. Both the battle and the ensuing settlement and apology have parallels in other parts of New Zealand. What is relevant is that such acts of aggression, like armed conflict in the past, highlight the way in which the Crown (in the form of successive New Zealand governments) was prepared to take up arms against its own subjects.

This event also serves to underscore the work of the Waitangi Tribunal as a postcolonial institution on the modern New Zealand political landscape. Almost thirty years ago, historian M. P. K. Sorrenson described the work of the Waitangi Tribunal as significant not only because of its role in bringing long-standing historical grievances to the point of legal and political resolution, but because it was casting light on Māori histories, ways of knowing, and Māori interpretations of the Treaty of Waitangi. Sorrenson stopped short of according the Tribunal a 'revolutionary' role, noting that then, as now, the Tribunal suffered from a particular political and legislative fragility.[7] Notwithstanding its position as a creature of statute, making it potentially vulnerable to the whims of elected governments, the Tribunal has continued to reveal 'new' histories of Māori–Crown encounters and has secured both its place and purpose in addressing longstanding Treaty grievances.

Alongside the work of the Tribunal and the subsequent emergence of its published narratives, especially those prioritising Māori perspectives of history, the story of New Zealand has typically been framed around the key tropes of invasion, conflict, colonisation, and development, usually documented in a linear and sequential fashion. The last habitable land mass on earth to be discovered and colonised by humans, New Zealand has variously seen itself (and has been seen by others) as tribal homeland, colonial outpost, settler society, and more recently as a modern bicultural nation. This narrative – which resonates with both Māori and Pākehā historical traditions – has been consolidated over the past century through a range of textual, printed, and discursive strategies. This is evident in published general histories of New Zealand, in addition to more popular narratives about the country's past. More poignantly, and as this volume investigates, New Zealand has been typically positioned as a site *of* colonisation, and as a victim of British imperial chauvinism and excess, rather than a colonial aggressor in its own right.

This chapter turns this interpretation on its head, arguing that New Zealand has another, lesser known and arguably more potent historical role – that of imperial dominion and colonising power. It argues that, not content with being a colony itself, 'New Zealand' (as embodied by its institutions, political structures, and legislative rubrics) has simultaneously acted as an imperial power as well as colonial outpost, to the extent of engaging in a sort of 'internal colonisation' of its own citizens. Indeed, it advances the idea that public and official apologies on behalf of the nation-state are evidence of this imperial desire and products of our particular postcolonial condition.[8] This proposes an alternative view of New Zealand's past, one that deliberately prioritises a postcolonial perspective on and *of* history and takes inspiration from historian Peter Gibbons' thesis on cultural colonisation.[9] The chapter argues that New Zealand's national apologies and declarations of regret, which have characterised much of the political discourse of the late twentieth and early twenty-first centuries, are evidence of its little-acknowledged historical role as an imperial power. State-sanctioned public apologies have been most obvious in the modern Treaty claims settlement process, in the apologies made to Māori on behalf of the New Zealand Crown for breaches of the 1840 Treaty of Waitangi. In recent years the New Zealand government has also offered apologies to the New Zealand Chinese community and to the people of Sāmoa for colonial indiscretions, prejudice, and neglect. This chapter considers moments when the New Zealand Crown and successive settler governments, together constituting the New Zealand 'nation-state', have willingly engaged in public acts of contrition as a way of coming to terms with a less than ideal history characterised by violence and shame.

The age of apology

Since the end of the Second World War, the impulse – by governments, institutions, nation-states, and former regimes – to officially apologise (and be seen to be doing so) has developed as a powerful phenomenon. Governments and governing powers around the world have felt compelled to atone for historical injustices through processes of public apology, acts of contrition, and, in some cases, reparation. These injustices include, but are not limited to, wartime atrocities, gross infringements of human rights, and the failure to recognise and acknowledge Indigenous rights. Indeed, the idea and expression of apology has become a familiar trope in recent world history. This includes the work of the Truth and Reconciliation Commission in South Africa and commissions of inquiry in other parts of Africa, Asia, South and Central America; the Truth Commission established in Northern Ireland; and processes addressing Indigenous land rights in Canada, Australia, and elsewhere.[10] Commentators have been quick to identify this trend. In Australia, for instance, Bain Attwood argues that in order to understand the politics of the late twentieth century we need to appreciate the notion of apology.[11] In considering how and why Western states and institutions have sought to come to terms with their relationships to non-Western states and peoples, Mark Gibney and his co-authors go further, labelling the late twentieth century the 'age of apology'.[12] In his *Guilt of Nations: Restitution and Negotiating Historical Injustices*, Elazar Barkan offers a sweeping examination of modern processes of restitution and their impact on the interpretation of human rights around the world.[13] More recently, Melissa Nobles, Priscilla B. Hayner, and Martha Minow critically examine responses to mass violence, truth commissions, and the politics of official apologies.[14] In a wide range of international contexts, scholars are considering guilt and political redress, apology and 'truth-seeking' commissions, reparation in settler societies, and the philosophy and ethics of cultural devastation.[15]

Modern apologies have been offered both to victims of past decisions – those who experienced injustice, discrimination, and violence firsthand – as well as to those who are the inheritors of these actions. This is an important distinction and warrants closer examination. At first glance it might be assumed that apologies offered to the dead – actions stemming from past wrongs where there are no living victims – might be confined to the past. These include, for instance, declarations of colonial injustices and wrongs perpetrated by 'third parties'.[16] Similarly, apologies for contemporary wrongs, when the guilty parties come face to face with their victims (a particular feature of modern truth and reconciliation commissions), may bring more immediate redemption for the guilty party. These include apologies to victims who are still alive, such as apologies to the Stolen Generations in Australia, atonement for twentieth-century genocidal policies, actions, and intent, as well as recent declarations of regret on behalf of the Catholic Church.[17]

While it may be useful for the apologising party (and for the conventions of academic periodisation) to distinguish between 'historical' and 'contemporary' injuries, this differentiation often makes little sense to victims. While facing up to the injured party in person may benefit the wrongdoer – providing them with the promise of absolution and freedom from guilt – for the victims of such crimes, historical sins are often felt as keenly as contemporaneous damage.[18] This is particularly the case in regard to claims to Indigenous rights, where historical wrongs are passed on from generation to generation. As New Zealand's first Chief Justice Sir William Martin presciently observed in 1863, arguing against the proposed punitive land confiscations (or raupatu) against 'rebel' Māori: 'The example of Ireland,' he warned, 'may satisfy us to how little is to be effected towards the quieting of a country by the confiscation of private land; how the claim of the dispossessed owner is remembered from generation to generation, and how the brooding sense of wrong breaks out from time to time in fresh disturbance and crime.'[19] Past events are never divorced from present responsibilities. Moreover, it is not uncommon for claimants in the twenty-first century to present evidence and talk *as if they were* those individuals. Judith Binney and Nēpia Mahuika, among others, have observed this trope, and Bella Te Aku Graham has written on how this particular perspective has been embodied and enacted before the Waitangi Tribunal.[20] Indeed, as Miranda Johnson argues, oral testimony given before Tribunals (and by extension the courts) has perhaps not been accorded the legitimacy, context, and voice intended by Indigenous agents.[21] There are also crimes that can never be absolved, regardless of their historical or contemporary status. 'Guilt is a legal term; responsibility is a moral one', observes Thane Rosenbaum, writing in the *New York Times* on the Holocaust and the memory of Nazi genocide. 'Acknowledgment, truth, and apologies are moral imperatives; forgiveness is not, precisely because it suggests starting over with a clean slate, which, in this case, only the ghosts are empowered to grant.'[22]

Recent public apologies in New Zealand: the state comes clean

Without doubt, the domain of New Zealand public discourse where the concept of apology has been most palpable has been Treaty of Waitangi settlement negotiations, and more particularly, apologies made to Māori on behalf of the Crown and New Zealand governments, as part of the modern Treaty claims process. As noted earlier, the research that constitutes a crucial part of this process has also brought to light Indigenous histories of loss and dispossession that were hitherto unknown, forgotten or simply marginalised by the Pākehā mainstream. It is worth noting that Māori have always rehearsed, known and told these stories of damage and cultural dislocation: after all, such narratives form the basis of numerous claimant testimonies presented before the Waitangi Tribunal and tabled in the course of negotiations with Crown agencies in efforts for redress.

Since 1975 – and especially since 1985, when its jurisdiction was expanded to include historical matters – the work of the Waitangi

Tribunal, along with that of agencies engaged in the Treaty claims process, has led to a number of public apologies by the Crown to Māori claimants.[23] The 'dual focus' of the Tribunal (its concern with both past and present) is a function of its statutory duties and obligations as well as the result of its own developing jurisprudential practice. Māori have been taking their claims to the Crown for well over a century and have actively communicated their histories to successive audiences through a variety of media. The work of contemporary mechanisms in addressing these claims is therefore neither new nor novel.[24] While there has been a succession of government commissions of inquiry into land confiscations and other grievances, the Waitangi Tribunal and the settlement process of which it is a part has provided the most robust methodology for claimants to date. In its forty-year history, the Tribunal has released over a hundred reports on a variety of claims, from small claims through to multi-volume chronicles, which have reframed the ways in which we conceptualise the nature of the Māori–Crown encounter in the post-1840 world. These claims cover land loss and the alienation or denial of a wide range of rights guaranteed to Māori under the Treaty of Waitangi.[25]

By virtue of its enabling legislation, the Tribunal can only make findings and recommendations on any given claim (or group of claims) to the government of the day. The final arbiter of a claim – and the agency charged with drafting the official apology – is the Office of Treaty Settlements; ironically a Crown agency, albeit one expressly charged with providing advice on Treaty policy and strategy to the Minister for Treaty of Waitangi negotiations, consulting with and providing advice to claimants, in addition to taking responsibility for the implementation of Treaty settlements. The drafting of an official apology is the domain of this Office. While other critics have commented on the form and genre of these apologies, typically they are clear and unambiguous statements of regret, offered in full and final terms.[26] The apology is offered in order to seek closure for redress but also for the Crown to absolve itself and restore 'the honour of the Crown', a recurring theme in deeds of settlement. What is most apparent in Treaty discourse in New Zealand, however, is the *absence* of certain terms which are central to processes elsewhere in the world. In New Zealand, the term 'settlement' has supplanted references to 'reconciliation'; in the Crown's eyes, the settlement of grievances signifies a closure of the past and the beginning of a new relationship between the Crown and Māori.[27] This is more than mere semantics: language determines the mode of reparation. 'Settlement' carries with it fiscal responsibilities, while 'reconciliation' is a less easily defined, softer (and some might say, less binding) term.

The analysis of one recent apology serves to illustrate these themes. The descendants of those who took up arms against colonial forces at the Battle of Pukehinahina, Ngāti Ranginui, finally witnessed a deed of settlement in June 2012.[28] The deed, ratified by the New Zealand Parliament, includes a four-page 'Acknowledgements and Apology' statement at the end of the document.[29] While the acknowledgement details key historical breaches of the Treaty of Waitangi and its principles, the apology goes further to admit that past Crown actions seeded intergenerational disadvantage and injustice. The apology was made to the constituent hapū, as well as to 'your tūpuna and to your descendants'.[30] The Crown admitted its failure to recognise the authority of Ngāti Ranginui 'for many generations' and referred to 'the burden carried by generations of Ngāti Ranginui who have suffered the consequences of war and raupatu which they continue to feel today'.[31] This tribunal report extended its focus even further to suggest that its past actions had 'deprived [Ngāti Ranginui] of opportunities for development, caused significant harm to the social and economic development ... [and] undermined the wellbeing of the iwi and its hapu'.[32] The intent of the Crown was clear: it sought redemption and forgiveness and to remove the stains from past history. 'Through this apology,' the Crown admitted in the deed of settlement, 'the Crown seeks atonement for the wrongs of the past and to establish a new relationship with the hapu of Ngāti Ranginui based upon mutual trust, co-operation, and respect for te Tiriti o Waitangi/the Treaty of Waitangi and its principles.'[33]

There are of course other public gestures that have engaged with the concepts of apology, remorse, and reconciliation in New Zealand's recent political history. The official public apology to the New Zealand Chinese community in 2002 by the then Labour government was one such event. At the Chinese New Year celebrations held at Parliament on 12 February 2002, then Prime Minister Helen Clark formally and publicly apologised to the descendants of those Chinese immigrants on whom a discriminatory poll tax had been enforced in the late nineteenth century. While not peculiar to colonial New Zealand, this practice was one of the most pernicious and damaging ways in which past government administrators and their agents had implemented a 'white New Zealand' policy. As the research of Nigel Murphy and others has demonstrated, thousands of Chinese immigrants, lured to New Zealand by the prospect of a better life (as had been generations of British immigrants), were subjected to systematic economic and social discrimination which left lasting effects on their families, their wellbeing and their ability to thrive.[34] Prime Minister Clark delivered an address on this date which included the following statements:

In the nineteenth century, the New Zealand Parliament passed discriminatory laws against Chinese seeking to enter New Zealand ... I wish
to announce today that the government has decided to make a formal
apology to those Chinese people who paid the poll tax and suffered other
discrimination imposed by statute and to their descendants.[35]

The Prime Minister's speech acknowledged the personal cost of the
policy and the ways in which Chinese people and their families had
been affected:

With respect to the poll tax we recognise the considerable hardship it
imposed and that the cost of it and the impact of other discriminatory
immigration practices split families apart.[36]

In addition, the goal of reconciling with the past, and cleansing the
narrative of history, was clear:

Today we also express our sorrow and regret that such practices were once
considered appropriate ... We believe this act of reconciliation is required
to ensure that full closure can be reached on this chapter in our nation's
history ... The Government's apology today is the formal beginning to a
process of reconciliation ... To that end we wish to meet with key representatives of the descendants to discuss the next step in this process of
reconciliation.[37]

Notwithstanding the sentiments expressed in the apology, no doubt
sincerely felt by the Prime Minister herself, the economic and political
motivations of this gesture were abundantly clear.

Today's New Zealand Government both recognises and values the importance of the Chinese community in New Zealand. The community is
making a huge economic and social contribution to our country. The
many new Chinese migrants are also bringing new ideas, a strong work
ethic, and valuable contacts with their countries of origin.[38]

Not content with issuing apologies to victims of Crown actions on
New Zealand soil, the state has recently engaged in saying sorry to its
former dominions.[39] In June 2002, only a matter of months following
the apology to the New Zealand Chinese community, Prime Minister
Helen Clark used the occasion of a state luncheon in Apia marking
the fortieth anniversary of Sāmoan independence to offer an apology
to Sāmoa for deaths arising from the influenza epidemic in 1918. The
apology was also made regarding the deliberate suppression of a local
nationalist movement when the islands were under New Zealand
administration. This public and official apology included the admission
that New Zealand's early administration of Sāmoa was incompetent
and ineffectual, in particular the decision by New Zealand authorities
to allow a ship carrying passengers with the influenza virus to dock in

Apia in 1918. This decision led to the deaths of more than one fifth of Sāmoa's population, one of the world's worst outbreaks of the epidemic. The apology also referred to the shootings of non-violent protestors in Apia by New Zealand police in 1929, resulting in the deaths of at least nine people and the subsequent banishment of the Sāmoan leaders.[40]

Prime Minister Clark was reported as saying that the apology dealt with 'unfinished business' between the two nations and she hoped that it would lead to an even stronger relationship between New Zealand and Sāmoa.

> We come to acknowledge the contribution of independent Samoa to the wider regional and international communities of which we are part. We come to say thank you to Samoa for the gift to New Zealand of its people and for the part they are playing in our society.[41]

The Prime Minister went on to offer a clear statement of apology. 'On behalf of the New Zealand Government,' she stated, 'I wish to offer today a formal apology to the people of Samoa for the injustices arising from New Zealand's administration of Samoa in its earlier years, and to express sorrow and regret for those injustices.'[42] The apology itself was strongly future-focused and referenced the numerous links existing between New Zealand and Sāmoa.

> We are truly sorry. It is our hope that this apology will enable us to build an even stronger relationship and friendship for the future on the basis of a firmer foundation. New Zealand and Samoa are bound together by our geography, our history, our cultural and family links, and today by our trade and diplomacy.[43]

Again, the Prime Minister's statements included the hope that 'we' could 'move on' and put the past behind us, a popularly expressed sentiment.[44] Here, history is not only linear and progressive, but something to be momentarily embraced, then moved on and away from. As the remainder of this chapter argues, this is a common trope in officially sanctioned public apologies.

How to read apologies, or evidence of imperial excess

The proposition that post-Treaty Pākehā New Zealand has been a colonising power stems in part from the local contextualisation of what is meant by 'colonisation' and 'imperialism'. Often used synonymously, these terms, and the processes they connote, are nonetheless strikingly different. Imperialism is generally understood as a policy of extending the power and rule of a government or governing polity beyond its own boundaries and an attempt to dominate others by direct rule and settlement. Fundamental to this definition is the acquisition of resources, be that land, people or extractable commodities. On the other hand, colonisation refers, in this context, to the process of a country being taken over and becoming a colony of another, a process often involving force and subjugation of the local population.

Public gestures of apology in the wake of either an imperial or colonial act – where the performance of being seen to make the apology is often considered as important as the apology itself – raises the question why. Why do governments and nation-states feel compelled to apologise for historical as well as contemporary crimes? What motivates the need to atone for the past in the present? In terms of political expediency – the efforts by politicians and governments to appease or appeal to their constituencies – apologies on behalf of nation-states are often underwritten by a discourse of religiosity and motivated by a desire to seek atonement and (therefore) redemption. To offer an apology one must admit wrongdoing: apologies carry with them expressions of remorse and admissions of guilt. They are therefore confessional as well as healing spaces. The language of 'reconciliation', a strong feature of many public official apologies, touches on the mythic and the magical; it has obvious confessional and religious overtones.[45] While there is no broad consensus as to what 'reconciliation' actually means, it is a term that risks 'being all things to all people'. Perhaps most ambiguously (and alarmingly), much of the language around 'reconciliation' posits an end-point; some future historical moment or juncture when both victim and perpetrator will be 'reconciled'.

This raises serious questions around the ethics of apology and, in particular, problematises the issue of in whose best interest an apology is offered. Perhaps the most poignant essay edging around this topic is Jonathan Lear's *Radical Hope: Ethics in the Face of Cultural Devastation*. Lear's philosophical inquiry tackles the big question: How should or could we face the possibility that our culture might collapse? How might we live with this vulnerability? Can we make any sense of facing up to this challenge courageously? Drawing on the history of the Crow nation, Lear suggests this is a vulnerability that affects us all – in that we are all inhabitants of a civilisation, and civilisations are themselves vulnerable to historical forces.[46] Allied to this is the difficult matter of whether or not public (and continuous) acts of national atonement and redemption must automatically lead to forgiveness. It is true that the language of forgiveness and its antonyms carries with it an implied morality; that is, forgiveness is honourable and superior, while antipathy and hatred (the fuel of resentment) is seen as morally inferior and innately destructive. As Daniel Levy and Natan Sznaider have argued, it is often assumed, especially in the context of a truth commission, that simply uttering the truth of historical injustice will be liberating and will redeem the enemy.[47] Moreover, they remind us that expressions of atonement, fiscal compensation, and other redemptive matters do not necessarily imply forgiveness.[48] After all, it is not guilt that must be eternal, but the acceptance of moral responsibility. In this regard it was noteworthy that when negotiating the terms of settlement with the Crown in 2008, Ngāi Tūhoe included a 'Statement of Forgiveness', which was to refer to the relationship between the iwi and the Crown.[49]

As Richard Vernon has recently argued, there are several philosophical and practical challenges in considering historical claims of restitution, compensation and apology. These include the fact that dealing with events that happened in the past distracts us from the concerns of the present, and that contemporary moral and social mores as well as standards have changed. Vernon also points out that so many injustices happened in the past that it would be impossible to address them all.[50] The matter of historical standards is a controversial but important issue.[51] Taking an historical perspective demands (by definition) that we understand the differences between our own moral and ethical present and the standards observed in and practised by peoples in the past. Historians generally accept that standards change over time; they are as mutable as the individuals who comprise them. We acknowledge that there were certain historical acts, policies, and practices – once commonplace and considered acceptable – now condemned, and seen as unlawful, unjust, and even immoral. There is nothing wrong with bringing such judgements into our study of the past. By the same token, historians do not as a rule seek to impose their own anachronistic standards on the past; yet at the same time, we can never approach the past neutrally and devoid of interest (or indeed compassion). Historians might well attempt to refrain from making explicit ethical judgements about historical actors and agents, but if an interpretation and analysis is offered, there is always an ethical judgement involved. History is, after all, a more subjective discipline than most of us would care to admit.

Reflecting on the 150th anniversary of the Battle of Pukehinahina in 2014, Māori leaders and local civic dignitaries alike have been moved to put the past behind them.[52] 'Acknowledging and taking steps to put injustices right,' commented a community leader, 'has made our community stronger and gives us every reason to hope for a closer relationship between Pākehā and Māori and a mutual desire for a better future.'[53] Local Māori organisations, entrusted with managing the post-settlement resources and charting a new future for their people, have also released statements that echo similar themes of unity.[54] The commemoration of the Battle of Pukehinahina, as with the examples considered above, reveals a particular Western preoccupation with ideas of linear development and causality. In this context 'history' does not denote a process but a *place*: a site to be excavated, documented, and then left behind. The phrases 'moving on' and 'building a future' create a distance between the present and the past. This preoccupation with 'moving on' from the collectivised entity that is 'the past' reveals a perspective of, and preoccupation with, linear and progressive definitions of history.

Similarly, the withholding of an apology or the refusal to offer one is indicative of a wider reluctance to address the inequities created by historical decisions and events; in short, an unwillingness to 'pay' for past excesses or injustices. Political leaders may be unwilling to confront shameful histories and offer apologies for fear that the admission of liability carries with it the risk of reparation and cost. In other words, saying sorry for the past is one thing – but paying for it is another. Furthermore, although in New Zealand and in other former settler colonies, processes are in place to 'reply' to various allegations of historical wrongdoing, these processes are often highly complex and legalised and frequently invested with more expectations than they can realistically deliver. The denial of history and the erasure of the post-imperial memory is not only peculiar to this part of the world; it is a characteristic of the ways in which the brutality and violence of the imperial and colonial pasts have been successfully 'silenced' and estranged from the present. Caroline Elkins' study of the silences in the archival record regarding the 'end of empire in Kenya', and the work of Alessandro Triulzi and Maria Cristina Ercolessi revealing the 'failure' of Italian public memory to come to terms with its colonial past, demonstrate how the tendency to forget and remember the imperial past *selectively* is a larger transnational phenomenon.[55]

New Zealand's own radical counter-narrative has been increasingly exposed over the past three decades through a series of official apologies regarding a range of historical injustices. Through multiple admissions of wrongdoing, the Crown has admitted its failure to live up to the expectations of a faithful Treaty partner. Apologies offered by the New Zealand government to the Chinese community and the people of Sāmoa, and to their respective descendants, signal attempts to 'set the record straight' and recalibrate the dynamic of present relations. Regardless of motivation, the impulse to put the past behind and 'in its place' remains a strong one. Apologies are evidence that the New Zealand state has exercised imperial power in ways redolent of other, more established imperial regimes. It would also be fair to say that matters such as public and official apologies for past transgressions often stir up strong feelings about 'our collective past', and this generates a profound sense of anxiety about the relationship between present decisions and future actions. Will the decisions that are made today be overturned by future generations? How durable are our current moral and ethical standards? And might such feelings of unease simply be indicative of our postcolonial circumstance? In any case, it is clear that contemporary issues invoking 'history' continue to expose a deep sense of apprehension about the past. In settler societies such as New Zealand and Australia, this palpable public disquiet – a sort of 'southern discomfort' – towards history continues to fuel debates examining the ways in which Europeans and their descendants came to colonise other peoples and places. This in turn has increasingly forced us to reconsider the terms of our current and continued occupancy. Given the stains on our own short history, a little self-reflection might not be such a bad outcome.

Notes

1 The title of this essay takes its inspiration from M. P. K. Sorrenson's essay of the same name, published in 1987. See M. P. K. Sorrenson, 'Towards a radical reinterpretation of New Zealand history: The role of the Waitangi Tribunal', *New Zealand Journal of History*, 21:1 (1987), 173–88.

2 See, for instance, James Cowan, *The New Zealand Wars: A History of the Maori Campaigns and the Pioneering Period* (Wellington: Government Printer, 1922–23) and James Belich, *The New Zealand Wars and the Victorian Interpretation of Racial Conflict* (Auckland: Penguin, 1988).

3 I grew up and attended secondary school in the shadow of Pukehinahina. The stone cairn marking the battle site and the bright blue wooden church standing on top of the little hill are still the most visible markers of the battle site. Situated on the city's main arterial route, the site is well known but perhaps not particularly well understood.

4 The first claims were heard in February 1998 from the three main Tauranga Moana iwi: Ngāi Te Rangi, Ngāti Ranginui, and Ngāti Pukenga. See *Te Raupatu o Tauranga Moana: Report on the Tauranga Confiscation Claims* (Wellington: Legislation Direct, 2004).

5 In June 2012, the Minister for Treaty of Waitangi Negotiations signed a deed of settlement with Ngāti Ranginui at Pyes Pa; a deed of settlement was signed with Ngāti Pukenga on Te Whetu o Te Rangi Marae in Welcome Bay in April 2013; and in December 2013, a deed of settlement was signed with Ngāi Te Rangi and Ngā Potiki at Whareroa Marae in Mount Maunganui.

6 The best outline of the 150th commemorations can be found at the official website, www.battleofgatepa.com, accessed 18 April 2014.

7 The Waitangi Tribunal was first established under the Treaty of Waitangi Act 1975; an amending Act ten years later extended its powers of jurisdiction to consider historical matters. The findings of the Waitangi Tribunal are also limited by the imperative that the Tribunal must give 'practical application' to Treaty principles.

8 The term 'postcolonial' refers here to an ongoing engagement with, and interrogation of, the lasting effects of colonisation. It assumes that colonisation is a process still unfolding.

9 Peter Gibbons, 'Cultural colonization and national identity', *New Zealand Journal of History*, 36:1 (2002), 5–15.

10 See for instance, Philip G. Dwyer and Lyndall Ryan (eds), *Theatres of Violence: Massacre, Mass Killing and Atrocity Throughout History* (New York: Berghahn, 2012); Bronwyn Leebaw, *Judging State-Sponsored Violence, Imagining Political Change* (New York: Cambridge University Press, 2011); Linda Radzik, *Making Amends: Atonement in Morality, Law, and Politics* (New York: Oxford, 2009); and Jeffrey K. Olick, *The Politics of Regret: On Collective Memory and Historical Responsibility* (New York and Abingdon: Routledge, 2007).

11 Bain Attwood, *Telling the Truth About Aboriginal History* (Crows Nest, NSW: Allen & Unwin, 2005).

12 Mark Gibney, Rhoda E. Howard-Hassmann, Jean-Marc Coicaud, and Niklaus Steiner (eds), *The Age of Apology: Facing Up to the Past* (Philadelphia: University of Pennsylvania Press, 2007).

13 Elazar Barkan, *The Guilt of Nations: Restitution and Negotiating Historical Injustices* (Baltimore, MD: Johns Hopkins University Press, 2001).

14 Melissa Nobles, *The Politics of Official Apologies* (Cambridge: Cambridge University Press, 2008); Priscilla B. Hayner, *Unspeakable Truths: Facing the Challenges of Truth Commissions* (London and New York: Routledge, 2001); and Martha Minow, *Between Vengeance and Forgiveness: Facing History after Genocide and Mass Violence* (Boston: Beacon Press, 1998).

15 The literature is vast, but see for example, Elazar Barkan and Alexander Karn (eds), *Taking Wrongs Seriously: Apologies and Reconciliations* (Stanford, CA: Stanford University Press, 2006); John Torpey, *Making Whole What Has Been Smashed: On Reparations Politics* (Cambridge, MA: Harvard University Press, 2006); Michael Humphrey, *The Politics of Atrocity and Reconciliation: From Terror to Trauma* (London: Routledge, 2002); and Janna Thompson, *Taking Responsibility for the Past: Reparation and Historical Justice* (Cambridge: Polity Press, 2002).

16 Annie E. Coombes, *Rethinking Settler Colonialism: History and Memory in Australia, Canada, Aotearoa New Zealand and South Africa* (Manchester: Manchester University Press, 2011); Giselle Byrnes and David Ritter, 'Antipodean settler societies and their complexities: The Waitangi process in New Zealand and Native title and the Stolen Generations in Australia', *Commonwealth and Comparative Politics*, 46:1 (2008), 54–78; Rachel Buchanan, 'Decolonizing the archives: The work of New Zealand's Waitangi Tribunal', *Public History Review*, 14 (2007), 43–63; Daniel Levy and Natan Sznaider, *The Holocaust and Memory in the Global Age*, trans. Assenka Oksiloff (Philadelphia: Temple University Press, 2005); Jon Elster, *Closing the Books: Transitional Justice in Historical Perspective* (Cambridge: Cambridge University Press, 2004); and Lawrence Douglas, *The Memory of Judgment: Making Law and History in the Trials of the Holocaust* (New Haven, CT: Yale University Press, 2000).

17 On the Catholic Church, see www.theguardian.com/world/2000/mar/13/catholi cism. religion, accessed 20 April 2014, and Jason A. Edwards, 'Community focused *Apologia* in Pope John Paul II's Year of Jubilee discourse', in Joseph R. Blaney and Joseph P. Zompetti (eds), *The Rhetoric of Pope John Paul II* (Lanham, MD: Rowman & Littlefield, 2009). See also Jennifer Henderson and Pauline Wakeham (eds), *Reconciling Canada: Critical Perspectives on the Culture of Redress* (Toronto: University of Toronto Press, 2013); Graham Dawson, *Making Peace with the Past? Memory, Trauma and the Irish Troubles* (Manchester: Manchester University Press, 2011); Mona Oikawa, *Cartographies of Violence: Japanese Canadian Women, Memory, and the Subjects of the Internment* (Toronto: University of Toronto Press, 2012); Danielle Celermajer and A. Dirk Moses, 'Australian memory and the apology to the Stolen Generations of Indigenous people', in Aleida Assman and Sebastian Conrad (eds), *Memory in a Global Age: Discourses, Practices, and Trajectories* (Basingstoke: Palgrave Macmillan, 2010), pp. 32–58; Steven D. Roper and Lilian A. Barria, 'Why do states commission the truth? Political considerations in the establishment of African truth and reconciliation commissions', *Human Rights Review*, 10:3 (2009), 373–91; Eric Brahm, 'Judging truth: The contributions of truth commissions in post-conflict environments', in Noha Shawki and Michaelene

Cox (eds), *Negotiating Sovereignty and Human Rights: Actors and Issues in Contemporary Human Rights Politics* (Farnham: Ashgate, 2009); Elazar Barkan and Alexander Karn, 'Group apology as an ethical imperative', in Barkan and Karn (eds), *Taking Wrongs Seriously*, pp. 3–30; Daniel Levy and Natan Sznaider, 'Forgive and not forget: Reconciliation between forgiveness and resentment', in Barkan and Karn (eds), *Taking Wrongs Seriously*, pp. 83–100; Michael Humphrey, 'From victim to victimhood: Truth commissions and trials as rituals of political transition and individual healing', *Australian Journal of Anthropology*, 14:2 (2003), 171–87; Janna Thompson, 'Historical injustice and reparation: Justifying claims of descendants', *Ethics*, 112:1 (2001), 114–35; Matt James, 'Being stigmatized and being sorry: Past injustices and contemporary citizenship', in David Taras and Beverly Rasporich (eds), *A Passion for Identity: Canadian Studies in the 21st Century* (Scarborough, ON: Nelson, 2001), p. 55–75.

18 I deliberately exclude here the victims of institutionalised psychological and sexual abuse, violence and confinement where victims experience damage beyond the scope of this research.

19 Sir William Martin, 'Observations on the Proposal to take Native Lands under an Act of the Assembly', *Appendices to the Journals of the House of Representatives*, E2, (1864), pp. 7–8.

20 Judith Binney and Gillian Chaplin, *Ngā Mōrehu The Survivors: The Life Histories of Eight Māori Women* (Wellington, Bridget Williams Books, 1986), pp. 5–6; Nēpia Mahuika, '"Kōrero Tuku Iho": Reconfiguring Oral History and Oral Tradition', PhD thesis, University of Waikato, 2012; Bella Te Aku Graham, 'All Stand: Courtroom Classes and the Transmission of Māori Knowledge', unpublished paper presented at the NZARE Conference, Melbourne, 2000.

21 See Miranda Johnson, 'Making history public: Indigenous claims to settler states', *Public Culture*, 20:1 (2008), 97–117, and Miranda Johnson, 'Honest acts and dangerous supplements: Indigenous oral history and historical practice in settler societies', *Postcolonial Studies*, 8:3 (2005), 261–76.

22 Thane Rosenbaum, 'The price of forgiveness', *New York Times* (8 November 2003); see www.nytimes.com/2003/11/08/opinion/the-price-of-forgiveness.html, accessed 18 April 2014.

23 I refer here to The Treaty of Waitangi Act 1975 and The Treaty of Waitangi Amendment Act 1985. Claimant researchers and agencies such as the Crown Forestry Rental Trust, as well as the Office of Treaty Settlements, have produced a vast amount of historical research documenting the detailed and complex nature of Māori–Crown relationships as they relate to particular claims.

24 Richard Boast and Richard S. Hill (eds), *Raupatu: The Confiscation of Māori Land* (Wellington: Victoria University Press, 2009); Richard Boast, *Buying the Land, Selling the Land: Governments and Maori Land in the North Island 1865–1921* (Wellington: Victoria University Press and Victoria University of Wellington Law Review, 2008); and Michael Belgrave, *Historical Frictions: Maori Claims and Reinvented Histories* (Auckland: Auckland University Press, 2006).

25 See further www.justice.govt.nz/tribunals/waitangi, accessed 20 April 2014.

26 See further Julie C. Bellingham, 'The Office of Treaty Settlements and Treaty History: An Historiographical Study of the Historical Accounts, Acknowledgements and Apologies Written by the Crown, 1992 to 2003', MA thesis, Victoria University of Wellington, 2006.

27 It is clear that in New Zealand the term 'settlement' thoroughly imbues the language of Treaty negotiations, despite increasing acceptance that the Treaty is, in the words of the Waitangi Tribunal, an 'ongoing social contract'. It is interesting to note that in Australia, where of course there is no agreement comparable to the Treaty of Waitangi, the language is skewed towards 'reconciliation'.

28 Strictly speaking the parties were 'Ngā Hapū o Ngāti Ranginui and Trustees of the Ngā Hapū o Ngāti Ranginui along with the Crown. 'Ngā Hapū o Ngāti Ranginui and Trustees of the Ngā Hapū o Ngāti Ranginui Settlement Trust and The Crown, Deed of Settlement of Historical Claims, 21 June 2012', clauses 3.18-3.22, http://nz01.

terabyte.co.nz/ots/ DocumentLibrary/NgatiRanginuiDOS.pdf, accessed 18 April 2014.

29 'Ngā Hapū o Ngāti Ranginui and Trustees of the Ngā Hapū o Ngāti Ranginui Settlement Trust and The Crown, Deed of Settlement of Historical Claims, 21 June 2012', pp. 31–34.

30 'Ngā Hapū o Ngāti Ranginui and Trustees of the Ngā Hapū o Ngāti Ranginui Settlement Trust and The Crown, Deed of Settlement of Historical Claims', clause 3.18.

31 'Ngā Hapū o Ngāti Ranginui and Trustees of the Ngā Hapū o Ngāti Ranginui Settlement Trust and The Crown, Deed of Settlement of Historical Claims', clauses 3.19, 3.20.

32 'Ngā Hapū o Ngāti Ranginui and Trustees of the Ngā Hapū o Ngāti Ranginui Settlement Trust and The Crown, Deed of Settlement of Historical Claims', clause, 3.21.

33 'Ngā Hapū o Ngāti Ranginui and Trustees of the Ngā Hapū o Ngāti Ranginui Settlement Trust and The Crown, Deed of Settlement of Historical Claims', clause 3.22.

34 See further Manying Ip (ed.), *Unfolding History, Evolving Identity: The Chinese in New Zealand* (Auckland: Auckland University Press, 2003); and Nigel Murphy, *The Poll-Tax in New Zealand: A Research Paper Commissioned by the New Zealand Chinese Association (Inc)* (Wellington: Department of Internal Affairs, 2002). For a comparative perspective, see Ann Curthoys, '"Men of all nations, except Chinamen": Europeans and Chinese on the goldfields of New South Wales', in Iain McCalman, Alexander Cook, and Andrew Reeves (eds), *Gold: Forgotten Histories and Lost Objects of Australia* (Cambridge: Cambridge University Press, 2001), pp.103–24. The Chinese Immigration Act was passed by Parliament in 1881, introducing a 'poll tax' of £10. Although the Minister of Customs could, from 1934, waive the poll tax, it was not officially repealed in New Zealand until 1944, long after a number of other countries had abandoned this punitive law.

35 The full text of the apology is available here: www.stevenyoung.co.nz/the-chinese-in-new-zealand/Poll-Tax/Helen-Clark.html, accessed 20 April 2014.

36 www.stevenyoung.co.nz/the-chinese-in-new-zealand/Poll-Tax/Helen-Clark.html.

37 www.stevenyoung.co.nz/the-chinese-in-new-zealand/Poll-Tax/Helen-Clark.html.

38 www.stevenyoung.co.nz/the-chinese-in-new-zealand/Poll-Tax/Helen-Clark.html.

39 The year 2008 was significant in New Zealand in terms of public official apologies. A further noteworthy apology by the Clark government was made in May 2008 when the New Zealand government publicly apologised to Vietnam War veterans and their families, recognising that servicemen were not treated fairly when they returned home from war. This apology was agreed to in a memorandum of understanding between the government, the Ex-Vietnam Services Association and the Royal New Zealand Returned Services Association in 2006. In addition, a $30 million package resulted from a report on the veterans' concerns and included an ex gratia payment of $40,000 for those with prescribed medical conditions and a $25,000 payment to the spouses of veterans who had died.

40 See further Damon Salesa, 'New Zealand's Pacific', in Giselle Byrnes (ed.), *The New Oxford History of New Zealand* (Melbourne: Oxford University Press, 2009), pp. 149–72; and Sandra M. Tomkins, 'The influenza epidemic of 1918–19 in Western Samoa', *Journal of Pacific History*, 27:2 (1992), 181–97.

41 The full text is reproduced at www.nzherald.co.nz/nz/news/article.cfm?c_id=1&objectid= 2044857, accessed 21 April 2014.

42 www.nzherald.co.nz/nz/news/article.cfm?c_id=1&objectid= 2044857.

43 www.nzherald.co.nz/nz/news/article.cfm?c_id=1&objectid= 2044857.

44 See for instance, Ruth Berry, 'Saying sorry and moving on', *Evening Post* (5 June 2002), n.p.

45 See for example Michelle Grattan (ed.), *Essays on Australian Reconciliation* (Melbourne: Black Inc, 2000); and Ágnes Tóth and Bernard Hickey (eds), *Reconciliations* (Perth: API Network, 2005).

46 Jonathan Lear, *Radical Hope: Ethics in the Face of Cultural Devastation* (Cambridge, MA: Harvard University Press, 2006).

47 See further, Levy and Sznaider, 'Forgive and not forget', p. 83.

48 Levy and Sznaider, 'Forgive and not forget', p. 87.

49 www.ngaituhoe.iwi.nz/LinkClick.aspx?fileticket=_Ay37ykuUoY%3D&tabid=98, accessed 20 April 2014.

50 Richard Vernon, *Historical Redress: Must We Pay for the Past?* (London and New York: Continuum, 2012), pp. 7–13.

51 See further Jim McAloon, 'By which standards? The Waitangi Tribunal and New Zealand history', *New Zealand Journal of History*, 40:2 (2006), 194–213; and Giselle Byrnes, 'By which standards? History and the Waitangi Tribunal: A reply', *New Zealand Journal of History*, 40:2 (2006), 214–29.

52 See also www.battleofgatepa.com, accessed 19 April 2014.

53 Ross Paterson [Mayor of the Western Bay of Plenty], cited in 'Battle of Gate Pa, Series 5 – Looking to the Future', *Bay of Plenty Times* (March 2014), p. 3.

54 Te Runanga o Ngai Te Rangi Iwi Trust have publicly urged their people to draw 'a line in the sand with regards to addressing many of the grievances we have had in relation to the Treaty', to learn from history and 'use the knowledge of that battle [Pukehinahina] to fight a new campaign for equity and justice ... that positions Ngai Te Rangi with the same pride and honour that occurred at Pukehinahina 150 years ago'. See 'Battle of Gate Pa, Series 5 – Looking to the Future', *Bay of Plenty Times* (March 2014), p. 12.

55 Caroline Elkins, *Imperial Reckoning: The Untold Story of Britain's Gulag in Kenya* (Henry Holt, 2010); and Alessandro Triulzi and M. Cristina Ercolessi, *State, Power and New Political Actors in Postcolonial Africa* (Milan: Feltrinelli, 2004).

INDEX

Note: page numbers in *italic* refer to illustrations.

Aboriginal peoples 84–5, 92–3, 95, 101n.46, 131, 207, 212n.66, 219, 225, 227n.26
Adelaide (Australia) 78
Africa 73, 87n.41, 201, 205, 207, 248
  see also North Africa; South Africa; Sudan
African Americans 183, 186, 187
Aitutaki (Cook Islands) 57, 183–5, 187, 188
Alice Springs (Australia) 219
Americans 6, 7, 22, 23, 57, 61, 152, 253, 156–7, 179–91
  see also United States of America
Angas, George French 76, 81
Anglo-Saxons 81
Antarctica 1, 8, 229–42, *235*
  and International Antarctic Centre (Christchurch) 238
  and New Zealand IceFest 239
  and pou whenua 8, 240, *240*
  and Trans-Antarctic Expedition 230, 234–5, *235*
anthropology 52, 53–4, 56–8, 60, 62–3
  Pacific anthropology 57
  see also Peter Buck, ethnology
apartheid 201
Apia (Sāmoa) 131, 136, 137, 141, 142, 180, 181, 182, 237, 244n.40, 252–3
apology 8, 246, 247–56
Armstrong, Mary Ann 102, *103*, 108, 109–18, *109*, *111*, *117*, 122n.49, 122n.73
Atafu (Tokelau) 181, 183, 190
Auckland (New Zealand) 14, 15–16, 22, 25n.8, 28, 45, 71, 95, 98, 105, 106, 107, 119, *138*, 139, 148, 149, 151, 155, 156, 157, 197, 198, 200, 202, 205–9
Auckland Hospital 96

Australasia 3, 71–3, 78–9, 102, 104, 105, 106, 113, 114, 149–50, 167, 169–70, 213, 214
Australasian Federation 164–5
  and sport 225
  and tourism 224
Australia 8, 71, 104, 106, 113, 115, 116, 131, 149, 179, 190, 230, 233, 248, 257, 259n.27
  as travel destination 72–3, 156–8, 213–26
  Australian Federation 165
  colonies 78, 79, 80, 83, 84
  and Antarctica 234, 243n.28
  and climate 77
  and convictism 81–2, 93
  and France 165–70, 176n.16, 176n.27
  and gold fields 21, 79
  and law 91–4, 96, 100n.25, 100n.30
  and New Guinea 131
  and shipping 151–2, 155, 159
  and sport 199, 204, 206–9, 210n.6
  and travel writing 75–6, 78, 85
  and White Australia Policy 77
  see also Western Australia

Baden–Powell, Sir George Smyth 71–2, 78, 81, 86n.1
Ballantyne, Tony 5, 14, 23, 75, 85
Battle of Gate Pa / Te Whawhai o Pukehinahina (1864) 8, 245–6, 251, 255, 257n.3, 261n.54
Battle of Rosaires (1898) 6, 127, *128*, 142
Bay of Plenty (New Zealand) 245
Belich, James 21, 45, 49n.71, 56, 75, 77–8
Benton, Lauren 91, 98
Best, Elsdon 55–6, 63
Black Saturday Massacre (1929) 7, 141–2
Blackstone, William 91, 100n.16

Board of Maori Ethnological Research (BMER) 54–5, 57–8
Boehm, Joseph Edgar 32–3, *34*
Boer War, Second 28, 35
Bowen, Sir George (Governor) 28
Brisbane (Australia) 151, 207, 212n.66, 222
Britain 2, 4, 6–8, 22–3, 106, 129–30, 135–6, 142
   British Colonial Office 141–2, 233
   in Sudan 127
   and colonisation 21, 74, 75–8, 80
   and Fiji 149
   and law 91
   and vagrancy 89, 92, 94, 97
British Empire Games 7, 197–8
British Settlements Act 1877 (UK) *see* legislation
Browne, Thomas Gore (Governor) 14–15, 17, 23, 26n.20
Buck, Peter (Te Rangihīroa) 5, 51–64
   see also anthropology

Canada 3, 77, 156, 199, 208, 210n.6, 234, 243n.21, 248
Canberra (Australia) 221
Canberra Pact (1944) *see* legislation
Canterbury (New Zealand) 22, 28, 122n.73, 238, 239
Chatham Islands 132, 173
children 4, 7, 42, 91, 108, 129, 153, 179, 181, 184, 185–91, 194n.78, 206, 224
Chinese 247, 251–2, 256, 260n.34
   labour force 166–7, 176n.21
Chinese Immigration Act 1881 (New Zealand) *see* legislation
Christchurch (New Zealand) 28, 105, 110, 119, 197, 200–2, 224
   and Antarctica 230–1, 236–42
Churchill, Winston *128*, 143n.2
Clark, Helen (Prime Minister) 234, 251–3, 260n.39
Coates, Gordon (Prime Minister) 54, 132, 136–42
Cold War 229, 235–6
colonialism 13–14, 18–19, 75–8, 90, 174, 201, 209
Colonial Office 16, 20, 23, 141–2, 233

colonisation 2, 4, 6, 17, 36, 53, 60, 90, 94, 229, 234, 241, 243n.21, 246–7, 253–4, 257n.8
   see also decolonisation
commerce 5, 17, 233
Commonwealth 7, 197–8, 201–9, 230, 233–4
Commonwealth Games 7, 197–209, 210n.3, 212n.66
Contagious Diseases Act 1869 (New Zealand) *see* legislation
convictism 80–2, 90–6
Cook Islands 3, 6, 7, 51–62
Cox, James 97
Cresswell, Tim 89, 98
crime 80–1, 91, 94, 174
Crimean War 22–3, 25, 26n.20
Crown 2, 4, 8, 13–16, 19–22, 36–7, 95, 180, 245–56
customary culture 14, 19, 55
   see also ethnicity

Darwin (Australia) 218
Davies, Susanne 93
D'Avigdor, Elim Henry 80, 83, 93
decolonisation 44, 174–5
   see also colonisation
Department of External Affairs 61, 132, 167
Dilke, Charles 72–7, 81
Dominion Museum 54
drunkenness 37, 80, 95–6
Dunedin (New Zealand) 28, 58, 105, 106, 108, 112–19, 149, 152–3

Edinburgh, Duke of (Prince Albert) 31, 43, 110
Edmonds, Penny 83, 101n.46, 101n.48, 217
education 20, 54, 55, 180, 190, 220, 223
emigration 71–5, 86, 131, 215
   see also immigration; migration
Enclosure Acts *see* legislation
England 13–24, 76–85, 91, 170, 198, 210n.6
Erebus disaster (1979) 236–7
ethnicity 5, 224–5
   see also customary culture
ethnology 52–5, 62–3
   see also anthropology; Peter Buck

European 1, 3, 17, 18–20, 35–7, 41, 45, 53, 57–64, 74–6, 92, 95

Fairburn, Miles 95–7
Federation (Australia) 77, 165, 170
Fergusson, Charles (Major) 6, 8, *129*, 127–42
Fiji 3, 6, 78, 147–60, 180
  Fiji Tourist Bureau 154
  Galoa Harbour 150
First World War 77, 127, 153, 166, 179
France 22, 132, 181, 243n.28
  and Pacific territories 164–75
Fraser, Peter (Prime Minister) 132, 171
French Polynesia 164
frontier zones 7, 76, 95, 213–26
Froude, James 37, 75–82
Fuchs, Sir Vivian 234

gender 3, 5, 72, 152, 181
  see also masculinity; women
geography 73, 78, 135, 253
Germany 60, 80, 132, 133–5, 166, 179
Gibbons, Peter 247
globalism 5, 73–5, 80, 85–6, 99n.12, 104, 110, 213, 233, 242
Gold Coast (Australia) 222
Golden Jubilee, Queen's (1887) 28
gold fields 21–2, 77–80, 95, 108, 149, 220–1, 233
gold rushes 214, 217
Gordon, Sir Arthur (Governor) 149
Gove (Australia) 217, 219
Grey, Sir George (Governor) 14, 15, 36, 45, 49n.71, 75
guilt 248–9, 255

haka 202, 208, 212n.68
Hauraki Gulf (New Zealand) 115
Hawai'i 52, 60, 148, 147–60, 160n.5, 168
  Honolulu 106, 148, 150–1, 156–7, 159, 184
Henry, Noël 164, 171–5
heritage 53–4, 63, 72, 115, 226, 230, 237, 239–40
Hill, Richard 36, 94

Hillary, Edmund (Sir) 230, 233–5, *235*, 238
Hobart (Tasmania) 71
Holland, Harry 132
Holland, Sidney (Prime Minister) 171, 200
Honolulu *see* Hawai'i
Hot Lakes District (New Zealand) 84, 110, 115
House of Representatives (New Zealand) 22, 232

identity 3, 18, 58, 75, 77, 89, 96, 98, 102, 197, 199, 201, 202–9, 222, 226, 235, 239–42
  Māori identity 41, 54, 223, 228n.39
  national identity 4, 6, 8, 229, 231
illegitimacy 190
immigration 2, 32, 91, 97–8, 149, 154, 166, 251–2
  see also emigration; migration
Immigration Restriction Act 1901 (Australia) *see* legislation
imperialism 1–9, 29, 41, 90, 97, 115, 119, 142, 149, 155, 159–60, 163, 165, 168, 186, 229, 239, 240, 242, 253
India 23–4, 71, 73, 76, 132, 153, 198
  Indian rebellion 23–4
Indigeneity 4, 110
industrialisation 72, 92, 97, 110, 118–20, 174
influenza epidemic (Sāmoa) 7, 60, 131–3, 180, 252
insanity 80
institutions 52, 53, 56, 92, 96, 174, 247, 248
Ireland 2, 86
  Northern Ireland 248–9

Kalgoorlie (Australia) 220–1
Keesing, Felix 55, 56, 61–3
Kīngitanga *see* law
King Korokī 200

Labour government (New Zealand) 172, 251
labour 14, 91, 92, 97, 149, 151, 166–7, 176n.21, 182, 185, 214, 217
land alienation 95

landscape 5, 6, 71, 102–20, 220, 221, 225, 231, 237, 242
law 5, 20–1, 42, 133, 137–41, 159, 188, 232, 252, 260n.34
  immigration law 77
  lawlessness 217–19
  vagrancy laws 89–98, 100n.30, 101n.46
  and Kīngitanga 19
League of Nations (LON) 60, 130, 134–6, 140, 167–8, 180
  Permanent Mandates Commission (PMC) 130, 140
Lea'lofi, Tupua Tamasese 137
legislation
  British Settlements Act 1887 (UK) 232
  Canberra Pact (1944) 169, 190
  Chinese Immigration Act 1881 (New Zealand) 251–2, 260n.34, 260n.35
  Contagious Diseases Act 1869 (New Zealand) 94–5
  Enclosure Acts 92
  Immigration Restriction Act 1901 (Australia) 77
  Poor Laws 92
  Samoa Act 1921 (Sāmoa) 60, 131–2, 133
  Samoan Offenders Ordinance 1922 (Sāmoa) 133
  Statute of Westminster (1931) 233
  Vagrant Act 1866 (New Zealand) 94, 96
  Vagrancy Act 1824 (UK) 94
London (UK) 4, 28, 42, 75, 84, 105, 112, 114, 131, 133, 164, 169–70, 232

Malaya 198, 210n.6
Manawatū (New Zealand) 55
Māori 1, 2, 6, 7, 49n.61, 92, 115–16, 118, 132, 166, 172, 188, 190, 202, 205–6, 231, 240–2
  in Australia 214, 216, 219, 223–5, 227n.26, 228n.39
  and activism 207–8, 209
  and agency 4–5, 7, 8
  and apology 245–57, 259n.23
  and British colonialism 13–21
  and Christianity 13, 18–19, 21, 25
  and ethnology 51–64, 185
  and identity 199–200,
  and racial amalgamation 19–21
  and resistance 21–5, 132,144n.23, 245–6
  and tourism 84–6, 106–8, 110
  and vagrancy 95–6
  see also woodcarving
marines, US 180
masculinity 97, 217–18, 234, 237
  see also gender; women
Massey, William (Prime Minister) 166, 167, 168
Matson Steam Navigation Company (Matson Line) 155–60
Mau (Samoan League) 7, 60, 62, 131–42, 144n.23, 144n.24, 168, 180
Melbourne (Australia) 72, 78, 80, 82, 83, 101n.46, 101n.48, 102, 105, 109, 110, 112–20, 149, 176n.27, 207, 222
men see masculinity
migration 8, 149, 173, 214–26, 216
  see also emigration; immigration
military 22–3, 127, 132–3, 137, 138, 139, 169, 181–9, 204–5, 236, 245
missionaries 15, 19, 84–5, 105
mobility 2, 5, 8, 74, 76, 80–2, 89–98, 148, 155, 222

nationalism 71, 104, 115, 120, 198–200, 207–9
Native Department (New Zealand) 15, 16, 24, 56, 59–61
Nelson, Ta'isi O. F. 60, 134, 134–7, 141–2
New Caledonia 78, 166, 167, 169, 179
New Guinea 131, 183
New Hebrides (Vanuatu) 165–7, 170
New South Wales 8, 92, 93, 213, 216
New York 44, 106, 150
New Zealand Police Gazette (NZPG) 89, 101n.45
New Zealand Parliamentary Debates (NZPD) 89
New Zealand Wars 7, 31, 38, 44, 47n.7, 106, 116, 132, 245
Ngāi Tahu see Te Arawa Confederation (iwi)
Ngāi Tūhoe (iwi) 255

Ngarima, Ranui 241
Ngata, Āpirana (Sir) 5, 52–64
Ngāti-ākarana (iwi) 200
Ngāti Kahugnunu (iwi) 42
Ngāti Porou (iwi) 59
Ngāti Ranginui (iwi) 251, 257n.4, 257n.5, 259n.28
Ngāti Rangiwewihi see Te Arawa Confederation (iwi)
Ngāti Tarawhai see Te Arawa Confederation (iwi)
Ngāti Whakaue see Te Arawa Confederation (iwi)
Niue 57, 58, 173, 179
North Africa 169, 172, 173
see also Africa; Sudan
Northern Territory (Australia) 213, 216–17, 225
North Island (New Zealand) 97, 114
Nosworthy, William (Minister for External Affairs) 132, 135
nuclear testing 163–4, 174, 236
Nullabor Desert (Australia) 221

Ohinemutu (New Zealand) 4, 28–47, 82, 110

Pacific peoples 1, 3, 51–2, 57, 60–4, 214–15, 224
Papa-i-Ouru (marae) 31, 38, 43, 46
Parihaka (New Zealand) 132, 144n.23
Parliament 172, 180, 185, 251–2, 260n.34
Parr, Sir James (High Commissioner) 133, 138–40
Permanent Mandates Commission (PMC) see League of Nations
Perth (Australia) 218, 220–4
Pink and White Terraces (New Zealand) 84
police 35, 46, 62, 89, 91–8, 101n.45, 101n.48, 137, 207, 253
Polynesian culture 6, 51, 57–64, 131, 165, 173, 181, 183, 190, 206
Polynesian Society 54, 55, 57
Pōmare, Māui (Sir) 5, 54, 58, 60, 132, 144n.23
Poor Laws see legislation
postcolonialism 174, 202, 246–7, 257, 257n.8
pou whenua see Antarctica

poverty 91, 93, 97, 190
Poverty Bay (New Zealand) 114, 115, 116
Princess Te Puea Herangi 200
property 14, 17, 36, 84, 91, 93, 156
prostitution 94–6, 101n.48, 183, 186

Quail Island (New Zealand) 231, 232
Queensland (Australia) 79, 216

racism 24, 39, 45, 76–7, 85, 142, 167, 186, 205–6, 218–19, 224–5
Rainbow Warrior 163
Rarotonga (Cook Islands) 51, 59, 61, 157, 180
reparation 172, 247–50, 256
Richardson, George Spafford (General) 62n.57, 127, 129, 130, 131–40, 144n.24, 168n.31
Ringatu Church 38
Ross Dependency 173, 230, 232–3, 237, 239
Rotomahana (New Zealand) 110, 111, 112
Rotorua (New Zealand) 28, 38, 39, 42, 43, 84, 112

Salesa, Damon 6, 20, 155, 159, 163–4
Sāmoa
American Samoa 144n.24, 156, 180
German Samoa 166
Western Samoa (Mandated Territory of) 6, 7, 60, 127–43, 138
Samoa Act 1921 (Sāmoa) see legislation
Samoan League see Mau
Samoan Offenders Ordinance 1922 (Sāmoa) see legislation
San Francisco 71, 106, 150, 152, 156–9
Scotland 3, 16, 210n.6
Scott Base (Antarctica) 8, 237–42, 240
Scott, Robert Falcon 230–3, 232, 236, 238–9
Second World War 6, 7, 64n.3, 155, 159, 164, 169, 179, 191, 214
Serre, Paul Adolphe (Consul) 164, 167–9, 172–4, 176n.27
settler colonialism 71, 73, 75–9, 84–6, 90, 256
Seuffert, Anton 107–8

Shackleton, Ernest 230–1, 233, 234, 238–40
shipping 71, 78, 147–60, 184
Siegfried, André 163, 165
social class 5, 7, 83, 89, 91–4, 97, 151, 153
Solomon Islands 57, 185
Sorrenson, M. P. K. 246, 257n.1
South Africa 39, 77, 131, 132, 201, 205, 206, 210n.3, 210n.6, 243n.28, 248
South Island (New Zealand) 119, 132, 240, 241
South Pacific Commission 169, 170
Springbok Tour
 (1973) 201, 203
 (1981) 205
Statute of Westminster (1931) see legislation
Stedman Jones, Gareth 97
Stolen Generations (Australia) 248
Sudan 6, 127–43, 143n.2
 see also Africa; North Africa
suicide 189
Suva (Fiji) 148–60
Swan River (Australia) 71, 78
Sydney (Australia) 71, 78, 81, 82, 105, 110, 113, 149–51, 156–8, 162n.57, 220, 222

Tahiti 157, 169, 179, 184
Tamihana, Wiremu 19
Taranaki (New Zealand) 26n.20
Taranaki War (1860) 13, 14, 15, 18, 22, 132
Taroi, Wero 41
Tasmania 71, 76, 78, 80, 85, 242n.7
Tauranga (New Zealand) 31, 39, 245–6, 257n.4
Te Amohau, Paora 31
Te Amohau, Temuera 36
Te Arawa Confederation (iwi)
 Ngāti Rangiwewihi 36
 Ngāi Tahu 240–1
 Ngāti Tarawhai 29, 32, 38
 Ngāti Whakaue 31–47
Te Ati Awa (iwi) 13, 15
Te Kooti Arikirangi Te Turuki 38, 48n.41, 110, 116, 132
Te Rangihīroa see Peter Buck
Te Rangitāke, Wiremu Kīngi 13

Tohungaism 96
Tokelau 6, 7, 168, 173, 179–91
Tonga 149, 150, 165, 180
tourism see Australasia
 see also Māori
transcolonialism 75, 149, 222
transience 89, 91, 94, 97
transnationalism 104, 110, 120, 222, 256
Trans-Tasman Travel Arrangement 214
Treaty of Waitangi / Te Tiriti o Waitangi (1840) 2, 28, 36–7, 42, 44, 46, 205, 207, 245–57, 257n.5, 257n.7, 259n.23, 259n.27, 261n.54
 see also Waitangi Tribunal
Trollope, Anthony 37, 73, 77, 83
Turner, Frederick Jackson 217, 220

unemployment 93, 97
Union Steam Ship Company of New Zealand (USSCo) 106, 149–59
United Nations Trusteeship Council 170
United States of America 8, 76, 79, 80, 81, 105, 115, 132, 148–59, 179–91, 217–19, 225, 230–8, 241, 243n.28
 see also Americans
urban centres 74–7, 85, 92, 98, 104–5, 118, 164, 171, 214–15, 222

vagabonds 89, 91–4
vagrancy
 as crime 91, 92, 94–6
 and Australia 100n.30, 101n.46, 101.n48
 and laws 91–6, 99n.12
 and mobility 5, 89–90, 98–9
 and the poor 97
Vagrancy Act 1824 (UK) see legislation
Vagrant Act 1866 (New Zealand) see legislation
venereal disease (VD) 182–5
Vershaffelt, Park and Berendsen (VBP) Report 140–1
Victoria, Queen 4, 28–47, 29, 30, 32, 34, 40, 44, 45

Victoria (Australia) 92, 93, 101n.46, 108, 113, 151, 207, 208, 216
Victorian culture 74, 82, 104
violence 20, 22, 76, 84, 131, 136–7, 142, 184, 247–8, 256, 259n.18
von Haast, Heinrich Ferdinand 170, 177n.35

Waikato (New Zealand) 22, 27n.50, 224
Waitangi Action Committee 207
Waitangi Tribunal 245, 246, 249, 250, 257n.7, 259n.27
    see also Treaty of Waitangi / Te Tiriti o Waitangi (1840)
Waitere, Tene 29, 38, 39, 41, 43
Wanganui (New Zealand) 58, 95, 244n.40
Ward, Joseph (Prime Minister) 139–41
welfare 1, 90–2, 96–7, 215

Wellington (New Zealand) 5, 28, 31, 33, 52, 58, 95, 138, 140, 141, 157, 164, 169, 171, 173
Wellington Industrial Exhibition (1881) 35
Western Australia 81, 213, 216, 218, 220–1, 225
    see also Australia
Western Samoa (Mandated Territory of) see Sāmoa
Wevers, Lydia 71, 84
whaling 22–3, 182, 233
White Australia Policy see Australia
Whitiki, Patu 29, 41, 43
women 3–4, 6, 7, 38, 72–3, 95–6, 101n.46, 108, 152, 168, 179–91, 218, 237
    see also gender; masculinity
woodcarving 8, 28–46, 29, 30, 32, 40, 44, 45, 49n.45, 49n.61

Young Māori Party 5

EU authorised representative for GPSR:
Easy Access System Europe, Mustamäe tee 50,
10621 Tallinn, Estonia
gpsr.requests@easproject.com

www.ingramcontent.com/pod-product-compliance
Lightning Source LLC
Chambersburg PA
CBHW051955270326
41929CB00015B/2662